T0202673

Lecture Notes in Computer Science   11197

Commenced Publication in 1973
Founding and Former Series Editors:
Gerhard Goos, Juris Hartmanis, and Jan van Leeuwen

More information about this series at http://www.springer.com/series/7409

Marinos Ioannides · Eleanor Fink
Raffaella Brumana · Petros Patias
Anastasios Doulamis · João Martins
Manolis Wallace (Eds.)

Digital Heritage

Progress in Cultural Heritage: Documentation, Preservation, and Protection

7th International Conference, EuroMed 2018
Nicosia, Cyprus, October 29 – November 3, 2018
Proceedings, Part II

 Springer

Editors
Marinos Ioannides
Cyprus University of Technology
Limassol, Cyprus

Eleanor Fink
American Art Collaborative Linked Open
Data Initiative
Arlington, VA, USA

Raffaella Brumana ⓘ
Politecnico di Milano
Milan, Italy

Petros Patias
The Aristotle University
Thessaloniki, Greece

Anastasios Doulamis
National Technical University of Athens
Athens, Greece

João Martins ⓘ
CTS-UNINOVA
Caparica, Portugal

Manolis Wallace ⓘ
University of the Peloponnese
Tripoli, Greece

ISSN 0302-9743   ISSN 1611-3349 (electronic)
Lecture Notes in Computer Science
ISBN 978-3-030-01764-4   ISBN 978-3-030-01765-1 (eBook)
https://doi.org/10.1007/978-3-030-01765-1

Library of Congress Control Number: 2018956722

LNCS Sublibrary: SL3 – Information Systems and Applications, incl. Internet/Web, and HCI

© Springer Nature Switzerland AG 2018, corrected publication 2019
This work is subject to copyright. All rights are reserved by the Publisher, whether the whole or part of the material is concerned, specifically the rights of translation, reprinting, reuse of illustrations, recitation, broadcasting, reproduction on microfilms or in any other physical way, and transmission or information storage and retrieval, electronic adaptation, computer software, or by similar or dissimilar methodology now known or hereafter developed.
The use of general descriptive names, registered names, trademarks, service marks, etc. in this publication does not imply, even in the absence of a specific statement, that such names are exempt from the relevant protective laws and regulations and therefore free for general use.
The publisher, the authors and the editors are safe to assume that the advice and information in this book are believed to be true and accurate at the date of publication. Neither the publisher nor the authors or the editors give a warranty, express or implied, with respect to the material contained herein or for any errors or omissions that may have been made. The publisher remains neutral with regard to jurisdictional claims in published maps and institutional affiliations.

Cover illustration: Wall painting (end of 15th century) of the Virgin Mary, Orans between the Archangels Michael and Gabriel from the Church of the Monastery of Christos Antifonitis, Kalograia (on the apse's conch) after it had been destroyed, following the 1974 Turkish invasion and occupation. Used with permission of the Ministry of Transport, Communications and Works, Department of Antiquities, Lefkosia, Cyprus.

This Springer imprint is published by the registered company Springer Nature Switzerland AG
The registered company address is: Gewerbestrasse 11, 6330 Cham, Switzerland

Preface

EuroMed 2018, the traditional biennial scientific event, was held in the capital city of Cyprus, the island which has always been a bridge to three continents going back to the origins of civilization. It is a place where the fingerprints of several ancient cultures and civilizations can be found, with a wealth of historical sites recognized and protected by UNESCO.

Several organizations and current EU projects (such as the H2020 Marie Skłodowska Curie RISE Fellowship project TERPSICHORE, the H2020 Marie Skłodowska Curie ITN CHANGES, the H2020 R&I Reflective 7 – INCEPTION, the H2020 COOP 8 CSA Virtual Multimodal Museum, the H2020 Reflective 6 CrossCult, the H2020 REACH, the Research Infrastructure DARIAH-EU ERIC and DARIAH-CY, the COST Action Innovation in Intelligent Management of Heritage Buildings [i2MHB], the H2020 Teaming Excelsior, H2020 Teaming Medstach, H2020 Twinning Athena and H2020 ERA Chair Mnemosyne) decided to join EuroMed 2018 and continue cooperation in order to create an optimal environment for the discussion and explanation of new technologies, exchange of modern innovative ideas, and in general to allow for the transfer of knowledge between a large number of professionals and academics during one common event and time period.

The main goal of the event is to illustrate the programs underway, whether organized by public bodies (e.g., UNESCO, European Union, national states, etc.) or by private foundations (e.g., Getty Foundation, World Heritage Foundation, etc.) in order to promote a common approach to the tasks of recording, documenting, protecting, and managing world cultural heritage. The 7th European-Mediterranean Conference (EuroMed 2018) was definitely a forum for sharing views and experiences, discussing proposals for the optimal attitude as well as the best practice and the ideal technical tools to preserve, document, manage, present/visualize, and disseminate the rich and diverse cultural heritage of mankind.

This conference was held during the second half of the EU Framework Programme, Horizon 2020, which is the largest in the world in terms of financial support on research, innovation, technological development, and demonstration activities. The awareness of the value and importance of heritage assets have been reflected in the financing of projects since the first Framework Programme for Research and Technological Development (FP1, 1984–1987) and continues into the current HORIZON 2020 that follows FP7 (2007–2013). In the past 35 years, a large community of researchers, experts, and specialists have had the chance to learn and develop the transferable knowledge and skills needed to inform stakeholders, scholars, and students. Europe has become a leader in heritage documentation, preservation, and protection science, with COST Actions adding value to projects financed within the FP and EUREKA program and transferring knowledge to practice and support the development of SMEs.

The EuroMed 2018 agenda focused on enhancing and strengthening international and regional cooperation and promoting awareness and tools for future innovative research, development, and applications to protect, preserve, and document the European and world cultural heritage. Our ambition was to host an exceptional conference by mobilizing also policy-makers from different EU countries, institutions (European Commission, European Parliament, Council of Europe, UNESCO, International Committee for Monuments and Sites ICOMOS, the International Committee for Documentation of Cultural Heritage CIPA, the International Society for Photogrammetry and Remote Sensing ISPRS, the International Centre for the study of the Preservation and Restoration of Cultural Property ICCROM, and the International Committee for Museums ICOM), professionals, as well as participants from all over the world and from different scientific areas of cultural heritage.

Protecting, preserving, and presenting our cultural heritage are actions that are frequently interpreted as change management and/or change in the behavior of society. Joint European and international research yields a scientific background and support for such a change. We are living in a period characterized by rapid and remarkable changes in the environment, in society, and in technology. Natural changes, war conflicts, and man-made interventions and changes, including climate change, as well as technological and societal changes, form an ever-moving and colorful stage and pose a challenge for society. Close cooperation between professionals, policy-makers, and authorities internationally is necessary for research, development, and technology in the field of cultural heritage.

Scientific projects in the area of cultural heritage have received national, European Union, or UNESCO funding for more than 30 years. Through financial support and cooperation, major results have been achieved and published in peer-reviewed journals and conference proceedings with the support of professionals from many countries. The European Conferences on Cultural Heritage research and development and in particular the biennial EuroMed conference have become regular milestones on the never-ending journey of discovery in the search for new knowledge of our common history and its protection and preservation for the generations to come. EuroMed also provides a unique opportunity to present and review results as well as to draw new inspiration.

To reach this ambitious goal, the topics covered include experiences in the use of innovative technologies and methods as well as how to take the best advantage to integrate the results obtained so as to build up new tools and/or experiences as well as to improve methodologies for documenting, managing, preserving, and communicating cultural heritage.

We present here 97 papers, selected from 537 submissions, which focus on interdisciplinary and multidisciplinary research concerning cutting-edge cultural heritage informatics, physics, chemistry, and engineering and the use of technology for the representation, documentation, archiving, protection, preservation, and communication of cultural heritage knowledge.

Our keynote speakers, Dr. Ronald de Bruin, Director of the COST Association, Dr. Robert Sanderson (Getty Foundation), Prof. Craig Knoblock, USC Information Sciences Institute, Mrs. Diane Zorich, Director of the Smithsonian's Digitization Program Office (DPO), Dr. Charalambos Chaitas, Executive Director for Arts, Heritage, and Education for the Public Investment Fund, Saudi Arabia, Mr. Joan Cobb, Principal IT Project Manager at J. Paul Getty Trust, Mr. Harry Verwayen, Executive Director of EU Digital Library Europeana, Prof. Koen van Balen, KUL, UNESCO Chair on Preventive Conservation, Monitoring, and Maintenance of Monuments and Sites, and UNESCO CHAIR Disaster Mitigation for Urban Cultural Heritage, Japan, Mr. Brigadier General Fabrizio Parrulli, Carabinieri for the Protection of Cultural Heritage Commander, Mrs. Nada R. Hosking, Director, Programs and Partnerships, Global Heritage Fund, and Mrs. France Desmarais are not only experts in their fields, but also visionaries for the future of cultural heritage protection and preservation. They promote the e-documentation and protection of the past in such a way that it is preserved for the generations to come.

We extend our thanks to all authors, speakers, and those persons whose labor, financial support, and encouragement made the EuroMed 2018 event possible. The international Program Committee, whose members represent a cross-section of archaeology, physics, chemistry, civil engineering, computer science, graphics and design, library, archive, and information science, architecture, surveying, history, and museology, worked tenaciously and finished their work on time. The staff of the IT department at the Cyprus University of Technology helped with their local ICT and audiovisual support, especially Mr. Filippos Filippou, Mr. Lefteris Michael, and Mr. Stephanos Mallouris. We would also like to express our gratitude to all the organizations supporting this event and our co-organizers, the European Commission scientific and policy officers of the DG Connect Mr. Albert Gauthier, Mrs. Adelina-Cornelia Dinu, the COST director Dr. Ronald de Bruin, the officers Mrs. Federica Ortelli, Mrs. Estelle Emeriau, the director general of Europeana Mr. Harry Verwayen, the Getty Conservation Institute and World Monuments Fund, the Cyprus University of Technology, the Ministry of Energy, Commerce, Industry and Tourism especially the permanent secretary and digital champion Dr. Stelios Himonas and Mr. Constantinos Karageorgis, the Ministry of Education and Culture and particularly the minister Mr. Kostas Champiaouris, the director of the Cultural Services Mr. Pavlos Paraskevas, the director of the Cypriot National Library Mr. Demetris Nicolaou, the Department of Antiquities in Cyprus, all the members of the Cypriot National Committee for E-documentation and E-preservation in Cultural Heritage, and finally our corporate sponsors, CableNet Ltd, the Cyprus Tourism Organization, the Cyprus Postal Services, and Dr. Kyriakos Themistokleous from the Cyprus Remote Sensing Society who provided services and gifts of kind that made the conference possible.

We express our thanks and appreciation to the board of the ICOMOS Cyprus Section for their enthusiasm, commitment, and support for the success of this event. Most of all we would like to thank the organizations UNESCO, European Commission, CIPA, and ICOMOS that entrusted us with the task of organizing and undertaking this unique event and wish all participants an interesting and fruitful experience.

September 2018

Marinos Ioannides
Eleanor Fink
Raffaella Brumana
Petros Patias
Anastasios Doulamis
João Martins
Manolis Wallace

Acknowledgments and Disclaimer

The EuroMed 2018 Conference was partly supported by the Republic of Cyprus, by the Cyprus University of Technology, by the Cyprus Tourism Organization, by CIPA (http://cipa.icomos.org/), ICOMOS Cyprus, the aforementioned EU projects, the DARIAH-EU ERIC and DARIAH-CY, the H2020 INCEPTION, and H2020-ViMM projects.

However, the content of this publication reflects the authors' views only, and the European Commission, the Republic of Cyprus, CIPA, ICOMOS, ICOMOS-Cyprus, Getty, Cyprus University of Technology, and the EU projects H2020 Marie Skłodowska Curie RISE Fellowship project TERPSICHORE, the H2020 Marie Skłodowska Curie ITN CHANGES, the H2020 R&I Reflective 7 – INCEPTION, the H2020 COOP 8 CSA Virtual Multimodal Museum, the H2020 Reflective 6 CrossCult, the H2020 REACH, the Research Infrastructure DARIAH-EU ERIC and DARIAH-CY, the COST Action Innovation in Intelligent Management of Heritage Buildings (i2MHB), the H2020 Teaming Excelsior, H2020 Teaming Medstach, H2020 Twinning Athena, the UNESCO Chair on Digital Cultural Heritage at Cyprus University of Technology, and the EU H2020 ERA Chair Mnemosyne are not liable for any use that may be made of the information contained herein.

Organization

Conference Chairs

Marinos Ioannides
Eleanor Fink
Raffaella Brumana
Petros Patias
Anastasios Doulamis
João Martins
Manolis Wallace

Local Organizing Committee

Vasilis Athanasiou
Robert Davies
Simos Georgiou
Theodoros Gkanetsos
George Hadjidemetriou
Maria Katiri

Charalambos Leventis
Elias Nobilakis
Chrisanthos Pissarides
Christiana Polycarpou
Konstantinos Skriapas
Kyriakos Themistokleous

International Scientific Committee

Fabrizio Banfi, Italy
Luigi Barazzetti, Italy
George Bebis, USA
Marco Bertini, Italy
Matthaios Bimpas, Greece
Frank Boochs, Germany
Gumersindo Bueno, Spain
Lorenzo Cantini, Italy
George Caridakis, Greece
Ying-Mei Cheng, Taiwan
Jiri Chmelik, Czech Republic
Paola Condoleo, Italy
Jorbi Conzalez, Spain
Stefano Della Torre, Italy
Iason Diakoumakos, Greece
Nikolaos Doulamis, Greece
Charalambos Georgiadis, Greece
George Giannoulis, Spain

Angelo Giuseppe Landi, Italy
Andrina Granić, Croatia
Alberto Grimoldi, Italy
Sang-sun Jo, South Korea
Dimitrios Kaimaris, Greece
Nikos Karanikolas, Greece
Norman Kerle, The Netherlands
Dimitrios Kosmopoulos, Greece
Chiao-Ling Kuo, Taiwan
Fotis Liarokapis, Czech Republic
George Livanos, Greece
Federica Maietti, Italy
Konstantinos Makantasis, Cyprus
Maria Merchan, Spain
Pilar Merchan, Spain
Luisa Migliori, Italy
Daniela Oreni, Italy
Pedro Pereira, Portugal

Contents – Part II

Digital Applications for Materials Preservation in Cultural Heritage

Digital Cultural Heritage Learning and Experiences

Contents – Part I

3D Digitization, Reconstruction, Modelling and HBIM

Digital Cultural Heritage – Smart Technologies

The New Era of Museums and Exhibitions

Digital Cultural Heritage Infrastructure

Reconstructing the Past

Supporting the Automatic Extraction of HBIM Elements from Point Clouds

Javier Román Cembranos[1](✉), José Llamas Fernández[1],
Pedro Martín Lerones[1], Jaime Gómez García Bermejo[2],
Eduardo Zalama Casanova[2], and Marinos Ioannides[3]

[1] CARTIF, Parque Tecnológico de Boecillo, Valladolid, Spain
{javrom, joslla, pedler}@cartif.es
[2] ITAP-DISA, University of Valladolid, Valladolid, Spain
{jaigom, ezalama}@eis.uva.es
[3] Cyprus University of Technology, Limassol, Cyprus
marinos.ioannides@cut.ac.cy

Abstract. The purpose of this paper is just detailing a state-of-the-art procedure for the automatic recognition of specific 3D shapes from point clouds of immovable heritage assets supported on a tailored tool using PLY, PTX and PTS formats as input files. To make this tool functional and widely used, it is currently developed as a plug-in for the well-known and representative REVIT BIM software package.

The procedure is particularly applied to the Castle of Torrelobatón (Valladolid, Spain) to allow the automation in cataloguing of required elements, as illustrative example of the defensive architecture from the Middle age to the Renaissance in Europe, reason why it is one of the pilot sites of the INCEPTION project. Thus the HBIM process is enhanced, which is continuing right through to provide better services to technicians, scholars and citizens.

Keywords: HBIM · Façade parsing · BIM for existing buildings
Point cloud

1 Introduction

Many in the Architecture, Engineering and Construction fields will see new buildings as the main application for BIM, but a considerable percentage of projects are part developments or refurbishments of existing buildings, within heritage is included for sure (European Commission 2015). According to Arayici et al. (2017) and the Historic England report (2017), the built heritage poses two major issues: (1) the requirement to 3D record and retain many architectural features; (2) how the existing structure is brought into the BIM process.

3D surveying technologies (laser scanning or photo-based scanning) are probed as adequate in the heritage field for a significant number of years (Tommasi et al. 2016), but still today, the data, although collected in 3D, are delivered to the Architects and Engineers as 2D drawings across Europe. A number of factors drove this at the time:

© Springer Nature Switzerland AG 2018
M. Ioannides et al. (Eds.): EuroMed 2018, LNCS 11197, pp. 3–10, 2018.
https://doi.org/10.1007/978-3-030-01765-1_1

- Pure restoration remains the major consideration to ensure heritage sustainability.
- Limited understanding of point cloud data (3D surveying output) and the capability to handle large data sets.
- Stakeholders' ability and familiarity working with as-built parametric models.
- Software capabilities to deal with point clouds and models simultaneously.

As the awareness of the benefits of BIM is increasingly growing and software and hardware resources are intensified, a greater understanding of the tools available and their application is becoming clear as long as new tools are demanded (Bruno et al. 2018). Due to the recognised wide professional body specification to face an inclusive heritage approach, working with each other into collaborative BIM platforms is a must to understand particular requirements. Thus BIM specifications are essential to bring the existing data into those platforms by developing complementary processes and tools to define the family structure and the delivery method from point clouds.

There are precedents of semi-automatic feature extraction on 3D models with further exporting to *AutoCAD* (Martín et al. 2010). The question now is just widening to the BIM paradigm. It is a real demand for HBIM from point clouds, but it is still relegated to research due to the difficulty of practical realization.

Authors such as Wang et al. (2015) are restricted to the extraction of planes and their intersections to define walls, floors, ceilings, doors and windows for geometrically very simple buildings. Zolanvari and Laefer (2016) detect doors and windows by horizontal and vertical sectioning of a point cloud. Li et al. (2017) make a height based segmentation and labelling to define prismatic volumetric forms by intersection of planes. Although approaching a Cathedral as an example, the most complex parts are discarded.

Many projects concerning the protection, conservation, restoration, and dissemination of cultural heritage are being carried out through commercial BIM software, i.e. *REVIT*, *ArchiCAD* and *Tekla*. According to López et al. (2018) *REVIT* is an efficient BIM platform to accurately model irregular surfaces as well as geometric anomalies of the different elements. Moreover, the *REVIT* platform lets users to add new functions or *plug-ins* based on the application programming interface (API). The programming languages that could be used to code the *plug-ins* are C++, C# and Python.

There are some commercial plug-ins for efficiently using as-built point cloud data captured by laser scanners directly within *REVIT* to ease the BIM modelling of existing buildings. These plug-ins are conceived to let users get all the advantages of a high-performance point cloud application directly within *REVIT*, but restricted to specific point cloud formats according to brand and model of the laser scanner. *LEICA CloudWorx*[1] is a representative example, providing tools for accurate fitting of steel, flange, automatic pipe, and 2D lines mainly oriented to retrofit design and lifecycle asset management of the building. Also provide a virtual visit within *REVIT* with a complete view of the captured reality. In any case, such a kind of plug-ins are only oriented to 3D laser scanning data on recent building and civil works, but not to the built heritage, so they do not expressly meet related needs.

---

[1] *LEICA CloudWorx* for REVIT: https://leica-geosystems.com/products/laser-scanners/software/leica-cloudworx/leica-cloudworx-revit.

2 Tailored Tool for the Automatic Extraction of Primary HBIM Elements from Point Clouds

A novel tool has been developed to automatically detect a useful basic set of architectonic features from a given point cloud. The detected features are intended to be a common workspace where more complex and detailed objects can be added in a later stage of the digital reconstruction process for heritage immovable assets. The tool is further handled into the *REVIT* well-known BIM package to ensure functionality and actual usability by means of a specific tailored software tool (plug-in).

Suitable digital information sources are mainly 3D point clouds acquired by laser scanning or photo-based scanning. The 3D data, which is made up of geometry (XYZ coordinates) and color (RGB coordinates: real appearance), can be directly handled by the tool. The raw 3D point cloud of the building can be imported into PTX, PTS, PLY formats (ASCII or binary) to be accurately managed into *REVIT* as BIM worldwide representative software by means of a specific tailored plug-in, so called "3DASH tool". Figure 1 describes the process.

Fig. 1. Process for automatic shaping into REVIT through the 3DASH tool.

This specifically tailored plug-in for *REVIT* is programmed in C++ and supported by the *Point Cloud Library* (PCL) as standalone, large scale, open software project for image and point cloud processing. *3DASH* is able to precisely display the detected features in a unique working project (RVT/RFA).

The *Point Cloud Library* has a wide range of statistical algorithms to detect geometrical primitives such as planes, cylinders, spheres, cones or torus. The vast majority of the architectural geometries making up the built heritage can be modeled by means of these primitives. Theoretically, a point cloud can be completely processed with the proposed library.

In order to put the efforts into a practical example, the *3DASH* plug-in has been focused on the existing primitives at the Castle of Torrelobatón (Spanish demo case). Thus, cylinders and planes are automatically detected on the corresponding point cloud.

2.1 Point Cloud Parameterization Flow Chart

The flow chart diagram of the point cloud parameterization process starts with a statistical filtering in order to minimize potential problems during later stages of cloud processing. Once filtered, a downsampling process is applied to the cloud, which decreases the point density in the point cloud. This step, although optional, significantly reduces the processing time of subsequent steps.

The analysis of interdependence and intersection between primitives is a key topological problem. Proper segmentation of the point cloud is fundamental to make it more meaningful and easier to analyze by assigning a properties-label to every point. Thus, those with the same label share certain characteristics (Fig. 2).

Fig. 2. Segmentation of the point cloud upon the Torrelobatón castle's wall.

In the next step of the parameterization process, the clusters of points are analyzed by a classifier in order to assign a category for each one of these sub point clouds. The clusters can fall into two geometrical categories, namely, planes and cylinders. The classification process is done through a statistical algorithm called RANSAC that determines the points of the cluster are related to the geometrical primitive used as template. It is important to note that every single point cloud can be approximate in some degree by any type of primitive. Thus, the primitive that approximate the highest number of points of the cluster is considered as the sorting primitive for the analyzed cluster. In Fig. 3(a), clusters sorted as planes are represented in red while clusters sorted as cylinders are represented in blue.

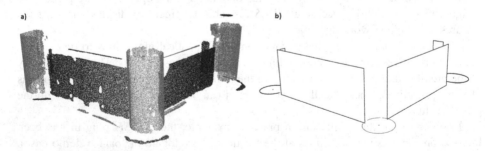

Fig. 3. Classification of the clusters of points into planes and cylinders (a) and advanced parameterization of the detected primitives (b). (Color figure online)

Once the clusters have been classified, the parameterization of the planes and the cylinders is done since the previous step only determined the general mathematical representation of the two primitives. For planes, the classifier determines the implicit equation of the plane, whereas for cylinders the point-slope equation of the centerline and the radius are estimated. These equations define an infinity geometrical primitive in which the limits must be set. Thus, a more advanced parameterization of the primitives is required.

The advanced parameterization step determines the primitive boundaries. This step is heavily related with REVIT as the parameterization of the primitives has to match the parameterization required by the BIM software. The coordinates of the vertices of the planes are the required for the complete definition of the walls whereas the coordinates of center of the base and the radius among other parameters are required for a complete definition of the round towers (Fig. 3b).

2.2 REVIT Plug-in

Before using the *3DSAH* tool, a new project needs to be created within REVIT in order to load a set of parametric elements to be used by the plug-in later on. Once it is loaded, a specific icon is created to allow the final user modifying some of the processing steps for the automatic shape recognition (Fig. 4, left).

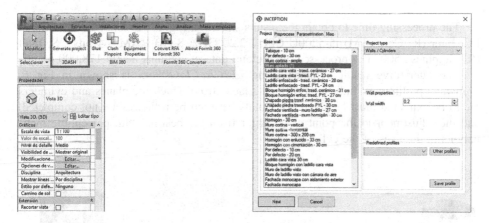

Fig. 4. 3DASH button into REVIT

Clicking on the button, all the functionalities of the *3DASH* tool are deployed according to the configuration parameters. These parameters cover the entire work flow of the automatic shape detection process, i.e. the region growing-based segmentation normal threshold, the percentage of remaining points in the point cloud after the downsampling process or the tolerances applied while searching common boundaries between different primitives (Fig. 4, right).

Once the parameters have been set, the point cloud can be loaded. The parametric elements automatically generated by the *plug-in* (Fig. 5) are part of the *REVIT* library loaded when the new project was created. Thus, the extraction can be readily exported to IFC from *REVIT* as well.

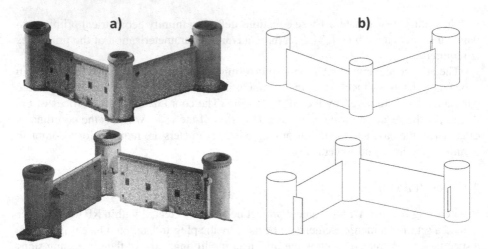

Fig. 5. Parametric extraction of walls and round towers. Loaded point cloud (a) and automatically generated BIM model (b).

The processing time to obtain the results shown in Fig. 5 was 5s in a conventional PC: Inter (R) Core (TM) i5-5200U CPU@2.20 GHz; 8 GB RAM; 64 bits OS; Intel (R) Graphics 5500. The processed point cloud dataset contains nearly 178,000 points.

The alternative result obtained using *LEICA CloudWorx* is shown in Fig. 6. A manual preliminary indication of the surfaces from which the planes and cylinders are to be extracted must be given. The joints between both figures are not completed, and the adjustment to the point cloud is far from the best-fit, with perceptible inclinations in the axes of the cylinders.

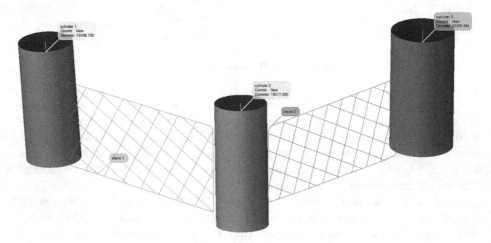

Fig. 6. Comparative result analyzed with PolyWorks 3D software solution

The complete process involving the 3DASH tool is described in a self-explanatory video at: https://www.youtube.com/watch?v=QpYiPX71Hms.

This tool is being refined under the INCEPTION European project of applied research on cultural heritage (www.inception-project.eu). The presented results are initial and need to be extended to the remaining 8 demonstrators to get proper feedback on user experiences and to share lessons learned.

3 Conclusions

Unlike the new-build construction sector, where BIM is increasingly applied at international level, with scores of relevant publications and online content, HBIM is a relatively new field of applied research and appears less popular in terms of adoption by heritage professionals despite strongly needing multi-disciplinary collaboration.

This is facilitated meeting specific demands as the case of tailored tool briefly explained in this paper, intended to automatically detect specific geometrical features to be part of a common workspace where more complex and detailed objects as well as semantics can be added in a later stage of the digital reconstruction process for heritage immovable assets. Therefore, HBIM documentation is favored according to the principle for non-invasive intrusions to ensure proper valorization.

Promising trends point out improving methods and tools for automatic conversion of point clouds in HBIM models, reducing inaccuracies and current severe simplifications, as well as extending the IFC standard to solve interoperability issues. The scarcity of research works reinforces the presented results and demands future developments.

Acknowledgement. This work is partially INCEPTION project (Inclusive cultural heritage in Europe through 3D semantic modelling), funded from the European Union's Horizon 2020 research and innovation programme under grant agreement No 665220.

References

Arayici, Y., Counsell, J., Mahdjoubi, L., Nagy, G.A., Hawas, S., Dweidar, K.: Heritage Building Information Modelling. Routledge, UK (2017)

Bruno, S., De Fino, M., Fatiguso, F.: Historic building information modelling: performance assessment for diagnosis-aided information modelling and management. Autom. Constr. **86**, 1–13 (2018)

European Commission: Getting cultural heritage to work for Europe. Report of the Horizon 2020 Expert Group on Cultural Heritage (2015). https://ec.europa.eu/programmes/horizon2020/en/news/getting-cultural-heritage-work-europe. Accessed 27 Apr 2018

Historic England: BIM for Heritage: Developing a Historic Building Information Model. Swindon, Historic England (2017). https://historicengland.org.uk/images-books/publications/bim-for-heritage. Accessed 27 Apr 2018

Li, Z., et al.: A hierarchical methodology for urban facade parsing from TLS point clouds. ISPRS J. Photogramm. Remote. Sens. **123**, 75–93 (2017)

Martín, P., Llamas, J., Melero, A., Gómez, J., Zalama, E.: A practical approach to making accurate 3D layouts of interesting cultural heritage sites through digital models. J. Cult. Herit. **11**(1), 1–9 (2010)

Tommasi, C., Achille, C., Fassi, F.: From point cloud to BIM: a modelling challenge in the cultural heritage field. Int. Arch. Photogramm. Remote. Sens. Spat. Inf. Sci. **41**, B5 (2016)

Wang, C., Cho, Y.K., Kim, C.: Automatic BIM component extraction from point clouds of existing buildings for sustainability applications. Autom. Constr. **56**, 1–13 (2015)

Zolanvari, S.I., Laefer, D.F.: Slicing method for curved façade and window extraction from point clouds. ISPRS J. Photogramm. Remote. Sens. **119**, 334–346 (2016)

López, F.J., Martín, P., Llamas, J., Gómez, J., Zalama, E.: A review of heritage building information medling (H-BIM). Multimod. Technol. Interact. **2**, 21 (2018)

Three Dimensional Modeling and Analysis of Ancient Indian Structures

Namratha Reddy Kondam, Balaphani Krishna Poddar,
Venkata Dilip Kumar Pasupuleti$^{(\boxtimes)}$, and Prabhakar Singh

Mahindra École Centrale, Survey no: 62/1A, Bahadurpally Jeedimetla,
Hyderabad 500043, Telangana, India
namratha1897@gmail.com, pkrishna172@gmail.com,
{Venkata.pasupuleti,Prabhakar.Singh}@mechyd.ac.in

Abstract. Ancient structures in India are the practical remains of the past. Exploring these structures helps to understand the structural significance of each and every part precisely and techniques used. The main objective of this research is to model and analyze the historical structural components, in terms of geometry and their arrangement to understand reasons for their higher stability. Columns are one of the major structural elements in transmitting the loads which have both aesthetic appeal and structural significance. For this study, columns and simple mandapas (pillared halls/sanctum) of structures at different ages in the past are considered and analyzed using the 3D models in Autodesk Inventor. The analysis includes mode shapes and stress distribution of these columns and mandapas under gravity. The results attained show the geometry of the structure plays a crucial role in its behavior when subjected to gravity loads. Further this research work will be fundamental for future studies to understand the effects of geometry on the stability of the structure and the scientific reason behind the usage of such designs.

Keywords: Ancient structures · Columns · Mandapas · Geometry
Autodesk Inventor

1 Introduction

India is considered to be one of the fastest growing countries in the world in terms of technology and infrastructure. It has advanced itself in various aspects which changed the working of society and the lifestyle of the people. Though many modern innovations have emerged in the recent years, not all of them are holistic in nature. There are few studies underway to understand the holistic construction of ancient structures which are still a mystery to current science. India has gone through various extreme cultural changes from the earliest civilization till the present modern day. Thus by diving back into the depths of time and by exploring the unexplored, it has started from the Indus valley civilization that provides a substantial evidence of efficient town planning. The Harappa and Mohenjo-Daro cities in Indus majorly depict the large scale building culture which includes town planning, advanced drainage systems and well planned roads [1]. As civilizations evolved, the purpose of construction has changed

M. Ioannides et al. (Eds.): EuroMed 2018, LNCS 11197, pp. 11–20, 2018.
https://doi.org/10.1007/978-3-030-01765-1_2

from need to exhibiting the greatness of the Empires. Around 300 BC the tradition of building structures using rock-cut method has started. This method was taken to a whole new level by the Dravidians whose structures consists of gigantic towers, vimanas and pillared halls. One such example that shows their finesses is Temple of Kailasa, Ellora caves is a megalith carved out of one single rock. It is double storied vertically excavated structure, built with a flat roof and a Dravidian Shikara [2]. The common structural forms in South Indian Temples are vimanam, mandapam, gopuram [3]. Due to various Islamic intrusions, many Muslim Emperors have conquered India which resulted in the introduction of Indo-Islamic style of building structures. The engineering features such as arches, domes, slender minarets were influenced from the Persian and Islamic building style whereas the inclusion of pillars and raised platforms were inspired from the Indian method of construction. Earlier in the past the major construction materials used were stones and bricks. Later metals, alloys, wood were prominently used in construction. Over the last 150 years; Archaeological Survey of India (ASI) has done a detailed work on conservation of ancient structures, monuments and sites in India [4].

History can no longer be treated as the study of dates or events. It shows the pattern of life. When paper hasn't come into existence, the works were documented on dried palm leaves, plates of copper and some were inscribed on pillars, walls, large rocks. These are evidences about past which can be seen and touched. Every structure has a unique significance when viewed in architectural point of view. Engineers in past studied the aspects of natures and incorporated them into their works. This resulted in structures standing for a long time without getting damaged. If similar techniques are adopted by today's engineers it is possible to design and build structures that are more durable and disaster resistant. One of the prominent structural elements in ancient Indian structures is high raised platforms to avoid natural calamities like floods and earthquakes. Sandbox technology was one of the foundation methods invented during Kakatiya rule to resist earthquakes [5]. The Rock Melting Technique has been used in the construction of Musical Pillars of Hampi which was built in 15th century [6]. These techniques during ancient times were so advanced that they match up with the present technology. Thus there might be many such undiscovered techniques which are more advanced and many more mysteries of such structural elements which are untouched are yet to be revealed. As the time passed various column and mandapam designs have emerged showing their stability and uniqueness. Therefore by studying these changes in design we might be able to understand the reason for the evolution.

2   Historical Structures

Our research team has visited various historical structures for visual inspection; some of the pictures are presented below.

2.1   Thousand Pillar Temple

The Thousand pillar temple as shown in Fig. 1 is located in Hanamakonda, Telangana State, India. It was added to the tentative list of World Heritage sites recognized by UNESCO [7]. This structure was constructed by the Kakatiya's in 14th century CE. The unique feature of this temple is that it consists of 1000 pillars which also act as walls of the temple. They used a unique foundation technique known as Sandbox technique for strengthening its foundation. In this technique a deep pit is dug and filled with sand and powder mixture of granite, jaggery and terminalia chebula which is covered with rock beams [8]. On this foundation the pillars were laid and the structure was constructed. This temple is constructed in such a way that the main idol is visible when viewed from any direction.

Fig. 1. Different views of thousand pillar temple

2.2   Konark Sun Temple

Konark Sun temple as shown in the Fig. 2 is located in Konark about 35 km northeast from Puri, Odisha in India. It was built using Kalinga architecture. It was declared as a world heritage site by UNESCO in 1984. The temple resembles a giant chariot pulled by 7 horses consisting of 24 wheels located at the base of the temple (12 wheels on each side). These horses depict the 7 days of the week and the wheels indicate 24 h in a day. Each wheel is designed based on the position of the sun. Out of which 2 wheels were proven to be acting as sundials designed to an accuracy of 1 min [9]. It is said that the main idol of the temple has been floating in air because of the arrangement of magnet during construction. The magnet was said to be arranged at the top of the temple and iron plates were placed after every two stones of the structure. But this technique used in the construction is yet to be proven.

2.3   Golkonda Fort

Golkonda fort as shown in the Fig. 3 is situated 11 km away from Hyderabad. It was first built by the Kakatiya's for the purpose of defense from invasions along the lines of Kondapalli Fort. The Qutb Shahi rulers expanded the fort, whose 7 km (4.3 mi) outer wall enclosed the city. Several dynasties ruled over golkonda over years and expanded the fort to current view. It is known for its alarm acoustic system. A hand clap at the entrance of the court echoes and can be heard at the highest point of the fort which is a kilometer away from the entrance. This technique requires the knowledge of sound echo and its amplification apart from geometry of the structure [10]. The diamond shaped indentations on the roof were specially designed for the vibration of sound. The series of arches were designed in such a way that they are smaller than the preceding one. The sound wave produced first gets compressed and bounces back amplified enough to reach considerable distance.

Fig. 2. Complete view of Konark sun temple showing chakra and main sanctum

Fig. 3. Eagle view of Golkonda fort and diamond shaped indentations on roof

3　Numerical Modeling

One of the major structural elements in Ancient structures of world is Column members. Columns play a vital role in providing stability to the structure by transferring the heavy loads from the superstructure to the foundation. In past, columns were studied in depth which resulted in unique innovations that still amaze the scientists and engineers of today. Few being Musical Pillars of Vitthala Temple in Hampi produce various sounds when struck [11], Panch Mahal of Fatehpur Sikri used the method of dual pillars [12], and Thousand Pillar temple in Warangal is majorly constructed of columns which even act as the side walls of the temple [13]. Many such type of columns needs to be studied in order to understand the proper use of material and technology. Different types of columns considered for this study are shown in Fig. 4.

In India from 5th century CE freestanding temples tend to have a mountain like spire, which can take the shape of a curving Shikar in North India and a pyramidal tower called a Vimana in South India. Roofs are fundamental to the integrity of a structure. It is the part of a structure which provides protection from rain, heat, wind and sunlight. Different types of roofs considered for this study are shown in Fig. 5.

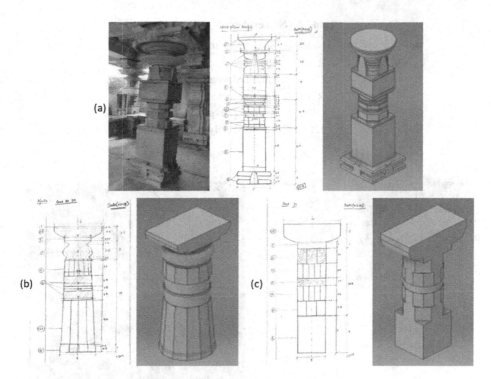

Fig. 4. Generation of 3D numerical models of columns (a) Thousand pillar temple column (b) Ajanta cave conical column (c) Ajanta cave square column

The column (a) is divided into 5 parts, column (b) and column (c) are single part. Modeling of all the case studies of three columns, roofs and nine mandapas has been done using Autodesk Inventor Software. The 2D sketches are drawn at the site with measurements upto scale. Then using scaling factors 3D models are generated from the 2D sketches (Tables 1, 2 and 3). The 2D sketches were drawn to show the keen geometric variations of the columns and roofs. The accuracy of the conversion from 2D to 3D is approximately 85–90%, as inclusion of minor details in 3D modeling is difficult and it needs high precision during meshing.

Table 1. Scaling factors and total height for columns

Case	Scaling factor	Total height (in meters)
a	0.12	2.85
b	0.14	2.8
c	0.135	2.8

Table 2. Nomenclature of shapes

Notation	Shapes/Geometry
R	Rectangular/cuboid
C	Circular/cylinder
R + C	Curved rectangle
O/8C	8 sided polygon
12C	12 sided polygon

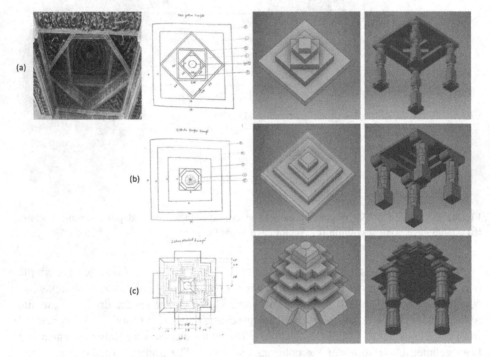

Fig. 5. Generation of 3D numerical models of mandapas (a) Roof of thousand pillar temple (b) Roof of Vitthala temple (c) Roof of Lotus Mahal temple

Table 3. Scaling factor and total dimensions of the roofs

Case	Scaling factor	Total height (m)	Length/Breadth (m)
a	0.2	1	3.8
b	0.2	1	3.8
c	0.46	2.53	4.692

As this research is preliminary, more focus is given to the geometry and dimensions. So, same material model is considered for all numerical models. All the structures considered in this research are primarily constructed using stone whose properties are given in Table 4. In this study only gravity loads have been considered to calculate the deformations and stress distribution. The scope of this research work deals with complete solids and behavior is assumed to be linearly elastic as deformations are small in nature. The base of the foundation is assumed to be fixed.

Table 4. Material properties

Material	Cases	Young's modulus (MPa)	Poison's ratio	Shear modulud (MPa)
Stone	a, b, c	$7.977 * 10^3$	0.25	$3.19 * 10^3$

With combinations of 3 different columns and 3 different roof arrangements nine various simple mandapas are generated. Modal and stress analysis are carried for all developed numerical models.

4 Analysis and Results

Modal and gravity analysis of the developed numerical models have been performed and the results are listed below. Analysis result of columns and two cases of mandapas are shown in Table 5 and Fig. 6 (shows first 3 modes of each mandapa in X and Y directions). Similarly analysis for all the nine mandapa cases has been done and the results are noted.

4.1 Modal Analysis of Columns and Mandapas

Modal analysis is been carried and fundamental frequencies are shown in the Table 5 and Fig. 6

Table 5. Fundamental frequencies of columns and mandapas

Columns	Mode 1 (Hz)	Mode 2 (Hz)	Mode 3 (Hz)
a	32.54	32.58	157.89
b	56.66	56.67	210.18
c	47.67	47.76	157.76
Mandapas			
a	36.27	41.04	53.13
b	13.59	13.60	21.98

Modal analysis is carried to understand the dynamic behaviour of the generated models and to know the kind of frequencies present in the structure. Table 5 shows the first three frequencies obtained for different numerical models. From the obtained results it can be observed that column model (b) column has high fundamental frequency when compared to other two. One of the major reason for having high frequency is uniform reduction in geometry from base to tip, due to its high stiffness. Similarly column (a) has less because of irregular distribution of mass.

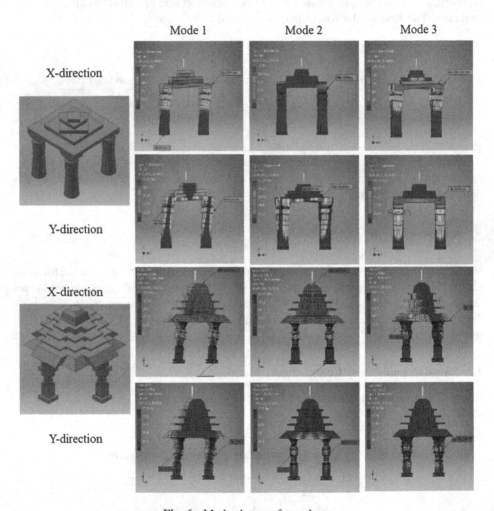

Fig. 6. Mode shapes of mandapas

4.2   Gravity Analysis of Columns and Mandapas

Geometry plays an important in the structural behavior of the structure. The column (a) has the largest maximum von-misses stress compared to column (b) and column (c), this is because of the large variation in geometry in (a) compared to other cases (Table 6). The maximum stress in (a) and (b) are observed where the change in geometry is very thin in shape and where there is sudden change in geometry is sudden or where thin sections are existed. In (c) the maximum stress is observed near the bottom part as the shaft of the column acts as its base. The maximum displacements in all the three cases are observed in the upper part of the column.

Table 6. Static analysis results of the columns

Column cases	Case (a)	Case (b)	Case (c)
Maximum von misses stress in MPa	0.833484	0.115008	0.117653
Maximum displacement in mm	0.00356381	0.00233279	0.00267813

In the mandapas the stress is seen in columns where the variation in geometry is more compared to the roof geometry. The maximum stress is observed in the roof where the geometry of roof is bulky, and it is present where there is a sudden change in geometry such as at the roof-column joint. The maximum displacement in most of the cases is observed in the roof part and at the roof-column joint (the upper part of mandapam). For the models whose roof is arranged in steps format the maximum displacement is seen in the bottom most step and at the edges of the roof.

5 Conclusion

Though there is a lot of research work carried around the world on historical structures it is still short in predicting the actual behavior of these structures, due to its complexity in modeling. One of the reasons is lack of availability of information regarding the dimensions, material, construction techniques and equipment used. The main objective of this research is considering geometry with precision, so this study considered the components as accurately as possible with the available information. The modeled components such as columns and simple mandapam were analyzed for their stability under the gravity loads.

The results conclude that the geometry plays a vital role in the response of structures under given loads. In this project linear material model is considered for all the three pillars and nine mandapas as the analysis is carried for only gravity loads. For the future work, realistic material properties will be considered and both static and dynamic analysis will be carried out (i.e. applying lateral loads and contact forces).

References

1. Kenoyer, J.M.: Ancient Cities of the Indus Valley Civilization.: American Institute of Pakistan Studies (1998)
2. Jain, P.: Dravidian Style of Architecture, 13 April 2017
3. Ronald, A.J., Prasad, A.M., Menon, D., Menon, A., Magenes, G.: Seismic Vulnerability of South Indian Temples, December 2008

4. Menon, A.: Heritage conservation in India: challenges and new paradigms. In: Pena, F., Chavez, M. (eds.) 9th International Conference on Structural Analysis of Historical Constructions, Mexico city, Mexico, 14–17 October 2014
5. Rateesh Kumar, P.: Kakatiyas used earthquake resistant construction technology in Ramappa temple – Sandbox, 22 May 2015
6. Pletcher, K.: Konark, 12 May 12 2014
7. UNESCO Home page.: http://whc.unesco.org/en/tentativelists. Accessed 30 May 2018
8. Baral, B., Divyadarshan, C.S., Rakshitha, M.D.: Warangal fort and temple architecture. NID, Bengaluru. http://www.dsource.in/resource/warangal-fort-and-temple-architecture/thousand-pillar-temple. Accessed 13 Feb 2018
9. FPJ Bureau: Get keen to know Konark, 23 September 2015
10. Nanisetti, S.: Ancient acoustic devices in the fort, 26 March 2012
11. The Mysterious India: The Musical Pillars of the Vittala Temple in Hampi, 5 August 2017
12. Nath, R.: Architecture of Fatehpur Sikri:forms, techniques and concepts. Historical Research Documentation Programme, Jaipur (1988)
13. Radhakrishna Sharma, M.: Temples of Telangana: Basker Ville Type by Director Department of Publication (1972)

A Framework for Semantic Interoperability in 3D Tangible Cultural Heritage in Taiwan

Chiao-Ling Kuo[1], Ying-Mei Cheng[2], Yi-Chou Lu[3], Yu-Chieh Lin[3], Wun-Bin Yang[3], and Ya-Ning Yen[3(✉)]

[1] Research Center for Humanities and Social Sciences, Academia Sinica, Taipei 115, Taiwan
[2] Department of Civil Engineering and Hazard Mitigation Design, China University of Technology, Taipei 116, Taiwan
[3] Department of Architecture, China University of Technology, Taipei 116, Taiwan
alexyen@cute.edu.tw

Abstract. Cultural heritage (CH) preservation and management play vital roles in conserving valuable properties and facilitating relevant historical studies on a country. The advanced technologies developed for CH preservation and management in recent years have made CH digitalization and documentation easy and have generated tremendous amounts of data for a wide range of applications. However, a great focus remains on the large amount of CH data, particularly on CH semantic interoperability, because various standards or schemas are applied during data generation. To achieve 3D CH semantic interoperability, this study proposes and comprehensively discusses an ontology-based approach for 3D tangible CH that includes 3D models, metadata, and their restoration information in the entire life cycle of the building information model (BIM). A tangible cultural heritage ontology is developed based on a top-level ontology, namely, the CIDOC conceptual reference model (CRM), for heritage information, metadata, and restoration. Access is achieved by mapping from the designated heritage in the national cultural heritage database with DC-based metadata to CIDOC CRM and from an enriched Heritage BIM with restoration information encoded as industry foundation classes (IFC) ontology to CIDOC CRM. The proposed framework can successfully combine a 3D model and its enriched information and is available for 3D model semantic accessing and integration. We focus on the discussion of Taiwan's traditional Southern Fujian architecture.

Keywords: Semantic interoperability
CIDOC conceptual reference model (CRM)
Heritage building information modeling (HBIM)
3D model · Tangible cultural heritage (TCH) · Restoration information
The taiwan's traditional southern fujian architecture

© Springer Nature Switzerland AG 2018
M. Ioannides et al. (Eds.): EuroMed 2018, LNCS 11197, pp. 21–29, 2018.
https://doi.org/10.1007/978-3-030-01765-1_3

1 Introduction

Cultural heritage (CH) preservation and management are crucial tasks for the conservation of valuable properties and facilitation of relevant historical studies on a country [1]. With the development of advanced technologies, CH digitalization or documentation for CH preservation and management has become easy, and massive amounts of CH data are generated for a wide range of applications. Presently, many organizations worldwide devote efforts to CH preservation and management. Examples include the United Nations Organization for Education, Science and Culture (UNESCO) [2], International Federation of Library Associations and Institutions (IFLA) [3], Aboriginal and Torres Strait Islander Cultural Heritage in Australia [4], National Institutes for Cultural Heritage in Japan [5], and International Research Centre for Intangible Cultural Heritage in the Asia-Pacific Region (IRCI) [6]. An evident challenge in handling massive amounts of generated CH information is CH semantic interoperability because various standards or schemas are applied during data generation. Ontology-based approaches are extensively employed to achieve CH semantic interoperability because ontology is defined as *an explicit specification of a conceptualization* [7]. The CIDOC conceptual reference model (CRM) [8] in CH is an ontology for describing concepts and relationships of CH and provides CH-related information, such as metadata, a common means of semantic representation.

We propose a framework that analyzes an existing national CH resource, namely, the national cultural heritage database (NCHDB) [9] with DC-based metadata, and extends the 3D model to Heritage Building Information Modeling (HBIM) that contains restoration information via a restoration analysis of CH for tangible cultural heritage (TCH) ontology development. The goal is to make CH information, including physical objects encoded as 3D models, metadata, and their enriched information (e.g., restoration information), semantically accessible and data exchangeable. Given that the proposed framework is based on a proposed TCH ontology that is extended from top-level cultural heritage ontology, CIDOC CRM and HBIM are transferred to ifcOWL [10] and mapped to CIDOC CRM. Then, 3D CH semantic interoperability can be achieved by ontology mapping and ontology integration. In this way, textual information and 3D models can be accessed semantically. We discuss Taiwan's traditional Southern Fujian architecture. The major contributions of this work are threefold.

1. A framework for presenting the semantics of TCH and combining the 3D model, metadata, and restoration information is proposed.
2. An HBIM model representing hierarchical components and the restoration information from LOD 0 to LOD 4 is proposed.
3. A 3D tangible cultural heritage ontology developed by integrating DC metadata, ifcOWL, and CIDOC CRM for tangible CH preservation is discussed.

The remainder of this paper is organized as follows. Section 2 presents related work. Section 3 introduces the proposed method and framework. Section 4 provides the conclusion.

2 Related Work

To achieve semantic interoperability in the CH field, many previous studies have adopted ontology-based approaches for semantic representation, semantic integration, and data exchange facilitation. In [11], a domain ontology, namely, monument damage ontology, was proposed to identify monuments and clarify relevant terms of monument damage. Reference [12] made a semantic annotation in CH preservation by using the multimedia ontology proposed in [13]. Aside from domain ontology proposed for a specific demand in a specific domain, top-level or core ontology has also been widely used as a mediator that assists in semantic representation and ontology integration. CIDOC CRM [8] is the most commonly utilized top-level ontology for CH semantic interoperability. CIDOC CRM in CH is event-centric and presents the relation among people, time, places, and so on. The authors in [14] employed semantic web technology to present archaeological information based on CIDOC CRM by mapping an archaeological dataset from a database or text to CIDOC CRM. Moreover, CIDOC CRM is applied to the semantic presentation of museums, libraries, and archives [15]. The authors in [16] extended the archaeology ontological model (CRM-EH) from CIDOC CRM to the archaeology domain to achieve archaeological semantic interoperability by data mapping and extraction. With regard to the integration approach, mapping methods for metadata integration that map EAD [17] and Dublin Core (DC) [18] to CIDOC CRM via path- and event-oriented approaches have been discussed. In addition to the textual information of CH, physical objects encoded as 3D models (e.g., 3D geographical information system or 3D GIS) are also vital CH resources for 3D information visualization, presentation, and application. Thus, the issue of 3D model semantic presentation has elicited considerable attention. BIM [19] has been widely discussed and used in recent years because it is beneficial for the efficiently planning, design, construction, and recording of entire life cycle information. Accordingly, an ontology for the BIM model, namely, ifcOWL [20], has been proposed for 3D model semantic representation. In [21], historic building information modeling based on the ifcOWL ontology was mapped to the corresponding CityGML [22] class to achieve the integration of ifcOWL and CityGML. Automatic CityGML LOD3 building models can also be generated from ifcOWL-based approaches [23]. The textual information and 3D models of CH are expected to be presented semantically. Thus, in this study, we aim to integrate the 3D model, metadata, and enriched information (e.g., restoration information) on the entire life cycle into BIM for comprehensive CH preservation and management.

3 Methodology

To make 3D TCH with enriched information, such as restoration information, semantically accessible and interoperable, a framework composed of two main parts is established. The two parts are (1) data resource analysis and design of HBIM, (2) development of the TCH ontology and TCH resource description framework (RDF) [24], and repository, which is illustrated in Fig. 1. A TCH ontology is proposed by adopting a schema-mapping approach based on an extensively used ontology, namely, the CIDOC CRM ontology, in the CH field. The TCH ontology was derived via the analysis of the NCHDB resource with DC-based metadata and an HBIM model with enriched management and restoration information designed from a 3D model resource. Subsequently, relevant TCH information is transformed and encoded as RDF data for semantic query and application to allow users to view 3D models and their enriched semantic information. We discuss Taiwan's traditional Southern Fujian architecture. Further details on this research are presented below.

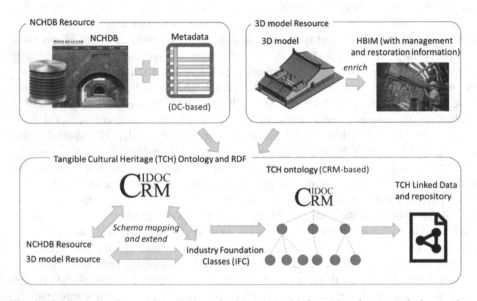

Fig. 1. Framework of a tangible 3D model with enriched information for semantic integration and application.

3.1 Data Resource Analysis and Design of HBIM

The NCHDB developed by the Bureau of Cultural Heritage, Ministry of Culture, in Taiwan encompasses designated CH information on tangible and intangible heritage, including monuments, historic buildings, settlements, historic sites, cultural landscapes, traditional arts, traditional folklore, antiquities and relics, and conservation techniques. The NCHDB is a relational database that stores above types of heritages with information such as the name, manager, official documents, criteria or laws for a heritage judgement, media, essay, designated types and reasons, etc. To make NCHDB accessible, a DC-based metadata extension from the original DC schema using the "field" attribute for tangible and intangible heritage in NCHDB was proposed in 2014. Each type of heritage is designed for a fitness metadata schema to fit its characteristics. For example, the metadata of a historic monument composed of normal elements, such as title, publisher, description, date, type, language, rights, and three extensions presenting information on class (assetsclassify), level (assetslevel), and type (assetstype-name) from the subject and four extensions presenting information on the location city (locationCity), address, or place (govDeptCity), longitude, and latitude are shown as Fig. 2, which also presents DC-based metadata with extensions of a historic monument called Cai Ancestral Shrines in Qionglin.

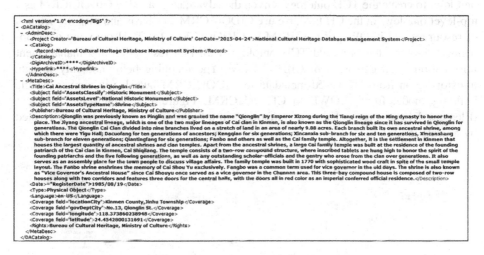

```
<?xml version="1.0" encoding="Big5" ?>
- <DACatalog>
  - <AdminDesc>
    <Project Creator='Bureau of Cultural Heritage, Ministry of Culture' GenDate='2015-04-24'>National Cultural Heritage Database Management System</Project>
    - <Catalog>
      <Record>National Cultural Heritage Database Management System</Record>
    </Catalog>
    <DigiArchiveID>****</DigiArchiveID>
    <Hyperlink>****</Hyperlink>
  </AdminDesc>
  - <MetaDesc>
    <Title>Cai Ancestral Shrines in Qionglin</Title>
    <Subject field='AssetsClassify'>Historic Monument</Subject>
    <Subject field='AssetsLevel'>National Historic Monument</Subject>
    <Subject field='AssetsTypeName'>Shrine</Subject>
    <Publisher>Bureau of Cultural Heritage, Ministry of Culture</Publisher>
    <Description>Qionglin was previously known as Pinglin and was granted the name "Qionglin" by Emperor Xizong during the Tianqi reign of the Ming dynasty to honor the
      place. The Jiyang ancestral lineage, which is one of the two major lineages of Cai clan in Kinmen, is also known as the Qionglin lineage since it has survived in Qionglin for
      generations. The Qionglin Cai Clan divided into nine branches lived on a stretch of land in an area of nearly 9.88 acres. Each branch built its own ancestral shrine, among
      which there were Yigu Hall; Dacuofang for ten generations of ancestors; Kengqian for six generations; Xincanxia sub-branch for six and ten generations, Xincanxiang
      sub-branch for eleven generations; Qiantingfang for six generations; Fanbo and others as well as the Cai family temple. Altogether, it is the settlement in Kinmen that
      houses the largest quantity of ancestral shrines and clan temples. Apart from the ancestral shrines, a large Cai family temple was built at the residence of the founding
      patriarch of the Cai clan in Kinmen, Cai Shiqiang. The temple consists of a two-row compound structure, where inscribed tablets are hung high to honor the spirit of the
      founding patriarchs and the five following generations, as well as any outstanding scholar-officials and the gentry who arose from the clan over generations. It also
      serves as an assembly place for the town people to discuss village affairs. The family temple was built in 1770 with sophisticated wood craft in spite of the small temple
      layout. The Fanbo shrine enshrines the memory of Cai Shou Yu exclusively. Fangbo was a common term used for vice governor in the old days. The shrine is also known
      as "Vice Governor's Ancestral House" since Cai Shouyu once served as a vice governor in the Chunnan area. This three-bay compound house is composed of two-row
      houses along with two corridors and features three doors for the central halls, with the doors all in red color as an imperial conferred official residence.</Description>
    <Date>="RegisterDate">1985/08/19</Date>
    <Type>Physical Object</Type>
    <Language>en-US</Language>
    <Coverage field="locationCity">Kinmen County,Jinhu Township</Coverage>
    <Coverage field="govDeptCity">No.13, Qionglin St.</Coverage>
    <Coverage field="longitude">118.373860238948</Coverage>
    <Coverage field="latitude">24.4542800131691</Coverage>
    <Rights>Bureau of Cultural Heritage, Ministry of Culture</Rights>
  </MetaDesc>
</DACatalog>
```

Fig. 2. DC-based metadata from NCHDM: a case of a historic monument called Cai Ancestral Shrines in Qionglin.

In addition to the textual information of CH, constructing a 3D model for a physical object from reality is another important task for CH preservation and management. 3D model construction using BIM [19] has been receiving considerable attention because it provides an efficient means for the design, planning, building management, and recording of entire life cycle information. The development of an HBIM that contains enriched information, such as restoration information, for detailed information representation aside from merely recording basic properties (e.g., name, issued year, and shape) is therefore vital. Furthermore, an ontology for the BIM model, namely, ifcOWL [20], has been proposed for 3D model semantic representation. Thus, we claim that 3D models encoded as HBIM assist in the subsequent semantic integration and application. In this research, we discuss Taiwan's traditional Southern Fujian architecture with preservation and management information, especially restoration information. The proposed HBIM model consists of two essential parts: hierarchical component and restoration information. The hierarchical component is proposed by referring to [25] and detailing building components (e.g., Cai Ancestral Shrines in Qionglin) to smaller components (e.g., "dougongs" or brackets). Specifically, the level of detail of HBIM encompasses LOD 0 to LOD 4. As to the principle of decomposing the components of a building to construct the components of HBIM, the following criteria of decomposition are adopted: from outer to inner, from front to back, from left to right, and from bottom to top. For restoration information, the ID, repair date and time, destroyed situation, repair craft, repair tools and materials, and name of repair craftsman are recorded in HBIM. The HBIM model is implemented with the AutoCAD Revit software [26].

3.2   TCH Ontology, TCH RDF, and Repository

After encoding the textual information and 3D model into the proposed HBIM, this step analyzes resources and maps the schema between resources and the existing ontology to create the TCH ontology. Given the advantages of using CIDOC CRM as a top-level ontology in the CH field, we use CIDOC CRM as a basis and map the schema of resources and ifcOWL of the HBIM to CIDOC CRM for TCH ontology development. Therefore, the proposed TCH ontology with rich restoration and management information is an extension of CIDOC CRM. The mapping helps not only in data transformation from DC-based metadata to CIDOC CRM but also in converting the building model from ifcOWL to CIDOC CRM. Figure 3 illustrates the fragment (Element_E18 is represented as a component in a building) of TCH ontology created by a protégé [27].

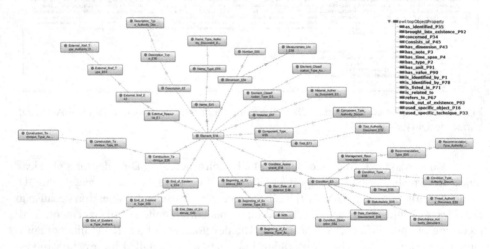

Fig. 3. TCH ontology.

After establishing the TCH ontology, the creation of RDF data is implemented. These data are then stored in an RDF repository, such as Virtuoso [28], to support semantic query and application. Furthermore, the 3D HBIM models with enriched information are available and can be accessed by the linking the UID between the component and RDF (the approach of accessing an image is the same by linking the image id between the component and an image) on a self-developed website based on three.js [29]. Figure 4 shows a 3D HBIM model example of Cai Ancestral Shrines in Qionglin.

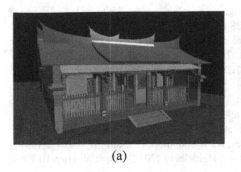 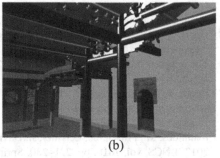

(a)   (b)

Fig. 4. HBIM model example of Cai Ancestral Shrines in Qionglin. (a) Outer appearance and (b) inner appearance.

4 Conclusion

Massive amounts of CH information are generated for CH preservation purposes, and solving heterogeneity and facilitating semantic interoperability among CH have become crucial tasks. In this research, we propose a framework that combines a 3D model, its metadata, and enriched information (e.g., restoration of TCH) for semantic accessibility by using a CIDOC CRM-based TCH ontology for metadata and restoration presentation. The 3D model can be accessed via HBIM. The proposed framework can present the semantics of a tangible 3D CH model and its enriched information, and it allows further for the involvement of intangible information of CH for a complete CH semantic presentation and application.

Acknowledgements. This work was supported by the Bureau of Cultural Heritage, Ministry of Culture, Taiwan (R.O.C.) [grant no. 107-05 and 107-06].

References

1. Doerr, M.: Ontologies for cultural heritage. In: Staab, S., Studer, R. (eds.) Handbook on Ontologies. IHIS, pp. 463–486. Springer, Heidelberg (2009). https://doi.org/10.1007/978-3-540-92673-3_21
2. The United Nations Organization for Education, Science and Culture (UNESCO). https://en.unesco.org/. Accessed 15 June 2018
3. The International Federation of Library Associations and Institutions (IFLA). https://www.ifla.org/cultural-heritage. Accessed 15 June 2018
4. The Aboriginal and Torres Strait Islander Cultural Heritage. https://www.datsip.qld.gov.au/people-communities/aboriginal-torres-strait-islander-cultural-heritage. Accessed 15 June 2018
5. The National Institutes for Cultural Heritage. http://www.nich.go.jp/english/. Accessed 15 June 2018
6. The International Research Centre for Intangible Cultural Heritage in the Asia-Pacific Region. https://www.irci.jp/. Accessed 15 June 2018

7. Gruber, T.R.: Toward principles for the design of ontologies used for knowledge sharing? Int. J. Hum.-comput. Stud. **43**(5–6), 907–928 (1995)
8. Doerr, M.: The CIDOC conceptual reference module: an ontological approach to semantic interoperability of metadata. AI Mag. **24**(3), 75 (2003)
9. The national cultural heritage database (NCHDB). https://nchdb.boch.gov.tw/. Accessed 15 June 2018
10. Beetz, J., Van Leeuwen, J., De Vries, B.: IfcOWL: a case of transforming EXPRESS schemas into ontologies. AI EDAM **23**(1), 89–101 (2009)
11. Blaško, M., Cacciotti, R., Křemen, P., Kouba, Z.: Monument damage ontology. In: Ioannides, M., Fritsch, D., Leissner, J., Davies, R., Remondino, F., Caffo, R. (eds.) EuroMed 2012. LNCS, vol. 7616, pp. 221–230. Springer, Heidelberg (2012). https://doi.org/10.1007/978-3-642-34234-9_22
12. Mallik, A., Chaudhury, S.: Acquisition of multimedia ontology: an application in preservation of cultural heritage. Int. J. Multimed. Inf. Retrieval **1**(4), 249–262 (2012)
13. Ghosh, H., Chaudhury, S., Kashyap, K., Maiti, B.: Ontology specification and integration for multimedia applications. In: Sharman, R., Kishore, R., Ramesh, R. (eds.) Ontologies, vol. 14, pp. 265–296. Springer, Boston (2007). https://doi.org/10.1007/978-0-387-37022-4_9
14. Eide, Ø., et al.: Encoding cultural heritage information for the semantic web. Procedures for data integration through cidoc-crm mapping. In: Open Digital Cultural Heritage Systems Conference (2008)
15. Gill, T.: Building semantic bridges between museums, libraries and archives: the CIDOC conceptual reference model. First Monday **9**(5) (2004)
16. Binding, C., May, K., Tudhope, D.: Semantic interoperability in archaeological datasets: data mapping and extraction via the CIDOC CRM. In: Christensen-Dalsgaard, B., Castelli, D., Ammitzbøll Jurik, B., Lippincott, J. (eds.) ECDL 2008. LNCS, vol. 5173, pp. 280–290. Springer, Heidelberg (2008). https://doi.org/10.1007/978-3-540-87599-4_30
17. Stasinopoulou, T., et al.: Ontology-based metadata integration in the cultural heritage domain. In: Goh, D.H.-L., Cao, T.H., Sølvberg, I.T., Rasmussen, E. (eds.) ICADL 2007. LNCS, vol. 4822, pp. 165–175. Springer, Heidelberg (2007). https://doi.org/10.1007/978-3-540-77094-7_25
18. Kakali, C., et al.: Integrating Dublin Core metadata for cultural heritage collections using ontologies. In: International Conference on Dublin Core and Metadata Applications (2007)
19. Azhar, S., et al.: Building information modeling (BIM): a new paradigm for visual interactive modeling and simulation for construction projects. In: Proceedings of the First International Conference on Construction in Developing Countries (2008)
20. Hietanen, J., Final, S.: IFC model view definition format. Int. Alliance Interoperab. 1–29 (2006)
21. Dore, C., Murphy, M.: Integration of historic building information modeling (HBIM) and 3D GIS for recording and managing cultural heritage sites. In: 2012 18th International Conference on Virtual Systems and Multimedia (VSMM). IEEE (2012)
22. Kolbe, T.H., Gröger, G., Plümer, L.: CityGML: interoperable access to 3D city models. In: van Oosterom, P., Zlatanova, S., Fendel, E.M. (eds.) Geo-Information for Disaster Management, pp. 883–899. Springer, Heidelberg (2005). https://doi.org/10.1007/3-540-27468-5_63
23. Donkers, S.: Automatic generation of CityGML LoD3 building models from IFC models (2013)
24. Klyne, G., Carroll, J.J.: Resource description framework (RDF): concepts and abstract syntax (2006)
25. Lee, Q.: 台灣古建築圖解事典 (Taiwanese Historical Architecture Picture Thesaurus (Translated from Chinese)), vol. 2. Yuan-Liou Publishing Co., Ltd. (2003)

26. Revit | BIM Software | Autodesk. https://www.autodesk.com/products/revit/overview. Accessed 15 June 2018
27. Protégé. https://protege.stanford.edu/. Accessed 15 June 2018
28. Erling, O., Mikhailov, I.: Virtuoso: RDF support in a native RDBMS. In: de Virgilio, R., Giunchiglia, F., Tanca, L. (eds.) Semantic Web Information Management, pp. 501–519. Springer, Heidelberg (2010). https://doi.org/10.1007/978-3-642-04329-1_21
29. three.js. https://threejs.org/. Accessed 15 June 2018

Reconstructing the Historic Landscape of Larochette, Luxembourg

Marleen de Kramer(ID), Sam Mersch(ID), and Christopher Morse(✉)(ID)

Luxembourg Centre for Contemporary and Digital History,
University of Luxembourg,
2 avenue de l'Université, 4365 Esch-sur-Alzette, Luxembourg
{marleen.dekramer,sam.mersch,christopher.morse}@uni.lu

Abstract. Cultural Heritage education relies on a solid foundation of scientifically validated knowledge. This case study shows how different disciplines come together to source, combine, and interpret data for a landscape reconstruction of Larochette, Luxembourg. It is the initial stage of a larger interdisciplinary project to create an educational game that highlights the tangible and intangible heritage that can be traced in the town's structures even today.

Keywords: Cultural heritage · Interdisciplinary · History
Reconstruction · Larochette · GIS · 3D modelling · Landscape
Tangible vs. intangible CH

1 Introduction

The reconstruction of the town and castle of Larochette, Luxembourg is a case study that shows how our expertise combines to create and validate a scientifically accurate model of a historical cultural landscape. This is the initial stage of a larger endeavour: to design an educational game that reveals the connection between a town's past and the names of its squares, streets, and even car parks—a visualisation of its intangible heritage. Our interdisciplinary approach, which draws on history, heritage science, linguistics, architecture, and interaction design, reveals the town to be a palimpsest, with traces of its history preserved within its structure.

It highlights the importance of context in heritage. Our changing perspective on history acknowledges that the castle did not exist in isolation; rather, it is part of the cultural and socioeconomic construct that is a fortified medieval/early modern town. Our analysis will attempt a snapshot of the landscape ca. 1550 in order to provide a backdrop for a reconstruction of the castle at the peak of its development, before it fell into ruin, and the town continued to develop independently [1].

This chapter was funded by the Luxembourg Fonds National de la Recherche.

The original version of this chapter was revised: Inadvertently the funding institution was not mentioned in the original chapter. A footnote for the explanation was added on the first page of the chapter. The correction to this chapter is available at https://doi.org/10.1007/978-3-030-01765-1_34

M. Ioannides et al. (Eds.): EuroMed 2018, LNCS 11197, pp. 30–37, 2018.
https://doi.org/10.1007/978-3-030-01765-1_4

The town of Larochette is located in the centre east of the Grand Duchy of Luxembourg and was already settled during the Roman era. The castle and the House of Larochette later rose to prominence during the High Middle Ages, but became less significant in early modern times. [2] Due to many divisions of the estate and internal squabbles, the castle fell into ruin. [3] Until the 20th century, the town was well renowned for its cloth manufacture, but today, its main industry is tourism, the picturesque ruins of the castle attracting visitors with outdoor pursuits like hiking and camping [4] (Fig. 1).

Fig. 1. Larochette castle and town, seen from the watchtower.

The Grand Duchy of Luxembourg is known for its linguistic diversity, as French, German, and the native Luxembourgish are all national languages. Luxembourgish is usually a spoken language, while French and German are primarily administrative. As a result, French and German have a lingering influence on the naming practices of places. Major place names have up to three official names[1], and minor place names were often transliterated into German rather than rendered in Luxembourgish when they were initially recorded[2] [5].

2   Data Overview

Our landscape—cultural or natural—is a *dramatype*,[3] an emergent pattern that evolves and adapts to its changing environment without ever being completely

---

[1] Such as the three official names for Larochette; *Larochette, Fels, Fiels.*

[2] We use the term *minor place names* or *micro-toponyms* for anything smaller than towns (e.g. fields). Their meanings are provided in idiomatic English for purposes of this article.

[3] In biology, a "dramatype" is an organism that adapts to changes in its environment directly, within the lifespan of a particular individual, as opposed to the phenotype, the expression of the genotype of a particular population that has developed within a particular environment. (See "The Principles of Humane Experimental Technique", W.M.S. Russell and R.L. Burch, 1958).

destroyed and rebuilt, so that the structure of the original can be read in the traces that remain. While some elements can change drastically in centuries, decades, or even years—buildings, land use, and, historically, the courses of rivers, and others remain fairly constant. Of course, the most persistent feature is the underlying geomorphology, but major roads, property boundaries and land-mark structures are also often remarkably slow to evolve—as a consequence, the landscape itself is our main primary source (Fig. 2).

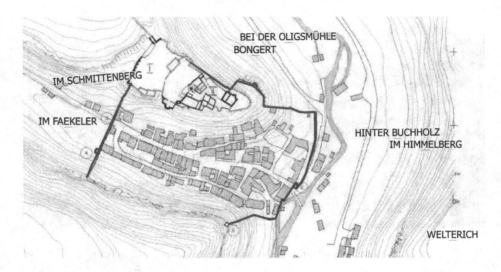

Fig. 2. Location of former town walls and place names.

Little scientific research pertaining to our case study has been published, so we amended our initial survey using other sources relating to historic landscapes. These include archaeology, place names, aerial and historic images, maps, local history and other related fields. As no official archaeological documentation was ever produced, we relied on the archaeological data on Larochette Castle pro-vided in ZIMMER (1996), a book that includes surveys of the castle ruins, but also overview maps of the town walls and other landscape features. Primary sources on the castle, the town, or the House of Larochette are found in the form of legal treaties. The open data portal of the Luxembourgish state (data.public.lu) and the website of the land registry office (http://geoportail.lu) gave us access to orthophotos, modern and historic maps, including the 1777 Ferraris map and historic cadastral maps, land use, toponymic and other geographic data. The two-volume special issue on Larochette of the journal *Cahiers Luxembourgeois* (1938), which includes articles on regional and local history and the toponomas-tic landscape, is a concise overview of secondary sources [6].

While much of this material dates from well after the period we are recon-structing, and although many descriptions are rather romanticising, rather than showing a contemporaneous reality, they were still useful in assessing the situation in Larochette, which has changed more significantly since the 1950s than in all the preceding centuries.

3   Methodology

3.1   Desk-Based Study

Our initial overview was a desk-based comparative study, combining data from our individual disciplines.This yielded enough material for a rudimentary assessment of the castle of Larochette and its immediate surroundings.

To give our data a spatial context, we conducted a GIS analysis. This allowed us to define our study area. A pragmatic decision was made to limit it to what can be seen from the castle itself. A viewshed analysis of the official 5 m resolution digital terrain model using observation points on all of the castle's towers[4] revealed that, due to the hilly terrain, nothing outside a 5 km radius was visible from the castle, and all man-made structures shown on historic maps fell within 2.5 km. Since the study focuses on the cultural landscape, the smaller circle was the obvious choice. Our work mainly focused on the area that is both visible from the castle and within the bounds of the town as shown in the original cadastral map [7].

To help identify features, the first cadastral maps of Larochette (1824) were georectified and layered over modern maps and orthophotos. Finally, we added the local minor place names, land use data, and drew in J. ZIMMER's hypothesised town wall as a linear feature.

3.2   Fieldwork

Although terrain maps and satellite images provide an overview, the importance of comparing data from primary and secondary sources to the modern terrain was immediately apparent when we visited the site. We acquired new data in the form of details not considered important by cartographers or impossible to reproduce in a map—the names of car parks, a GPS-tracked walk along the postulated town wall supplemented by photographs of turning points, a feeling for the steepness of the climb to the castle, details of watercourses, soil and vegetation.

3.3   Cross-Validation

Our analysis shows a striking contrast between the areas inside and outside the town walls—while the building footprints, streets, and property boundaries within the walled town remain remarkably constant, the area just outside the original town gate on the eastern wall on the other side of the river is quite volatile. Two roads are combined into one, property boundaries disappear as

---

[4] The observer's height above the ground was roughly estimated from the number of stories in each part of the building.

fields become houses, the river is straightened and partially paved over, a new square is created, the town gate gives way to a wider bridge and a new road leading through the town, and a larger church is built along the eastern edge of the valley.

But how can we draw conclusions about the 16th-century town based on its 19th-century state? Industrialisation had a much larger and much more sudden impact on the landscape than previous developments. The town's population, reasonably steady throughout the preceding centuries [8], suddenly grew, farming gave way to industry, and a railway connected the town to the rest of the Grand Duchy. The landscape before the industrial revolution, which arrived in Luxembourg in the 1840s, is more similar to the 16th-century landscape than it is to the present day [9].

In fact, even the modern place names may not necessarily be historically correct. For cross-validation of our theories, we can refer to other data points. Minor place names are a good indicator of the previous use of a particular piece of land. The medieval town wall has angles built to accommodate an existing building. Surviving medieval documents refer to the town, its landscape, and its early industry.

The importance of cross-validation of sources to eliminate false conclusions can be demonstrated using the example of the place name *Schmittenberg* (i.e. smith's mountain) in Larochette town, near the western gate close to the castle, which at first glance implies a smithy. Its absence in the first map does not necessarily suggest that there was no such place, just that it might not have been important enough to be put on the map. However, the value of a field survey soon became apparent, as we found an inscription above the door of a nearby house that identified the owner as one *Johannes Schmitz*, who presumably lent his name to the street.

4   Historic Land Use

As in any medieval town, the majority of Larochette's landscape was dedicated to agriculture, primarily subsistence farming. Our knowledge of this comes primarily from minor place names designating fields, streams, hills, etc. Many of these indicate crops and the demarcation of certain fields set aside for planting. These include *auf dem fischten Stück* (i.e. on the forward-most plot), *in den Theilen* (i.e. in the section of fields). Others evoking the elongated shape of a plot—such as *Langfeld* (i.e. long field)—evidence crops like wheat, as they suggest ploughed fields [10]. The valley and river have names relating to wetlands, such as *auf dem Wasser* (i.e. on the wetland) or *im Weiher* (i.e. in the pond) [10].

Situated close to the city walls, *Bongert* and *Oligsmuehle*, also relate to agricultural production, the former referring to an orchard, the latter to an oil mill. The earliest evidence of these names is the first cadastral map that dates to the early 1800s, but the names themselves and their locations suggest an earlier usage.

Livestock farming is evidenced by names such as *auf dem grossen Driesch* (i.e. on the big common), *Platzwies* (i.e. a meadow) or *Bourenpesch* (i.e. pasture close to water, from lat. *pascua*, pasture), while others relate to woods, like *Weltrich* (i.e. rich in forest) or special trees, such as *Bürkelt* (i.e. birch field). Beyond such toponyms as *hinter Buchholz* (i.e. behind the cleared land), the oil mill that was formerly a sawmill evidences the production of timber [12].

Numerous mills in Larochette attest to early industry, but the most important by far is also the oldest, the *Bannmühle* (i.e. bound mill). The name attests to a mill soke (*banalité du moulin* in French), meaning that locals were required to use only that mill to grind grain. This law gave the House of Larochette economic control over the villages under its dominion. A 16th-century edict dictates a hierarchy for use of the mill, which was broken down by social status and rank, and gave first use to the town providing the millstones [11].

Larochette was known even in the 20th century for its textile industry, whose roots date at least as far back as the 14th century. King John the Blind of Bohemia (*1296-†1346) granted the right to erect four looms with frames suitable for cloth with a length of 25 ells (a Parisian fleece ell was about 0.61 m). Four looms were a significant asset at this time, with most towns being granted only one [13]. Among the town's many mills were a fulling mill (Luxembourgish *Follmillen*) for the production of good woolen cloth or fine leather, dating at least into the 15th century [11].

Medieval town life centred around the market and the church. Today's church is located well outside the walls, along the eastern slope of the valley. However, older maps and depictions of the town show a small church and adjoining graveyard in the southeastern corner of the old town. A further clue is, once again, in the name: the street leading through it is the *Rue St. Nicolas*, and the car park itself is named *Kierfecht* (i.e. graveyard) [14].

There is no room for a market within the bounds of the former city wall, the only open space being a walled garden on the northeastern corner, nor is one shown on the 19th-century maps and engravings. Instead, most commercial buildings cluster around the road leading to the bridge across the *Ernz blanche* (White Ernz) river and into the main gates of the town, suggesting that the wide meadow in the east was in use as a market. One engraving shows a high-ceilinged non-residential building in the middle of a square, which could well have been a covered market.

4.1 Certainty of Results

We apply a four-tier hierarchy of certainty to our reconstruction work:

relict-interpolated-extrapolated-speculative

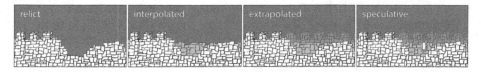

"Relict" covers elements for which evidence survives from the time of their creation. "Interpolated" refers to consulting several nearby data points, e.g. filling a gap in a wall along an existing foundation. Where this "interpolated" result is a line between two points, an "extrapolated" one is a vector, using a solid point of reference augmented with secondary and tertiary sources. "Speculative" results are obtained using only secondary and tertiary sources, e.g. comparing with similar sites or drawing on expertise from other fields, like estimating heights of walls using engineering knowledge.

Our conclusions fall into the third to fourth tier; we are using existing data points to draw conclusions about former states, and presenting the results as our working hypothesis. Comprehensive documentation is a critical element in the development of our reconstruction. It summarises research decisions, tracks sources, and affords the opportunity to re-examine our conclusions if new, contradictory information comes to light. Grounding the reconstruction within the scientific method guarantees a duplicable process and an adaptable model.

5   Prospects for Virtual Reconstruction

Moving beyond the traditional "artist's impression" toward a reconstruction that is researched, validated, and documented, we support a broader movement that integrates emerging technologies into heritage science, providing tools for the outreach and dissemination of knowledge to the public.

We are developing the Larochette learning game using A-Frame[5], a web framework for virtual reality applications. Players will be positioned inside a reconstruction of one of the rooms in the Criechinger Haus on the eastern side of the castle, overlooking the valley below. They will be tasked with combining graphic representations of the name elements of local minor place names in Luxembourgish (e.g. Bann + Mühle) and locating them on a map of the valley. Correctly combining and placing the names will reward players with a three-dimensional symbol in the virtual landscape. Suitable names were chosen based on visibility, variety, and natural separation into distinct elements.

Drawing on learning models designed for cultural heritage, such as the *Sandbox Serious Games* (SBSG) model described by BELLOTTI ET AL. (2012), the Larochette game will engage users while simultaneously encouraging the creation of "well-connected knowledge structures representing relationships among facts and concepts" [15]. This approach, based originally in cognitive science and reconceptualised for use in cultural heritage contexts, extends the project's reach to general audiences and brings the cultural landscape and its tangible and intangible heritage to life.

References

.1. Cf. Majerus, N.: Die Luxemburger Gemeinden nach den Weistümern, Lehenerklärungen und Prozessen, Vol 4. St. Paulus, Luxembourg (1963). Meyers, J.: Studien zur Siedlungsgeschichte Luxemburgs. De Gruyter, Berlin (1932)

---

[5] https://aframe.io/.

2. Cf. Majerus (1963). Diederich, A.: Notes généalogiques sur la Famille de Larochette. Les Cahiers luxembourgeois **1**(2), 21–28 (1938). Ries, N.: Les Seigneurs d'Ouren. Les Cahiers luxembourgeois **1**(2), 29–32 (1938). Schroell, P.: Le Château-Fort et les Seigneurs de Larochette. Les Cahiers luxembourgeois **1**(2), 33–40 (1938). Ries, N.: Puissance et Privilèges des Seigneurs de Fels. Les Cahiers luxembourgeois **1**(2), 41–44 (1938)
3. Cf. Dasburg, V.: Die Schlossruinen von Fels. Les Cahiers luxembourgeois **1**(2), 57–79 (1938). Dasburg, V.: Kurzer Abriss der Geschichte der Herrschaft von der Veltz. Les Cahiers luxembourgeois **1**(2), 100–144 (1938). Zimmer, J.: Burgen des Luxemburger Landes, vol. 3. Saint-Paul, Luxembourg (1996)
4. http://www.larochette.lu/presentation.html. https://www.visitluxembourg. com/de/ansicht/castle/schloss-larochette. http://www.associationchateaux.lu/ francais/larochette/index.html. Accessed 28 May 2018
5. Cf. Géportail. https://geoportail.lu. Accessed 28 May 2018Cf. also Gilles, P.: Dialektausgleich im Lëtzebuergeschen. Niermeyer, Tübingen (1999), Goetzinger, G. et al.: Lëtzebuergesch—"eng Ried, déi vun allen am meeschtem ëm ons Kléngt". CNL, Mersch (2001). Meyers (1932)
6. Ashton, M.: Interpreting the Landscape. Batsford, London (1989), 13–20. Hardt, M.: Burgfriede zu der Felz, 1. Juni 1399. PSH **5**, 10–26 (1850). Hardt, M.: Luxemburger Weithümer. Bück, Luxembourg (1870). Holbach, R., Pauly, M.: Das "Lützelburger Duch". In: Pauly, M. (ed.) Schueberfouer 1340–1990, pp. 71–111. Saint-Paul, Luxembourg (1990). Cf. also Pauly, M.: Geschichte Luxemburgs. Beck, München (2011). Cf. also Zimmer (1996). La plate-forme de données luxembourgeoise, https://data.public.lu. INSPIRE. https://data.public.lu/fr/search/? q=INSPIRE. Géportail. https://geoportail.lu. Accessed 28 May 2018
7. Zimmer (1996). First cadastral Map of Larochette. http://map.geoportail. lu/theme/main?fid=256_1011. Open Street Map. https://download.bbbike.org/ osm/bbbike/Luxemburg/. Google Street Map, https://www.google.com/maps. Also used via the QGIS Google Street Map Web Layer. Minor Place Names of Luxembourg. https://data.public.lu/fr/datasets/region-names-from-the-digitized-cadastral-map-pcn/. Accessed 28 May 2018
8. Cf. Courrier du Grand-Duché de Luxembourg, Nr. 154, 2. Juli 1865. Development of population density. https://data.public.lu/fr/datasets/densite-de-la-population-par-canton-et-commune-habitants-par-km2-1821-2017/. Accessed 28 May 2018
9. Economic Development. http://www.luxembourg.public.lu/en/le-grand-duche-se-presente/histoire/histoire-mots/essor-economique/index.html. Accessed 28 May 2018. Gengler, Cl.: La nouvelle géographie du Luxembourg, In: Trausch, G. (ed.) Histoire du Luxembourg, pp. 275–297. Privat, Luxembourg (2003)
10. Cf. Erpelding, É.: Die Mühlen des Luxemburger Landes. Saint-Paul, Luxembourg (1981). Anen, P.: Luxemburgs Flurnamen und Flurgeschichte. Saint-Paul, Luxembourg (1946). Cf. Ashton (1989)
11. Erpelding (1981)
12. Cf. Erpelding (1981)
13. Cf. Pauly (1990)
14. Rausch, D.: Panorama von Fels, Engraving. Lithographie Erasmy, Luxembourg (accessed by courtesy of the Bibliothèque Nationale de Luxembourg)
15. Bellotti, F.: A serious game model for cultural heritage. J.: Comput. Cult. Heritage **5**(4), 17:1–17:27 (2013)

Digital Preservation of the Nottingham Ichthyosaur Using Fringe Projection

Petros Stavroulakis[1]($\boxtimes$) (ID), Yael Bis-Kong[2], Elodie Doyen[2],
Thomas Hartman[3], and Richard Leach[1]

[1] Manufacturing Metrology Team, University of Nottingham,
Nottingham NG8 1BB, UK
`petros.stavroulakis@nottingham.ac.uk`
[2] École Nationale d'Ingénieurs de Saint-Étienne, 42100 Saint-Étienne, France
[3] School of Life Sciences, University of Nottingham,
Nottingham NG7 2RD, UK

Abstract. Natural heritage is an important part of cultural heritage. More specifically, the protection and preservation of the unique biodiversity of flora and fauna in a specific region is an important part of preserving and celebrating the cultural diversity and identity of a region and of a nation. Nottingham is a home of pre-historic natural heritage and specifically of the 'Nottingham Ichthyosaur'; a new species *Protoichthyosaurus applebyi* named in 2017 which was discovered in the area, probably in the early part of the 19th century. The near-complete type specimen of the species is on display at the Life Sciences building of the University of Nottingham. In this work, we describe the process which was used to digitally preserve the specimen which, it is hoped, will be lodged in an appropriate museum. The purpose of the digital preservation would be to aid teaching and research purposes as well as exploit the data for further distributed research by other natural scientists. To digitise the fossil, which was embedded, in cement a commercial fringe projection system was used to register the bone structure and grayscale imaging was used to register the texture of the bones on display.

Keywords: Natural heritage · Ichthyosaur · 3D form metrology
Fringe projection

1 Introduction

Optical areal non-contact 3D measurements techniques normally developed for industrial applications have been proving useful in scientific areas such as archaeology [1], architecture [2], cultural heritage [3, 4] and life/medical sciences [5]. Non-contact digital dimensional preservation using non-contact optical technologies can be performed on a range of scales, from small to medium objects [3], all the way up to large structures of interest to cultural heritage curators (temples [2], caves [1] and amphitheatres [6]).

The benefits of digitisation in the field of Life Sciences ranges between enabling simultaneous study of the same object by multiple researchers at the same time, to

© Springer Nature Switzerland AG 2018
M. Ioannides et al. (Eds.): EuroMed 2018, LNCS 11197, pp. 38–44, 2018.
https://doi.org/10.1007/978-3-030-01765-1_5

providing a teaching aid for educators by supplying a virtual object or a 3D printed replica. Additionally, the production of replicas via 3D printing from the data acquired can be used for promotional/marketing activities and provide an extra source of income to museums and curators of cultural heritage.

In this work, an example of digital preservation performed on a circa 140 million year old fossil of an Ichthyosaur available at the Life Sciences building at the University of Nottingham is presented.

2 Methodology

The Ichthyosaur fossil is a nearly complete skeleton in a limestone matrix that has been embedded in a thick layer of concrete for structural integrity and security and, therefore, it was available for digitisation from one side only. The system used to perform the measurement was a commercial fringe projection setup (SIDIO XR from NUB3D).

2.1 3D Metrology Specifications

The SIDIO XR fringe projection system used has four measurement volumes which are shown in Table 1.

Table 1. The four measurement volumes supported by the SIDIO XR fringe projection kit.

Measurement volume	Length/mm	Width/mm	Depth/mm	Accuracy/μm
1	120	80	60	~9
2	190	150	90	~12
3	340	260	200	~15
4	550	390	240	~19

The accuracy figures are not stated in the product specifications. They are the nominal values acquired after repeated calibration cycles at each of the measurement volumes. The reason that accuracy increases with measurement volume has to do with the fact that the same camera is used for all volumes and therefore the measurement resolution drops as the distance to the object increases.

2.2 Spatial Restrictions

The part of the Ichthyosaur that was available for measurement was restricted, so movement of the fringe projection system around the fossil was challenging. This meant that there was also a restriction on the angles and points of view from which the fossil could be measured. We selected three general directions which were in the plane vertical to the spine and spaced angularly as far apart as possible in order to acquire the fossil from as many directions as possible. Each direction was used to scan the fossil along its length and the various scans were aligned during post processing.

2.3   Scan Strategy

As a general rule of thumb and as discussed in Sect. 2.1, the smaller the measurement volume selected, the higher the lateral resolution and depth accuracy. However, in this case, the Ichthyosaur had large out-of-plane features (with respect to the accuracy achievable) and, therefore, it did not need to be measured with the smallest measurement volume to achieve the highest accuracy. As it was not critical which measurement volume was used, the largest measurement volume (550 mm × 390 mm × 240 mm) was selected in the interest of stitching together the least amount of measurements, as none of the measurement volumes could acquire the full Ichthyosaur at once (stitching together a large amount of 3D measurements is prone to the accumulation of alignment errors).

For two parts of the fossil in particular (the head and the fin), the measurement was repeated at higher resolution, as it was requested that it be studied in more detail. This is important because several diagnostic features of the different species are found in the forefin. In the publication defining this fossil as the type specimen [7], six features of the arrangement of the bones in the forefin are cited as being critical in distinguishing this as a new, distinct species. An image of the fin is shown in Fig. 1.

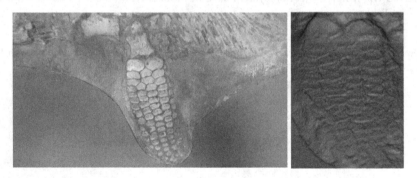

Fig. 1. Image of the arrangement of the bones on the forefin of the Ichthyosaur at the University of Nottingham and accompanying 3D surface mesh of the 3D topography.

3   Results

As noted, the Ichthyosaur was measured longitudinally from three different directions. The data from each longitudinal measurement taken from a specific direction needed to be stitched together for the full length of the Ichthyosaur. In general, however, the actual data which were added to the final measurement after each overlapping scan was kept to a minimum. The reason for keeping overlapping data to a minimum is that it increases the chance of data 'blurring'. Data 'blurring' is the effect of having multiple point clouds of the same area overlapped onto each other [8]. The reproduction accuracy drops when compared to a single shot of the same area as slight misalignments between the overlapped point clouds create a 'fuzzy' point cloud which can reduce high spatial frequencies present in the measurement and, therefore, replicate the object with lower fidelity.

It was, therefore, decided that the first measurement would be kept in its entirety and useful segments from overlapping scans would be kept in areas where the first measurement was lacking data, as discussed, to minimise data 'blurring'. Minimising the overlapping data also results in minimising the size of the dataset and is, therefore, more practical when post-processing the data.

3.1   Scan Stitching

To assemble the complete point cloud of the Ichthyosaur, multiple alignment operations were required. The first operation was stitching the components of each measurement together to create a full Ichthyosaur for each scan. The coarse stitching was performed by selecting corresponding points in overlapping segments of the measurements and the fine alignment was performed in the overlapping regions by an iterative closest point (ICP) algorithm available in a point cloud processing software called Cloud Compare [9]. An example of a completed Ichthyosaur measurement is shown in Fig. 2.

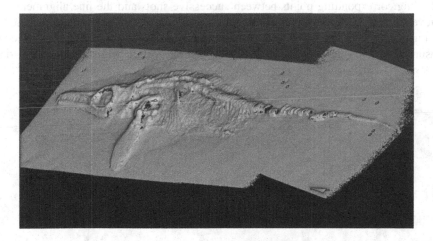

Fig. 2. Image of the point cloud created after stitching the parts of the first scan together.

To assist in the initial coarse alignment procedure, circular target stickers were attached around the fossil (Fig. 3). The 3D shots taken in each measurement were overlapped in such a way as to ensure that at least three targets were visible between successive shots to allow for quick and efficient coarse point cloud alignment when post processing the data.

Fig. 3. Image of the fossil with circular sticker targets placed around it to ease coarse alignment.

3.2 Selective Void Filling

The second operation required was to align the measurements to each other in order to identify which parts were missing form each measurement and could, therefore, be 'filled-in' to allow for a more complete representation of the fossil. As discussed, the alignment process between measurements comprised of two stages, a coarse alignment and a fine alignment stage. The coarse alignment between measurements was achieved by finding corresponding points between successive shots and the fine alignment was achieved though ICP. An example of selective void filling is shown in Fig. 4, where the missing points from the top of the skull and the spine were acquired from the second measurement and, therefore, improved the overall result whilst minimising data overlap.

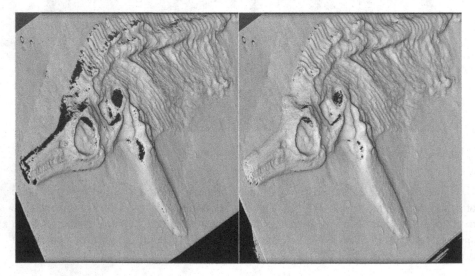

Fig. 4. Example of the void filling technique, the missing points from the top of the skull and spine which were missed by the first scan were saved after overlapping and aligning the next scan and selecting the missing regions to add to the dataset.

3.3   Data Tagging and Storage Strategy

The data were stored in ASCII point cloud files. The 3D coordinates of each point were stored in three columns each representing the XYZ coordinates respectively. There was a simple file naming and numbering schema used to tag the individual point cloud passes with the metadata required for the reconstruction of the complete Ichthyosaur point cloud at the end of the 3D measurement.

The data is stored on the University of Nottingham's research drive (R: drive) which is backed up daily at multiple sites clones in order to ensure backup and preservation of the data.

4   Conclusions

Life sciences, archaeology, architecture, cultural heritage and other scientific areas have much to gain from the use of non-contact dimensional form measurement equipment. In this example we achieved the digital preservation of the morphology of a fossil via optical means and in particular via fringe projection.

Multiple measurements were required to acquire a complete point cloud of the object to the accuracy required as the fossil had lots of corrugated self-occluding features. The dataset acquired will be sent for 3D printing and the digital replica will be used as a teaching aid as well as a marketing tool when the fossil will be lodged in an appropriate museum.

This work shows the advanced simplicity and speed of preserving fossils digitally using fringe projection compared to photogrammetry which is normally used for this work. Real-time feedback of the acquired areas and areas which are missing from the scan is immediately known in fringe projection therefore the amount of data and measurements that need to be taken can be minimised. In our case each pass of the Ichthyosaur was required 4 measurements, and the complete point cloud of the fossil was performed in total with only 12 measurements. In photogrammetry, the operator takes images 'blindly' around the object. Therefore to ensure that they will be enough to cover all the self-occlusions during post processing a lot more such photos are taken compared to fringe projection [10]. Finally, the post processing time required to reconstruct them can rise to in some cases to ~ 12 h depending on the number of photographs taken [10].

4.1   Future Work

The 3D printed replica will be evaluated in terms of accuracy with the CAD created as well as functionality appropriateness. The three functions investigated for the 3D printed replica are for it to serve as a teaching aid, scientific 'digital double' (i.e. for researchers to use the 3D model instead of the real fossil to conduct research), and as a marketing tool to promote publicity and interest into the specific fossil and palaeontology in general.

References

1. Lerma, J.L., Navarro, S., Cabrelles, M., Villaverde, V.: Terrestrial laser scanning and close range photogrammetry for 3D archaeological documentation: the Upper Palaeolithic Cave of Parpalló as a case study. J. Archaeol. Sci. **37**, 499–507 (2010)
2. Pavlidis, G., Tsiafakis, D., Koutsoudis, A., Arnaoutoglou, F., Tsioukas, V., Chamzas, C.: Preservation of architectural heritage through 3D digitization. Int. J. Archit. Comput. **5**, 221–237 (2007)
3. Hermon, S., Polig, M., Driessen, J., Jans, G., Bretschneider, J.: An integrated 3D shape analysis and scientific visualization approach to the study of a Late Bronze Age unique stone object from Pyla-Kokkinokremos. Cyprus. Digit. Appl. Archaeol. Cult. Herit. **10**, e00075 (2018)
4. Themistocleous, K., Ioannides, M., Agapiou, A., Hadjimitsis, D.G.: The methodology of documenting cultural heritage sites using photogrammetry, UAV, and 3D printing techniques: the case study of Asinou Church in Cyprus. In: Proceedings of SPIE - The International Society for Optical Engineering, vol. 9535, p. 953510 (2015)
5. Frankowski, G., Hainich, R.: DLP-based 3D metrology by structured light or projected fringe technology for life sciences and industrial metrology. In: Hornbeck, L.J., Douglass, M.R. (eds.) Proceedings of SPIE - The International Society for Optical Engineering, vol. 7210, p. 72100C (2009)
6. Agapiou, A., Hadjimitsis, D., Alexakis, D., Themistokleous, K., Cuca, B.: Integrated method for tracking changes in archeolandscapes using remote and close-range technologies: monitoring of change and risk assessment methodologies. In: 2013 Digital Heritage International Congress (DigitalHeritage), pp. 231–234. IEEE (2013)
7. Lomax, D.R., Massare, J.A., Mistry, R.T.: The taxonomic utility of forefin morphology in Lower Jurassic ichthyosaurs: Protoichthyosaurus and Ichthyosaurus. J. Vertebr. Paleontol. **37**, e1361433 (2017)
8. Olsen, M.J., Johnstone, E., Kuester, F., Driscoll, N., Ashford, S.A.: New automated point-cloud alignment for ground-based light detection and ranging data of long coastal sections. J. Surv. Eng. **137**, 14–25 (2011)
9. Cloud Compare homepage. http://www.danielgm.net/cc/. Accessed 28 June 2018
10. Falkingham, P.L.: Acquisition of high resolution three-dimensional models using free, opensource, photogrammetric software. Palaeontol. Electron. **15**, 1–15 (2012)

Resilience and Preservation of Cultural Heritage After Natural Disasters: Case Study of City of Volos, Greece

Mprouzgou Maria[✉] and Coccossis Harry

Department of Planning and Regional Development, School of Engineering,
University of Thessaly, Pedion Areos, 38334 Volos, Greece
mbrouzarch@gmail.com

Abstract. Natural disasters and their interaction with cultural heritage are a global phenomenon that has come to the attention of the scientific community the last decade. Preventive measures and policies have been developed in order to protect the natural and cultural environment of the humanity. The current study aims at the identification of cultural heritage, its interaction with natural disasters and the up-to-dated developed policies for Volos city in Prefecture of Magnesia, in Greece. "The social and economic implications of a heritage at risk", are corroborated by the example of the '50s earthquake at Magnesia Prefecture. The current research indicates that Greek policies are not well targeted, and they are without a vision. Additionally the preventive taken measures are not cost effective and the local community is not aware of the existing risk. Thus, in the current research are proposed a few non-constructive measures such as: (i) the creation of a local natural disaster and cultural heritage data-base, (ii) the enhancement of the public awareness concerning the natural disasters and its effect on cultural heritage and (iii) the promotion of cultural heritage and its value. Aiming at cultural resilience and sustainable development of the region, the proposed measures must also be supported by a strong legal framework.

Keywords: Cultural heritage · Cultural resilience · Preventive measures
Sustainable communities · Greece · Prefecture of Magnesia · City of Volos

1 Tangible Cultural Heritage - Sustainable Communities

Nowadays, it has been recognized that heritage conservation can contribute significantly for developing sustainable communities, leading therefore to a sustainable future. The four main components of sustainable communities are: (i) the economic, (ii) cultural, (iii) social and (iv) environmental sensitivity, awareness and success. It is important to highlight that the conservation of cultural heritage have several positive impacts to the long-term community sustainability. Some of them are the increased property values, the development of heritage tourism, the reuse of buildings and structures and the enhancement of the local economy.

Natural disasters are one of the most common factors that are responsible for the destruction not only of the cultural buildings, but also of the disappear of local cultural communities. In the following sub-sections are discussed the connection between

M. Ioannides et al. (Eds.): EuroMed 2018, LNCS 11197, pp. 45–52, 2018.
https://doi.org/10.1007/978-3-030-01765-1_6

natural disaster and cultural identity along with the policies that have been taken up-to-date for the cultural heritage protection and conservation [1, 2].

1.1 Natural Disasters and Cultural Identity

Cultural heritage expresses the history and the specificities of a community, having a catalytic impact on its economic prosperity, its coherence as well as on the formation of its national identity. More specifically, the cultural heritage's inseparable relationship with the environment is important as it defines, emerges and sets the purpose of its existence expressing the past, the present and the future. Any disturbance of this relationship from destabilizing factors, such as natural disasters, can affect directly and at a great extent the identity of cultural heritage [3].

The tendency of man to preserve the elements that have been bequeathed by his ancestors is an impulsive tendency expressed due to his need to connect with his natural environment and its cultural elements. Thus, changes to the balance of the relationship 'cultural heritage-nature', can lead to the disorientation of the local community, the displacement of its members from their point of reference, the devaluation of local community present and past as well as to the reduction of the chances of recovery.

The impacts of a natural disaster can be evident in the faults of a building structures, by altering its constant cultural elements which constitute factors that create the historical and cultural identity of the building structures [4]. Those can vary and can be multifaceted, influencing different aspects of life and are categorized into direct and indirect impacts. Being more specific, direct impacts of a natural disaster refer to material damage of measurable size, while the indirect refer to the perceived ones after the incident being of immeasurable size and recognized in the wider environment, after a reasonable time [5].

Therefore, the achievement of the restoration of a community, from all aspects, after natural disasters is an inherent need and can be partially achieved through the protection of its cultural heritage and the shaping of its new identity by assimilating the effects of dangerous natural phenomena. The use of existing and new cultural elements for the revival of a community is a direction of modern development strategy policies in an effort to maintain the cohesion of a society in times of crisis [6]. In the next subsection the policies that have been developed towards this direction, are discussed.

1.2 Policies for the Protection and Preservation of Cultural Heritage from Natural Disasters

Natural disasters so far are treated as individual and independent events. Particularly in European territory, addressing this issue varies from country to country as well as from one region to another. Most of the preventive measures that have been taken concern mainly International cultural elements that are scarce and of great significance.

According to the recent European Commission's report [7], lists and databases have been created in occasional cases, but they are not up to date or complete. Each country's action plans are used and updated in their theoretical context without put into practice due to lack of qualified staff and the formation of the appropriate bodies of action.More specifically the EU's final remark has been: «*serious gap in the collective approach to creating and promoting fully effective resilience policies. Cultural heritage is persistently omitted, and this need must be addressed*» [7].

However, over the past decade great efforts have been made from some EU countries to implement a wider protection of the cultural elements of a community. The protection of the cultural elements of a community can contribute significantly to the development of sustainable communities and consequently of sustainable environments [7].

The most important policies that have been taken from the EU are: (i) the increase of funds from 5.3 million to 25 million of euros in 2019 to transform historic urban areas into hubs of social and cultural integration, (ii) the increase of funds to mitigate the impacts of climate change and natural hazards on cultural heritage and (iii) the development of international networks for cultural heritage innovation and intercultural diplomacy [8].

In the Greek territory the application of protection measures is non-existent and whatever action had been taken was the result of individual mobilization and sensitivity of the humans without a clear planning. Moreover, the lack of finance as well as of the comprehensive plans that for protecting any cultural heritage of natural disasters constitutes a fact [9].

Thus, the aim of the current research is to recognize the necessity of protecting the cultural heritage of city of Volos, located in Prefecture of Magnesia, in Greece, from natural disasters.

The main objectives are:

- To link the notions of durable cultural heritage - Durable society - Cultural identity - Sustainable development in the case of Volos city
- To identify the magnitude of natural disasters impacts on the cultural heritage of the Volos city
- To identify and suggest policies that can ensure Volos cultural heritage continuity.

2   Cultural Heritage and Natural Disasters: Case Study of Volos City, Greece

2.1   Location of Volos City

Volos is a city of Thessaly, built in Pagasitikos gulf, near the site of ancient Iolkos and on the foothills of the Pelion mountain in Greece (see Fig. 1). It is one of the largest cities including one of the most important ports of Greece. According to the 2011 census, the permanent population of the Municipality of Volos was 86,046 inhabitants,, which reaches the 125,248 inhabitants, when the inhabitants of the rural area are taken into consideration.

The area of Volos (ancient Magnesia) is among the first areas inhabited in Greece. The settlements discovered in the nearby villages of Sesklo and Dimini dated back to the 7th millennium BC, while the cultural presence in the area is still compelling as it is discussed in the following sub-section.

Fig. 1. Location of city of Volos, Prefecture of Magnesia, Greece [10].

2.2 The Most Important Cultural Heritage of Volos City

Prefecture of Magnesia owns a rich cultural heritage that reflects the region's history, myths and legends, the social changes and the economic influences of every age. The location of 99 important archaeological sites within the administrative unit of Magnesia, the 21 Monasteries and the number of religious buildings, the 24 Traditional Settlements of Pelion and the 300 buildings of architectural heritage in Volos, constitute a multifaceted cultural landscape capable of becoming a decisive factor in the region's sustainability [11].

The vulnerability of the above-mentioned rich heritage had been endangered in the past by varied natural phenomena, mainly by earthquakes and floods. Their inadequate infrastructure (resistant to natural phenomena) was another factor enhancing their vulnerability and, by extension threatening to alter the cultural identity of the place [12, 13]. Therefore, cultural heritage protection should be a primary concern for the local authorities and the local community.

The Ancient Theater of Demetriades is one of the characteristic examples of Hellenistic theaters, located west of the urban center of Volos, at the site of Dontia, within the boundaries of the walls of the ancient city, in Pagasses. Against the palace of the Macedonian kings where the hero of the Chiefs and Builders of the city of Demetrias was built. The use of the theater ends in the 4th century. A.D. and since then has been exposed to many natural and manual disasters. The theater was discovered in 1901, while in 2017 the building parts of the Roman technique, the orchestra, the hollow and the frescoes were revealed [14].

The areas of Dimini (4,800 BC) and Sesklo (6,800 BC) are considered to be two of the most important prehistoric settlements in Greece during the Neolithic period. Dimini was discovered by Lolling and Wolters in 1886, by the identification of the Mycenaean vaulted tomb. The excavations that followed brought into surface important findings about the region's culture and its evolution into the years. Sesklo was excavated by Tsunta revealing the Acropolis (Kastraki) and a variety of clay objects [15].

Finally the archaeological site on the hill of Goritsa is considered an authentic monument of the Hellenistic period. The buildings that were discovered are the city's footprints, strategically located by Kassander between 316–298 BC. and which was abandoned some years later. It is claimed that had lived between 3,000 and 3,500 inhabitants, uilding 400–500 houses according to the Hippodamian system. The Hippodamian system originates to the ancient Greek architect and it is an urban planning concept that organizes the layout of cities and towns into a system of straight roads and streets intersecting each other at a 90° angle [16].

2.3   Natural Disasters Impacts on the Cultural Heritage of Volos City

The archaeological site of Goritsa it is located in the pine forest, so being in constant danger of a possible fire. A characteristic example is the 1994 fire which posed the archaeological site into a serious danger. Furthermore, the Goritsa hill's archaeological site due to the fact that up-to-date remains unprotected and exposed to natural phenomena, such as rain, is being flooded continuously on (see Fig. 2). The lack of the appropriate infrastructure, for flood and fire protection, in combination with the lack of public awareness and the negligence of local authorities, enhance the impacts of natural disasters [17].

Fig. 2. Archeological site on the hill of Goritsa in Volos, Prefecture of Magnesia, Greece (a) flooding and uncovered, (b) covered with panels [18].

In 2018, the archaeological service installed panels (see Fig. 2) for maintenance purposes, but since then has not been developed and specific project to protect the area. The historical city remains exposed to the weather, with the risk of flooding, fires and disintegration of materials over time.

In its turn, the City Hall (see Fig. 3) remained intact until 1970 when it suffered considerable damage after a great earthquake. From 1909 until the earthquake housed the services of the Municipality of Volos, while in 1939 it was donated by Maria Skerderanis to the general public. In the 1990, in its place a multi-storey building of dubious architectural value was built, covering any sign of cultural heritage (see Fig. 3).

2.4   Contemporary Policies and Projects on the Protection of Cultural Heritage from Natural Disasters in Volos City

According to the results of the current investigation, the Volos Structure Plan and the Volos Residential Environmental Protection Plan, the Volos General Urban Plan, the Urban Spatial Planning and Spatial Planning Scheme and the Strategic Development Plan of Magnesia are some of the recent projects considering the protection of the city.

Fig. 3. The ex City Hall of Volos City, Prefecture of Magnesia, Greece (left picture: before earthquake, right picture: today) [19].

The projects that have been implemented or are planned to be implemented are projects for the restoration of selected historic buildings or infrastructure projects. In 2005, the characteristics of the land using regulatory plans, according to which tourist concentrations, archaeological sites and traditional settlements were identified and reported officially (44357/2005-FEK:1502/B/1.11.2005). This can be said that is the first movement of recognizing the necessity of identifying all the historical sites all over the Greece.

In its turn the Sustainable Urban Development Plan of Volos is another project which is consisted of 27 sub-projects of 15 million euros worth value (funding from NSRF program). Some of the most important works are the reconstruction of the old Port Authority and the Panepistimiou Square (700,000 euros).The antiseismic construction of the Municipal Theater (NSRF - 2,200,000 euros) is considered another important project of the city in order to maintain its cultural heritage.

Additionally, within the framework of the Regional Operational Program of Thessaly, 2007–2013, the financing for the maintenance of the train of Pelion mountain was approved. It worths being mentioned that the train of Pelion was constructed in 1892 and was a creation of the father's greatest painter Giorio De Chirico that inspired him for many of his initial paintings.

However, all the above-mentioned projects concerned only the reconstruction and not the protection of natural disasters. The unique programme that has been developed concerning the protection of cultural heritage from natural disasters is the Eufofinet-Civil Protection Program (2011–2014). This aims to exploit the already well-proven good practices in the field of forest fires, in order to create a competent exchange network knowledge and response models at National and regional level.

3   Conclusions

In the case of city of Volos, many historical significant sites and buildings that are the cultural identity of the city have been identified. Some of the most important sites are the Goritsa hill, the ancient theater of Demetriades and others. According to the current research many of them more than once time have suffered by natural disasters, such as earthquake and floods. However, even after those impacts of natural phenomena the local authorities even today have not shown the appropriate attention.

Moreover, even recent natural phenomena, e.g. flooding of archeological sites, have not led to preventive measures even to a future project. This fact highlights the lack of the knowledge of the cultural heritage importance and at the same time the presence of a loose National legal framework concerning cultural heritage. For this reason it is suggested a project that all the historical sites and buildings will be recorded in a respective map. Moreover the creation of a database that will record every natural disaster from the past to the present for each site, respectively, would be very useful for the implementation of future projects in order Volos city's cultural heritage to be protected by natural phenomena.

References

1. Coccossis, H.: Sustainable development and tourism: opportunities and threats to cultural heritage from tourism. In: Cultural Tourism and Sustainable Local Development, pp. 65–74. Routledge (2016)
2. Coccossis, H., Kallis, G.: Theoretical reflections on limits, efficiency and sustainability: implications for tourism carrying capacity. In: the Challenge of Tourism Carrying Capacity Assessment (Routledge), pp. 31–52 (2017)
3. King, T.F.: Our Unprotected Heritage: Whitewashing the Destruction of Our Cultural and Natural Environment. Routledge, New York (2016)
4. Van Vugt, M., Hart, C.M.: Social identity as social glue: the origins of group loyalty. J. Pers. Soc. Psychol. **86**, 585 (2004)
5. Jha, A.K.: Safer Homes, Stronger Communities: A Handbook for Reconstructing After Natural Disasters. World Bank Publications, New York (2010)
6. Kiriama, H.: The community and sustainable heritage management: the Rabai Kayas of coastal Kenya La communauté et la gestion durable du patrimoine: La Kaya de Rabai sur la côte kényane. Living with World Herit Africa **56**, 2 (2012)
7. European year of cultural heritage E for culture-EC: Safeguarding cultural heritage from natural and man-made disasters a comparative analysis of risk management in the EU (Brussels) (2018)
8. European Parliament directorate-G for IP of the U: Protecting of the cultural heritage from natural disasters-Policy Department Structural and Cohesion Policies (2007)
9. European Comission. http://www.europarl.europa.eu/RegData/etudes/etudes/join/2007/369029/IPOL-CULT_ET(2007)369029_EN.pdf
10. Heritage EC-C: Policies, publications and funding details to support preserving Europe's cultural heritage (2017)
11. European Comission. https://ec.europa.eu/research/environment/index.cfm?pg=cultural
12. Organization P. https://pelionparadise.com/wp-content/uploads/2017/01/greece-magnesia-blue.jpg
13. Deffner, A., Metaxas, T.: Shaping the vision, the identity and the cultural image of European places (2005)
14. Papazachos, B.C., Panagiotopoulos, D.G., Tsapanos, T.M., Mountrakis, D.M., Dimopoulos, G.C.: A study of the 1980 summer seismic sequence in the Magnesia region of Central Greece. Geophys. J. Int. **75**, 155–168 (1983)
15. Ambraseys, N.N.: Value of historical records of earthquakes. Nature **232**, 375 (1971)
16. Ferrara, F.M.: Demetriade in Tessaglia a la polis il palazzo reale macedone. Archeol. Class. **65**, 181–226 (2014)

17. Darling, J.K.: Architecture of Greece. Greenwood Press, London (2004)
18. Blogspot A: A visit to Goritsa Hill (2014). http://artanis71.blogspot.gr/2014/01/blog-post. html
19. Tassopoulou, K.: Historical builidings that were regretfully destroyed (Κτίρια που ο Βόλος γκρέμισε και το έχει μετανιώσει) (2015). https://e-thessalia.gr/185497-2/

Visualisation, VR&AR Methods and Applications

The Epigraphic Museum of Athens Revisited

Athanassios Themos[1], Eleni Zavvou[1], Eirene-Loukia Choremi[1], and Nikolaos Dessipris[2(✉)]

[1] Epigraphic Museum, Tositsa 1, 10682 Athens, Greece
{ema, ezavvou}@culture.gr, echoremi@gmail.com
[2] Institute of Communications and Computer Systems (ICCS),
Zografou Campus, 9, Iroon Politechniou Str, 15780 Zografou, Greece
nikos.dessipris@iccs.gr

Abstract. The main ideas behind the re-exhibition of the permanent collections of the Museum and the use of digital media are presented. For the first time in the Museum, the re-exhibition is supported by digital means. The Museum has focused on touchscreen displays together with mobile devices for organising and supporting the visitors. The Museum tablet application presented, allows the user to get a multilingual integrated approach for each item on display. The plans of the museum are focusing on augmented reality applications running on visitors' smartphones. It is also shown that despite the restricted nature of the museum artifacts (fragments of stones with partial inscriptions) digital presentations can be successfully created, if complementary combined information from other archaeological fields and published research is employed.

Keywords: Inscriptions · Tablet · Augmented reality

1 Introduction

The re-exhibition of Room 11 is developed in two topics (each one having three sections), whereas Room 9 has one topic (with ten sections). Both the printing and digital material accompanying the exhibition are presented, with a focus on the novel *'Epigraphic Museum tablet application'*. This short paper closes with a description of direction for the future digital museum projects.

2 About the Epigraphic Museum

The Epigraphic Museum houses the largest collection of ancient Greek inscriptions, the primary historical sources that provide valuable information for the economic, politic, religious and social life of ancient times. It stores 14.078 inscriptions on stone, deriving mostly from Attica, but also from other areas of the ancient Greek world dating from the 8th cent. BC. till the later times (most of them in ancient Greek language). The Museum is housed in the south wing of the basement of the building of the National Archaeological Museum.

© Springer Nature Switzerland AG 2018
M. Ioannides et al. (Eds.): EuroMed 2018, LNCS 11197, pp. 55–63, 2018.
https://doi.org/10.1007/978-3-030-01765-1_7

3   The Renovation of Gallery 11

The main concept for the renovation of Gallery 11 is *the history through the stones*, i.e. the historical and social information obtained from the inscribed monuments and their importance for the knowledge of the various aspects of the ancient Greek life.

The exhibition creates a clear and structured narrative course based on both the chronological organization of the archaeological material and the development of individual topics. Forty inscribed monuments are exhibited in Room 11[1].

The Exhibition of Room 11 is developed in 2 topics (Topic 1 & 2 below):

Topic 1: the birth and the development of writing, includes 3 sections:

Section 1: *'The provenance of the Greek Alphabet and the Early Greek Inscriptions'* of topic 1, informs the visitors about the pre-alphabetic scripts of the Aegean, the provenance of the Greek alphabet from the Phoenician and the types of the earliest preserved ancient Greek inscriptions.

Section 2 *'Ways of Writing'* the different ways of writing and arranging texts in the archaic Greek inscriptions are presented through four monuments.

Finally in Sect. 3, *'the Local Alphabets'* (Fig. 1) presents examples of early Greek alphabets from different regions of Greece (Thira, Corinth, Amorgos, Argos).

Topic 2: Main categories of inscriptions in the Archaic period (three sections).

The first section presents *'laws and sacred laws'*. Of great importance is a copy of stele VI of the Law Code of Gortys, the largest and most important Greek law code, was written initially in the Cretan alphabet (480–460 BC).

The second section *'Dedicatory inscriptions'* includes a total of 17 inscribed Attic monuments. In the center of the gallery, a scenic setting is formed that represents the open space of a sanctuary (Fig. 2). Around the altar that was dedicated to the sanctuary of Apollo Pythios (SW of the Olympeion) by Peisistratos, the homonymous grandson of the famous tyrant, eight archaic dedicatory monuments (mainly statue – bases) are set up. In the northwest corner of the room, this section closes with *the craftsmen's offerings,* inscriptions mentioning the occupation of the dedicator or the sculptor who created the dedication.

The third section *'Funerary inscriptions of the Archaic period'* are inscriptions from graves (placed on either side of the hallway's corridor as an imitation of the road to an ancient cemetery). The six statue-bases, placed as signs on the grave of the dead, preserve funerary epigrams (verse inscriptions) providing evidence of the diseased.

4   The Renovation of Gallery 9

Ten topics under the general title *'Aspects (Views) of Public Life'* are presented here:

---

[1] The conservation of the inscriptions and the order of their location in galleries 11 and 9 were coordinated by the head of the Laboratory of Conservation Stergios Tzanekas and the conservator Theodoros Mavridis. The bases and the presentation of room 11 with wooden partitions were designed by the architect-engineer Nikolaos Kyriakopoulos. The general coordination of the works was done by the architect-engineer Dr. Marianna Savrami.

Fig. 1. Sections: *'the provenance of the Greek alphabet and the early Greek inscriptions', ways of writing'* and *'local alphabets'* at the south side of Gallery 11. In a showcase at the left, the earliest preserved Attic inscription on stone.

Fig. 2. The section 'Dedicators and Dedications' with central exhibit the altar of Peisistratos. Around it, eight archaic dedicatory statue-bases are arranged in the center of the gallery 11.

Section 1 presents four of the *'oldest written texts of Ancient Athens'*: (a) The oldest known decree (resolution) of the people's Assembly of Athens (510–500 BC), (b) The sacred law of Hekatompedon, which includes regulations on the use of the sacred vessels of the Hekadompedon temple and the protection of the sanctuary, (c) Re-publishing of Draco's earlier law on homicide (408 BC) and (d) The so-called *'Themistocles decree'* from Troizen (3rd cent. BC), probably a copy of a decree in

Fig. 3. The "ancient decree" section and the drawer on the west side of the gallery

which Themistocles seems to propose significant measures to protect the city of Athens against the Persians before the naval battle of Salamis.

Section 2 *'the Ancient Decree'* presents the proceedings for the adoption of resolutions (decrees) by the Athenian Boule (Parliament) and by the Assembly of the People (demos) through five monuments (Fig. 3).

Section 3 *'Selection procedure for the Athenian rulers and the distribution of judges by drawing lots'* includes a kleroterion, an allotment machine used by the Athenians during the democracy to select officers and citizens serving public bodies by lot.

Section 4 *'Honorary Decrees'* informs the visitors about the award of honours to Athenian and foreign citizens, who had provided services and benefited the Athenian state either financially or morally.

Section 5, *'Worship section'*, informs the visitor on various aspects of the religious life of ancient Athens, such as the types of offerings to the gods and the sacrifices, the management and the account of the property of the sanctuaries (Fig. 4).

Section 6: *'Choregic Monuments'*: The institution of choregia was one honorable and sumptuous liturgy of ancient Athens (established in Athens in the 5th century BC), whereby wealthy Athenians were assigned the financial responsibility of producing a dithyrambic, tragic or comic chorus for a festival of the city (Fig. 4).

In Sect. 7 *'Public Funerary Monuments'* stelai are exhibited with the names of the fallen Athenian warriors listed according the official series of tribes, either in the same stele or in a number of stelai on a common base (Fig. 5).

The exhibition closes with 3 more sections: Sect. 8 *'Various Monuments'*, Sect. 9 *'The Institution of Ephebeia'* and Sect. 10 *'Monuments of the Roman Period'*.

Fig. 4. The 'Worship' section in the southwest corner of gallery 9 the 'Choregic Monuments'

Fig. 5. The 'Choregic Inscriptions' and the 'Public funerary monuments for the fallen warriors' sections.

5   Supporting Printed and Digital Material

5.1   Printing and Digital Material

New short captions of the monuments were drawn up in Greek and English, which took into account the recent bibliography. Installation of wall-mounted information panels in Greek and English at the beginning of each topic, enhanced the exhibition.

A special digital application was created with information material, also in Greek and English, which is accessible through 6 interactive touch screens placed in the central parts of the two galleries. It will soon be accessible by handheld touch screens (tablets).

5.2   The Epigraphic Museum Tablet Application

The highly user-friendly application presents a comprehensible record for each monument, (photo, a short caption and basic information).

The user touches the screen on the tablet and is driven to the basic selection of the room. The menu currently includes English and Greek and will be expanded in German. Upon selecting Room 9 (Fig. 6 left), the user faces the first of the two screens covering all exhibits of this Gallery (Fig. 6 right).

Fig. 6. The first screen in two languages, after launching the application. On the right the first screen with the exhibits of gallery 9 based on the museum inventory number (blue room). (Color figure online)

By selecting any number, a standard object tab appears (Fig. 7a).

The standard tab of the exhibit includes: the *inventory number* in the Museum's collection, a *caption* with a brief description of the exhibit, a *return button* to the menu of the corresponding room, together with *information for each exhibit arranged in four buttons*, corresponding to the following: 1. Ancient text; 2. Translation; 3. Short comment; 4 Extensive comment (Fig. 7a). Only buttons with content are active. At this stage, there is no extensive (bibliographic) commentary on any of the exhibits; however it will be filled in future projects.

Figure 7 shows the overall presentation of each exhibit. Users can move and zoom in on texts of screens (b), (c) and (d) so that text can be read regardless of its length (supporting also people with impaired vision). The museum is experimenting with these technologies, with the help of visiting school classes and University students.

6   Future Work

Since 2010, the Epigraphic Museum has applied augmented reality technologies, using $360°$ panoramas, digitizing permanent and periodical exhibitions (Fig. 8, [1]).

Recent research work, (EU supported programs [2]), shows a direction in both personalized presentations and virtual and augmented reality applications [3–7].

An interesting technology named as situation simulation [8] has been developed by the University of Oslo and has been implemented in both a number of battles and reconstructions of archaeological sites, and events. (i.e. Falassarna site and battle

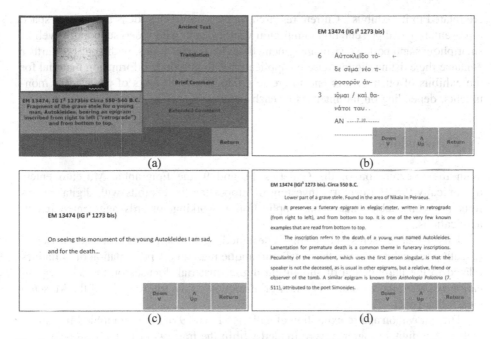

Fig. 7. Typical presentation of each exhibit: (a) the exhibit card based on museum inventory number, (b) the ancient text, (c) the translation from ancient Greek and (d) the short comment

Fig. 8. Augmented reality for documenting exhibitions: a case study at the Epigraphic Museum of Athens based on [1] (left opening screen; right typical room).

reconstruction [9]). This technology allows the user with a smartphone to open a window in the past and watch in real 3D houses and events (i.e. battles) by moving the device in situ with impressive results [10]. Digital applications have been also developed to allow freezing of the screen and selection of hyperlinks to enrich the information provided [11].

As the next research activity, the Museum has already starting selecting material to create three-dimensional virtual spaces based on situated simulations applications that are related to its exhibits[2]. Current research focuses on various ideas for optimal space representation and presentation to museum visitors, both with video support, as well as smartphones and portable virtual/augmented devices applications, with goals: to further enhance the existing digital museum applications; to introduce information material for the exhibits of other venues and to create guided thematic tours of preselected monuments, depending on the interests of each visitor.

7   Conclusions

With the re-exhibition of the Galleries 11 and 9, the Epigraphic Museum enters dynamically the 21st century, investing in supporting the exhibits with digital means (touch screens, tablet/smartphone applications), working towards augmented reality applications.

This paper presents the main (redesigned) exhibition areas of the Museum, revealing the rich content of this small but unique museum. A presentation of initiatives related to the introduction of supporting digital material, focuses on the tablet application targeting the museum visitor. A brief section on the future plans of the Museum closes this paper.

The renovation and re-exhibition of galleries 11 and 9 of the Epigraphic Museum as well as the digital programs were funded within the framework of the European Programme 'Attika 2013–2015'.

References

1. Mendoni, L.G.: 'Το ιστορικό πλαίσιο της πολιτικής ένωσης των πόλεων της Κέας στον 4ο και 3ο αι. π.Χ.' In: Lagogianni-Georgakarakou, M. (ed.) Πολιτεύεσθαι του Κείους κατά πόλεις: Athens, pp. 22–28 (2007)
2. H2020 home page. https://ec.europa.eu/programmes/horizon2020/
3. iMARECULTURE: Advanced VR, iMmersive serious games and Augmented REality as tools to raise awareness and access to European underwater CULTURal heritagE. https://imareculture.eu/
4. EMOTIVE: Emotive virtual cultural experiences through personalized storytelling. https://www.emotiveproject.eu/
5. GIFT meaningful personalization of hybrid virtual museum experiences through gifting and appropriation. https://gift.itu.dk/
6. ViMM Virtual Multimodal Museum. https://www.vi-mm.eu/
7. PLUGGY: Pluggable social platform for heritage awareness and participation. https://www.pluggy-project.eu/
8. Liestøl, G.: Sequence and access, storytelling and archive in mobile augmented reality. In: Goodman, L., Addison, A. (eds.) 2017 Proceedings of the 23rd International Conference on Virtual System and Multimedia (VSMM), Dublin, Ireland, pp. 1–7. IEEEXplore Digital Library (2018)

---

[2] One such case is the inscription related to the construction of the skeuotheke (arsenal) of Philon in the port of Piraeus, where the equipment battleship was stored [12].

9. Phalassarna sitsim app. https://www.youtube.com/watch?v=lphW5YbQaEo
10. Liestøl, G.: Storytelling with mobile augmented reality on Omaha beach: design considerations when reconstructing an historical event in situ. In: Proceedings of Museums and the Web 2018 MW18, Published 16 February 2018. Consulted 26 March 2018
11. Situated Simulations *(SitsimLab)*, Designing a Mobile Augmented Reality platform for experimentation with locative storytelling and new genres. http://www.sitsim.no/
12. Inscription relating the conditions for the construction of the sheuotheke of Philon. http://odysseus.culture.gr/h/4/eh430.jsp?obj_id=4545

A Roman in Venice
3D Documentation and Digital Restoration of an Endangered Roman Altar

Gaia Trombin$^{(\boxtimes)}$ and Antonio Bonaldo

Venice, Italy
gaia.trombin@gmail.com, antonio.bonaldo@gmail.com

Abstract. Digital documentation of cultural heritage is important especially for endangered monuments. Nowadays fast and low-cost SfM techniques are available, but it is not always possible to digitally acquire the whole artefact, because it is fragmentary or not totally accessible. Combining the 3D acquisition of the object with the 3D modeling of the missing parts allows the hypothetical reconstruction of the original aspect of the monument. A case study will be presented here, regarding a Roman altar reused in Venice.

Keywords: Structure from motion · Virtual reconstruction
Digital 3D documentation · Digital archaeology and epigraphy
Endangered cultural heritage · Roman altar

1 The Project

This work wants to be an experiment of 3D documentation and 3D virtual restoration, combined together, of a Roman altar reused in Venice, Italy. This is an example of a procedure that could be extended to the whole archaeological heritage, especially to the finds in reuse and exposed to weathering and damages. A case study will be presented here, starting from some considerations about the artefact and then explaining the sequence of operations used to produce a 3D model of it. This project is meant to be a proof of concept, demonstrating a possible approach to virtual conservation of endangered cultural patrimony. Many assumptions have been made during the virtual reconstruction, which is, therefore, purely hypothetical.

2 Reused Artefacts: Through Space and Time

On the island of Venice, in the area of the city called Castello, a Roman funerary altar is visible embedded in a building near the bridge "dei preti" (Fig. 1).

The stone monument has been placed at the corner of two perimeter walls that overlook the street called "fondamenta dei preti" and the canal "rio del

© Springer Nature Switzerland AG 2018
M. Ioannides et al. (Eds.): EuroMed 2018, LNCS 11197, pp. 64–73, 2018.
https://doi.org/10.1007/978-3-030-01765-1_8

Fig. 1. The Roman altar.

pestrin". For this reason only its front and one side are visible, while the remaining surfaces are hidden. The front of the altar bears six lines of a funerary latin text, the front and the side are both decorated. The inscribed monument was included by Theodor Mommsen in the *Corpus Inscriptionum Latinarum* (CIL) in [6], and analyzed in details by Paola Zamarchi Grassi (CIL, V, 2269; Zamarchi Grassi [10]). It appears to be datable to the first century AD.

This is one of the many Roman *spolia* located in the Venetian lagoon. During the medieval and post medieval ages many buildings of Venice and of other smaller islands in the Venetian lagoon were constructed reusing large quantities of old stones and bricks (Calvelli [1]; Trombin [9]; Calvelli [2]). The reuse of Roman artefacts, widespread and known as a characteristic of post classical times, seems to have reached a particular intensity in the Venetian area, due to the lack of local stone, the availability of the material of earlier Roman settlements in the near mainland, and a peculiar attitude of the Venetians. The closest Roman town had been *Altinum* and it should have provided most of these *spolia*.

The fact that this type of artefacts traveled through time and space, belonging not only to the culture that created them, but also to the one that reused them, makes them particularly valuable and interesting from a historical point of view. In the case of the Roman altar walled in the palace of Castello, it was created by some Roman artisans for the tomb of a freedman of the *gens Statia* and therefore placed in a Roman cemetery; later it was reused in the Venice settlement as a building material. Considering its position, it is clear that it has been selected from ancient ruins and displayed in the building of Venice not only for a practical and functional purpose, but also for an aesthetic and ideological choice. In fact it is easily seen by people passing by on the adjacent *fondamenta*.

This epigraphic monument can provide information about the Roman society that created it, but also about the medieval and post-medieval inhabitants of Venice: their settlement choices, tastes, ideologies, identities.

3   An Endangered Altar

This altar is one of the four reused Roman inscribed monuments recorded by Mommsen in the Venetian lagoon that are still *in loco*. A large number of reused monuments whose inscriptions were recorded in the CIL have somehow disappeared in less than two centuries and are now regrettably lost (Calvelli [1]).

Nowadays the funerary altar of Castello is in a poor condition of preservation. The right column of its front is not complete: it was partially cut off when the altar was enclosed in the wall. Meteorological phenomena during centuries of exposition wore out the limestone surfaces, smoothing the decoration and the carved inscription, today both readable with difficulty. More recent human activities increased the decay. In fact static problems of the building have required the use of some metal bars; one of them has been inserted in the inscribed surface, so part of the monument and of its text is missing.

It appears urgent to document so an important artefact in so an altered condition. This documentation could greatly benefit from modern digital 3D technologies. Besides being exhaustive and thorough, they produce an accurate, effective, objective, easily shareable representation of the object in a non-destructive way.

4   The Visible and the Invisible

The project has aimed not only to document the visible part of the item, applying 3D technologies, but also to cope with the invisible, that is what is hidden, obliterated by the wall, or has actually been destroyed. The second goal of the project was in fact the production of a 3D virtual restoration or at least an hypothetical simulation.

Regarding the visible part, the 3D acquisition technology of choice has been Structure from Motion (SfM), because, compared to laser scanning, it is much more affordable, does not require expensive or heavy equipment and is still able to produce accurate and high-quality models. Moreover when applied to stone objects, a not very homogeneous material, this technique may achieve very good results. This particular type of semi-automatic photogrammetry, offers some advantages in terms of rapidity and convenience in respect to traditional photogrammetry[1].

As for the invisible part of the altar it was necessary to understand what it could have looked like. That type of funerary altar, although not the most

---

[1] The relationship between traditional photogrammetry and SfM is partially controversial (Paris [8]).

popular, is well attested in the Roman Empire, in some variants (Zamarchi Grassi [10]; Dexheimer [4]). The upper part, especially, could come in many different shapes, e.g. with a complex top ornament, with a cavity for the ashes, or with a flat top. Not knowing the exact conformation of the Venetian altar it was decided to digitally reconstruct the top face in the simplest possible shape, that is a flat surface. The same considerations held for the base and the back of the find. The hidden side of the monument could have sported the same decoration of the visible side, so we decided to make it this way. The missing part of the inscription was restored following the integration given by the scientific literature (CIL, V, 2269; Zamarchi Grassi [10]; EDR 99269).

5   The Workflow

The workflow employed in this project consisted of the following phases:

1. the photographic campaign
2. the point cloud computation
3. the surface reconstruction (mesh) of the visible portion
4. the texturing process from photographs
5. the 3D modeling of the hidden/missing parts
6. the creation of a texture for the hidden/missing parts

The first four phases regard the data collection and post processing needed to produce the digital 3D model of the visible part. For these operations we have used mainly free, open source software (Python Photogrammetry Toolbox and Meshlab), integrated for some specific tasks with commercial software (Geomagic by 3D Systems).

In the last two steps a 3D modeling software and a photo retouching software (Blender and GIMP), both open source and free, have been used.

6   Modeling the Visible

First of all a photographic campaign was conducted. The device used for the digital image acquisition was a smartphone camera[2]. No professional camera is strictly needed for this task, because compact cameras or the ones integrated in recent smartphones are generally sufficient to obtain a good result. A set of digital photographs was shot from various points of view, although the location of the Roman monument permits a limited freedom of movement. In fact one side of the altar overlooks a canal and it is therefore impossible to move around it. To obtain a 3D reconstruction it is important that the pictures have a large degree of overlap and that each particular portion of the object appears in at least 3 photos. During this campaign a very large number of photographs were taken and then reviewed, discarding the blurry and the shaky ones, since they are

---

[2] The camera used was a GT-I9300, shooting in JPEG format at 8 MP resolution.

useless or even harmful to the algorithms later involved. In the end, a selection of 100 photos was used to compute the model.

In the next phase the set of photos was processed with Python Photogrammetry Toolbox (PPT), an open source and free software composed of a bundle of algorithms implemented by Python scripts (Moulon, Bezzi [7]). This software extracted from the 100 pictures, in a semi-automatic way, the geometric and chromatic information required to build a photorealistic 3D model. PPT has then returned a dense point cloud representing the three-dimensional coordinates (X, Y, Z) of points on the surface of the object (Fig. 2a). Although PPT can run on different systems, it appears to offer better performance on Linux than on Windows, so this stage was performed on a Linux machine.

The point cloud was then imported into the open source and free software MeshLab to be cleaned (Cignoni et al. [3]). The points that did not belong to the monument were removed.

The next step was the creation of the polygonal mesh, that is the geometric representation of the surface of the object, made of tiny triangles having the points of the cloud as vertexes (Fig. 2b). Although MeshLab is equipped with surface reconstruction algorithms (e.g. Poisson), the commercial software Geomagic was preferred to create the mesh, because it uses the Wrap algorithm that preserves more details (Ippoliti et al. [5]). Geomagic also includes convenient repair functions such as "Fill holes", and a tool, "mesh doctor", for the correction of anomalies such as, for example, non-manifold edges, spikes and self-intersections. The resulting polygonal surface was saved in the Ply format to be imported in MeshLab.

The photorealistic texture for the mesh was created with this open source software, projecting the photographic images on the surface. In this case, the output was saved in the Obj file format because it maintains the association between the surface and its texture, besides being importable by a wide range of open source and commercial 3D modeling software.

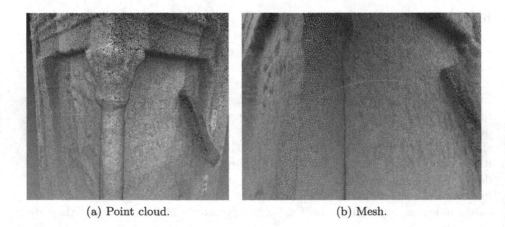

(a) Point cloud.   (b) Mesh.

Fig. 2. Digital representation of the altar's surface.

For the final cleaning of the reconstructed polygonal surface we preferred to use Geomagic, due to its convenient and advanced cleaning and editing functions.

7   Modeling the Invisible

The mesh of the survived and visible portion of the altar was imported in the software Blender and was scaled to the actual dimensions, using some measurements taken on the find as references. The metal bar was removed by selecting and deleting its triangles in the mesh, leaving a hole in its place (Figs. 3a and b).

(a) Wireframe view.   (b) Textured view.

Fig. 3. Removal of the metal bar.

The missing right side of the funerary altar was reconstructed by duplicating and mirroring the left one. Although we tried to align the model as precisely as possible along the X, Y, Z axes, the artisanal nature of the artefact implicated that the new face did not meld and blend perfectly with the rest of the model. In order to better adapt and join this face to the front of the model, Blender's "knife project" tool was employed. Projecting the outline of an object (in this case the front face) on another object (the right side aligned to the edge of it), the tool permitted to cut the latter precisely, removing any overlap (Fig. 4a).

Nevertheless a gap still existed, in particular along the join of the two parts of the column shaft, due to the inevitable geometrical differences. The resulting Obj file was therefore imported back into Geomagic to fill the gap between the two parts of the right column, to fill the hole left by the removed metal bar, and to easily create the remaining surfaces of the monument, i.e. the back, the base and the top.

While the parts of the model derived from the initial scan (front, left and right sides) had their photorealistic texture correctly mapped to the mesh, the new reconstructed surfaces did not. Geomagic applied the same texture to them, but with a random mapping, and the result was far from optimal (Fig. 4b).

(a) Adapting the right side. (b) Reconstructing the missing parts.

Fig. 4. Phases of the reconstruction.

Back in Blender, a series of manual improvements have been performed to the model. First of all, we corrected the unevenness along the "scar" at the join between the front and the right side. The reconstructed portion of the shaft of the column has been slightly rotated around the X axis and slightly scaled along the X and Y axes. Further enhancements to the scar involved the use of some advanced tools available in Blender's *sculpt mode*:

- fill: to fill the grooves
- smooth: to correct creases, spikes and other deformations generated by the editing of the column shaft
- sculpt (in subtract mode): to correct unwanted deformations generated by the editing of the column shaft, in particular to the capital of the column
- inflate/deflate: to fix deformations in the area of the capital of the column

The last step of the workflow consisted in texturing the reconstructed part of the Roman monument. Hence this part (as well as other small parts where the original texture appeared stretched) has been selected and a new virtual "material" has been created and assigned to it (Fig. 5a).

The procedure to create a photorealistic material involves defining its color, roughness, and other properties like translucency, transparency and reflectance. For the first two items it is possible to obtain a very natural and realistic result using, as a starting point, a picture of a real object made of the actual material, e.g. stone. This picture is then processed, for example scaled, and attached onto the mesh with a "mapping" operation, in which to every triangle of the mesh is associated a portion of the image.

In this case, due to the large extent of the surface to be covered with the texture, we used an image processing software called GIMP to prepare a large raster cloning small parts of the original photos. The resulting image has been used both to give the color information and to model the roughness of the surface. As for the other properties we have tried to make the material not too shiny. The reflection of the light appeared an undesirable effect, while on the contrary the ability to cast shadows could be useful to simulate the grazing light conditions and emphasize the inscription.

(a) Partitions for texturing.

(b) Reconstructed inscription.

Fig. 5. Other phases of the reconstruction.

The portion of the model corresponding to the metal bar inserted in the real altar was virtually restored. After the virtual removal of the bar and the filling of the resulting hole, a new texture was specifically created using a technique slightly different from the one described above. Exploiting Blender's clone tool in the "texture paint" mode, it was possible to recreate not only a realistic stone surface but also the portion of the missing text (a complete A letter and the upper end of the preceding S) directly painting on the model. Also in this case the chromatic contents were used to create both a texture and a microrelief, therefore giving to the letters an engraved effect (Fig. 5b).

8   What Now?

3D techniques, such as SfM, can produce a comprehensive, metrically accurate, low cost documentation which responds to the needs of the recording and the conservation of cultural heritage. The 3D model in fact digitally stores the geometrical, morphological, chromatic features of the find.

Combining the acquired model of the object with the virtual restoration it is possible to reconstruct the original aspect of the monument, or an hypothetical configuration, that is in any case a valuable, high-impact instrument for understanding and disseminating archaeological contents (Figs. 6a and b).

(a) Front-right view.

(b) Front-left view.

Fig. 6. Final model.

This type of digital documentation may offer many advantages compared with traditional ones: it is more manageable, durable, interactive, shareable, versatile. 3D documentation can therefore be the base for different activities:

– *Studies, analysis.* Digital tools can be effective means of investigation. It is possible for example to rotate and zoom in and out of the model, examining it from different viewpoints. We can simulate different light conditions, including grazing light, and display just the raw form of the object, without the texture, which sometimes can be misleading. Such a digital environment provides tools for measurement, for geometrical analysis and even for relief enhancement.

– *Prototyping/3D printing.* It is possible to create high quality replicas using a 3D printer. In museums they can be used for tactile experiences and for accessibility reasons, they can also substitute the originals when their display is not possible.

– *Geographic Information Systems.* The 3D models can be archived in a GIS, showing each item in the context it was found (e.g. Venice) or crafted (e.g. *Altinum*).

– *Virtual galleries or museums.* Digital collections can be displayed in a physical building or just virtually, e.g. on the web.

– *Animations, augmented reality, virtual reality.* Creating videos and interactive digital environments can be effective ways to deliver and communicate cultural heritage contents.

– *Traditional graphic documentation (2D)*. From the 3D representation it is easy to produce still 2D images from any desired angle, and also orthogonal projections like plans and elevations.

This POC suggests how a mixed approach can sometimes overcome challenging situations where parts of the artefacts are missing or, like in this case, not accessible. Building upon both acquired physical data and historical knowledge a realistic reconstruction can be proposed with an accuracy that is suitable for most Cultural Heritage applications.

How and where the models will be physically stored, which metadata will be associated with them, and in which formats they will be available depend on the specific uses that are to be enabled. As of today no particular infrastructure has been prepared to host, manage or share the Roman altar model.

References

1. Calvelli, L.: Da Altino a Venezia. In: Altino antica, pp. 184–197. Venice (2011)
2. Calvelli, L.: Iscrizioni esposte in contesti di reimpiego: l'esempio veneziano. In: L'iscrizione esposta, pp. 457–490. Faenza (2016)
3. Cignoni, P., Callieri, M., Corsini, M., Dellepiane, M., Ganovelli, F., Ranzuglia, G.: MeshLab: an open-source mesh processing tool. In: Sixth Eurographics Italian Chapter Conference, pp. 129–136. Salerno (2008)
4. Dexheimer, D.: Oberitalische Grabaltäre, Oxford (1998)
5. Ippoliti, E., Meschini, A., Sicuranza, F.: Digital photogrammetry and structure from motion for architectural heritage. In: Handbook of Research on Emerging Digital Tools for Architectural Surveying, Modeling, and Representation, pp. 124–181. L'Aquila (2015)
6. Mommsen, T.: Corpus Inscriptionum Latinarum, V, Part 1, Berlin (1872)
7. Moulon, P., Bezzi, A.: Python Photogrammetry toolbox: a free solution for three-dimensional documentation. In: ArcheoFoss, pp. 1–12. Naples (2011)
8. Paris, L.: Fotogrammetria e/o fotomodellazione. In: Geometria descrittiva e rappresentazione digitale, pp. 55–62. Rome (2012)
9. Trombin, G.: Analisi e restauro virtuale di un'iscrizione ante cocturam su un mattone romano. In: Torcello scavata, pp. 151–165. Venice (2014)
10. Zamarchi Grassi, P.: Da Altino a Venezia: osservazioni su un altare funerario romano. In: Studi di Archeologia della X Regio in ricordo di Michele Tombolani, pp. 437–446. Rome (1994)

Virtual Reality for Cultural Heritage Monuments – from 3D Data Recording to Immersive Visualisation

Thomas P. Kersten[(⊠)] [iD], Felix Tschirschwitz, Simon Deggim, and Maren Lindstaedt

Photogrammetry and Laser Scanning Lab, HafenCity University Hamburg, Überseeallee 16, 20457 Hamburg, Germany
{Thomas.Kersten,Felix.Tschirschwitz,Simon.Deggim, Maren.Lindstaedt}@hcu-hamburg.de

Abstract. Recent advances in contemporary Virtual Reality (VR) technologies are going to have a significant impact on everyday life. Through VR it is possible to virtually explore a computer-generated environment as a different reality, and to immerse oneself into the past or in other virtual environments without leaving the current real-life situation. Cultural heritage (CH) monuments are ideally suited both for thorough multi-dimensional geometric documentation and for realistic interactive visualisation in immersive VR applications. Furthermore, VR is increasingly in use for virtual locations to enhance a visitor's experience by providing access to additional materials for review and deepening knowledge either before or after the real visit. Using today's available 3D technologies a virtual place is no longer just a presentation of geometric environments on the Internet or a virtual tour of the place using panoramic photography. Additionally, the game industry offers tools for interactive visualisation of objects to motivate users to virtually visit objects and places. This paper presents the generation of virtual 3D models for different cultural heritage monuments and their processing for data integration into the two game engines Unity and Unreal. The workflow from data acquisition to VR visualisation using the VR system HTC Vive, including the necessary programming for navigation and interactions, is described. Furthermore, the use (including simultaneous use of multiple end-users) of such a VR visualisation for CH monuments is discussed.

Keywords: 3D · Game engine · HTC vive · Modelling · Reconstruction

1 Introduction

Virtual Reality (VR) is defined as the representation and simultaneous perception of the reality and its physical characteristics in an interactive virtual environment, generated by a computer in real time. This technology will change our everyday future and our working life. It is already obvious that this new technology will offer great opportunities for many applications such as medicine, technics, engineering, computer science, architecture, cultural heritage and many others. VR typically refers to computer

© Springer Nature Switzerland AG 2018
M. Ioannides et al. (Eds.): EuroMed 2018, LNCS 11197, pp. 74–83, 2018.
https://doi.org/10.1007/978-3-030-01765-1_9

technologies that use software to generate realistic images, sounds and interactions that replicate a real environment, and simulate a user's physical presence in this environment. Furthermore, VR has been defined as a realistic and immersive simulation of a three-dimensional environment, created using interactive software and hardware, and experienced or controlled by movement of the user's body or as an immersive, interactive experience generated by a computer. VR offers an attractive opportunity to visit objects in the past [1] or places, which are not easily accessible, often from positions which are not possible in real life. Moreover, these fundamental options are increasingly being implemented today through so-called "serious games", which embed information in a virtual world and create an entertaining experience (edutainment) through the flow of and interaction with the game [2, 3]. One of the first virtual museums using the VR system HTC Vive as a HMD for immersive experiences was introduced in [4].

In this contribution the workflow from 3D data recording to the generation of a VR application is presented using different practical examples, which were created by the Photogrammetry & Laser Scanning lab of HafenCity University (HCU) Hamburg.

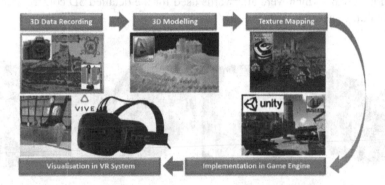

Fig. 1. Workflow for the generation of VR applications at HafenCity University Hamburg.

2   Workflow

The workflow for the production of a VR application at HCU Hamburg is schematically represented in Fig. 1. The data acquisition of real objects takes place with digital photogrammetry and/or with terrestrial (TLS) and airborne laser scanning (ALS), while for objects which no longer exist, historical sources such as maps and perspective views are used. The acquired 3D data is mainly modelled in AutoCAD with geometric primitives, in order to avoid using memory-intensive surface models with high number of triangles. The texture mapping of the CAD models is carried out in both the software Autodesk 3ds Max and directly in the game engine. After importing the data into the game engine they are further processed and prepared for visualisation. The implementation of the data in the game engine also includes appropriate programming of navigation and interactions for the user in the VR environment. The interactive visualisation of the created VR environment was then produced using the VR system HTC

Vive. Edler et al. [5] present a different workflow for the construction of an interactive cartographic VR environment using open-source software for exploring urban landscapes.

3 Data Recording and Processing

For the 3D recording of historic buildings digital photogrammetry and terrestrial laser scanning are used. The photogrammetric data acquisition and 3D modelling of North German castles and manor houses, for example, are described in [6]. The combined evaluation of photogrammetric and terrestrial laser scanning data for the construction of a CAD model of the Old-Segeberg Town House in Bad Segeberg, Germany is published in [7] (Fig. 2). The wooden model of the main building of Solomon's temple, which was constructed from 1680 to 1692 in Hamburg and is exhibited today in the museum for Hamburg's history. A photo series was taken with a DSLR camera Nikon D800 from the outside and also from the inside after dismantling of the building into its individual parts. Using these photo sequences scaled point clouds were generated in Agisoft PhotoScan, which were afterwards used for the detailed 3D construction of the temple building in AutoCAD (Fig. 2).

Fig. 2. 3D CAD models of historic buildings generated from photogrammetry and terrestrial laser scanning– f.l.t.r. CAD model Old-Segeberg Town House and main building of Solomon's Temple, meshed 3D model and reconstructed CAD model of Almaqah Temple.

The Almaqah temple located in Yeha in northern Ethiopia exist today only as ruins. The foundation walls of the temple remain upright above the ground, while only ancient remains of the monumental building are visible. These are the subject of a current excavation of the Sana'a branch office of the Orient department of the German Archaeological Institute. Point clouds from terrestrial laser scanning were used by an architect and a geomatics engineer as the basis for a virtual reconstruction of the two buildings (Fig. 2 right) [8].

For the virtual 3D reconstruction of the entire town Segeberg in the year 1600 both previously constructed, detailed building models of the Old-Segeberg Town House and of the church St. Marien, and historical sources such as maps and perspective views were used in combination with the expert knowledge of a historian (Fig. 3). From the previously constructed Town House twelve different variants were derived and virtually distributed throughout the environment, while special buildings such as the castle,

Fig. 3. Positions of historic buildings of Segeberg in Google Earth (left), detailed reconstructed church St. Marien and Old-Segeberg Town House (centre), reconstructed model of the historic lime mountain and its integration in the latest terrain model (right).

town hall, monastery, storehouse and others were constructed using information of the Braun-Hogenberg perspective view of the town in the year 1588 and the historian's expert knowledge [9]. The positions of the buildings, which are overlaid onto Google Earth (Fig. 3 left), originate from historical maps. The reconstruction of the approximately 300 buildings was carried out in AutoCAD and the texture mapping of the objects was accomplished in 3ds Max. The terrain model of Segeberg and the surrounding environment is based on airborne laser scanning data, which was provided by the Federal State Office for Surveying and Geo-Information Schleswig-Holstein in Kiel, Germany. The historical lime mountain, which no longer exists, was physically modelled and reconstructed on the basis of historical sources from 1600 using butter first (initial model) and then gypsum. The gypsum model was later photogrammetrically recorded from image sequences, in order to derive the scaled historical lime mountain model from point clouds (Fig. 3 right), which was finally integrated in the latest laser scanning terrain model [10].

4 Game Engines and VR System

4.1 Game Engines Used

A game engine is a software framework designed for the creation and development of video games for consoles, mobile devices and personal computers. The core functionality typically provided by a game engine includes a rendering engine for 2D or 3D graphics to display textured 3D models (spatial data), a physics engine or collision detection (and collision response) for the interaction of objects, an audio system to emit sound, scripting, animation, artificial intelligence, networking, streaming, memory management, threading, localisation support, scene graph, and may include video support for cinematics. For the projects at HCU Hamburg the Unreal Engine 4 (UE4) from Epic Games and the game engine Unity from Unity Technologies are used. Both products allow the development of computer games and other interactive 3D graphics applications for various operating systems and platforms. All necessary computations using the game engines run in real-time. UE4 was selected due to the opportunity to develop application and interaction logics using a visual programming language called Blueprints. Visual programming with Blueprints does not require the writing of machine-compliant source code. Thus it provides opportunities for non-computer scientists to program all functions for a VM using graphical elements. The two game engines are free for non-commercial use and very well-suited to the development of virtual reality application of cultural heritage monuments.

4.2   VR System Used

For the visualisation of the VR application the Virtual Reality System HTC Vive is used (Fig. 4 left). The HTC Vive, developed by HTC and by Valve Corporation, was released on April 5, 2016. It offers a room scale VR experience through tracking the Head Mounted Display (HMD) and the motion controller, which control interactions in the virtual environment, using "Lighthouse" technology. The Lighthouse technology guarantees a very precise and temporally high-resolution determination of the current position and orientation of the user within the interaction area of 4.6 m × 4.6 m (Fig. 4 right). The visual presentation happens in the VR glasses with a resolution of 1080 × 1200 pixel per eye using a frame rate of 90 Hz.

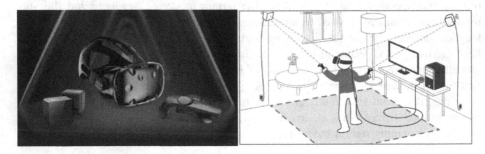

Fig. 4. Components (left) and schematic setup (right) of the VR system HTC Vive (www.vive. com).

5   Implementation and Generation of VR Applications

5.1   Data Reduction for VR Applications

All modelled and textured objects are transferred from 3ds Max into the game engine using appropriate file formats such as FBX. The CAD modelling is carried out by solid modelling based mainly on photogrammetric and TLS data. These CAD elements are divided into triangles and quads after the transfer to 3ds Max and/or into the engine, which significantly increases the data volume. In principle, more triangles and/or quads require more computing power, which in turn calls for high performance PCs with powerful graphics cards for VR visualisation. Thus, the general tendency exists to try to reduce the data set on one hand, but there is also a conflicting drive to obtain a visually attractive representation of the object. Therefore, it can be essential for data reduction to replace geometrical details with appropriate textures in order to still represent required details. In addition, the settings for export/import into different software packages should be compatible with the modelling and texture mapping of the objects.

Thus, the number of polygons of the Selimiye mosque had to be substantially reduced in order to guarantee homogeneous movement of the user without latency and interactions in the virtual 3D model using the VR system HTC Vive (Fig. 5). In the first step the number of polygons was reduced from 6.5 to 1.5 million. Interactive visualization thereby permits an investigation of the 3D data in intuitive form and in previously unseen quality. Through the free choice of the viewing angle, similar to the real, human movement, the 3D objects are observed from different distances, so that modelling errors are easily identified. The following modelling errors were visible after the visual inspection of the virtual Selimiye mosque in the VR system HTC Vive: (A) gaps and shift of textures, (B) double surfaces of object elements, (C) missing elements, which are available in the original data structure of the mosque, and (D) errors in the proportionality of items compared to the original structure of the mosque. After correction of all detected errors the number of polygons could be reduced to 0.9 million, which was acceptable for the visualisation of the virtual Selimiye mosque in the VR system [11].

Fig. 5. Selimiye mosque in Edirne, Turkey – data set with reduced number of polygons (left) and perspective views in the VR application (centre, right).

5.2   Landscape Design

Another substantial aspect of VR is the environment of the building/monument to be visualised. If a real digital terrain model (DTM) is available, it is then possible to integrate the DTM in form of a height-coded greyscale image as a so-called height map into the engine. For the generation of terrain the Landscape module of the Game Engine is used, which in UE4 allows intelligent and fast presentation via adaptive resolution of the terrain (level of detail) including vegetation objects such as trees. Since the engine, however, generally does not work with geodetic coordinate systems, scale adjustment is required with respect to the scaling of area sections as well as height data. Nevertheless, geodetic professionals demand that all geodata is represented in correct relative positions and in the correct dimensions. This is very essential for VR applications, since all objects are presented on a 1:1 scale in the viewer.

5.3 Locomotion and Navigation in VR

Most VR applications use HTC Vive for natural, human locomotion in which real movements are converted into virtual motion, while the spatial restriction of the inter-action area is extended by teleportation. The teleportation function is driven by the motion controller, which enable VR visitors to bridge larger distances (Fig. 6 left). The speed of bridging space for very large distances can be increased and the user can also click at configured hotspots to jump directly to the requested and pre-defined place in VR.

Fig. 6. Locomotion in VR – navigation using the developed teleportation function in UE4 (left) and using the flight modus by permanent pressing of a trigger button of the motion controller in Unity (right).

Due to the immense spatial expanse of many generated VR environments, such as the mosque or the temple, the flight option was developed as a further artificial movement for the user. Using the motion controller the user can guide the direction and the speed of the flight, whereby the flight mode is activated by permanently pressing the trigger button of the motion controller (Fig. 6 right). The movement function for the VR application of the mosque in Edirne and Solomon's temple was implemented based on the SteamVR package of the Unity Asset Store.

5.4 Interactions and Animations in VR

For the control of interactions and for the release of animations the VR system HTC Vive supplies two controllers, for which the configuration of the buttons is accordingly programmed. For the virtual museum Old-Segeberg Town House the following interactions and animations were integrated in the VR application (Fig. 7): 52 info boards with text and photos, animation of the architectural history of the building over six epochs, and animations of objects that no longer exist in the building, such as fire-places [4]. They are controlled with the right hand, while the left hand is only used for the mobile display of information.

For the production of a VR application of the astronomical observatory Hamburg-Bergedorf the two buildings Meridian Circle and Equatorial were constructed (Fig. 7 right). These two modelled buildings are no longer active in use since the telescopes are no longer *in situ*. Therefore, two non-original telescopes were integrated in each virtual building, in order to watch the starlit sky using the telescope after interactively opening the dome of the building.

Fig. 7. Interactions and animations in der VR application – f.l.t.r. Virtual Museum Old-Segeberg Town House using the controller for the request of information by clicking the info sign and animating the history of building construction phases, the building Meridian Circle of the astronomical observatory Hamburg-Bergedorf with the interactively opened dome for watching the starlit sky with the telescope.

5.5   Multiple Users in VR

Using a HMD for the virtual reality application significantly increases the immersive experience, since all senses are sealed off from the external world around the user. In order to bring a social component into the VR application, several users can meet each other in the VR environment, in order to investigate together the virtual object, while each user is at another location in the real world (Fig. 8). Therefore, each other user appears as an avatar in the appropriate virtual position. The independent network solution Photon (Photon Unity Networking) is used to synchronize the movements of the different users. The voices are recorded by the microphone integrated in the HMD and played for all users relative to the position of the speaker (spatial audio). Photon also provides server infrastructure, which is free for use up to a certain user number. The functionality for several users was used for the VR application of the Selimiye mosque and the city model Duisburg 1566, when four users visited the virtual model at the same time at different locations in order to examine and discuss together the geometrical quality of the modelled 3D data. During the common virtual visit the VR visitors could communicate via the integrated microphones. Since the user groups were located at two different locations in Hamburg, Istanbul and Bochum respectively, travel expenses could be saved for these meetings.

Fig. 8. Multiple user as avatars in VR in the Selimiye mosque (left) and in front of the entrance to Solomon's temple (right).

5.6 Developed Virtual Applications

Since August 2016 some VR applications were already developed for projects in the Laboratory for Photogrammetry & Laser Scanning of the HafenCity University Hamburg and in lectures, which are illustrated in Fig. 9. Selected VR applications are currently presented at scientific conferences and trade fairs, in demos at the Photogrammetry & Laser Scanning lab and in the museum Old-Segeberg Town House (virtual museum and Segeberg 1600).

Fig. 9. Different VR applications of cultural heritage monuments developed at HCU Hamburg – f.l.t.r. Selimiye-mosque Edirne, Duisburg 1566, bailiwick Pinneberg, Solomon's Temple (top), astronomical observatory Hamburg-Bergedorf, West Tower Duderstadt and Segeberg 1600, and Almaqah temple in Yeha, Ethiopia (bottom).

6 Conclusions and Outlook

In this contribution the workflow from 3D data acquisition of an object over 3D modelling and texture mapping up to immersive, interactive visualization of the generated objects in a programmed VR application was presented showing different examples. Following lessons have been learned: Both game engines Unity and Unreal demonstrate their great potential for the development of VR applications. However, the game engine Unreal allows non-programming experts the easy-to-use option visual programming to avoid direct code writing. The file format FBX is the best choice for data transfer into the game engine. The VR system HTC Vive supplies a real immersive experience, which permits the users to dive into a virtual environment without having ever seen the object in real life or experienced in the real scale. The functionality of the VR system enables simultaneous visits by multiple users thus supporting new possibilities such as holding common discussions within the virtual model about aspects of architecture, structural analysis, history, virtual restoration of the object and many others. Moreover, the VR application permits a detailed geometrical quality inspection of the 3D models in the framework for a visual inspection using the high degree of mobility and unusual perspectives of the viewer. The development of VR applications also offers capabilities for difficult areas such as complex buildings, dangerous zones, destroyed cultural heritage monuments and tunnels, in order to simulate and train disaster control operations. Beyond that, such VR applications can also offer possibilities for therapy to humans with claustrophobia, acrophobia and aviophobia.

Not only individual cultural heritage monuments, (historic) buildings or building ensembles are suitable for interactive VR visualisations, but also whole towns and cities as soon as they are available as 3D models. Since the winter semester 2016/2017 Virtual Reality is also included in the lecture module Visualisation of the master study program Geodesy and Geoinformatics at HafenCity University Hamburg.

References

1. Gaitatzes, A., Christopoulos, D., Roussou, M.: Reviving the past: cultural heritage meets virtual reality. In: Proceedings of the Conference on Virtual Reality, Archaeology and Cultural Heritage, pp. 103–110 (2001)
2. Anderson, E.F., McLoughlin, L., Liarokapis, F., Peters, C., Petridis, P., De Freitas, S.: Developing serious games for cultural heritage: a state-of-the-art review. Virtual Reality **14** (4), 255–275 (2010)
3. Mortara, M., Catalano, C.E., Bellotti, F., Fiucci, G., Houry-Panchetti, M., Petridis, P.: Learning cultural heritage by serious games. J. Cult. Herit. **15**(3), 318–325 (2014)
4. Kersten, T., Tschirschwitz, F., Deggim, S.: Development of a virtual museum including a 4D presentation of building history in virtual reality. In: The International Archives of the Photogrammetry, Remote Sensing and Spatial Information Sciences, 42-2/W3, pp. 361–367 (2017)
5. Edler, D., Husar, A., Keil, J., Vetter, M., Dickmann, F.: Virtual Reality (VR) and Open Source Software: A Workflow for Constructing an Interactive Cartographic VR Environment to Explore Urban Landscapes. Kartographische Nachrichten – Journal of Cartography and Geographic Information, issue 1, pp. 5–13, Bonn, Kirschbaum Verlag (2018)
6. Kersten, T., Acevedo Pardo, C., Lindstaedt, M.: 3D Acquisition, Modelling and Visualization of north German Castles by Digital Architectural Photogrammetry. In: The International Archives of Photogrammetry, Remote Sensing and Spatial Information Sciences, 35(5/B2), pp. 126–132 (2004)
7. Kersten, Th., Hinrichsen, N., Lindstaedt, M., Weber, C., Schreyer, K., Tschirschwitz, F.: Architectural Historical 4D Documentation of the Old-Segeberg Town House by Photogrammetry, Terrestrial Laser Scanning and Historical Analysis. In: Lecture Notes in Computer Science, vol. 8740, pp. 35–47, Springer Internat. Publishing Switzerland (2014)
8. Lindstaedt, M., Mechelke, K., Schnelle, M., Kersten, T.: Virtual reconstruction of the Almaqah temple of yeha in ethiopia by terrestrial laser scanning. In: The Internat. Archives of Photogrammetry, Remote Sensing & Spatial Inform. Sciences, 38(5/W16) (2011)
9. Deggim, S., Kersten, T., Tschirschwitz, F., Hinrichsen, N.: Segeberg 1600 – reconstructing a historic town for virtual reality visualisation as an immersive experience. In: The International Archives of the Photogrammetry, Remote Sensing and Spatial Information Sciences, 42(2/W8), pp. 87–94 (2017)
10. Deggim, S., Kersten, T., Lindstaedt, M., Hinrichsen, N.: The return of the Siegesburg - 3D-reconstruction of a disappeared and forgotten monument. In: The International Archives of the Photogrammetry, Remote Sensing and Spatial Information Sciences, 42(2/W3), pp. 209–215 (2017)
11. Kersten, T., et al.: The Selimiye Mosque of Edirne, Turkey – an immersive and interactive virtual reality experience using HTC Vive. In: The International Archives of the Photogrammetry, Remote Sensing and Spatial Information Sciences, XLII-5/W1, pp. 403–409 (2017)

A Project for Museo Civico Castello Ursino in Catania: Breaking Through Museum Walls and Unlocking Collections to Everyone

Cettina Santagati[1]([✉]), Valentina Noto[2],
and Federico Mario La Russa[1]

[1] Department of Civil Engineering and Architecture, University of Catania,
Catania, Italy
Cettina.santagati@dau.unict.it, fedelarussa@live.it
[2] Museo Civico Castello Ursino, Piazza Federico di Svevia 2, Catania, Italy
valentina.noto@comune.catania.it

Abstract. This paper presents the preliminary ideas for the improvement of the cultural offerings' standard and fruition of the Museo Civico Castello Ursino in Catania. In conceiving the project, the requests of the European Commission, the European Digital Agenda, and the Directive on Public Sector Information (PSI) have been taken into consideration. In particular, the digitisation of cultural heritage (embedding museums, libraries, and archives) and its accessibility on a large scale. Among the aims of the project, there are the creation of a digital archive; 3D digitalisation of the museum's collections and their online accessibility; and the use of immersive and interactive solutions for a better audience involvement.

Keywords: Digital cultural heritage · Digital photogrammetry
Virtual reality

1 Introduction

The primary function of museums is to contribute to the society's cultural growth and promote a sense of belonging to the existing heritage of a country. One of the major challenges faced by museums today [1–3] comes in the form of opportunities offered by digital technologies in terms of digitisation, accessibility of collections, and communication to the public.

This paper presents the preliminary ideas for the improvement of the cultural offerings' standard and fruition of the Museo Civico Castello Ursino in Catania. The project is part of the actions taken by the Sicilian region (Action 6, PO FERS 2014–2020) on the promotion of assets of cultural heritage. In conceiving the project, the requests of the European Commission, the European Digital Agenda, and the Directive on Public Sector Information (PSI) have been taken into consideration. In particular, the digitisation of public information and cultural heritage (embedding museums, libraries, and archives) and their accessibility on a large scale.

Although in the past years, the Museo Civico Castello Ursino has opened up to the use of digital technologies through its participation in digitalisation, projects

M. Ioannides et al. (Eds.): EuroMed 2018, LNCS 11197, pp. 84–92, 2018.
https://doi.org/10.1007/978-3-030-01765-1_10

concerning epigraphic heritage (project EPICUM [4]), 3D crowdsourced digitalisation of sculptural heritage (#invasionidigitali3D [5]), or through the creation of the izi. TRAVEL guide [6]. Till date, no overall digital strategy has been developed, which provides adequate responses with regard to the current needs of the museum.

Among the aims of the project there are the creation of a digital archive; 3D digitalisation of the museum's collections and their online accessibility; the use of immersive and interactive solutions for a better audience involvement.

This article is structured as follows: first a description of the project context (Sect. 1) has been provided, followed by an analysis of the needs that have to be met (Sect. 2). Subsequently, a description of the project proposal (Sect. 3) is given, which is followed by an in-depth analysis of the creation of digital assets, their sharing on the web, and their use for the museum (Sect. 4). Lastly, a few comments are mentioned about the first experiments conducted (Sect. 5) and the conclusion has been presented.

2 The Project Context: The Museo Civico Castello Ursino

The Castello Ursino, built in 1239 by Frederick II of Swabia, is one of the oldest buildings of Catania that remained nearly intact during the 1669 eruption and survived the 1693 earthquake. It became the residence of the Aragonese kings and of the Spanish Viceroy (XVI century). Furthermore, it served as a prison until 1934 when the castle, under the direction of the archaeologist Guido Libertini [7, 8], was transformed into the current Museo Civico Castello Ursino. Today, it is one of the principal cultural attractions of the city, a prestigious venue for training and orientation meetings as well as a place that is suitable for creating networks and a sense of national identity.

Castello Ursino has a double historical/monumental identity. It is one of the most important historical testimonies of the medieval period in the city of Catania and hosts, preserves and exhibits the major local and non-local collections (Fig. 1).

Fig. 1. View of the 3D textured models of the exterior and the courtyard of Castello Ursino.

The heritage of the museum consists of more than 13,000 artefacts. It was established in 1826 with the bequest of 123 paintings by G.B. Finocchiaro. Later, in 1866, the municipality acquired the collection of Benedictine monks, one of the most important and richest collections in Catania. Of equal importance is the art collection of Ignazio Paternò Castello Principe di Biscari, which became a part of the municipal heritage between 1927 and 1930. These two collections [9] constitute the nucleus of the civic collection with works of different types, belonging to archaeology, sculptures, paintings, numismatics, weapons, scientific instruments and natural sciences.

In addition to this, over a period of time, there have been various donations from collectors (Ing. Francesco Mirone, Baron Zappalà Asmundo, Ing. Natale Balsamo) and the heirs of artists (Natale Attanasio, Giuseppe Sciuti).

The museum has a policy of rotating its permanent collections in order to promote the vast heritage of minor arts (arms, numismatics, prints), as well as the archaeological and pictorial heritage of the country.

3 Identifying Needs and Requirements

In order to start the design phase in a participatory and shared way with the users, questionnaires for evaluation were prepared and submitted. Their analysis shows the need for the public to approach the collection in a more direct way, often requesting personalised visits and the possibility to find more information about the castle and its collections on the website, even before the visit begins.

Moreover, as is often the case with most museums, of the enormous quantity of the museum's historical and artistic heritage, only a small part of it is exhibited, while most of the works are kept in the warehouses and see the light of the day cyclically, depending on the rotation planned.

The intervention foresees a series of measures aimed at improving the fruition and the diffusion of knowledge of the Museo Civico Castello and its collections in three primary directions:

- Creating a management platform (back-end) dedicated to the Museum and its artistic and cultural heritage.
- Encouraging a greater and more extensive – also online – knowledge and accessibility of the collections according to the paradigm of open science.
- Making the visit engaging by stimulating the user in the knowledge of the "museum container" and its "content" using innovative technologies.

The project is therefore aimed at citizens, tourists, occasional visitors, history lovers, scholars, researchers, students of various levels, universities, and research centres.

Among these categories, some specific target groups such as the resident population and schools of all levels, which express the need for knowledge of the territory and the need to find in the museum a place of identity of the collective historical memory of the city, have also been identified.

4 A Project for Museo Civico Castello Ursino

The The project envisages the 3D digitisation of the museum's collections and a part of the building itself, and the creation of a cataloguing and management platform (back-end) for internal use and an app (front-end) dedicated to visitors.

To this end, the project will aim at the realisation of the following activities:

- Creation of a back-end platform for the management of the collections that allows the classification and organisation of information relating to these items: the cataloguing sheets will be created according to the ICCD (Italian Institute of Cataloguing and Documentation) standards, reviewed according to the ARIADNE project; data and metadata schemas (i.e., EDM) will be verified to be compliant with Linked Open Data [10]; the recording of information/activities related to the museum management will consider the management of information relating to the castle, history, collections, key service information, and works exhibited in theatres and works on loan.
- 3D digitisation of the museum's collections through the integrated use of 3D scanning techniques (digital photogrammetry and laser scanning); 3D reconstruction of the castle's environment (courtyard, entrance hall, towers) for a better storytelling of the history of the building, the architecture and the construction techniques; 3D reconstruction of some of the sites where the artefacts were found (explorable with VR visors) to facilitate the recontextualisation of the exhibits.
- Online diffusion of the museum's heritage through available 3D model-sharing platforms, according to the logic of the Green Public Procurement (GPP).
- Creation of an App for mobile and desktop devices connected to the back-end platform, which would be able to make the museum heritage accessible in a more engaging and interactive way through a system of exploration, scanning, and gamification.
- Setting up of two interactive consultation kiosks on-site to view the virtual gallery of some of the most valuable pieces that are not on exhibition.
- Training of hall and office staff.
- Evaluation of the user experience.

5 3D Digitisation and Web Sharing

The creation of digital content has taken into account the different uses that these resources would have had within the project, from the insertion in the back-end platform to the dissemination on the web, to the support for the realisation of interactive and immersive visit experiences.

As far as the 3D acquisition of the collections was concerned, we opted for the use of 3D techniques such as laser scanning and digital photogrammetry [11, 12], as well as for the experimentation of low-cost solutions such as the use of latest generation devices (i.e., Sony Xperia ZX1), which is very effective for the dissemination on the web [13].

The collections span over centuries of the city's history – artefacts from the Greek and Roman periods concerning both objects from daily life (vases, coins, statues, epigraphs, portraits, busts, oil lamps, sarcophagi and lids) as well as objects from the thermal baths and the roman theatre (engravings, prints, sacred vestments and ornamental artistic object, Byzantine tablets, oils on canvas from the 19th century).

The collections will be subdivided by their different types (physical, material and dimensional characteristics) in order to identify the best techniques for their 3D acquisition (setting up photographic sets to ensure optimal lighting conditions).

The 3D models obtained will be retopologised [14], optimised and lightened for their inclusion on disseminative platforms on the web.

With regard to the web accessibility of the models, various solutions were examined, including the use of Europeana, 3DHop, and Sketchfab. Europeana allows you to upload 3D PDFs of objects, while 3DHOP (3D Heritage Online Presenter), an open-source software package for the creation of interactive web presentations of high-resolution 3D models [15], requires the programming of web pages.

The online platform Sketchfab.com was chosen as it is the most widespread platform used by various museums (British Museum, Musée d'Archeologie Nationale and others), for the ease of embedding 3D content on websites and other platforms, for the possibility of direct access to social networks or the connection to guided tour apps (GuidiGO), and finally in the context of the GPP. In fact, Sketchfab has recently decided to support museums by offering the possibility of using a free business account. In addition, the models can also be enriched with textual annotations and audio content, allowing a more engaging use of the collections on exhibit through a dynamic exploration that is multisensory and particularly effective.

However, the 3D models' metadata will be structured following the EDM (Europeana Data Model) schema in order to allow a future link with Europeana.

6   Results

In order to start the campaign of digitisation and the sharing of models on the web, preliminary tests were carried out on the technologies to be used (photogrammetry/low cost sensors), dividing the collection by type (large sculptures, busts, vases, etc.), and the subcategories related to the material and surface finishing (Fig. 2).

A comparison was made between the use of photogrammetry (Agisoft Photoscan) and the 3D Creator App of the Sony Xperia ZX1 mobile device. It was found that the models obtained with the latter can be acquired faster, have a good texture but a low polygon content that is unable to describe the richness of the detail of some sculptural elements [13]. Moreover, the limits of both the technologies have arised where photogrammetry has failed with reflective metallic elements, the 3D Creator App has been able to complete the acquisition, and the vice versa, where in the presence of materials such as ceramics, the use of photogrammetry has proved to be successful (Fig. 3).

At the same time, the 3D models of the castle's environments (courtyard, entrance hall, towers) and 3D reconstructions of the sites of origin of some significant items of the collection have been created.

Afterwards, the workflow related to the optimisation of the models through retopology techniques was tested, using the Z-Brush software combined with Agisoft Photoscan. Through sculpting and smoothing the operations, the noise caused by the shooting was eliminated and some signs on the sculptures have been highlighted.

Furthermore, the retopology operation from triangular meshes obtained through photogrammetry to quadrangular (quad) meshes has involved a reduction in the faces

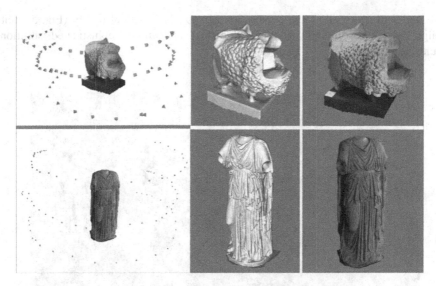

Fig. 2. 3D models of different types of items created through digital photogrammetry technique.

of 1/5, compared to the original (Fig. 4), without losing the visual detail of the mesh and the texture. The transformation to mesh quads also allows one to use the models in interactive virtual reality and gaming platforms such as UnReal Engine and Unity.

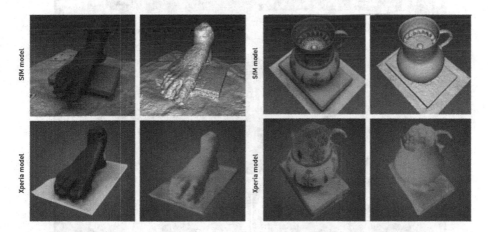

Fig. 3. Comparison between Sony Xperia ZX1 3D Creator App and Agisoft Photoscan on a bronze foot (left) and on a terracotta Samovar (right)

Finally, the procedure for uploading models to the Sketchfab online platform was tested, verifying the different file formats allowed (OBJ, PLY, FBX, etc.). From the editing, windows were identified as the different parameters to be applied to the models for effective visualisation, as well as annotations for the enrichment of information, audio and settings to allow the exploration of models in virtual reality (Fig. 5), both through low-cost solutions (google cardboard) and more sophisticated solutions (Oculus Rift).

Fig. 4. From the triangular mesh model to the retopologised model

Fig. 5. Virtual Reality settings in Sketchfab

7 Conclusions and Future Works

The preliminary ideas for the project respond to the need of the OpenGLAM (Open Galleries, Libraries, Archives, and Museums) initiative promoted by the Open Knowledge Foundation, which encourages free access to the digital heritage of galleries, libraries, archives, and museums. The large-scale diffusion of the 3D models of the museum collection will have positive effects not only from the perspective of the museum's visibility but also from the cultural and scientific perspective.

Further experimentation will be conducted with the aim of linking the "container" to the "content" according to the information modelling approach through the creation of a single model that manages geometric/spatial, environmental, plant engineering, maintenance, micro-climatic, and security information, which can be linked to a management database. This can pave the way for new forms of maintenance, and the optimisation of the design processes of the set-ups and of each user experience, facilitating the development of a dynamic information model, to evaluate alternative scenarios and to test its effectiveness through different narrative paths.

References

1. Antinucci, F.: Comunicare nel museo. Edizioni Laterza, Rome-Bari (2014)
2. Candy, L., Ferguson, S. (eds.): Interactive Experience in the Digital Age. Springer, New York (2014). https://doi.org/10.1007/978-3-319-04510-8
3. Hossaini, A., Blankenberg, N. (eds.): Manual of Digital Museum. Planning Rowman and Littlefield Publishers, Lanham (Maryland) (2017)
4. Agodi, S., Cristofaro, S., Noto, V., Prag, J.R.W., Spampinato, D.: Una collaborazione tra museo, enti di ricerca e scuola: l'epigrafia digitale e l'alternanza scuola-lavoro. Umanistica Digitale 1, 207–224 (2018)
5. Inzerillo, L., Santagati, C.: Crowdsourcing cultural heritage: from 3D modeling to the engagement of young generations. In: Ioannides, M., et al. (eds.) EuroMed 2016. LNCS, vol. 10058, pp. 869–879. Springer, Cham (2016). https://doi.org/10.1007/978-3-319-48496-9_70
6. Bonacini, E.: #iziTRAVELSicilia, a Participatory Storytelling Project/Process: Bottom-Up Involvement of Smart Heritage Communities. IJICST 7(2), 24–52 (2017)
7. Libertini, G.: Il Castello Ursino e le raccolte artistiche comunali di Catania. Catania (1937)
8. Patanè, G.: Castello Ursino-Museo Comunale. Catania. Rivista del Comune VI 5, 253–262 (1932)
9. Giarrizzo, G., Pafumi, S. (eds.): Oggetti, uomini, idee. Percorsi multidisciplinari per la storia del collezionismo. Fabrizio Serra Editore, Pisa-Roma (2009)
10. https://openglam.org/
11. Guidi, G., Micoli, L.L., Gonizzi, S., Navarro, P.R., Russo, M.: 3D digitizing a whole museum: a metadata centered workflow. In: 2013 Digital Heritage International Congress (DigitalHeritage), Marseille, pp. 307–310 (2013)
12. Stanco, F., Tanasi, D., Allegra, D., Milotta, F.L.M.: 3D digital imaging for knowledge dissemination of Greek archaic statuary. In: Proceedings of the Conference on Smart Tools and Applications in Computer Graphics (STAG 2016), pp. 133–141. Eurographics Association, Goslar, Germany (2016)

13. Santagati, C., Lo Turco, M., Bocconcino, M.M., Donato, V., Galizia, M.: 3D models for all: low-cost acquisition through mobile devices in comparison with image based techniques. potentialities and weaknesses in cultural heritage domain. In: International Archives of the Photogrammetry, Remote Sensing and Spatial Information Sciences, vol. XLII-2/W8, pp. 221–228 (2017)
14. Palestini, C., Basso, A.: The photogrammetric survey methodologies applied to low cost 3D virtual exploration in multidisciplinary field. Int. Arch. Photogramm. Remote Sens. Spatial Inf. Sci. **XLII-2/W8**, 195–202 (2017)
15. Potenziani, M., Callieri, M., Dellepiane, M., Corsini, M., Ponchio, F., Scopigno, R.: 3DHOP: 3D heritage online presenter. Comput. Graph. **52**, 129–141 (2015)

Archaeological Landscape Heritage: Museums' Systems Between Narrative Techniques and Multimedia Tools

Biancardi Michela, Massarente Alessandro[✉] [ID], and Suppa Martina

TekneHub and Department of Architecture, University of Ferrara, Ferrara, Italy
{michela.biancardi, alessandro.massarente,
martina.suppa}@unife.it

Abstract. The new information and communication technologies (ICT) are playing an increasingly predominant role in contemporary society. We must provide the opportunity to experiment and to develop new possible interactions between narrative techniques and multimedia tools able to promote our Cultural Heritage.

Actually, it's very important to focus our attention on trying to get over knowledge from generation to generation, through ICT. This work shows the results of a research project, implemented in close partnership (named Eridano museum network) among a University laboratory of Emilia-Romagna High Technologies Network (TekneHub), Regional Museum Pole Emilia-Romagna, two National Museums, four civic Museums, one Archaeological dig and a creative enterprise (TryeCo 2.0 srl).

The study primarily investigates how ICT can contribute to enhancing Cultural Heritage Education, adding value to cultural and didactic activities in museums. In this perspective, all Museums of Eridano network have tested innovative learning and teaching tools, thanks to user-centered design methodology, focusing virtual views, interactive technological platforms, games and immersive experiences. The researchers' team builds a web platform, using VR cardboards linked to the innovative YouTube's feature, 3D-VR-360 videos, through which is possible to discover ancient archaeological landscapes on Eridano river.

Then this research aims to investigate new possible interactions between these tools and methodological approaches in the development of FOSS (Free and Open Source Software) Tools, especially OpenWebGIS (Geographic Information System), considering the growing social demand to have an inclusive fruition of cultural and landscape heritage.

This new approach highlights the importance of a clearly defined communication strategy able to be inclusive for the different stakeholders of the Cultural Heritage, from museum workers to museum users.

Keywords: Inclusive communication strategy · OpenWebGIS
Cultural heritage · Archaeological landscape · Museum network

© Springer Nature Switzerland AG 2018
M. Ioannides et al. (Eds.): EuroMed 2018, LNCS 11197, pp. 93–102, 2018.
https://doi.org/10.1007/978-3-030-01765-1_11

1 Introduction

Today in Italy we are witnessing change in museums' governance and communication policy. In fact, museums have gained an administrative independence in 2015, allowing new and smart experiences to promote their cultural landscapes and communities.

Nevertheless, in a national museum context so different from case to case, there are still some problems which exist in relation with their territories, concerning in particular the way of organization and communication of their cultural tasks. This is down to the fact that the conditions of work in museums are more difficult because of their scarcity of human and economic resources. In particular, these conditions are more different if we compare national museum's accessibility to local museum's one.

Eridano museum network wants to cross over this critical issue making an interactive and a dynamic museum' system, where are included different types of cultural places as: Archaeological National Museum in Ferrara, Abbey and Museum in Pomposa like National Museums, Civic Archaeological Museum in Stellata, Civic Museum in Belriguardo, Territory Museum in Ostellato, Museum of Ancient Delta in Comacchio like local museum, and also the Archaeological dig of Terramara in Pilastri.

Therefore, the goal is transforming different museum characteristics in added cultural value: it seems useful to propose a pilot study to test, to examine and to widen the use of innovative technologies concerning the management of territorial cartographic data information related to the representation of the territory as form of communication and social inclusion [1].

In this perspective, the research project[1] is composed by strongly multiple and interconnected aspects, related to material and immaterial heritage. So, the research wants to look into the innovative methodologies of analysis and the ICT's impact, in relation with the different scales and uses of the diffused *Cultural Heritage*. According to European directives [6], the research project aims at: (a) reading of the different dimensions of the heritage (cultural, physics, digital, environmental, human and social); (b) the necessity to build relationships among technology, innovation and exploitation of the cultural landscapes; (c) the heritage's ability to promote social integration through the regeneration of outlying and weak territories; (d) the heritage's digitization and the opening of a common databases net of transformation's actions of territory; (e) the modernization of heritage's sector, increasing the ability to involve new actors; (f) the necessity to apply a strategic innovative approach to the search, promoting the exchange of knowledge and the creation of specific territorial specializations.

In particular, the research project is based on a user-centered design approach, where the ICT tools - FOSS tools for VR Virtual Reality and AR Augmented Reality, cardboards and interactive media design - become instruments to narrate the archeological stories, landscape, sites and values of the old river Po, that was named Eridano.

---

[1] The research project (2017–2018) was financed by italian Ministry MiBACT Ministero dei beni e delle attività culturali e del turismo Direzione generale Musei, MuSST Musei e sviluppo dei sistemi territoriali, Museums and development of territorial systems, direction Mario Scalini, scientific coordination Alessandro Massarente and Paola Desantis.

This system is planned to expand an inclusive and innovative fruition of the whole network, especially for small and local museums, building a virtual net structured on family targets, to bring together children, young people and their parents. In fact, one of the focus of this study is to approach the common people, especially young one, to the archeological world, that many time is been a field of culture only for experts and archaeology lovers for a long time.

The project is structured on two levels of planning and communication, studying a technological system of interaction to valorize the enclosed contents in every museum: the first level has developed multimedia contents into totem-indoor devices; the second level has implemented the museum's education activities, developing 3D VR 360 videos, immersive realities and games (Fig. 1).

In this perspective, totem-indoor devices have an interface for adult user and contain different information of the Eridano museum network, structured in layers: the first layer shows the archaeological data related to every museum; for each of them they were picked five archaeological finds (icons) to illustrate the relative historical period assigned to every Eridano network museum; a second layer shows relationship between archeological sites, museums, the Delta landscape and historical values, memories and local knowledge and skills.

Ergo, they were been built interactive maps, through OpenWebGIS - Geographic Information System allowing to analyze stratifications and interactions between different Cultural Heritage's values. This approach moves by the European directives in the field of preservation of Cultural Heritage and landscape, underlining the actions and the different aspects to integrate conservation and development of this area, through multi- and inter-scale approach [5]. In a context of Cultural Heritage, clearly, is necessary that the mapping over crosses the metric data, looking to the processes that bind people to the places in which heritage is conserved and its landscape is visible [4].

Consequently, the key idea is to realize games and video VR to design an innovative and collaborative online platform, especially for children and young people. The virtual reconstruction is an output of a cooperative work between university research team (TekneHub), creative enterprise for 3D modelling (TryeCO 2.0 s.r.l), and the museums. Therefore, the project changes the traditional approach by providing a collaborative simulation web platform, where the user can interact in 3D space, sharing different contents related to the various museums of the network. In fact, thanks to the cardboards, that are 3D viewers launched by google, the user can allow to visit specific museums' contents, giving an exciting immersive experience in ancient Delta landscape. This is a peculiar innovative aspect in archaeological museums, because enriches them giving a holistic vision and a 3D open reconceptualization of objects, sites and landscapes from a multi-scale point of view [1].

The VR becomes the mean to show the "relics" in its context, because furnishes important details non immediately enjoyable and allows the visitor to visualize antiquities correlated, creating some real emotional runs.

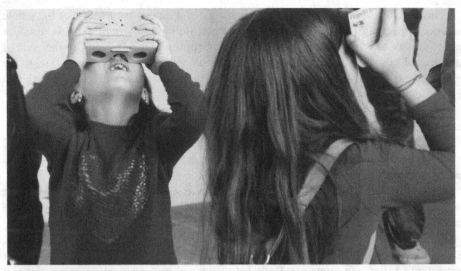

Fig. 1. The picture shows graphic cardboards and one of the moments of immersive Eridano Labs

2 Diffused Cultural Heritage: Eridano Museums' System and Its Valorization

The most innovative content of the case study is to increase the interoperability of survey systems, realizing an exclusive dataset of Eridano network, designing maps, through the QGIS tools, where the cultural, natural and logistic systems of Ferrara's area (material data) are intertwined with historical and archeological values of the same area. These cartographies support the application totem devices and, crossing the different metadata, coming from national and international datasets [2, 3, 7, 11], allow an assessment of the problems and potentials about a smart fruition of the qualitative aspects of landscape and Cultural Heritage of the examined area.

In this perspective, the landscape survey becomes an interactive tool, in which there is underlined the relationship between user/actors and objects, places, landscapes and their intrinsic value. So it changes the dialogue between tangible and intangible heritage: on the one hand, geographic material data, population and places, and on the other hand identity values of a territory [10]. The issues of different survey systems are over crossed working on the same platform, that includes a great amount of geo-referenced data and, then, developing an interactive design to have a wider digital inclusion [9]. So, these maps represent one of the most innovative content of the projects, because they act as cross media tools, allowing to the users to manage the landscape objects, through a multi and inter space-time dimension of the territory. In fact, the focus of this research is building a scenario of a part of Ferrara territory that is accompanied by the ability to include non-qualitative reading in relation with this tasks' set: (a) practice of active and direct people participation; (b) gathering and sharing of experiences related to diffuse cultural heritage; (c) analysis of the forms of perception of cultural heritage by different users of Eridano museum network.

Therefore through metadata, fundamental component of every user's GIS implementation, which is a summary document including content, quality, type, creation, and spatial information about a data set, are created thematic maps, taking the meta information from database record ESRI.[2] These data set stored in any format such as a text file, Extensible Markup Language (XML), allows to build different cartographies, split in specific layer. Merging some of these layer it's possible to get a clearer scan Eridano area, achieving to create digital cultural itineraries. A dataset of Ferrara's area is built, where are archived information about metric, morphologic, geographic and cultural data, thanks to the open data system it's possible to implement in every time the information, generating new layer (Fig. 2). Through these maps, users can browse in Eridano network, where they can see: cultural heritage places and landscapes related whit metric territorial data, coming from different sources; georeferencing of roads, slow mobility networks, railways, rivers and canals, wet areas, protected natural areas (i.e. Natura 2000 sites, national and regional parks as Parco Delta del Po) with simple and clear readability and usability (Fig. 3). This aspect is a good mark to develop new Heritage Information's tools, because it widens the local people and tourist's participation through an interactive design and digital inclusion.

Anyway, another innovative aspect of the research is the proposal to create new didactic labs employing the cardboards. They are simple and economic visual media, that are customizable cardboard boxes and allow the users to visualize an image in 3D on the proper smartphone (Android or Apple), through devoted applications: the application starts on smartphone, the users can answer to the instructions for the use

---

[2] Technology that supports metadata creation and editing, includes these tools in the core software products, sharing geographic information and building communities through shapefiles.

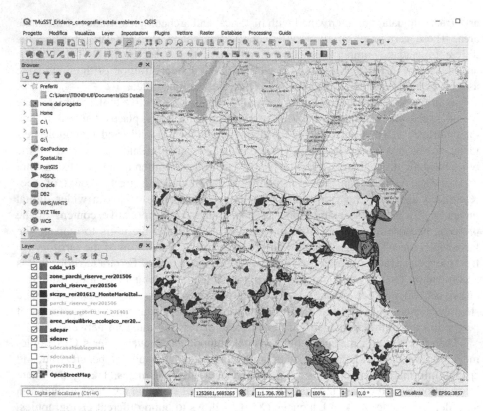

Fig. 2. The picture shows a QGIS map, that is focus on aspects relating to natural protected areas in Ferrara territory.

and to automatically modify the sight when the user moves its own head and the viewer.

Unlike other viewers, that are very more complex and expensive, through the cardboards, the Virtual Reality is lived in a fascinating immersive way. In fact, in spite of the Beacons technology, initially select, that allow to transmit and to receive small messages within brief distance only by Bluetooth, through messages strictly correlated to physical place in which are installed, the cardboard allows to view the contents anywhere and anytime: you can access, if you are at home or in the museum or in another place, to YouTube the channel seeing 3D VR 360 Eridano videos.

A customized graphic designed is apply on every single cardboard, studying an *ad hoc* packaging design for identifying the Eridano museum system, allowing the user not only to bring the memory of the immersive visit in the museum, but also having a gadget, that will be reuse in another place to relive or to tell the experience lived.

Part of the 3D interactive contents are enjoyable online: Eridano has 3D VR 360 video YouTube channel dedicated. The choice to have YouTube channel is dictated by a need to have a digital platform able supporting 3D VR 360 videos connected to cardboards use. In fact when TryeCO team decides to adopt this technologies, only YouTube is able to achieve an interactive archive of 3D VR 360 videos allowing

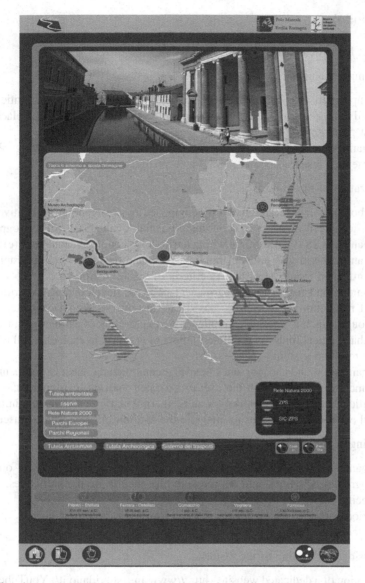

Fig. 3. The picture shows Eridano map supporting the application totem devices: in this the archeological areas are connected with Natura 2000 sites (zps and sic)

immersive experiences where users can observe, interpret, verify and understand cultural contents, using their capacity of reading the information and knowledge that are linked, through the identification of multidimensional relations.

In spring 2018 these cardboards are experimented through six laboratories of the museums' network, where are chosen the family as experimental target: the children with their parents participated to a particular day, when they test totem device and live an immersive experience, connected to education activities organized by the host museums.

3   Methodology

The project has articulated in four macro phases

A. - preliminary analysis:

- composition of a documents' collection about researches and activities developed in the territorial museum system, putting in relationship to the places' nets, that promote Cultural Heritage;
- organization and carrying out of technical co-planning meetings between museums, researchers and private enterprises.

B. - realization of the project:

- elaboration of a feasibility Study composed by: (a) general illustrative report; (b) technical report; (c) economic-financial evaluation; (d) cartography in OpenWebGIS (QGIS) of the whole territory object of investigation; (e) creation of an acronym and project branding; (f) planning of distinctive graphics and coordinated image according to criteria of visual identity;
- planning and realization of permanent benefits: development, experimentation and realization of a website, based on Responsive Web Design technology, through which it's possible an interactive exploration of cartography, museums, archaeological finds, over different filters of enquiry, in each one of the knots of the museum system;
- organization and carrying out of experimental didactic labs: experimentation of immersive visits through the use of dedicated viewers (cardboards);
- participative process, realization and experimentation of apparatus informative and communicative faces to integrate the fruition of the Eridano museums net.

C. checking *in itinere* and evaluation *ex post* of the project's results:

- organization of activities and public seminars to test the carrying out of the programmed actions and to measure the results of the initiatives, through specific indicators of resulted (output);
- periodic control of the planned tools, through specific indicators of impact (outcome);

D. - diffusion and sharing of the results:

- creation of a dedicated website - http://www.musst-eridano.it/; YouTube VR360 Eridano- https://www.youtube.com/channel/UC2rfhZkr-or-EJM8Ju47jG_A - musst-eridano; Facebook account and page - www.facebook.com/Musst-Eridano, page MuSST Eridano; Instragram profile - www.instagram.com/musst.eridano/; Twitter profile –MuSSTEridano; creation of a #mussteridano hashtag;
- digital publication (to be developed).

4 Results

The research project aims to realize interoperable web-tools to make a territorial analysis and to promote the diffused cultural and landscape heritage's fruition with simple and clear readability and usability, both for specialists and for generalist users. All of the aspects of data's management (representation, information, communication) are planned with an incremental web approach, in which all the intermediary products are immediately available on the project's web site or totem devices, thought as an evolutionary searchable multi-level database.

Furthermore, in the scientific research, is tested that the use of web tools, that have the specific focus to effectively widen the diffusion and the shared use of FOSS tools, took successful results at the condition that is possible to show users possible positive relapses related to managing's processes. But also, the present research project wants to investigate, through VR tools, the relation between digital system and users.

The new approach allows to refocus public attention on spaces of Cultural Heritage: Eridano network wants to respond to the collective need to know the archeological heritage of Ferrara's territory becoming a specific component of collective fruition for the regional tourism. In fact it offers an original solution to visiting requirements of different types of public. Visitors can customize its itineraries: selecting a specific cultural direction they can browse a step of Eridano contents, that are translated into English, allowing a best accessibility for tourists.

Therefore, some *in itinere* assessments show how ICT has been positively accessed by visitors and museums staff, giving a new and positive influence on the visit's quality and encouraging visitors to return at the museum to see further specific contents. Especially immersive experiences and interactive games has highlighted a good level of involvement by children of all ages. Eridano shows how a communicative approach using ICT tools during a visit at a museum or in a territory bring some advantages, like promoting specific aspects of the cultural surrounding environment and fruition of information, not always available.

The use of media tools achieve to share a large and varied amount of georeferenced information, to customize the contents, to propose a new education approach to realize a new way of fruition, revolutioning the people experience of museum visit. Furthermore, social networks, web site and YouTube channel represent a best opportunity to share Eridano contents, increasing the involvement of visitors and other museum actors. In this prospective, in few months, great results have been achieved thanks to the cooperation of Eridano partners.

The project is a first step to construct a partnership about diffused Digital Cultural Heritage in Ferrara's and Emilia-Romagna area, allowing to strengthen future research's possibility in this field and to widen future interchange among other possible partners, promoting a common advanced level of skills, a growth know-how about Digital Cultural Heritage including ICT and FOSS tools, a communicative development in the governance's processes of Cultural Heritage.

In this prospective, Eridano network can become an important cultural attractor, increasing the tourist offer in the territory of Ferrara

With its dynamic, open and flexible nature, based on the co-planning criteria among the different stakeholders of the territory, Eridano represents a best practice to replay practices achieving a wide fruition of museums and relative cultural and landscape heritage.

References

1. AA.VV.: Archaeology and virtual environments. From excavations to virtual museums and web communities. Alinea, Firenze (2008)
2. CGU - Carta Geografica Unica della provincia di Ferrara. http://visore.cgu-ferrara.it/. Accessed 03 June 2017
3. Dataset – European Data Portal. https://www.europeandataportal.eu. Accessed 27 Sept 2017
4. European Commission, European Landscape Convention, Art. 1 (2000)
5. European Commission – MiBACT, JPI Cultural Heritage and Global Change Strategic Research Agenda, Roma (2014)
6. European Commission, Towards an Integrated Approach to Cultural Heritage for Europe, Brussels, 22 July 2014
7. GeoER - Geoportale Emilia-Romagna. https://geoportale.region.emilia-romagna.it/it. Accessed 11 Dec 2017
8. Trisciuoglio, M., Barosio, M., Ramello, M. (eds.): Architecture and Places. Progetto culturale e memoria dei luoghi, Celid, Torino (2014)
9. Villa, D.: WebGis Qualitativi nel rilievo dei paesaggi culturali e del patrimonio diffuso. Note da un'esperienza italo-svizzera. In: Italian Survey and International Experience, pp. 1039–1046. Gangemi Editore, Parma (2014)
10. Villa, D., Manfredini, F.: From location-aware technologies to open data: toward a new urban research agenda. In: Seventh International Conference on Informatics and Urban and Regional Planning INPUT 2012, pp. 1127–1138. FrancoAngeli Edizioni - e-book, Cagliari (2012)
11. WebGIS del Patrimonio culturale dell'Emilia-Romagna, http://www.patrimonioculturale-er.it/webgis/. Accessed 03 Mar 2018

A Case Study of Digital Preservation of Motion Capture for Bā Jiā Jiāng Performance, Taiwan Religious Performing Arts

Yun-Sheng Syu$^{(\boxtimes)}$, Li-o Chen, and Yu-Fang Tu

Department of Digital Multimedia Design, China University of Technology,
Taipei, Taiwan, R.O.C.
hysaint@gm.cute.edu.tw

Abstract. Bā Jiā Jiāng (eight generals) are performers painted their faces, playing four generals Gan, Liu, Xie, Fan, and the Four Seasons God and other characters. When the celebration festival parade, as Lord God's the guardian team. It is an intangible cultural heritage of Taiwan's important religious and performing arts.

This project sponsored by Bureau of Cultural Heritage, Ministry of Culture (BOCH), Taiwan in 2017, the subject of study was Sheng De Temple, a traditional Bā Jiā Jiāng troupe of Beigang, Yunlin, Taiwan. The project uses optical motion capture technology to digitalize two Bā Jiā Jiāng actors performing in the parade and square, recording to three-dimensional digital motion information, and creating virtual reality software to present the results of technological applications. This is a interdisciplinary integrated project that includes religious folklore, performing arts, and digital technology.

Keywords: Motion capture · Taiwan Bā Jiā Jiāng (eight generals)
Festival parade · Intangible cultural heritage

1 Introduction

1.1 Optical Motion Capture System

Motion capture is also known as "Mocap". At present the most important capture technology is passive optical system. Advantages are high accuracy, high degree of freedom of movement, large range, high versatility (such as props, facial expressions, etc.). You can record multiple sets of data at the same time. Although expensive, but has been widely used in digital content production. Usually used in medical analysis, motion measurement, performing arts, visual effects, character animation and video games and other uses.

Optical motion capture technology uses multi special cameras to take a series of reflective images of moving images, the marker is placed in the human body, objects and other capture targets. After tracking and analysis, calculate the coordinate information in the three-dimensional space, and then solve the skeleton movement for further application. Because the mark is passive reflection of light, so called "passive" optical system.

M. Ioannides et al. (Eds.): EuroMed 2018, LNCS 11197, pp. 103–110, 2018.
https://doi.org/10.1007/978-3-030-01765-1_12

1.2   Motion Capture for Intangible Cultural Heritage Preservation

Intangible cultural assets are also known as intangible cultural heritage, including the following: (1) oral traditions and manifestations, including the language of intangible cultural heritage media; (2) performing arts; (3) social practice, rituals, festivals Activities; (4) knowledge and practice about nature and the universe; (5) traditional crafts.

Intangible cultural assets in the performance of the arts, in the past to save the performance of the action, mostly by the mentor oral dictation or through the text and image records. Often because the learner of learning is different from memory. And different types of performances or even different factions, using a different way of learning records. Such as the field of dance in the so-called Labanotation and other recording systems, now most of using photography or video to record performance.

Digital technology has now become an important knowledge and tools for the preservation of cultural assets. Motion capture technology can record analogical motion as digital data. Used in the traditional performing arts, can record accurate and realistic action information. Compared with the traditional abstract text or 2D image and video records, 3D digital action information, can be a better all-round display of the characteristics of the performance of the stage and get the scientific analysis of data, more conducive to the digitization of intangible assets Preservation, learning, animation, interactive performances and other purposes.

1.3   Taiwan "CHÊN T'OU" Culture and Bā Jiā Jiāng

"CHÊN T'OU" is a Taiwanese folk culture parade. In the temple incense, celebration, wandering, funeral and other occasions, the people composed of performance team, to participate in the parade. "CHÊN T'OU" combines visual arts and performing arts, which includes folk music, dance, martial arts, art and craft … and so on.

"Jiā Jiāng (General regiment)" is an important religious performance team in Taiwan in Fig. 1. Refers to a form of expression, painted in the face, wearing a dress and helmet of God, hand holding instruments, play God general patrol. In the important religious procession, you can see the general performance. Bā Jiā Jiāng (eight generals) is one of the most well-known and the oldest Jiā Jiāng General regiment.

The traditional Bā Jiā Jiāng (eight generals), including Gan, Liu, Xie, Fan known as the four generals, with the spring and summer autumn and winter god, known as the four seasons gods. Coupled with the leader and two messenger, arranged in the team. Bā Jiā Jiāng (eight generals) is the guard of God and the police, when the Lord God patrol, they walk in front of the god's chair, performance patrol, capture ghosts and other tasks.

In the past, after the farming work, men gathered in the square to practice the 8 Generals posture, on the one hand can learn martial arts physical, protect the hometown, on the other hand can promote harmony and cooperation, and is an important social activity.

But with the industrial and commercial social development, fertility decreased. Such as the research subject Yunlin Beigang Sheng De Temple of the General regiment, has few people willing to inherit the action, footsteps, rituals and traditional

Fig. 1. Bā Jiā Jiāng (eight generals)

norms, so Bā Jiā Jiāng (eight generals) is already an urgent need to preserve the intangible cultural assets of Taiwan.

2 Cast Study - Bā Jiā Jiāng

This study take the "eight generals" of the "Sheng De Temple in Beigang, Yunlin, Taiwan as the research subject. The optical motion capture system will be used to record performances on the intangible cultural heritage of Taiwan's traditional performing arts for 3D digital preservation. The first section is to conduct field surveys, interview masters, and analyze plans for "eight generals" to perform and plan and capture. The Sect. 2 is to study motion capture hardware and software technologies to develop equipment and space requirements for the study. The Sect. 3 is to capture the action of "eight generals" and establish a three-dimensional digital motion database. The Sect. 4 is to use motion data to develop VR experience software as a feasibility test for future use of intangible assets.

2.1 Performance Analysis

This study mainly focuses on the capture of the eight generals' basic movements. Before entering the studio to capture movements, it is necessary to analyze the performance movements in order to develop appropriate capture methods. After field investigation and film analysis, we learned that the Action of " Sheng De Temple eight Generals" is more traditional, simple, soft and slow, not too fancy move, attention and consistent with the action show tacit understanding.

In general, due to the limitations of space, equipment, and post-processing capabilities, it is better to perform single-player motion capture as much as possible to improve the quality and stability of data.

However, most of the eight generals' performances were performed by two performers. Therefore, after many rehearsal tests, we decided to capture the performances of the two performers simultaneously for the best performance, so as to reduce the problem of post-processing alignment. Actors holding a feather fan, one hand holding instruments, including a flag, token, board, yoke and so on. In order to avoid the body cross, the performance of weight, the actors need to hold a props to capture.

2.2 Motion Capture on Set

Our project uses a passive optical motion capture system at the Department of Digital Multimedia Design, China University of Technology. There are a total of 6 MotionAnalysis Raptor-H digital cameras and 8 Osprey cameras. The camera resolution is 640 * 480, capture speed to 1/250 s, can provide precise high-frequency motion capture capabilities. The effective capturing space is: 3 m (length) * 2.5 m (width) * 2 m (high), which can provide a full-body motion capture of 2 actors and an on-site realtime preview (without facial expressions and finger movements).

According to the schedule, we performed three motion captures in the studio. The period of motion capture is between 4 and 6 h, including system settings and dress up. Considering the actor's status, recording about 8 to 10 sets of movements and recording 1,000 s of performance on average (Fig. 2).

Fig. 2. Motion capture on set

2.3 Data Processing

There are mainly two kinds of motion capture data according to its technical principles: The first is the relative rotation information of the joint system. The second is the absolute position information of the markers, an optical system is first recorded the position data and solved data to joint rotation value of each level.

Although the passive optical motion capture system has the advantages of accurate high frequency, high versatility, and less impact on performers. However, because the system captures reflected light and is susceptible to environmental noise, and the actor

Fig. 3. 3D character model and animation

loses marker images due to physical shadowing during exercise, the distance between the markers is too close to or similar, etc., often causing confusion in marker numbers. Get the right movement information.

It is necessary to manually correction, data interpolation, and data filtering at the later stage to become effective use of 3D data and solve it to skeleton information. In particular, the eight generals perform fast-vibrating motions such as fanning, shaking, and percussion. It is easy to be regarded as noise bursts in the data. If excessive processing results in a decrease in the strength and rhythm of movement, must pay special attention.

3   Animation and VR Application

In order to verify the results of technology use, we use digital motion data to create 3D character animations (Fig. 3) and use virtual reality (VR) immersive interactive technologies to overcome the limitation of time and space to experience the demonstrations of the eight generals (Fig. 4.)

Fig. 4. Virtual reality experience application

4   Conclusion

This project sponsored by Bureau of Cultural Heritage, Ministry of Culture (BOCH), Taiwan in 2017. This is the result of the first phase. This is an interdisciplinary integrated project that includes religious folklore, performing arts, and digital technology. The conclusions of this phase of the study are as follows:

4.1 The Combination of Intangible Cultural Assets and Digital Technology

The use of motion capture technology to capture the movement of traditional arts performing arts can record accurate and realistic movement information. However, the performances of The "Eight Generals" have traditionally been relayed by mentor in an oral presentation and demonstration mode. They rarely leave records. Compared with the two-dimensional space photo or video recording method, the three-dimensional digital motion information obtained in this study can more fully demonstrate the characteristics of body movement performance and obtain scientific analysis data, which is more conducive to intangible assets. Digitized preservation, teaching and learning, animation, interactive performances and other value-added applications.

4.2 The Using of Motion Capture Technology in Performing Arts

Through this research process, it is also the mutual learning of traditional culture and technology. For example, although the motion capture technologies are all the same, different performance types and actions are still different. For example, the design of the mark, the setting of the capture space, and the planning of the capture process must all be adjusted according to the type of performance. During the research process, the motion capture technicians need to have a deep understanding of the intangible cultural assets and interact with the performers. Intangible cultural assets are the soul. Digital technology is a tool. Each takes its own strengths to achieve the record of performances with the best quality.

4.3 The Inheritance of Intangible Cultural Heritage

The "Eight Generals" is not only the visual arts of masks, costumes and props, but also the art of performing arts for team dance parades. Taiwan's folk folklore contains rich cultural spirit and emotions. It is already part of the people's lives and is an intangible cultural asset of Taiwan's important religious and performing arts. The use of motion capture technology is only one of the digital records, and it cannot replace live performances. For example, performers also pointed out that they did not paint their faces and wear costumes. Not all generals performed together. Even at different venues, the feeling of performance was different. In addition, the group performance is not just performing art. The traditional generals must be vegetarian and cultivate their bodies before patrolling, and the artist's facial make-up, shaman's spells, etc. have strict rituals and symbolism. This is indeed an intangible cultural heritage that Taiwan needs to continue to study and preserve.

References

1. Wang, T.-X., Liu, Z.: Intangible cultural heritage protection: strategy and dilemma. J. Chongqing Univ. Arts Sci. (Soc. Sci. Ed.) (7) (2006)
2. Peng, D.-M., Pan, L.-S., Sun, S.-Q.: Digital protection—intangible cultural heritage, new means of protection. Art Res. (1) (2006)

3. Pan, N.-Y.: Practice from Congjiang County, Guizhou, observing the protection and use of ethnic minority intangible cultural heritage. Theory Contemp. (6) (2005)
4. Yang, X.-M.: Digital museum and related issues. Chin. Original Art. (1) (2006)
5. China Intangible Cultural Heritage Protection Online Exhibition Hall. http://www.china.com.cn/chinese/zhuanti/bh/1116783.htm
6. Lu, J.-M.: 《Generals' Duties》.Green Travel Cultural Foundation
7. Lu, J.-M.: 《Lead Generals》. Tangshan Publisher
8. Tobon, R.: The Mocap Book: A Practical Guide to the Art of Motion Capture (2010)
9. Kitagawa, M., Windsor, B.: MoCap for Artists: Workflow and Techniques for Motion Capture. Taylor & Francis, Abingdon (2008)
10. Menache, A.: Understanding Motion Capture for Computer Animation. Elsevier, New York (2011)
11. Wang, M.-Z.: Animation Production: Motion Capture Technology Fundamentals. Tsinghua University Press, Beijing (2013)
12. Hsu, Y.-S.: A study of appling Taiwan folklore hero characters in computer animation arts— a case study of the Pat-ka Chiòng characters. National Taiwan University of Arts Multimedia Animation Arts Institute (2005)
13. Huang, Z.-L.: Infinite beauty imagination- talking about dance and technology. Aesthetic Education No. 174 (2010)
14. Huang, Q.: When Avatar meets Yang, Gui-Fei-Wang, Guan-Qiang Director, talking about digital 3D technology and drama training. Guoguang Electronics News No. 129

Interactive Media Art Based on Location and Motion Tracking of Multi-performers

Haeyeon Won[ID] and Jeongmin Yu[(⊠)][ID]

Department of Cultural Heritage Industry, Graduate School of Cultural Heritage,
Korea National University of Cultural Heritage, Buyeo-gun,
Chungcheongnam-do, Korea
{mile18, jmYu}@nuch.ac.kr

Abstract. In this study, we present a novel interactive media art framework on the theme of culture heritage. From existing research and case studies, interactive media art has shown that the audience be build their own identity through interaction during the process of the artwork, and aesthetic experiences are possible through the origin of folk games. The combination of folk play and interactive media art is considered to have aesthetic commonalities, and it can be presented as a new direction for using traditional culture and the possibility of interactive media art. In this paper, we proposed a framework that is designed for interactive media based on location and hand-motion of multi-performers. Otherwise, from existing methods, we reproduce the changing aspects of folk play that develop from the game, and the interactive media art is performed by a collaboration of multiple performers. To this end, we introduce a conceptual framework for verifying its feasibility.

Keywords: Interactive media art · Folk play · Multi-audiences

1 Introduction

Advanced technology in modern society has brought about a change in art. Digital technology-based methods and the development of a variety of content have led audiences to approach these works from a new perspective. There are many interactive media artworks, which are mainly conducted through touch or hand motion tracking, or body motion tracking. This may lead to communication with the audience, but it could only be a temporary effect, which focuses more on the perception of individual behavior, despite the fact that there will be more individuals than groups. Therefore, this study will recognize motion at the same time as location of the audience, and actively induce audience participation so that the work can be composed with other audiences.

The study aims to present the possibility of attempting various productions through interactive media art combined with traditional culture, and to present elements to be used in content development. We review the existing research and preceding studies that combine media art with cultural assets, and analyze the meaning of the communal characteristics of folk games. In addition, by considering the most important feature of interactive media, the interactive element, we can derive the meaning of

M. Ioannides et al. (Eds.): EuroMed 2018, LNCS 11197, pp. 111–117, 2018.
https://doi.org/10.1007/978-3-030-01765-1_13

communication between audience and traditional culture. In the proposed framework, we combined motion and location of performers, based on tracking technology, with projection mapping, using Kinect2 and beacon to devices for the work. Projection mapping creates a new virtual space by projecting video or images onto the surface of a wall or object. The open source mapping tool vvvv is used to track the behavior of the audience with a Kinect2, recognize the location of the audience with beacon, and present the art direction to express its behavior with other audiences.

2   Related Works

2.1   Traditional Culture and Media Art

First at all, conventional media art combined traditional patterns and the coincidences of fractal images. [1] created media art by combining an ultrasonic sensor and projection mapping, fusing the spatial characteristics of *Dancheong* with the commonality of projection mapping [2]. [3] interpreted the amulets with pictures and letters, and [3] focused on the expression and artistic use of amulet graphics. [4] presented a system that plays a flute and digitally draws a *mookjookdo*, representing the direction of new interactive media art [5]. In this visualization of traditional culture, most viewers are in a passive but reflective position [6]. Therefore, in this study, we will recognize movement at the same time as considering the location of performers, thereby attracting active participation, so that multiple performers can produce the work at the same time.

2.2   Media and Cultural Content

In [7], the characteristics based on the "thought world" are "mutually subjective" by the entity of the writer and audience of media art, which combines the process of establishing subjectivity with the process of establishing identity. In other words, we need to understand how subjects and interaction appear in different genres of cultural content. The characteristics seen in the "symbolic world" are "interacting" in the relationship-oriented structure of writers, media, and audience. Realistic worlds are areas of things that cannot be expressed, and thus a place where the self meets inexpressible joy. This can be seen as a fundamental factor in "enjoying" the cultural content of various genres. Interaction in media art focuses on communication and highlights the concept of art as an experience. The experience means knowledge or information obtained by participating in an observing activity or event.

In this paper, we attempt to see how people interact with the audience in the example of interactive media art that's perceived and tracked. In Fig. 1(a), we watched the image of the pond containing the four seasons show the flow of time by recognizing the spectators, and letting the spectators themselves examine the relationship between the images. In Fig. 1(b), the butterfly implemented various interactions, such as moving away from the framework of the work and being affected by other works, or losing energy depending on the behavior of the audience, such as moving away from the framework of they work. The system is designed to prevent the same scene from occurring as the interaction with the viewer results in continuous changes in the work.

Fig. 1. (a) *Kimchanggyum* water shadow four season2, (b) *Teamlap* a borderless group of butterflies

The work of Fig. 2(a) consists of a system that converts images of crushed soil particles and pottery into illusions and accelerates what is repeated. However, it does not produce the same accumulations and recordings; it produces an infinitely random variable under limited conditions. The work of Fig. 2(b) is one of the examples in which *Daegeum*, reflecting a user's performance, presents a new direction for inter-active art using a new medium as of a bamboo drawing.

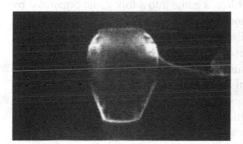

Fig. 2. (a) Yang Min Ha-nonlinear accumulation, (b) Traditional culture experience art research-Mookjookdo

If conventional art required passive and reflective methods, the biggest character-istic of the digital age is interaction. Art interaction is about the basis of the experience of the audience and highlights the basic element of art as communication. This change in the art, based on this human-centered experience, means that communication with the audience is complete and works actively considering the relationship with the audience appear. Traditional interactive media art has shown that while media changes were driven by temporary behavior considering audience interaction, this study has led to continuous interaction. Those actions, not one change, will accumulate and appear in the work.

2.3   The Origin of Folk Play

John Dewey [8] referred to aesthetic experiences that are not accumulated from passive senses, but are closely related to everyday life and driven through interaction, not just within the environment. If you look at the way folk games are played, you can easily find that games originated in many aspects of life. Farming depends on the changes of nature at any time, so it is common to pray to the gods of nature for a good harvest. In Korea, farming rites include harvest ceremonies between January, June, and July, and harvest ceremonies for the month of the year, typically called the *Jeongwol Dae-boreum*, where various games are played in hopes of a good harvest [9]. For this reason, Korean folk games often originated from festivals to pray for the well-being of farming and villages and to dance and sing. Based on this, various folk games were developed.

3   Proposed Framework

3.1   Intent of Planning

The experience of using fire by humans may have begun with an open mind. In this case, lighting is a method of using light from fire. Humans may have lived their lives learning materials through their experience with using fire and lighting up dark places.

The *Jwibullori* is transformed from a children's game into a folk game organized by a village community, such as a torch fight and burning a moon house. What these folk games have in common is a kind of rite, which is to pray for the well-being of farming and villages [10]. By drawing light from these origins, the work was implemented in a new way by inducing the cooperation of visitors. The reason why the form of the work is composed of semicircular figures is that this is the original form often used in Korean festivals. The symbol of the sun and the moon is part of the worship of nature. The distance of the sun from *Haji* increases little by little, which is why ancient people regarded the sun as sacred and held a festival [11].

3.2   The Overall Proposed System

When the audience comes in with their cell phones, they send a Bluetooth signal from their cell phones. The Bluetooth signal is continuously sent to an Arduino (open-source computing platform based on microcontroller boards) and an approximate location can be obtained using the signal's strength. The depth sensor of the Kinect perceives human movement. When an infrared IR laser beam detects people, pixels are measured. The image processor processes the data and recognizes the behavior of the performer. A signal from the beacon is received by the Bluetooth module and is connected to the Arduino. A signal is sent to the PC via the PC recognize the signal, visualizing the location and motion information and sending it to the projector (Fig. 3).

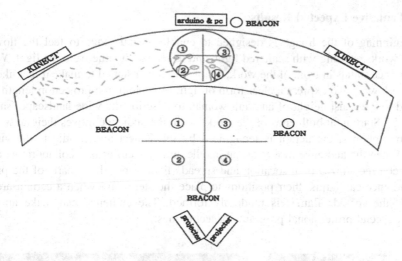

Fig. 3. The overall proposed system of interactive media art

4 Initial Experiment

4.1 Hardware and Software Configurations

To recognize the movement of the human body, we analyzed skeletal tracking information from two Microsoft Kinect sensors to get more accurate tracking of audience actions. Using the beacon and the smartphone held by the audience, the Bluetooth signal is recognized and the part of the piece can be configured with the location after being tracked. To do this, Kinects and beacons are connected to an Arduino to send a signal to a PC, which is then sent to the projector by the project tool vvvv (Fig. 4).

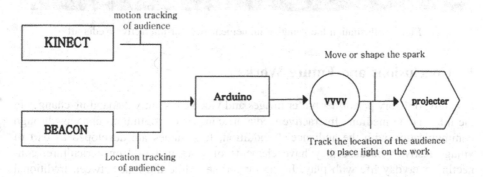

Fig. 4. Detail system diagram for the proposed interactive media art

4.2   Tentative Expected Results

The beginning of the image is designed to enable the audience to feel the flow of natural works, starting with scattered light, and to realize the line from the light. When the audience stands in front of the work, a large cloth is installed to make it feel like the wind is blowing. To express a clear form of light on a cloth, the projection length was planned to the waist height of an adult woman to describe the wide landscape (shown in Fig. 5). Starting at both ends of the work, when the audience moves their arms with their smartphones, the action is recognized by the Kinect and it adjusts the virtual flame. When the audience moves to the middle and gets closer to a collaborative area, the beacon recognizes their location and spreads flames into those parts of the piece. The audience can adjust their positions to place the stem, and when a certain area is formed, the spreads flames is randomly formed. The audience can make artwork without special professional programs or techniques.

Fig. 5. Illustration the tentative implementation for interactive media art

5   Conclusions and Future Works

Recently, ordinary performer prefer images and video constantly demanding changes in the information medium. Interactive media art consists of continuous changes through communication with the audience. In addition, folk games are developed as part of village festivals because they have elements of worship based on agriculture, connecting everyday life with play. In the meantime, while the link between traditional culture and interactive media art has been based on individuals, the proposed method in this study has been designed for the active participation of large audiences.

Our proposed system consists of beacons, a Kinect, an Arduino, a PC (vvvv), and a projector, to try to interact with multiple audiences. It tracks the audience's movements to create and transform sparks, and converts interactions to parts of the picture depending on location. It combines interactive media art with community elements, of traditional culture, to propose a new approach to media art and traditional culture.

The limitations of this study have not yet been analyzed, so it is difficult to know the recognition accuracy and speed. Therefore, in future studies, we plan to test the accuracy and speed of motion and location recognition after the work is implemented and to investigate user experience through surveys from the audience.

Acknowledgement. This research is supported by 2018 Support Project for Academic Research on Traditional Culture in Korea National University of Cultural Heritage.

References

1. Kim, S.H., Joo, H.J.: A study on process development of media art through fusion of fractal and traditional patterns formative media. Korea Illustr. Soc. **16**(2), 39–46 (2013)
2. Moon, J.H., Kim, H.J.: Using traditional symbols of dancheong and projection mapping in interactive media art - based on the work "this moment". J. Korean Soc. Media Arts **15**(3), 75–92 (2017)
3. Jin, X.: A study on the interaction of the leading in media art - focused on the interrelation and transformation of hexagrams. Res. Basic Des. **17**(1), 101–114 (2016)
4. Oh, Y.J.: Study on graphic art as the art of lines focused on the graphics of talisman. Bull. Korean Soc. Basic Des. Art **14**(2), 219–229 (2013)
5. Kim, Y.M.: Traditional culture experience art research. Korea Sci. Art Forum **17**, 95 (2014)
6. Kim, J., Kim, J., Kim, E.-K., Kim, C.: Production of 3D mongyudowondo with reinterpretation of traditional paintings. J. Korea Inst. Inf. Commun. Eng. **13**(6), 1234–1240 (2009)
7. Kim, S.: A study on the interrelationship between media art and cultural content global cultural content, (22), 55–57 (2016)
8. Dewey, J.: Art as Experience, p. 13. A Perigee Books, New York (1980)
9. Lim, J.H.: The victory and function of folk play as a community culture (2008)
10. Kim, G.: Folk science. Daewonsa (2014)
11. Pyo In Joo: The physical experience and symbolic meaning of ui fire in folklore (2016)
12. Kim, S.: Chapter 1 Korean folk playing theory. Central Folklore (1), 24 (1989)

Ego-Centric Recording Framework for Korean Traditional Crafts Motion

Eunsol Jeong⬤ and Jeongmin Yu(✉)⬤

Department of Cultural Heritage Industry, Graduate School of Convergence
Cultural Heritage, Korea National University of Cultural Heritage, Buyeo-gun,
Chungcheongnam-do, South Korea
{solsolssi, jmyu}@nuch.ac.kr

Abstract. The transmission and safeguarding of intangible cultural heritage
(ICH) follow an apprenticeship manner for education. However, people have
problems that cannot continue to implement education because of time, space,
economic and environmental constraints. Utilizing information and communication technology (ICT), these problem can be settled. Particularly, in this paper,
we propose a novel 3D hand motion recording framework to record the motions
of the craftsperson in the ego-centric view using Leap-motion vision sensors. In
contrast to the existing 3D hand motion recording frameworks, we adopt a head-
mounted Leap Motion for recording the ego-centric view of handcraft motions
and use the other Leap Motion to solve the problem of severe self-occlusions
between the fingers. For the target content for recording, we select Nubi, which
is a traditional sewing technique in Korea, and a Nubi craftsperson is designated
as the ICH of Korea. From the preliminary experiments, we confirm that the
proposed framework can be applied to recording the various sewing hand
motions effectively.

Keywords: Ego-centric view · Intangible cultural heritage · Craftsperson
Nubi

1 Introduction

Intangible cultural heritage (ICH) is transmitted by gestures and word of mouth and
easily modified or disappears as time goes by. Mechanization also poses a greater threat
to the survival of the ICH crafts field because of mass production. Moreover, globalization links the world, but many communities lose their traditions. To prevent these
threats, many organizations have opened schools and conducted projects to support
craftspeople and encourage education. And also digitalization has been considered a
potential solution.

On the other hand, the digital contents of ICH are made infrequently, and it not
enough to implement practical education for transmission and safeguarding. Practical
education through apprenticeship training is base step of ICH transmission [1]. In
addition, the ICH is preserved while learning orthodox skills. However, the recorded
and utilized digital ICH contents do not have the educational elements noted above. [2]
recorded a Chinese ICH named "Tujia brocade" using Leap Motion and Kinect for

© Springer Nature Switzerland AG 2018
M. Ioannides et al. (Eds.): EuroMed 2018, LNCS 11197, pp. 118–125, 2018.
https://doi.org/10.1007/978-3-030-01765-1_14

target ICH transmission and safeguarding. They recorded the craftsperson's motions directly but just provided a rough animation of the process. They also adopted multi-sensors, but did not address the problems of the hand's self-occlusions and different points of views. There was no accurate recording, and there was no interaction, so it could not be used to play an educational role at all. [3, 4] also did not represent educational elements. Sculpture and pottery game contents were implemented for entertainment purposes, but there was little content that users can use for educational purposes.

In this paper, we propose a framework of ICH crafts hand-motion recording for making educational contents. The target subject is called "Nubi", a Korean traditional quilting craft. For recording detailed hand motions and to reduce the confusion of mental rotation, we used a head-mounted Leap Motion vision sensor because the best view of education is from the standpoint of the craftsperson (i.e., the ego-centric view). For the first time in the literature of ICH fields, the ego-centric 3D recording is performed. In addition, to resolve self-occlusions between the hands and fingers, we used another Leap Motion from the frontal view. This framework can contribute to improving the accuracy of recording and improving educational effectiveness.

This paper is organized as follows: Related works for recording crafts motion are described in Sect. 2, the proposed Nubi craft-motion recording framework is described in Sect. 3, tentative expected results are shown in Sect. 4 and a conclusion is given, and future works are suggested in Sect. 5.

2 Related Works

2.1 Recording of Hand Motions

It is important in recording the field of crafts to record the hands, but this is a great challenge because the hands consist of many connected parts and joints that make various movements.

Physical Sensor-Based Methods. Physical sensor-based methods include gloves [5, 6], bands [5], and markers that are wearable or attached to the hand. These methods were used frequently in the early development stage but are not used often these days because of drawbacks such as cost and inconvenience. In addition, marker-based motion capture does not work well for hand motion recording because there are missing data from markers' occlusions [7].

Vision-Based Methods. Compared with physical sensor-based devices, vision-based methods are low cost and easy to mount in different environments. They are marker-less motion capture technologies based on a real-time depth sensing system. A two-dimensional video using a monocular camera recognizes the hand's low-level features, such as skin color or shape, acquired from hand motion images [8]. However, it focuses on hand detection at the level of analyzing hand gestures in images rather than hand motion tracking. Therefore, it does not extract the z axis, so does not produce reliable hand recording. Meanwhile, the development of infrared (IR) cameras, such as Leap Motion, and RGB-D cameras, such as Microsoft Kinect and Asus Xtion, has enabled people to track complex hand motions in real time [9]. Leap Motion uses two IR cameras and three IR LEDs to obtain 3D position data and specialized tracking of hand motions. While RGB-D cameras, such as Microsoft Kinect and Asus Xtion, have been made for efficient human pose reconstruction, they are weak at detecting hands. [10] also shows that Leap Motion's capabilities of hand motion tracking are more accurate and fasted than Microsoft Kinect. The biggest drawbacks of a vision-based optical recording system is occlusion by angle and finger it selves. In this situation, using multi-cameras is obviously efficient at detecting hand motions. [11] use two Leap Motion sensors to cover the blind zone, and [12] use Leap Motion and an RGB-D camera (ex, Intel RealSense F200) to solve the occlusion problem and achieve virtual reality.

2.2 Digitalization of ICH

The digitalization approach to ICH presents a new method and solution for safeguarding and transmitting. However, most digital recording is still proceeded like filming a documentary, as it used to be. Archiving ICH in 3D is rarely performed, and it is too early to expect the educational use of that content.

In [3], the ICH weaving process of China was recorded and animated using multi-sensors. A Leap Motion was placed on the work desk for recording hand motions, and a Kinect was positioned on the craftsperson's left side for recording body movements. They used multi-sensors, however cannot solve the self-occlusion problem. And the animation without interaction cannot be used for education purposes. [4] achieved interaction using Leap Motion but did not have crafts motions for training. In addition, [5] made a pottery game focused on the implementation of making ceramics with hand gesture control. These game contents just focused on finishing the work, such as doing handicrafts; thus, these are not sufficient for training students.

For the approach of the digitalization of ICH playing a role of safeguarding and transmitting, the lack of educational elements in ICH contents will have to be resolved. Additionally, to improve the shortcoming of an education factor, this study presents an ego-centric recording framework. It emphasized using the craftsperson's view (i.e., the egocentric view) and multi-Leap Motion to record authentic information.

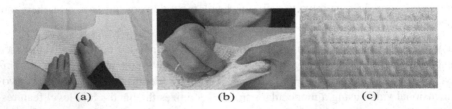

(a)   (b)   (c)

Fig. 1. Images of Nubi performance: (a) stitching on fixed layered fabrics like contemporary method, (b) rolling the layered fabrics around a bar from one side and stitching like the traditional method, (c) example of Nubi progress; using different-colored thread with fabrics for distinction.

3 Proposed Method

3.1 Recording the Target Nubi Content

Origin of Nubi. Nubi, a Korean traditional quilting method, is a process of stitching together two layers of fabric. Nubi originates in monks' lifestyle. They had abandoned the mundane world and led secluded lives deep in the mountains for years. They performed Nubi work on their tattered robes to avoid worn-out clothes. After cotton was first cultivated, Nubi flourished in the public. Since Nubi required much labor and time, Nubi clothes were tailored for the royal household and nobility at first. In time, however, ordinary households gradually took up the practice. Nubi became especially popular for winter clothes because of its warmth and durability [13].

Difference from Quilts. Nubi is similar to quilts with a supplementary operation. Both use cotton or fur between two layers of fabric. However, they are different in some elements. Quilts use colorful fabrics that are stitched on grids and curves. Quilted fabrics are used for bedspreads generally. In contrast, Nubi uses single, same-color fabrics and thread and sews horizontally or vertically. Nubi is mainly used to make clothes and is considered a luxury product in recognition of the difficulty involved in handcrafting [14].

Nubi Method. Traditional Nubi work is all hand-sewn. To obtain regular intervals of stitch lines, the craftsperson needs to hook a strand in the middle of the outer layer of the fabric and put it back in again. Then, a fine line is drawn, but any damage is found. The next step is fixing the layered fabrics tautly. The traditional Nubi method uses a bar to roll around the layered fabrics together tautly from one side, and Nubi work is started from the other side. Contemporary Nubi, however, is slightly deformed due to fixing the fabrics with tongs on a work desk for convenience. The last step is a broad stitch along the line. This is a repetitive task but requires concentration because meticulous and straight sewing is important [15] (Fig. 1).

3.2 The Proposed Framework

The framework records the crafting hand motion in 3D using an optical depth camera, Leap Motion, and includes steps for calibrating the accuracy and precision. The main Leap Motion is mounted on the performer's head for recording in the ego-centric view. If the recorded depth information from egocentric view has errors larger than the set threshold, error correction is conducted by another Leap Motion and IR reflector's xyz axis. Error is caused by self-occlusion or the accuracy of the Leap Motion equipment. After correcting the error, the recorded information undergoes the data fusion step. Then, modeling is started and an AR simulation program is created for training (Figs. 2 and 3).

Ego-Centric View. The head-mounted Leap Motion records crafting hand motions at the viewing angle of the craftsperson. In other words, it is an ego-centric view recording. We consider it to resolve the hand being concealed by fabric and to improve educational effectiveness. First, concealment by fabric happens because of Nubi work's

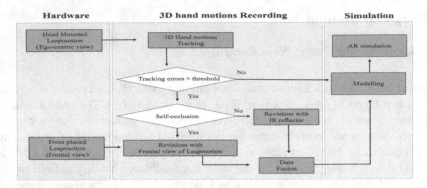

Fig. 2. The proposed recording framework of hand motions.

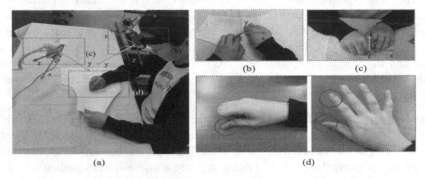

Fig. 3. Overall system configuration: (a) Hardware configuration of designed hand motion recording system, (b) view of head-mounted Leap Motion (i.e., egocentric view), (c) view of front-placed Leap Motion, (d) attached IR reflector on fingertips.

features. The craft work starts with layered fabrics, which are setting like a cover on the work desk. Therefore, setting the Leap Motion in midair is suited for recording crafting hand motions and it is suggested that it is mounted on the head. Another reason for setting Leap Motion in the ego-centric view is to provide educational benefits to users. This is related to mental rotation and cognitive load. Mental rotation is carried out when a person wants to understand what the rotated objects are and where they belong [16]. A larger rotation degree of objects leads to cognitive load, which causes slow perception [17]. [18] explains that the reason people turn a map is to support mental rotation. Additionally, according to [18], cognitive load from a larger view increases the possibility of an accident. Summing up the above examples, the ego-centric view, which matches the degree of rotation between humans and objects, helps people learn efficiently and fast.

Error Correction. After recording the motion using the head-mounted Leap Motion, if the error is above the threshold, it will undergo the error correction process. There are two types of errors. The first is caused by concealment. There are two problems from concealment: being covered by an object and being covered by the hands and fingers (i.e., self-occlusion). In the Nubi recording process, the problem of concealment with an object appears due to the underlying fabric. This problem, however, is solved by the head-mounted Leap Motion, which is set in relation to the structure so that the hand is always visible. Meanwhile, there is another problem when self-occlusion occurs due to interference from the hands and fingers. This problem happens because of the angle of the optical camera; thus, we suggest using a multi-camera. We set two Leap Motions considering the aliasing between camera references by [13]. The second type of error is due to the accuracy of the tracking of the equipment. Leap Motion detect the craft motion less accurate than an ideal, static palm pose. Furthermore, the Leap Motion that takes it is also shaking because it is attached to the head. It is therefore necessary to calibrate the position using ancillary equipment. We use an IR reflector to perform hand position revision. [19] marked retro-reflective dots on the workspace in a real-world position and calibrated three depth cameras as reference points. Similarly, the reflector was attached to the thumb and index finger's fingernail and used as a reference point to modify the skeleton position.

4 Tentative Expected Results

The results of the initial implementations are shown in Fig. 4. The first step is to have a framework that can accurately record the hand gestures of the craftsperson. Align according to coordinates, some errors in detecting hand motion are shown. Through this experiment, we found that the performance of Leap Motion is not perfect for movement at a certain angle. However, we also found that the head-mounted Leap Motion and front-placed Leap Motion have a complementary relationship because at least one Leap Motion worked normally.

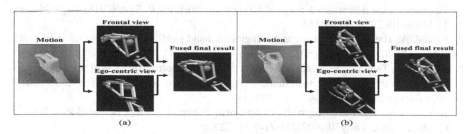

(a)   (b)

Fig. 4. Final 3D recording results: (a) hand motion of a holding needle, (b) hand motion of a pulling thread.

5 Conclusion

For the transmission and safeguarding of ICH, the best method is education from person to person. However, people cannot continue to implement education because of time, space, economic and environmental constraints.

This study emphasizes the recording of a Korean ICH named "Nubi" from an ego-centric view, unlike the existing method of recording from an external view. This is because it has the advantage of detail and immersion. This recording framework is based on the fact that a head-mounted device is essential for virtual space immersion and this experience, while ICH education has never been recorded in the ego-centric view. The hand gestures were obtained in 3D by Leap Motion and underwent the error correction process by using another Leap Motion and an IR sticker manually.

While our framework suggests the possibility of ego-centric view digitalization in ICH and performs error correction manually, our study did not consider automatic error correction, which would improve the accuracy of hand motion recording. In future work, we will record accurate handcrafting motions and try to calibrate the camera. This will help correct errors automatically. In addition, an AR simulator for Nubi crafts will be created for training all users in ICH.

Acknowledgement. This research is supported by 2018 Support Project for Academic Research on Traditional Culture in Korea National University of Cultural Heritage.

References

1. Seo, J.: A study on the role of masters craftstman in traditional crafts education-based on the case of the crafts department of Konkuk University. Korean Assoc. Mus. Educ. **15**, 27–55 (2016)
2. Gang, Z., Hui, Z., Bingbing, D., Yali, Y., Wenjuan, Z.: Research on tujia brocade craft visualization based on unmarked motion capture technique. In: CYBConf, pp. 1–5 (2017). https://doi.org/10.1109/cybconf.2017.7985803
3. Vosinakis, S., Koutsabasis, P., Makris, D., Sagia, E.: A kinesthetic approach to digital heritage using leap motion: the cycladic sculpture application. In: VS-GAMES, pp. 1–8 (2016). https://doi.org/10.1109/VS-GAMES.2016.7590334
4. Dimitropoulos, K., et al.: A multimodal approach for the safeguarding and transmission of intangible cultural heritage: the case of i-Treasures. IEEE Intell. Syst. (2018). https://doi.org/10.1109/MIS.2018.111144858
5. Rashid, A., Hasan, O.: Wearable technologies for hand joints monitoring for rehabilitation: a survey (2018). https://doi.org/10.1016/j.mejo.2018.01.014
6. Chossat, J., Tao, Y., Duchaine, V., Park, Y.: Wearable soft artificial skin for hand motion detection with embedded microfluidic strain sensing. In: ICRA, pp. 2568–2573 (2015). https://doi.org/10.1109/ICRA.2015.7139544
7. Aristidou, A.: Hand tracking with physiological constraints. Vis. Comput. **34**(2), 213–228 (2016). https://doi.org/10.1007/s00371-016-1327-8
8. Burns, A.-M., Mazzarino, B.: Finger tracking methods using EyesWeb. In: Gibet, S., Courty, N., Kamp, J.-F. (eds.) GW 2005. LNCS (LNAI), vol. 3881, pp. 156–167. Springer, Heidelberg (2006). https://doi.org/10.1007/11678816_18
9. Shotton, J., et al.: Efficient human pose estimation from single depth images. Trans. Pattern Anal. Mach. Intell. **35**(12), 2821–2840 (2013). https://doi.org/10.1109/TPAMI.2012.241
10. Guna, J., Jakus, G., Pogačnik, M., Tomažič, S., Sodnik, J.: An analysis of the precision and reliability of the leap motion sensor and its suitability for static and dynamic tracking. Sensors **14**(2), 3702–3720 (2014). https://doi.org/10.3390/s140203702
11. Jin, H., Chen, Q., Chen, Z., Hu, Y., Zhang, J.: Multi-LeapMotion sensor based demonstration for robotic refine tabletop object manipulation task. CAAI Trans. Intell. Technol. **1**, 104–113 (2016). https://doi.org/10.1016/j.trit.2016.03.010

12. Ferche, O., Moldoveanu, A., Moldoveanu, F.: Evaluating lightweight optical hand tracking for virtual reality rehabilitation. Rev. Romana de Interactiune Om-Calculator **9**(2), 85–102 (2016)
13. Cultural Properties Administration.: Korean Intangible Cultural Properties Traditional Handicrafts. Hollym corporation, Korea (2001). ISBN-13: 978-1565911505
14. Park, S.: Nubi: Korean Traditional Quilt. Korean Craft&Design Foundation, Seoul (2014). ISBN-13: 978-9111913690
15. Park, S., Kim, H., Kim, I.: Nubijang. National Research Institute of Cultural Heritage, Daejeon (2008). ISBN-13:978-8956386850
16. Cho, K., Cho, M., Jeon, J.: Fly a drone safely: evaluation of an embodied egocentric drone controller interface. Interact. Comput. **29**, 345–354 (2017). https://doi.org/10.1093/iwc/iww027
17. Park, Y., Kwon, S., Koo, B., Kim, H., Jang, J., Cho K.: Evaluation of a new egocentric smartwatch interface. Extended Abstracts of HCI Korea, pp. 80–82 (2016)
18. Reichenbacher, T.: Adaptive egocentric maps for mobile users. In: Meng, L., Reichenbacher, T., Zipf, A. (eds.) Map-Based Mobile Services, pp. 141–158. Springer, Heidelberg (2005). https://doi.org/10.1007/3-540-26982-7_1
19. Wilson, A.D., Benko, H.: Combining multiple depth cameras and projectors for interactions on, above, and between surfaces. In: UIST 2010 Proceedings of the 23nd Annual ACM Symposium on User Interface Software and Technology, pp. 273–282 (2010). https://doi.org/10.1145/1866029.1866073

Digital Workflow for Virtual and Augmented Visit of Architecture

Cecilia Maria Bolognesi[✉]🆔

ABC Dep., Politecnico of Milan, Via Ponzio 31, 20131 Milan, Italy
cecilia.bolognesi@polimi.it

Abstract. This paper adopts Virtual and Augmented reality experiences to be enjoyed in a historical place as tools and bust for the knowledge and dissemination of the culture of a landscape.

The development of this virtual pipeline is focused on some Neoclassical architecture built in the monumental park of the Reggia of Monza and considers the semantic modeling of the digital survey to support a virtualized and augmented environment for culture production and culture dissemination.

The workflow described regards: construction of semantic relations between the various architectures of the case history; survey of the same buildings with advanced technologies; modeling of point clouds to create parametric 3D models of the existing through digital modeling of elements and buildings; experiments of virtual environments; experiences of augmented reality. It considers the buildings as virtual hubs to describe their history and the landscape they set up, where one is related to the other in the same Park by perspective green paths as a spread museum; the aim is a fruition renewed by immersive realities to be enjoyed in situ [1] brought to public, to smart users, for a better knowledge of Cultural Heritage. Due to the integration and interoperability among different technologies many issues grow during the research, [2] and it considers them steps necessary to be investigated.

Keywords: HBIM · 3D models · Virtual augmented environment

1 State of the Art

1.1 Following the Evolution of a Concept

Recent digressions on Virtual Museum have pushed us towards further evolutions of the original paradigm, offering new ideas for applied research.

From its very beginning, Virtual Museum gradually embodied different opportunities: from the digital fruition of existing collections [3], to digital catalogues on line, to digital simulations of new environments with new semantic meanings added.

At the beginning of the 2000s, the discussion has been enlarged and web sites, Virtual tours, apps integrated within the physical museums and digital catalogs concentrated under the same concept [4]. The following boost to the evolution of the Virtual Museum concept in the field of Cultural Heritage is now strengthen by the development of new survey technologies and visualization. Advantages are evident: 3D modeling offers the possibility of representing monumental structures that could hardly

© Springer Nature Switzerland AG 2018
M. Ioannides et al. (Eds.): EuroMed 2018, LNCS 11197, pp. 126–133, 2018.
https://doi.org/10.1007/978-3-030-01765-1_15

be host in small places in any place; 3D digital models can convey cultural experiences to smart audience in large and spread environment also; immersive, Virtual, augmented and mixed realities expand fruition to any smart device also. The transition from a channel for further dissemination of content as the first Virtual Museum to new opportunities for the production of knowledge such as Virtual reconstruction, especially in the field of Cultural Heritage, is short [5]. Advent and progressive growth of the 4.0 era pushes definitively towards new conceptual models the relation between Cultural Heritage and Virtual Museums, for a new integrated paradigm [6].

1.2 The Possibility of a Experimentation

The possibility of a new semantic representation for knowledge and use of Cultural Heritage of a territory is the basis of the research carried out through a study of trainees and undergraduates still in progress at Milan Polytechnic regarding the Reggia and its Park in Monza; both of them were recently provided by digital communication tools such as a web site and an app with thematic botanical or architectural paths typical of the first digital activities of communication of CH.

Our research aims: to deepen a semantic path with digital experiences by the neoclassical buildings in the Park, driving public through a series of green perspectives from one architecture to the following one; to create a story tale that makes comprehensible to a wider audience landscapes inside Royal Monza Park; to disseminate its culture by making available to a wider public the relations existing between its architecture and the context, its designers and other contemporary architecture (such as the Scala of Milan, completed by Piermarini himself during the years of work at the Reggia of Monza) with Virtual and Augmented reality experiences.

The driver for all these action is supposed to be 3D modeling of the buildings taking advantage of VR and AR technologies; also maps, generally analytical tools, can be considered narrative atlases, geolocalize stories, host models to gather the multiplicity of points of view [7]; both 3D models and maps can be good Virtual db with new semantic meanings where geo-referencing and implementable systems from users are opportunities constantly growing also.

2 Historical Background

2.1 A Case Study: The Royal Villa and the Park

Monza Park formally represents the union of several large green areas: the first one is strictly annexed to the Ducal Palace commissioned by Austrian Archduke Ferdinand, who chose the place to make the residence of the Asburgo enchanted by his beauty and helped by the presence of previous family properties.

After the construction of the Reggia Ferdinand shared his desire to realize the gardens with Giuseppe Piermarini, at the beginning of the 80s [8], a year before his finishing the construction of the Scala in Milan. He conditioned his first formal choices in a strictly geometric construction project of the landscape according to the principles of the French school. Later on the cultural evolution of Piermarini was directed towards the experimentation of landscaped gardens simulating romantic naturalness in the Garden of the Reggia (Fig. 1).

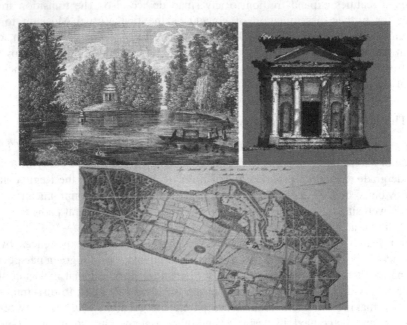

Fig. 1. Francesco e Carolina Lose, Promenades dans le Parc Imperial et Royal et Les Jardins de Monza, 1825 in "Monza nelle sue stampe", Mulazzani G., Crespi A., 1985 and a DP of the temple by the lake, dense cloud. Luigi Canonica, Il Parco unito alla Cesarea R., 1808. From A. Maniglio Calcagno "the Birth of the Park".

The second part of the formal realization of the Park starts from Bonaparte arrivals at the Reggia in 1805; it regards a series of lands acquired after the palace was built, whose general configuration project is entrusted to Luigi Canonica. Bonaparte himself decrees the construction of the great Park, finalizing it to functions of representation as well as pleasure or agricultural production. At this time the pre-existing architectures were connected through a network of specific optical paths and green perspective. Canonica organized the structure of the large Park assuming axis of connection directed towards Milan, connecting the most artificially designed and the most agricultural parts of the lands with a series of minor green perspective; several trees were planted to trace formal connection between the Park and its architectures in a unique design [8].

Canonica and Tazzini realized a series of new buildings or restored pre existing ones with agricultural or residential features within the Park: approximately 26. The reality of the pre-existences, shape up to be with roles different from those previously held in the territory become a determining factor in the general narration of the system of perspective references [9]. Typology reflects the typical characters of destinations: the buildings are equipped with loggias, porticoes and pronai according to their destiny such as temple, residence, farmhouse, menagerie. For all these reasons, the Park as a whole represents a place of extraordinary value for understanding that concept of landscape that proceeds by conceptual models where architecture and nature coexist in mutual exaltation and provides the heart of our possible narration.

3 Digital Modeling for CH: VR and AR Experiments

3.1 The Architectures Modeled

The first pipeline chosen as a test for this experience regards 3D digital models and involves three different buildings, related to three different architecture of the Park, all linked by green perspectives, considering at this first step the visitors naturally moving from one to the other one: the neoclassical temple in the perspective of the little lake, the perspective point of the axis of Villa Mirabello that is villa Mirabellino, the double-fronted farmhouse on the double levels of the park Cascina Casalta. The pipeline considers to transform the advanced survey of the architecture of the park into Virtual hubs, using 3D models with VR and AR supports [10] for an enriched semantic open air path. The introduction of the term Scan-to-BIM (or Point-to-BIM), generally used to indicate this first part of the workflow, begins from the generation of a Terrestrial Laser Scanning (TLS) and Digital Photogrammetry (DP) point cloud to be then modeled into specific geometric object (i.e. not relying on libraries); this frame is already a normal path in any CH modeling study, useful to exchange data through model representation [11] (Fig. 2).

Fig. 2. DP dense clouds of Cascina Casalta (top) and Villa Mirabellino (down). The first includes three loggias directed to different axis in the landscape. Villa Mirabellino, on a hill is the end point of a green perspective axis from Villa Mirabello (Color figure online)

3.2 The Pipeline: from TLS and Photogrammetry to HBIM Model

The exteriors of the buildings were surveyed using both Terrestrial Laser Scanning (TLS) and digital photogrammetry (DP): while the first technique grants a reliable metric model, the second one is mainly dedicated to architectural details and textures. Sensor size of the camera, focal length and the morphology of the objects determined distances of the capture scenes in order to satisfy horizontal covering, and consequently the number of images needed. For this survey it was decided to accept an error within the centimeter, assuming an average scale of representation of 1:50, with a GSD = 1 cm/4 = 2.5 mm/pixel, that is each pixel of the image represents 2.5 mm of the actual object detected. The generated point clouds were imported for a strong decimation into a specific software (Recap) and then in a modeling software (Autodesk Revit), scaled and enriched with levels to be correctly modeled; HBIM models have been modeled with specific parametric families and objects, self-aware of their architectural identity and conscious of their mutual semantic interactions [12]; every object was shaped overlapping it on the cloud to control its right feature. A HBIM model can be considered as an ideal Data Base where elements, from the whole building to the smallest detail, can be related to heterogeneous data, keeping track of their relationships and roles in the global construction [13].

3.3 From the HBIM Model to Virtual Fruition

The HBIM models are necessary to test the second track of the pipeline: Virtual and Augmented experiences. The software modeler allows plug in to test both Virtual as Augmented Reality [14], to widen the opportunity to use our buildings as Data Base for information, taking advantage of real time rendering capability. The first tests were carried out with Enscape program, a plug in to browse the model and experiment Virtual tours inside it using optical viewers (Oculus Rift and HTC lives) once the perimeter for the Virtual walk is set with the appropriate equipment. The solutions requires plug in and modeler working simultaneously and a good a connection between the viewer and a computer with excellent performance; this makes this choice more advisable for indoor fruition. An additional test on Virtual reality was processed with 360° images realized through "Rendering cloud" function of the modeler which allow a view of the architecture embedded using simple smartphones. The modeler's server mainly processes the data necessary for the production of the images using views previously set up and collecting them; once the project has been processed the rendered image can be opened and shared with the smartphone via URL or QR-code. In order to view the image in VR, it is necessary to use a browser enabled such as Google Chrome Dev.

Panorama images can, however, allow the user to immerse himself in the building context in a simple but effective way even if as the first example with proprietary software (Fig. 3).

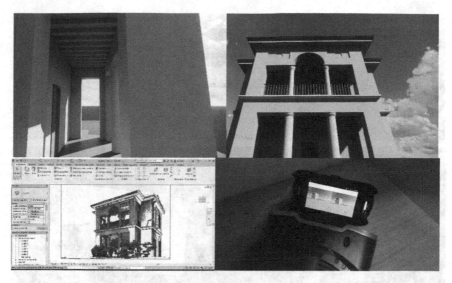

Fig. 3. Stereo VR panorama through Enscape plug in (up) and 360° image (down)

3.4   From the BIM Model to Augmented Reality

Augmented Reality was tested to take advantage of additional information as a corollary of the knowledge of the single architecture and history [15].

There is no unique workflow to generate an Augmented Model as technology is continuously progressing. However, it is possible to define a series of processes that are necessary to obtain as a result the generation of an augmented reality environment [16].

In order to go and exploit our Revit models in an Augmented Reality environment we chose to test Sketchfab platform which allows embedding both point clouds imported in .Las extension from Photoscan software than Collada files, generated from Revit software. Advantages are: the possibility to add information to the model itself such as texts, images, links to websites while browsing the model dynamically and visit it in an immersive reality as well. Disadvantage is that all the images must be previously collected in a dedicated Data Base as a storage to be upload in the model.

Augmentecture is another plug in for Revit software that allows to visit models on smart devices: it works with an application downloadable for Android or iOS operating system and an online server that connects the smartphone to the software used for modeling with a generated QR code.

When QR code is scanned by the device the model appears because already loaded into the proprietary server accessible only through the creation of a private account, making it user friendly and a possible app for visitors of architectures (Fig. 4).

Technology regarding display appears to be functioning satisfactory, landing the model on the QR code or as a second possibility on a map generated for the building.

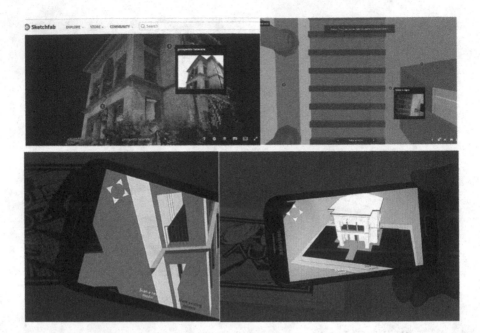

Fig. 4. Test model for augmented reality in Sketchfab; .Las extension and Collada embedded. Below a visualization through generated QRcode and Augmentecture with smartphone.

4 Conclusion

A monumental environment can benefit from Virtual or Augmented Reality to communicate the value of its architecture as a Virtual Museum can do with its collections. Studies from the phases of advanced survey of small buildings to their modeling for usable Virtual or Augmented reality offers many peculiar opportunities each with different difficulties. Limits related to interoperability among platforms, proprietary software, too big file, storage data that we could share to enrich any digital model actually still influence communication of semantic meanings in CH such as in the case of the architecture we considered. A model necessary to support Heritage restoration, a HBIM model, is not necessarily what is technically required to communicate his value or the relationship between it and the surroundings. In order to take advantage of Virtual or Augmented reality, it is advisable to create models dedicated to this purpose containing less information but with an appreciable graphic feedback [17]. This observation guided us towards specialized pipelines to organize the model fruition according to different aims starting from a typical geometric model. Relationship between architectures for a unique digital project is to be explored yet and it will be next in-depth analysis [18].

Aknowledgments. This work was developed with the help of student now engeneer Yuri Seiti of Politecnio of Milan.

References

1. Chiabrando, F., Lo Turco, M., Rinaudo, F.: Modeling the decay in an HBIM starting from 3D point clouds. In: International Archives of the Photogrammetry, Remote Sensing and Spatial Information Sciences, vol. XLII-2/W5 (2017)
2. Apollonio, F.I., Gaiani, M., Sun, Z.: BIM-based modeling and data enrichment of classical architectural buildings. SCIRES-IT **2**(2), 41–62 (2012)
3. BRITANNICA.   http://www.britannica.com/EBcheched/topic/630177/Virtual-museum. Accessed 11 May 2018
4. TRECCANI.   http://www.treccani.it/enciclopedia/museo-virtuale_%28XXI-Secolo%29/. Accessed 11 May 2018
5. Caspani, S., Brumana, R., Oreni, D., Previtali, M.: Virtual museum as digital storytelling for dissemination of built environment. In: The International Archives of the Photogrammetry, Remote Sensing and Spatial Information Sciences, vol. XLII-2/W5 (2017)
6. Teferaa, Y., Poiesia, F., Morabito, D., Remondino, F., Nocerino, E.: 3DNOW image based. 3D reconstruction and modeling via WEB. In: The International Archives of the Photogrammetry, Remote Sensing and Spatial Information Sciences, vol. XLII-2 (2018)
7. Banfi, F., et al.: L'intermediazione geospaziale per la valorizzazione del paesaggio e lo sviluppo di sistemi museali multimediali. In: Proceedings of ASITA (2015)
8. Salerno, R.: La fortuna iconografica dei Giardini e del Parco della Villa Reale di Monza. In: Il Parco di Monza. Itinerari storico naturalistici, pp 42–53. Bellavite, Missaglia (2014)
9. Maniglio Calcagno, A.: La Villa i giardini e il Parco di Monza nel fondo disegni delle Residenze Reali Lombarde. Skirà, Milano, (2010)
10. Valero, E., Adan, A., Huber, D., Cerrada, C.: Detection, modeling, and classification of moldings for automated reverse engineering of buildings from 3D data. In: Proceedings of the International Symposium on Automation and Robotics in Construction (2017)
11. Stanga, C., Spinelli, C., Brumana, R., Oreni, D., Valente. R., Banfi, F.: A N-D virtual notebook about the Basilica of S. Ambrogio in Milan. In: The International Archives of the Photogrammetry, Remote Sensing and Spatial Information Sciences, vol. XLII-2/W5 (2017)
12. Dore, C., Murphy, M.: Integration of historic BIM (HBIM) and 3D GIS for recording and managing cultural heritage sites. In: Proceedings of the 18th International Conference on Virtual Systems and Multimedia (VSMM). IEEEXplore Digital Library, Milano (2012)
13. Murphy, M., McGovern, E., Pavia, S.: Historic building information modeling – adding intelligence to laser and image based surveys of European classical architecture. ISPRS J. Photogramm. Remote. Sens. **76**, 89–102 (2013)
14. Chionna, F., Argese, F., Palmieri, V., Spada, I., Colizzi, L.: Integrated building information modelling and augmented reality to improve investigation of historical buildings. Conserv. Sci. Cult. Herit. **15**, 149–161 (2015)
15. Williams, G., Gheisari, M., Chen, P., Irizarry, J.: BIM2MAR: an efficient BIM translation to mobile augmented reality applications. J. Manag. Eng. **31**(1) (2014). https://doi.org/10.1061/(ASCE)ME.1943-5479.0000315
16. Bertocci, S., Ventimiglia, M.: Augmented reality for the documentation of Villa Adriana in Tivoli, Vienna. In: International Conference on Cultural Heritage and New Technologies (2015)
17. Seung, Y.J., Mi, K.K., Han, J.J.: Space management using a mobile BIM-based augmented reality system. Arch. Res. **1**, 19 (2017)
18. Zaher, M., Greenwood, D., Marzouk, M.M.: Mobile augmented reality applications for construction projects. Constr. Innov. **2**, 18 (2018)

Usage Scenarios and Evaluation of Augmented Reality and Social Services for Libraries

Zois Koukopoulos[(✉)] and Dimitrios Koukopoulos

University of Patras, 30100 Agrinio, Greece
zkoukopu@upatras.gr

Abstract. Libraries are cultural environments that aggregate large volumes of cultural content accessible by experts and the broad public. The continuous attraction and engagement of visitors, along with the production of revenue for the institute are two of the biggest challenges in such an environment. In this work, we propose the provision of Augmented Reality and social services trying to address those challenges. We implement and use as a testbed Active Visitor, a system that offers such services aiming at investigating services' acceptability by visitors and librarians. We propose and implement a series of usage scenarios that use such services in order to facilitate the user activities within a library environment. A specific evaluation methodology is applied to stress the strength of the presented services. The evaluation results provide a first positive indication about the benefits that Augmented Reality and social services introduce in a library environment.

Keywords: Libraries · Augmented Reality and social services
Evaluation

1 Introduction

Libraries, public and academic, are accustomed to incorporate new technologies as a means to improve their services, a reality that guided such institutes to adopt mobile technology in order to offer modern services as anticipated by their visitors [4–6]. Augmented Reality (AR) is a rising new technology that promises to change the world as we know and comprehend it [7, 12]. Many excellent AR systems, applications and tools have already been introduced to the libraries field [8–11]. A big question though is lurking. How can we be sure that such a technology will be beneficial for a library? Can we decide to spend a part of a library's budget to design and implement specific AR services? The need for a thorough evaluation of the AR services' application within a library environment instantly appears.

In this work we attempt to evaluate the use of AR and social services within a library from the perspectives of a visitor and a professional librarian. We are interested in finding out whether such services are interesting, useful, attractive and engaging for a visitor. We try to explore the visitors' intention to use or pay to use such services during a library visit and the visitors' intention to disseminate the library services to peers or strangers. Also, we are interested in extracting the opinions of professional librarians about the use of AR services in their libraries. In order to evaluate AR and

© Springer Nature Switzerland AG 2018
M. Ioannides et al. (Eds.): EuroMed 2018, LNCS 11197, pp. 134–141, 2018.
https://doi.org/10.1007/978-3-030-01765-1_16

social services in libraries we use Active Visitor (AV), a system which we designed and implemented targeting library environments for the provision of AR and social services on-demand. The system supports the real-time digital interaction of a visitor with the book she/he is reading by allowing the user to create and view AR annotations associated with specific phrases in the book. The system automatically creates a personalized electronic version of the library book and creates AR annotations for, which can be purchased by the user at the end of the visit with respect to the electronic book's copyrights. AV supports the direct communication of concurrent visitors that read the same book by allowing them to create ad-hoc social networks and participate in digital discussions concerning the particular book. Evaluation procedure was designed and implemented separately for each user group (librarians and visitors). Users' opinions were quantified through carefully structured questionnaires and then filtered using open-type semi-structured interviews. Evaluation results suggest that visitors intend to use the system AR and social services while librarians' questionnaires indicate that the system services are important and useful for a library.

2 Related Work

Notable scientific efforts have been recorded in the field of digital systems for libraries that offer AR services concentrating around real-time navigation inside a library [13], book recommendation based on visitor's book choices [9] or book recognition for augmented information presentation [10]. [13] proposes NODE (NO Donkey e-Learning) a system that utilizes AR and indoor positioning technology to provide real-time navigation in a library. [9] introduces an AR application that recognizes a book by its call numbers and recommends relevant library books that are not shelved nearby. Authors in [10] implement an AR application that performs real-time book recognition on a library shelf based on the book's spine information. Many researchers have focused their studies on the evaluation of indoor AR services in various fields and in the field of cultural institutions [2, 3, 15]. As far as libraries are concerned, there are some attempts to evaluate AR services [8, 11, 14]. [8] hosts a thorough investigation of current literature on AR services for library environments and initiates a discussion with librarians in order to discover the actual benefits of using AR technology in a library space. The author reveals that such a technology has a positive influence on increasing user engagement. AR services and personalization is discussed in [14]. Authors discover that personalized services along with system quality affect user satisfaction and intention to disseminate AR applications. [11] explores the use of AR services at the Uppsala University libraries as a marketing tool.

3 Active Visitor – AR and Social Services for Libraries

AV is a system that offers AR and social services to libraries transforming the traditional library to a modern, engaging, immersive, personalized and social space where visitors can exchange opinions about a book or create digital annotations on a book in real-time (Fig. 1). The system offers an AR annotation service allowing users to create

AR annotations on the book they are reading via a mobile AR application (ARA module) installed in their mobile devices. Those annotations can be marked as personal (can be accessed only by the user who created them) or public (can be viewed publicly). Through the ARA, users can retrieve all the personal and public AR annotations associated with the book they are reading. Annotations appear as modal windows (red for personal and green for public annotations) with the annotation text embedded in the camera view of the user's device and registered over the associated phrase. The system notifies users about concurrent visitors that read the same book permitting users to invite other ones in forming an ad-hoc social network. If a user accepts the incoming invitation, the two users become members of the social network and exchange text messages engaging in a digital discussion concerning the book they are reading. AV can work properly only by the assumption that the library staff submits to the system all library content (book information). Apart from the AR annotation service which aims at enhancing the leisure experience of visitors, AV attempts to create a sustainable library environment by implementing an exploitation service based on the AR annotation service. When a user creates a new AR annotation, the annotation text is automatically embedded in a digital copy of the physical book that the user reads. In this way, a personalized digital version of the physical book is created and it is associated with that user. The user can ask the library staff to purchase the personalized digital copy of the physical book containing all the personal and/or public annotations. The purchasing service is feasible only with respect to book's electronic version copyrights.

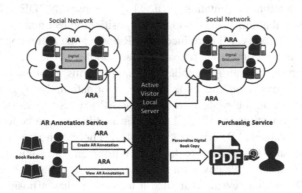

Fig. 1. Active visitor system services (Color figure online)

4   Usage Scenarios

Scenario 1: A user creates an AR annotation on a book. In order to create an AR annotation on a book phrase, the user opens the ARA, navigates to the "Annotation Creation" screen (Fig. 2) and submits the book title, page and row above which she/he wants the annotation to appear. The user submits the annotation text and marks the annotation as personal or public. The user clicks on the "Capture Book Detachment" button opening the device camera and taking a clear picture of the phrase above which the AR annotation will appear. This step is critical for the procedures of AR tracking and registration because the captured image is going to be used as the Image Target. Annotation creation is finalized by clicking the "Create Annotation" button.

Fig. 2. ARA annotation creation screen

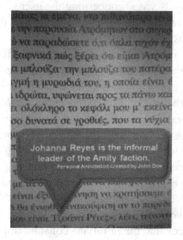

Fig. 3. Screenshot of the AR annotation service

Scenario 2: A user views an AR annotation. A user activates the ARA in order to view personal AR annotations on a book, navigates to the corresponding ARA screen and she/he is informed that the book is associated with personal AR annotations in specific pages and rows (dropdown). When the user reads a page that contains an AR annotation, she/he focuses the device over the phrase containing the annotation. The ARA performs the AR tracking procedure by using the current view of the camera in comparison to the annotation's captured image. After AR tracking is complete, the ARA performs the AR registration procedure where a modal window appears, embedded in the camera view above the related book phrase, containing the annotation text and the annotation owner (Fig. 3). *Scenario 3: Users engage in a digital discussion.* A registered user wants to be informed about concurrent registered users (visitors) that read the same book and invites them in a digital discussion about the book. The user activates the ARA and navigates to the corresponding screen where she/he is informed about the users that read the same book. The user chooses to send invitations to those users forming a social network. The invited users are notified via the ARA with an android notification. When an invited user opens the ARA, she/he views the corresponding screen and chooses to accept or reject the invitation. The users that accept the invitation form a social network and exchange text messages. *Scenario 4: A librarian submits library content to the system.* A librarian opens the system desktop application navigating to the corresponding screen. The user submits content-based information (book title, writer, publisher, publication year, abstract, genre etc.) and context-based information (section, floor, corridor, shelf, hard copies number, digital availability, purchasing ability, copyright, directory path of the book's digital copies).

5 Evaluation Results

The proposed research model and hypotheses attempt to investigate whether the system fulfills its scope concerning the user groups of librarians and visitors. We are interested in investigating visitors will to use the system AR services during a library visit proposing the hypothesis H_1: *Visitors intent to use the system services.* We are interested in finding out if the system offers engaging services to visitors proposing the hypothesis H_2: *The system offers engaging services to visitors.* We are interested in finding out if the system offers personalized services to visitors proposing hypothesis H_3: *The system supports the personalization of book reading according to visitors.* We are interested in investigating visitors will to disseminate the library proposing the hypothesis H_4: *Visitors would disseminate the system to peers or strangers.* We are interested in finding out if visitors would like to use the purchasing service proposing the hypothesis H_5: *The system offers an interesting exploitation service for visitors.* We are interested in finding out if the system promotes social involvement proposing the hypothesis H_6: *The system promotes social interaction and involvement among visitors.* We are interested in finding out if the system offers services that the librarians consider important for their library proposing the hypothesis H_7: *Librarians believe the system services are important for a library.* We are interested in finding out if the system offers useful services for the librarians proposing the hypothesis H_8: *Librarians believe the system services are useful for a library.* We are interested in finding out if the system is considered easy to use by the librarians proposing the hypothesis H_9: *The system is easy to use by librarians.* We are interested in finding out if the librarians believe that the system offers attractive services that will increase the number of visitors at their libraries proposing the hypothesis H_{10}: *Librarians consider the system services attractive for visitors.* We are interested in finding out if the librarians believe that the system services would engage the visitors in longer visits proposing the hypothesis H_{11}: *Librarians consider the system AR services engaging for the visitors.* We are interested in finding out if the librarians believe that the system's purchasing service would produce revenue for the library proposing the hypothesis H_{12}: *Librarians believe that the library can generate revenue by the system use.*

In order to study the validity of the research model hypotheses, we use qualitative and quantitative evaluation tools (questionnaires, personal interviews). Questionnaires investigate all research hypotheses. Personal interviews revealed the attitude of the librarians and visitors towards AR services. This study used a non-random sampling technique (convenience sampling) to collect data [1]. The experiment team formulated a user group of librarians and another one of potential visitors. The librarians group consisted of 19 professionals (<30 years of experience) that work in public or university libraries. The visitors group consisted of 27 individuals of various age groups that visit academic or public libraries from once a year to several times a week. The visitors sample was selected to be small due to the controlled evaluation environment limitations and our goal to investigate the very first impression such system services cause. The evaluation procedure was divided in 3 stages which took place in a controlled environment. In stage 1, the supervisors initiated a discussion about the application of AR and social services within a library and responded to questions concerning such services. In stage 2, focus group members were separated in two different groups (librarians and visitors). Supervisors discussed thoroughly the scope, characteristics and services of the AV system to each group and presented the 4 usage scenarios in practice. In stage 3, the experiment team distributed 2 evaluation questionnaires, one for each group. The questionnaires covered the 12 research hypotheses. Each hypothesis was approached by a series of statements for which the users stated their agreement or disagreement. Moreover, the experiment supervisors interviewed each individual personally to extract their opinion about the system services. Visitor and librarian questionnaire results are displayed in Tables 1 and 2 respectively. The reliability of the questionnaires' results was confirmed by the calculation of the Cronbach's Alpha measure which was 0.81 for visitors' and 0.72 for librarians'.

Table 1. Library visitors questionnaire results.

Questionnaire statements	Agree	Disagree
S_1 The existence of AR services would attract you into visiting a library	96%	4%
S_2 You would use existing AR services while visiting a library	96%	4%
S_3 You would like to be able to use AR services while visiting a library	100%	0%
S_4 There are positive aspects using AR services in a library	96%	4%
S_5 The system AR services would be beneficial for a project you work	93%	7%
S_6 You would download and install a mobile AR application (without cost) created by the library you are visiting	81%	19%
S_7 You would visit a library with the system's AR annotation service	85%	15%
S_8 The AR annotation service would be uninteresting to you	7%	93%
S_9 You would spend more time in a library if you used AR services	93%	7%
S_{10} You would prolong a library visit if using the annotation service	59%	41%
S_{11} You would like to obtain a digital copy of the book you are reading in a library along with the AR annotations you created	93%	7%
S_{12} You would like to view the AR annotations you created embedded in the camera view of your mobile device while reading a book	93%	7%
S_{13} The system's AR annotation would be useful to you in order to complete a personal professional task	88%	12%
S_{14} You would notify your peers about system AR service positively	93%	7%
S_{15} You would notify the public through the social media about your visit in a library that offers the system's AR services	35%	65%
S_{16} You would notify the public through the social media about your visit in a library that offers you the opportunity to engage in digital discussions about a book you are reading	67%	33%
S_{17} You would pay a small fee in order to use AR services in a library	37%	63%
S_{18} You would pay a small fee in order to use the system's AR service	41%	59%
S_{19} You would share personal AR annotations with other visitors	93%	7%
S_{20} You would read other users' AR annotations for the same book	81	19%
S_{21} You would participate in a digital discussion focusing on the book you are reading in order to exchange opinions with other library visitors	56%	44%

Table 2. Librarians questionnaire results.

Questionnaire statements	Agree	Disagree
S_1 System services are important for a library	42%	58%
S_2 System services are useful for a library	83%	17%
S_3 System services are positive for a library	100%	0%
S_4 The system operation in your library would make your work harder	17%	83%
S_5 You could successfully guide the visitors to use the system services	92%	8%
S_6 A library that offers users the opportunity to use the system's modules and services would increase the number of its visitors	75%	25%
S_7 Visitors would appreciate the existence of AV in a library	100%	0%
S_8 Visitors would spend more time in a library that hosts AV	64%	36%
S_9 The system purchasing service would generate revenue for a library	0%	100%
S_{10} You would charge the visitors for using the library's AR equipment	18%	82%

In order to validate hypotheses H_1 to H_6 we asked the visitors to agree/disagree with statements S_1–S_8 (H_1), S_9–S_{10} (H_2), S_{11}–S_{13} (H_3), S_{14}–S_{16} (H_4), S_{17}–S_{18} (H_5) and S_{19}–S_{21} (H_6) (Table 1). Questionnaire results provide a strong indication that all hypotheses are confirmed. Notable observations derived from visitor answers are: (i) more than half of the visitors confirmed H_3 indicating that the number of engaged users could further increase under real conditions, (ii) the system offers interesting personalization services to visitors, (iii) users are slightly more open to disseminate the system social service than the AR one, (iv) 37% of the visitors responded that they would pay for AR services while 41% of the visitors expressed their will to pay for using the AR annotation service, demonstrating the exploitation potential of AV; (v) users acknowledge that AV promotes social involvement.

In order to validate hypotheses H_7 to H_{12} we asked the librarians to agree/disagree with statements S_1 (H_7), S_2–S_3 (H_8), S_4–S_5 (H_9), S_6–S_7 (H_{10}), S_8 (H_{11}) and S_9–S_{10} (H_{12}) (Table 2). Questionnaire results provide a strong indication that all hypotheses are confirmed. Notable observations derived from librarians answers are: (i) all the professionals believed that visitors would appreciate the system's existence in a library, (ii) the majority of the librarians agreed that visitors would engage in longer visits if using the system services, (iii) librarians believe that the system is not exploitable. In our opinion, the professionals cannot visionize at the moment the system's exploitation potential. On the other hand today's users constantly become familiar with the idea of purchasing useful services with a rational cost (confirmation of H_5).

6 Conclusions

This paper attempted to evaluate the use of AR and social services within a library based on the opinions of visitors and librarians. In order to extract the users' opinions, we implemented Active Visitor, a system that offers specific AR and social services to visitors. Through a carefully designed evaluation methodology we managed to portray a first positive overview of the users' opinions about AR and social services.

References

1. Emerson, R.W.: Convenience sampling, random sampling, and snowball sampling: how does sampling affect the validity of research? J. Vis. Impair. Blind. **109**(2), 164–168 (2015)
2. Peng, F., Zhai, J.: A mobile augmented reality system for exhibition hall based on Vuforia. In: 2nd International Conference on Image, Vision and Computing, pp. 1049–1052. IEEE, Chengdu, China (2017)
3. de Oliveira, L.C., Andrade, A., de Oliveira, E.C., Soares, A., Cardoso, A., Lamounier, E.: Indoor navigation with mobile augmented reality and beacon technology for wheelchair users. In: IEEE EMBS International Conference on Biomedical & Health Informatics, IEEE, Orlando, USA, pp. 37–40 (2017)
4. Haugh, D.: Mobile applications for libraries. In: Costello, L., Powers, M. (eds.) Developing In-House Digital Tools in Library Spaces, vol. 4, pp. 76–90. IGI Global, USA (2017)
5. Lo, P.: Use of smartphones by art and design students for accessing library services and learning. Libr. Hi Tech **34**(2), 224–238 (2016)
6. Wong, K.P.: Library services for mobile devices: the national institute of education library experience. Libr. Hi Tech **30**(9), 7–11 (2013)
7. Azuma, R.: Making augmented reality a reality. In: Proceedings of OSA Imaging and Applied Optics Congress, San Francisco, CA (2017)
8. Massis, B.: Using virtual and augmented reality in the library. New Libr. World **116**(11/12), 796–799 (2015)
9. Hahn, J.F., Ryckman, B., Lux, M.: Topic space: rapid prototyping a mobile augmented reality recommendation app. Code4Lib J. 30 (2015). https://journal.code4lib.org/articles/10881
10. Chen, D., Tsai, S., Hsu, C.H., Singh, J.P., Girod, B.: Mobile augmented reality for books on a shelf. In: Proceedings of the 2011 IEEE International Conference on Multimedia and Expo, ICME 2011, Barcelona, Catalonia, Spain, pp. 1–6 (2011)
11. Vidlund, I., Petersson, C.: Use marketing as a strategy for skill development tablets, QR, AR – our journey from printed book collections to a social place. Qual. Quant. Methods Libr. QQML **3**, 583–589 (2014)
12. Azuma, R.: A survey of augmented reality. Teleoperators Virtual Environ. **6**(4), 355–385 (1997)
13. Huang, T.C.: Get lost in the library? An innovative application of augmented reality and indoor positioning technologies. Electron. Libr. **34**(1), 99–115 (2016)
14. Jung, T., Chung, N., Leue, M.C.: The determinants of recommendations to use augmented reality technologies: the case of a Korean theme park. Tour. Manag. **49**, 75–86 (2015)
15. Chung, N., Lee, H., Kim, J.Y., Koo, C.: The role of augmented reality for experience-influenced environments: the case of cultural heritage tourism in Korea. J. Travel. Res. **57**(5), 627–643 (2017)

Evaluating the Impact of a Virtual Reality Application in Raising Awareness Toward the Destruction of Cultural Heritage Sites

Christos Hadjipanayi[1]([✉]), Eleni Demitriadou[1], Haris Frangou[1],
Maria Papageorgiou[1], Christina Zavlanou[2], and Andreas Lanitis[2,3] [iD]

[1] Department of Multimedia and Graphic Arts,
Cyprus University of Technology, Limassol, Cyprus
christos.hadjipanayi@gmail.com,
jelenadiml995@gmail.com, xarisfrangou@gmail.com,
papageo.met@gmail.com
[2] Visual Media Computing Research Lab,
Department of Multimedia and Graphic Arts, Cyprus University of Technology,
Limassol, Cyprus
cg.zavlanou@edu.cut.ac.cy, andreas.lanitis@cut.ac.cy
[3] Research Centre on Interactive Media Smart Systems and Emerging
Technologies, Limassol, Cyprus

Abstract. The aim of our work is to investigate the applicability of Virtual Reality (VR) in raising awareness of users in relation to the destruction of important monuments. The proposed methodology involves the exposure of users to three virtual environments displaying the original state of a monument, the current state and the predicted future state of the same monument in the case that the monument is not maintained. The exposure to the three states of the same building allows the user to experience the "glorious days" of a monument and compare them to the current and future states in an attempt to realize the level of destruction that could occur to the building if the monument is not maintained properly. As part of a pilot case study, a number of volunteers were asked to navigate in virtual environments depicting the three chronological states of a landmark building. Preliminary results indicate a significant increase of the intensity of negative emotions of the users, indicating the applicability of VR in alerting the society toward the destruction of important monuments.

Keywords: Virtual reality · Cultural heritage · Visualization techniques

1 Introduction

Virtual Reality (VR) is defined as "an interactive three-dimensional environment that is created on the computer and in which the user can be immersed" [1]. Recent progress of science and technology resulted in affordable and efficient hardware and tools [2] that enables the design and implementation of engaging applications that can be used in a variety of different fields, resulting in an increased popularity of VR in different application domains [3]. A key issue to enable efficient interaction of users with a 3D

© Springer Nature Switzerland AG 2018
M. Ioannides et al. (Eds.): EuroMed 2018, LNCS 11197, pp. 142–149, 2018.
https://doi.org/10.1007/978-3-030-01765-1_17

virtual environment is the "presence" and "immersion" [4] of the users, i.e. the illusion of users that they are in the virtual environment, physically and mentally [5]. Immersive applications engage the users emotionally in a similar way like the exposure to real environments [6] maximizing in that way the impact of a VR application.

The aim of our work is to investigate the applicability of VR in raising awareness of users in relation to the destruction of important monuments. The proposed methodology involves the exposure of users to three virtual environments displaying the original state of a monument, the current state and the predicted future state of the same monument in the case that the monument is not maintained. The exposure to the three states of the same building allows the user to experience the "glorious days" of a monument and compare them to the current and future states in an attempt to realize the level of destruction and the size of the potential loss in the case that the monument is not maintained properly. As part of an experimental investigation changes in the emotions of the users are registered to assess the emotional impact of the application.

In the remainder of the paper we present a brief literature review of the use of VR in Cultural Heritage applications, a description of the VR application and the experimental evaluation. In Sect. 5 conclusions and plans for future work are presented.

2 Related Work

Virtual reality can be exploited in various areas of human activity. One of these is the design of sites and buildings that are hardly reachable by visitors either due to distance or area configuration [7]. For example, Behr et al. [8] simulated the cathedral of Siena, Italy. The virtual environment, including a virtual avatar-style guide, dressed in traditional costume, allows users to explore the site and draw important historical information about the temple and its architecture.

Virtual reality could be also used to rebuild buildings and ruins of cultural heritage, to restore their original state in all details [9], thereby promoting the feeling of change of spaces and buildings over time [8] while enabling users to research what they could previously research only by descriptions [10]. Christofi et al. [7] reconstructed the historic site of Choirokitia, in Cyprus, based on true information, aimed at assessing the learning performance of the users and examining whether their interest in archaeological sites is increasing.

Kontogianni et al. [9] reconstructed the Middle Lodge in the Ancient Agora, dating back to the 2nd century BC, situated northwest of the sacred rock of the Acropolis of Athens. The building today does not exist and visitors can see only its foundations. The implementation of the project relies on a bibliographical survey, reconstruction studies, plans, three-dimensional reconstruction of the foundations, as well as considering assumptions of the site's managers working in the Ancient Agora.

Loizides et al. [11] describe an evaluation of user experience in relation to the use of VR in presenting Cultural Heritage sights. According to the findings the use of VR for the presentation of VR is highly appealing for the users and as a result it can cause emotional engagement of the users. However, the most important drawback of this approach was the user nauseousness that may cause discomfort to users. Fortunately, improvements in VR hardware resulted in noticeable decrease of nauseousness symptoms to VR users, improving the applicability of VR to different application domains.

3   VR Application

In this section we provide information related to the site used in the case study, along with the details related to the implementation of the VR application.

3.1   Case Study

The case study considered in this paper, relates to the abandoned hotel "Berengaria", a landmark building in the Troodos area of Cyprus. The hotel was completed in 1931 and it used to be a point of reference for the whole region [12]. During 1984 the operation of the hotel was suspended and since then the impressive building is following a continuous deterioration that will eventually lead to its complete destruction. The hotel is linked to numerous mysterious stories and myths and as a result it is considered a key site for the local region.

3.2   Virtual Representation of the Hotel

For the needs of the experimental investigation it is required to have three models showing the building while it was in operation, the current state of the hotel and a model showing the prediction of its future appearance. It should be noted that for all three cases there is no need to create a geometrically correct 3D model; a close approximation of the appearance of the building is sufficient for the needs of the experiment. Hence this paper is not focused on techniques and methodologies suitable for photorealistic 3D reconstruction.

The 3D modeling process started with the capture of photographs and measurements of the building. This material formed the basis of generating a 3D model of the facade and part of the interior of the building that can be used for generating the 3D models corresponding to the three chronological phases under investigation. To generate the 3D model showing the past appearance of the building, an extensive literature search was carried out in order to collect photographic material showing the interior and exterior of the hotel during its "glory" days. Photographic material collected on site was used to recreate and texture the 3D model based on the current hotel appearance. Since the hotel was abandoned for several years, the current appearance shows the depressing views of worn out walls, destroyed doors and windows, damages from graffiti and nests for reptiles in the building's interior. Because of erosion due to aging, a fire that broke out in 2001 and vandalisms, it is foreseen that the building is in immediate danger of collapsing, hence the model showing the future state of the building was created by using special effects where photographs from the current state and the 3D models are deformed to show the building almost-demolished.

It should be noted that this work is still in progress. Currently the 3D model showing the past appearance was generated, but the generation of the complete 3D models showing the current and future appearance is still in progress. For the needs of the preliminary experimental investigation, a panorama of photographic material was used to generate the illusion of a 3D model showing the current and future state of the building.

3.3   Implementation of the Application

The main software tools used for the generation of 3D models and the implementation of the application were the Autodesk Maya, Unity 3D and Adobe Photoshop 2018. The necessary soundtrack, that includes the provision of aural information about the site, was recorded through Ice-cream screen recorder and edited via Adobe Premiere. The final application works with an Oculus Rift CV1 head mounted display with touch controllers so that the level of immersion of users in the simulated environment [13] is maximized. The user of the application can navigate the site using the VR touch controllers, in first person view. During the navigation information about the hotel is presented to the users through audio channels.

A total of three scenes were planned in the environment. In the first scene, the user was transported to the "glorious" past by looking at the facade. From the main entrance, the user had the option to be transported from the reception area to the mezzanine through the central staircase, and then to the balcony area. In the second scene, the user was confronted with the tragic current state of the building, by looking at the facade. In the third and last scene, the user could witness nothing but scattered relics of the ever-imposing building. Then, moving into the interior, the user could only see the debris that will remain if the state of the building is not maintained. Screenshots from the three scenes depicting different chorological states of the site are shown in Fig. 1.

Fig. 1. Facade of the hotel as it was in the past as well as the interior of this hotel (top), current state of the facade (bottom left) and the predicted future appearance (bottom right)

4   Experimental Evaluation

An experimental evaluation was carried out to investigate whether the exposure of users to the three VR environments could affect the emotional state of the users in a way that indicates increased awareness and concern related to the need for preventing the destruction of the building. This was accomplished through the examination of changes in the emotional states of the users, before and after the exposure to the VR environments. A description of the experiment and the results are presented hereunder.

4.1   Participants

The selection of participants in the survey was made by convenience sampling [14]. Twenty adults, 8 male (40%), 12 female (60%), 18–45 years old, with a mean of 26.5 (SD = 6.243) took part in the experiment. Among the sample 17 (85%) participants live in urban areas and 3 (15%) in semi-urban. Twelve (60%) of the participants were graduates of a Higher Education Institution, three (15%) high school graduates, three (15%) holders of a postgraduate diploma and two (10%) PhD holders. All survey participants use the internet, with the majority of them, namely 18 (90%) on a daily basis. Most of the participants (85% of the sample), knew what virtual reality is, while half of them had a previous experience with it. Most of them, 13 (65%) also believe that, through the virtual world, they can live and experience similar experiences as in the real/natural world.

4.2   Data Collection

Data collection was achieved through two questionnaires [15]. The first questionnaire was completed by the participants at the beginning of the experiment, before they use the application. The first questionnaire had four parts with closed-ended questions. The first part concerns the demographic data of the participants (sex, area of residence, age, education) and the second part examines the participants' experience with virtual reality. Specifically, the second part of the questionnaire included questions related to the computer literacy of the participants and their previous experience with virtual reality. In the third part of the questionnaire users had to quote the intensity of their current six basic emotions (Anger, Fear, Disgust, Happiness, Joy, Sadness) on the Likert scale where 1 indicates minimal intensity of the corresponding emotion and 5 indicates maximum intensity of the corresponding emotion. The last part of the questionnaire examines the participants' knowledge of basic facts related to the building such as facts related to the location, opening and closing date, background of its naming and other historical facts.

The second questionnaire was given to the participants after they used the VR application for about five minutes. The questionnaire consisted of four parts. In the first part, there were questions about the user experience in the virtual environment. In the second part feelings of the users were recorded in the same way as in the first questionnaire, in order to detect changes in the intensities of the emotions. The third part of the questionnaire examines the knowledge that users gained through the experience. It should be noted that during the navigation in the VR environment participants were presented with aural information about the site. In this case the aim was to compare the knowledge gained by participants during their overall VR experience. In the last part of the questionnaire, participants had to answer three open questions related to their willingness to help to maintain and restore the building. Participants also stated how they planned to contribute to the maintenance of the site.

4.3 Data Analysis and Results

The SPSS statistical packet was used to analyze the quantitative data. Descriptive statistics and the t-test statistical criterion were applied, and paired comparisons were made to determine whether there were statistically significant changes in emotions. The results (see Table 1) indicate that negative emotions of the users were affected. Specifically, there is a strong variation detected and statistical significance (p < 0.05) in the feelings of anger, disgust, sadness and fear. On the contrary, positive emotions, such as joy and happiness, did not change significantly. The increase of the negative emotions is a strong indication of the success of the application in raising awareness towards the destruction of the building. Results also indicate a significant improvement in the knowledge gained about the building, and the willingness of the volunteers to contribute to the effort of maintaining/restoring the building.

Table 1. Comparing the average of emotions before and after users experience with the planned environment (emotion names in bold indicate the emotions with significant change in intensity)

Emotions	Mean (SD)	Mean (SD)	T	p-value
	Before	After		
Anger	1.60 (0.883)	2.10 (1.165)	2.127	**.047**
Fear	1.80 (1.005)	2.35 (1.137)	3.240	**.004**
Disgust	1.40 (.995)	2.35 (1.268)	4.790	**.000**
Happiness	3.20 (1.105)	3.25 (.967)	170	.887
Joy	3.25 (1.020)	3.10 (.912)	.767	.453
Sadness	1.40 (.681)	2.45 (1.191)	4.273	**.000**
Surprise	2.35 (1.309)	2.70 (1.129)	1.234	.232

5 Conclusions and Future Work

A preliminary investigation in the use of a VR application for raising awareness towards the destruction of important buildings is described. As part of the experiment, users were exposed to virtual environments showing the past, current and future pre-dicted appearance of a building in the case that the building is not maintained properly. Significant increase of negative emotions of the users was recorded, indicating that such a VR application can have an important impact on users contributing in that way to efforts for preserving Cultural Heritage sites. The use of VR as a means of creating highly immersive and affective applications, can be applied for other Cultural Heritage sites to help raise interest among policy makers and the public. Although other means of raising awareness for the destruction of CH sites could be employed (i.e. utilization of campaigns through social media), we envisage that VR tools can be more effective for this particular application due to the immersive nature of VR technology.

Based on the promising results of this preliminary investigation we plan to carry on with the 3D modeling phase so that complete 3D models of the three chronological periods are generated. Although so far for the needs of the experiment we did not use photorealistic 3D models of the site, in the future we plan to investigate the impact when geometrically correct models are used in similar applications. We also plan to incorporate damage simulators [16] in order to get better predictions of the foreseen future state of a site. Furthermore, more sophisticated EEG-based methods [17] for recording changes in emotional states will be used so that more accurate results in relation to the impact of the application are recorded. We also plan to further investigate the intensity of awareness raised among the participants in relation to the increase of negative emotions recorded and the content presented in the VR application. We also plan to use the same principle on other sites in order to verify the findings in different scenarios and to contribute to the efforts of preserving Cultural Heritage monuments.

References

1. Conn, C., Lanier, J., Minsky, M., Fisher, S., Druin, A.: Virtual environments and interactivity: windows to the future. ACM SIGGRAPH Comput. Graph. **23**(5), 7–18 (1989)
2. Coburn, J.Q., Freeman, I., Salmon, J.L.: A review of the capabilities of current low-cost virtual reality technology and its potential to enhance the design process. J. Comput. Inf. Sci. Eng. **17**(3), 031013 (2017)
3. Huang, H.M., Rauch, U., Liaw, S.S.: Investigating learners' attitudes toward virtual reality learning environments: based on a constructivist approach. Comput. Educ. **55**(3), 1171–1182 (2010)
4. Sanchez-Vives, M.V., Slater, M.: From presence to consciousness through virtual reality. Nat. Rev. Neurosci. **6**(4), 1–34 (2005)
5. Muhanna, M.A.: Virtual reality and the CAVE: Taxonomy, interaction challenges and research directions. J. King Saud Univ.-Comput. Inf. Sci. **27**(3), 344–361 (2015)
6. Diemer, J., Alpers, G.W., Peperkorn, H.M., Shiban, Y., Mühlberger, A.: The impact of perception and presence on emotional reactions: a review of research in virtual reality. Front. Psychol. **6**(26), 1–9 (2015)
7. Christofi, M., et al.: A tour in the archaeological site of Choirokoitia using virtual reality: a learning performance and interest generation assessment. In: Ioannides, M., Martins, J., Žarnić, R., Lim, V. (eds.) Advances in Digital Cultural Heritage. LNCS, vol. 10754, pp. 208–217. Springer, Cham (2018). https://doi.org/10.1007/978-3-319-75789-6_15
8. Behr, J., et al.: The Digital Cathedral of Siena–Innovative concepts for interactive and immersive presentation of cultural heritage sites, pp. 57–71 (2001)
9. Kontogianni, G., Georgopoulos, A., Saraga, N., Alexandraki, E., Tsogka, K.: 3D virtual reconstruction of the Middle Stoa in the Athens Ancient Agora. ISPRS-Int. Arch. Photogramm. Remote. Sens. Spat. Inf. Sci. **40**, 125–131 (2013)
10. Guidi, G., Russo, M.: Diachronic 3D reconstruction for lost cultural heritage. Int. Arch. Photogramm. Remote. Sens. Spat. Inf. Sci. **38**(W16), 371–376 (2011)
11. Loizides, F., El Kater, A., Terlikas, C., Lanitis, A., Michael, D.: Presenting cypriot cultural heritage in virtual reality: a user evaluation. In: Ioannides, M., Magnenat-Thalmann, N., Fink, E., Žarnić, R., Yen, A.-Y., Quak, E. (eds.) EuroMed 2014. LNCS, vol. 8740, pp. 572–579. Springer, Cham (2014). https://doi.org/10.1007/978-3-319-13695-0_57
12. Andreou, A.: Berengaria, The Hotel of the Kings. iWrite, Nicosia (2016)
13. Goradia, I., Doshi, J., Kurup, L.: A review paper on oculus rift & project morpheus. Int. J. Curr. Eng. Technol. **4**(5), 3196–3200 (2014)
14. Babbie, E.: The Practice of Social Research, 13th edn. Wadsworth, Belmont (2013)

15. Papanastasiou, K., Papanastasiou, E.: Educational Research Methodology, 1st edn. Private, Nicosia (2005)
16. Barbat, A.H., Moya, F.Y., Canas, J.: Damage scenarios simulation for seismic risk assessment in urban zones. Earthq. Spectra **12**(3), 371–394 (1996)
17. Baka, E., Stavroulia, K.E., Magnenat-Thalmann, N., Lanitis, A.: An EEG-based evaluation for comparing the sense of presence between virtual and physical environments. In: Proceedings of Computer Graphics International, pp. 107–116 (2018)

Using Linked Data for Prosopographical Research of Historical Persons: Case U.S. Congress Legislators

Goki Miyakita[1]([✉]), Petri Leskinen[2], and Eero Hyvönen[2,3]

[1] Research Institute for Digital Media and Content, Keio University, Tokyo, Japan
`5ki-miyakita@kmd.keio.ac.jp`
[2] Semantic Computing Research Group (SeCo), Aalto University, Espoo, Finland
[3] HELDIG – Helsinki Centre for Digital Humanities, University of Helsinki, Helsinki, Finland
`http://seco.cs.aalto.fi`, `http://heldig.fi`

Abstract. This paper shows how biographical registries can be represented as Linked Data, enriched by data linking to related data sources, and used in Digital Humanities. As a use case, a database of 11 987 historical U.S. Congress Legislators in 1789–2018 was transformed into a knowledge graph. The data was published as a Linked Data service, including a SPARQL endpoint, on top of which tools for biographical and prosopographical research are implemented. A faceted browser named U.S. Congress Prosopographer with visualization tools for knowledge discovery is presented to provide new insights in political history.

Keywords: Linked Data · Visualization · Biography
Prosopography · Digital Humanities · American history

1   Prosopographical Method

Person registries and biographies are widely used to document and describe life stories of historical people, with the aim of getting a better understanding of their personality, actions, and motivations in history. In *biography* [17] the focus is on individual protagonists, while in *prosopography* [21] life histories of groups of people are studied in order to find out some kind of commonness or average in them. Here persons are studied in the context of communities. The prosopographical research method [21, p. 47] consists of two steps. First, a target group of people is selected that share desired characteristics for solving the research question at hand. Second, the target group is analyzed and compared with other groups to solve the research question.

This paper shows how the prosopographical method can be used in practice in Digital Humanities by presenting an interface and application based on the Linked Data (LD) paradigm [5] in the Cultural Heritage (CH) domain [7]. It is shown how faceted search and data visualization tools can be integrated with a SPARQL endpoint allowing the end user to (1) filter out target groups of people,

M. Ioannides et al. (Eds.): EuroMed 2018, LNCS 11197, pp. 150–162, 2018.
https://doi.org/10.1007/978-3-030-01765-1_18

and (2) then to study them. A key novelty of this paper is the idea to support comparing analyses and visualizations based on different target subgroups. The paper extends substantially our earlier short four page paper [14] that focuses on the application demonstrator.

As a use case, a database about the United States Congress Legislators[1,2] were used. We pulled and linked two different datasets: (1) a dataset of the members of the United States Congress and (2) a dataset based on ICPSR ID[3] accompanying Congress numbers[4], as a basis. It contains biographical records of 11 987 persons who served in the U.S. Congresses from the 1st (1789) to the 115th (2018) one. We converted and extracted the data into RDF, and developed a SPARQL compliant data service and an online application named *U.S. Congress Prosopographer*[5] to complement both quantitative and qualitative inquiry in American political history.

As shown in Fig. 1, after data preparation, the paper presents a data model we used in representing person registries and a data service for publishing the registry data as Linked Open Data. After this, the user interface (tools) for using the data service for biography and prosopography are presented. The interface allows the users to browse different data segments with multiple visualizations, and a set of use cases are described. In conclusion, contributions of the work are summarized in relation to related works, and directions for further research are suggested.

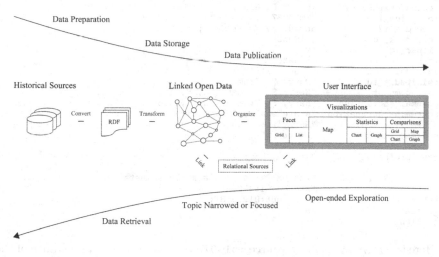

Fig. 1. Research pipeline

---

[1] https://github.com/unitedstates/congress-legislators.
[2] http://k7moa.com.
[3] The Inter-university Consortium for Political and Social Research (ICPSR) ID number.
[4] https://www.senate.gov/reference/Years_to_Congress.htm.
[5] https://semanticcomputing.github.io/congress-legislators.

2   Data Model and Linked Data Service

Data Model. The ontology model representing people and their biographical information is based on the schema.org vocabulary[6] [3]. Legislators are modeled as instances of the class `schema:Person` with properties expressing their biographical data. Places are represented as instances of `schema:Place`. The data model of schema.org is extended by additional properties and classes in the domain specific namespace[7] of the underlying data service (to be described below). To illustrate the model, an example of data resources in the Turtle format[8] is given below:

```
@prefix :        <http://ldf.fi/congress/> .  # Domain name space
@prefix schema:  <http://schema.org/> .
@prefix wd_ent:  <http://www.wikidata.org/entity/> .
@prefix xsd:     <http://www.w3.org/2001/XMLSchema#> .
@prefix skos:    <http://www.w3.org/2004/02/skos/core#> .
@prefix rdfs:    <http://www.w3.org/2000/01/rdf-schema#> .
@prefix geo:     <http://www.w3.org/2003/01/geo/wgs84_pos#> .
@prefix dbr:     <http://dbpedia.org/resource/> .

:p10079  a       schema:Person ;    # A person instance
   schema:familyName      "Truman" ;
   schema:givenName       "Harry" ;
   schema:gender          "Male" ;
   schema:birthDate       "1884-05-08"^^xsd:date ;
   schema:birthPlace      wd_ent:Q572172 ;
   schema:deathDate       "1972-12-26"^^xsd:date ;
   schema:deathPlace      wd_ent:Q41819 ;
   :bioguide_id           "T000387" ;
   :dbpedia_id            dbr:Harry_S._Truman ;
   :govtrack_id           "410956" ;
   :icpsr_id              "9487" ;
   :type                  "Senator" ;
   :wikidata              wd_ent:Q11613 ;
   :wikipedia_id          "Harry S. Truman" ;
   rdfs:comment           "Harry S. Truman (May 8, 1884 ..."@en ;
   schema:description     "Harry S. Truman (May 8, 1884 ..."@en ;
   schema:hasOccupation   "statesman" , "politician" ;
   schema:image           "HarryTruman.jpg" ;
   schema:memberOf        "Democrat" ;
   schema:state           "MO" ;
   skos:prefLabel         "Truman, Harry" .

wd_ent:Q41819  a         schema:Place ;    # A place instance
   rdfs:label            "Kansas City"@en ;
   schema:containedInPlace  wd_ent:Q127238 ;
   geo:lat               39.05 ;
   geo:long              -94.583333333 .
```

Here the *Harry Truman* resource `:p10079` is represented as an instance of the class `schema:Person`. All basic biographical data (family name, gender, given name, etc.) are modeled using the schema.org namespace, and all the data relating to his career are in the domain namespace. The resources can be linked to external databases or services, such as DBpedia, Wikidata, Wikipedia, and

---

[6] http://schema.org/docs/schemas.html.

[7] http://ldf.fi/congress/.

[8] https://www.w3.org/TR/turtle/.

Twitter, for more information. There are 11 987 legislator resources like this in the knowledge graph.

The data example also shows the place resource of *Kansas City*, wd_ent:Q41819. The place ontology data in our domain was extracted from DBpedia[9]. The dataset contains 7865 place resources, including all places mentioned in the United States Congress Legislators data. Each place entry contains the place name, the latitude and longitude, and a link to a larger scale place containing the current place, a linkage that constructs a topological hierarchy. Property :icpsr_id is used to identify and classify each person according to the Congress(es) (s)he served/serves.

Data Service. The data is available as a Linked Open Data service at the Linked Data Finland platform[10] [8] in an open SPARQL endpoint[11] with resolvable URIs, using the W3C Linked Data publishing principles and best practices [5]. For example, the URI http://ldf.fi/congress/p10079 refers to Harry Truman (1882–1972), and can be used for retrieving the related RDF data or for Linked Data browsing depending on the need and HTTP protocol header data used.

The data in the service contains altogether ca 830 000 triples, 790 000 in the people graph and 40 000 in the place graph.

3   Supporting Biographical and Prosopographical Research

This section describes the functionalities of the interface *U.S. Congress Prosopographer* from the end-user's perspective. To support the first step in the prosopographical method, a faceted search application view is provided for finding legislators of interest and their groups. To support the second analysis step in the prosopographical method, the interface contains separate application views for (1) visualizing the target group on a map, (2) analyzing it using statistics, and (3) for making comparisons between two target groups. In below, these features are explained in more detail. All application views can be selected from the menu bar of the system using corresponding link buttons that open the selected application view.

Faceted Search View. Figure 2 depicts the main faceted search interface of the interface. Its upper part allows the user to filter the target group of interest in the prosopographical method, based on filters and hierarchical facet ontologies shown on the top. The lower part visualizes the target group retrieved as a matrix grid. Its cells contain an image of the person (if available) and below it metadata about the person with links to additional data sources. The matrix can alternatively be viewed in list form by clicking the link "List" on the menu bar instead of "Grid". The use case of this application view is to find groups of persons of interest, and then by selecting one of them, to get more information about him/her on a

---

[9] http://dbpedia.org.
[10] http://ldf.fi.
[11] http://ldf.fi/congress/sparql.

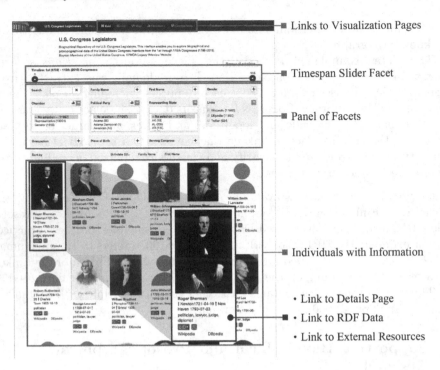

■ Links to Visualization Pages

■ Timespan Slider Facet

■ Panel of Facets

■ Individuals with Information

• Link to Details Page
■ Link to RDF Data
• Link to External Resources

Fig. 2. Faceted search view (search interface)

Details Page (a kind of "home page") (cf. Fig. 2). For biographical research, the Details Page of each person entry contains a description of the person, based on the original database, with additional data links. The description is also enriched by a short textual biograph extracted from Wikidata, when such an article is available.

In the data filtering part, there is first a timespan slider by which the range of congresses (1st–115th) in focus can be constrained. Below that there is generic search box filter, like in Google basic search box. After this comes facets for faceted search.

The idea in faceted search [20], called earlier also view-based search [6,16], is to index data items along orthogonal category hierarchies, i.e., facets [12] (e.g., places, times, document types, etc.) and use them for searching and browsing: the user selects in free order categories on facets, and the data items included in the selected categories are considered search results. After each selection, a count is computed for each category showing the number of results, if the user next makes that selection. In contrast to static filters, facets interact with each other; facets have also been called dynamic ontologies [19]. In this way, search is guided by avoiding annoying "no hits" results. Moreover, hit distributions

---

[12] The idea of facets dates back to the Colon Classification system of S. R. Ranganathan in library science, published in 1933.

on facets provide the end-user with data-analytic views on what kind of items there are in the underlying database. Faceted search is especially useful on the Semantic Web where hierarchical ontologies used for data annotation provide a natural basis for facets, and reasoning can be used for mapping data to facets [6].

Following facets are available in the Panel of Facets of Fig. 2: personal attributes (Family Name, First Name, Gender, Occupation, and Place of Birth), political characteristics (Chamber, Political Party, Representing State, and Serving Congress), and external datasets he or she has been linked to (Wikipedia, DBpedia, and Twitter).

People often distinguish between what data is indelible and what is ephemeral. Therefore, it is important to acknowledge that every aspect of historical entities yields information that may be of use to certain users. The faceted interface gives the user the freedom to make filtering choices freely, which provides flexibility needed in biographical and prosopographical research.

Map Visualization View. By selecting link "Map" in the menu bar of the user interface (Fig. 2), a map visualization application depicted in Fig. 3 on the left is opened. It illustrates the intellectual mobility of Congress members through the places of their birth and death. Blue circles show birth places, red circles death places, and the diameter of the circle indicates the number of births and deaths in the place. By clicking on a circle, a pop-up window listing legislators who were born or died at the place is shown with links to their home pages in the application. This process is illustrated graphically in the right hand side of Fig. 3. The same filters and facets (on the left in Fig. 3) as in Fig. 2 can be used for filtering the target group visualized on the map. Angular Google Maps[13] is used in this visualization on top of the SPARQL endpoint.

The use case of this application view is prosopographical: the idea is to locate, map, and explain historical trends of legislator groups in the geographical space.

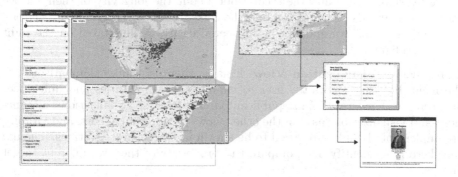

Fig. 3. Map visualization view (places of birth and death of a filtered target group)

---

[13] http://angular-ui.github.io/angular-google-maps/.

Statistical Visualization View. By clicking the link "Statistics" in the menu bar of Fig. 2, two data analytic application views to the data can be opened: one based on (1) charts (pie charts and a sankey chart), and (2) one using graphs (histograms). In both cases, the target group can be filtered in the same way as in the previous views.

To examine the data through structured charts, and to provide glanceable overviews of the temporal features of the legislators, this page generates statistics using Google Chart diagrams[14] based on the extracted filtering results. For example, Fig. 4 LEFT illustrates the political party (Republican, Federalist, Jackson, Adams, etc.) and occupation (politician, lawyer, judge, diplomat, etc.) distributions of the legislators of the first 20 congresses, totaling 1567 members.

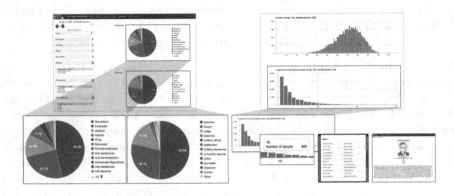

Fig. 4. Statistical visualization view (LEFT: pie charts, RIGHT: histograms)

Statistics based on histograms provide yet another perspective to the data. For example, the first histogram of Fig. 4 RIGHT depicts the age distribution of the legislators (up) and the second one about the longevity of their service (down) in years. By clicking on a bar, the links to the corresponding legislators' home pages are shown and can be inspected easily, as illustrated on the right side of the figure.

Comparison Visualization View. Finally, there is a link "Comparisons" in the menu bar that allows the user to examine the similarities and differences between the Democratic and Republican parties. In these visualizations, all functions and visualizations used in the other views (Grid, Map, Chart, and Graph), are implemented, and customized to be shown in two separate sections. The use case here is to identify and compare the properties of the two different target groups.

For example, all four comparison views are depicted in Fig. 5 illustrating the differences between the members of the Democratic and Republican parties without any further filter and facet selections made.

---

[14] https://developers.google.com/chart/.

Grid (Individuals)   Map   Chart   Graph

Fig. 5. Comparison visualization view (four comparison views)

Use Case Examples. The comparison visualizations can be used in different research studies. For example, it can be shown that during the Reconstruction era from the 38th through the 45th Congresses (1863–64 to 1877–78) there is a large difference in the locations of birth and death of the legislators. Most legislators were born and died in the eastern side. However, the distribution reveals a further clear tendency during this period: while the Democrats have a longitudinal spreading, Republicans remain in the Northeastern megalopolises (cf. Fig. 6).

Fig. 6. Birth and death places (TOP: democrats, BOTTOM: republicans)

Another example is from the 84th through the 89th Congresses (1955–56 to 1965–66) when the federal government aimed to revitalize cities though funding urban renewal programs.[15] During this period of time, the poor were displaced and suffered from the series of policies. However, comparing with the overall trend in longevity of service of legislators which continuously decreases (cf. Fig. 7 LEFT), there is a wide variation in the longevity during 1955–1966 (cf. Fig. 7 RIGHT). This indicates that incumbent re-election rates were extremely high in both parties during this time, despite the fact that the social situation was very unstable.

It is also possible to narrow down the target groups (through filtering) and investigate the changes in a longer time period. For instance, in the sequence of decades from the 97th through the 115th Congresses (1981–82 to 2017–18), the end-user is able to examine the changes in women's occupations over the years. In

---

[15] Widely known as "The Urban Renewal Projects".

Non-Filtered (1st through 115th Congresses)   Filtered to 84th through 89th Congresses

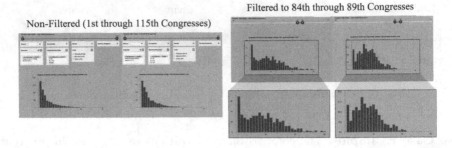

Fig. 7. Longevity of service (LEFT: non–filtered, RIGHT: filtered)

Fig. 8, the pie charts show the change of occupations in every ten years. Although the number of women is quite small in comparison to men, the result shows that the types of occupations are growing ever more diverse. Furthermore, by taking a closer look at the occupational categories from the 2000's, *social worker* and *nurse* are ranked high in Democrats (although *politician* and *lawyer* accounts for a large percentage in both parties). On the Republican side, the results are more dispersed, and *rancher* follows after *politician* and *lawyer* in the 2010's, which does not appear in the Democrats' occupations.

1981-1990   1991-2000   2001-2010   2011-2018

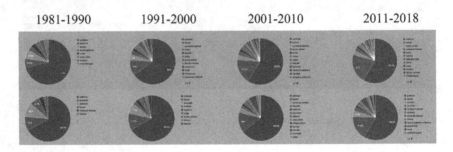

Fig. 8. Changes in women's occupations (TOP: democrats, BOTTOM: republicans)

Through revealing such correlated continuities and changes, these examples demonstrate how historical patterns correspond to biographical information and further intertwine with politics, economics, and historical knowledge.

4   Implementation

U.S. Congress Prosopographer was implemented by extending SPARQL Faceter [11], an interface for creating faceted search interfaces on top of a SPARQL endpoint. AngularJS[16] framework was used to organize Linked Data

---

[16] http://angularjs.org.

together with a timespan slider[17] that is included as a canonical facet for the user to specify a desired range of congresses based on their interest. Based on our experiment, SPARQL Faceter could be fairly easily combined with various means and tools for visualization with leaving a large space for customization. Modifying SPARQL Faceter itself for new features, e.g., to use functionally new kind of facets, requires expertise is using AngularJS, but just adapting the existing system to a new dataset is more straightforward. In our case, an old SPARQL Faceter application [9] was used as a template to start with.

The interface *U.S. Congress Prosopographer* contains two separate components: (1) The Linked Open Data service for machines that supports the LD publishing principles [5]. The data used in the application is available as Linked Open Data at the "7-star" Linked Data Finland platform. (2) The user interface with application views for humans which are implemented completely on the client side as a Rich Internet Application.

Detaching the data service from applications is beneficial: the data service can be re-used by anyone for other application purposes easily without server side programming and concerns. In this way, also the computational burden of doing analyses can be distributed from the server to the clients. However, the data has to be transferred from the server to the clients for analysis, which can be problematic, when transferring and analyzing very large target groups.

5   Related Work and Discussion

There are a number of prior studies related to American or Congress history [1,2,4,15]. However, these works have limitations in their generality and usage, restricted to particular subject, time frame, or resources (e.g., non-machine readable formats). The research of this paper stands unique in providing a comprehensive coverage of U.S. Congressional biography from its beginning until today, distributed in a Linked Open Data structure, and further enabling access through its "rich-prospect interface" [18] to enhance the user's understanding and exploration in American political history.

Applying Linked Data principles to cultural heritage data [7] and historical research [13] is a promising approach to solve the interoperability problems of isolated and semantically heterogeneous data sources. Linked Data has been used before also for representing and studying biographical data about the U.S. legislators [12]. Consistent with, but extending from this past research, the novelty of our work is bringing in the facet-based tooling with integrated visualizations together with a generous [22] and rich-prospect interface.

Thorough representing and visualizing temporal data in a Linked Data format, this research allowed the users to interact with diverse data elements on both micro to macro levels. The visualizations provide both practical and comprehensive insights into the long history of the United States. On the other hand, the interface *U.S. Congress Prosopographer* explores different ways to support

---

[17] https://github.com/angular-slider/angularjs-slider.

prosopographical research. While the usability as well as the functionality must be tested and evaluated in further studies, its different types of visualization establish context and maintain orientation while revealing details also about the individuals. This combination of macro- and microscopic viewpoints offers both qualitative and quantitative understanding of the biographical and proso-pographical aspects of the Congress legislators.

This paper showed that Linked Open Data can be used as a flexible basis for representing biographical registries, for filtering out target groups of persons of interest, and for conducting biographical and prosopographical research. According to our practical experiences, the technology is useful, stable and handy with having the basis in Linked Data publishing standards and principles. Alongside the SPARQL querying infrastructure, the interface conveys prosopographical insights in different ways, depending on the user's curiosity and interests. In practice, assembling biographies as well as prosopographies based on Linked Data has its potential to align with traditional humanities research, not only to form research questions, but also to stimulate exploration in every individual through enriching the very foundation of historical entities.

Like in other areas of data-driven research, the resulting interface established a robust infrastructure to explore historical records. Yet, additionally, this paper provides a new method in interpreting intangible cultural heritage resources through the dynamic integration of querying and visualizing Linked Data under one single system.

6   Future Work

In future work, we hope to do more experimental studies on using the interface with experts on political history of the United States. On the technical side, solutions for showing new types of visualizations, such as linguistic analyses of biographical texts or social networks of politicians, could be studied. Also, to understand broader implications and the potential influence of U.S. Congress legislators on a global scale, this research can leverage and link across other fields and domains, e.g., congressional bills, cultural enhancements, or heritage datasets of other countries.

Although the research of this paper has focused on one particular dataset, the versatility of the presented general framework can be fully applied to other large scale datasets, and further give rise to new perspectives and paradigms in exploring cultural and historical spheres. Indeed, alongside with the research presented in this paper, we have transformed the National Biography of Finland, 13 000 short textual biographies of notable Finns, into a Linked Data service, and created a semantic portal for biographical and prosopographical research on top of it [10].

Acknowledgements. Thanks to Erkki Heino for implementational help regarding extending the Faceter SPARQL tool for our case studies, to Jouni Tuominen for discussions related to data modeling and Linked Data services, and to Brian Keegan and Thea Lindquist (University of Colorado, Boulder) regarding the U.S. Legislator data and research questions related to it. Goki Miyakita was supported by a mobility scholarship at Aalto University in the frame of the Erasmus Mundus Action 2 Project TEAM, funded by the European Commission. Our research was also supported by the CSC computing services and the Severi project (http://seco.cs.aalto.fi/projects/severi) funded mainly by Business Finland.

References

1. Congressional biographical directory, United States (2002). http://bioguide.congress.gov/biosearch/biosearch.asp
2. Culpepper, J.: Chronicling America: historic American newspapers. Ref. Rev. **21**(7), 52–53 (2007)
3. Guha, R.V., Brickley, D., Macbeth, S.: Schema. org: evolution of structured data on the web. Commun. ACM **59**(2), 44–51 (2016)
4. Harward, B.M., Moffett, K.W.: The calculus of cosponsorship in the U.S. Senate. Legis. Stud. Q. **35**(1), 117–143 (2010)
5. Heath, T., Bizer, C.: Linked data: evolving the web into a global data space (1st edition). In: Synthesis Lectures on the Semantic Web: Theory and Technology. Morgan and Claypool (2011). http://linkeddatabook.com/editions/1.0/
6. Hyvönen, E., Saarela, S., Viljanen, K.: Application of ontology techniques to view-based semantic search and browsing. In: Bussler, C.J., Davies, J., Fensel, D., Studer, R. (eds.) ESWS 2004. LNCS, vol. 3053, pp. 92–106. Springer, Heidelberg (2004). https://doi.org/10.1007/978-3-540-25956-5_7
7. Hyvönen, E.: Publishing and Using Cultural Heritage Linked Data on the Semantic Web. Synthesis Lectures on the SemanticWeb: Theory and Technology. Morgan and Claypool, Palo Alto (2012)
8. Hyvönen, E., Tuominen, J., Alonen, M., Mäkelä, E.: Linked data Finland: A 7-star model and platform for publishing and re-using linked datasets. In: Presutti, V., Blomqvist, E., Troncy, R., Sack, H., Papadakis, I., Tordai, A. (eds.) ESWC 2014. LNCS, vol. 8798, pp. 226–230. Springer, Cham (2014). https://doi.org/10.1007/978-3-319-11955-7_24
9. Hyvönen, E., Leskinen, P., Heino, E., Tuominen, J., Sirola, L.: Reassembling and enriching the life stories in printed biographical registers: Norssi high school alumni on the semantic web. In: Gracia, J., Bond, F., McCrae, J.P., Buitelaar, P., Chiarcos, C., Hellmann, S. (eds.) LDK 2017. LNCS (LNAI), vol. 10318, pp. 113–119. Springer, Cham (2017). https://doi.org/10.1007/978-3-319-59888-8_9
10. Hyvönen, E., Leskinen, P., Tamper, M., Tuominen, J., Keravuori, K.: Semantic national biography of Finland. In: Proceedings of the Digital Humanities in the Nordic Countries 3rd Conference (DHN 2018), CEUR Workshop Proceedings, vol. 2084, pp. 372–385, March 2018
11. Koho, M., Heino, E., Hyvönen, E.: SPARQL Faceter–Client-side faceted search based on SPARQL. In: Troncy, R., Verborgh, R., Nixon, L., Kurz, T., Schlegel, K., Vander Sande, M. (eds.) Joint Proceedings of the 4th International Workshop on Linked Media and the 3rd Developers Hackshop, CEUR Workshop Proceedings, vol. 1615 (2016). http://ceur-ws.org/Vol-1615/semdevPaper5.pdf

12. Larson, R.: Bringing lives to light: biography in context, Final Project Report, University of Berkeley (2010). http://metadata.berkeley.edu/Biography_Final_Report.pdf
13. Meroño-Peñuela, A., et al.: Semantic technologies for historical research: a survey. Semant. Web **6**(6), 539–564 (2015)
14. Miyakita, G., Leskinen, P., Hyvönen, E.: U.S. congress prosopograher - a tool for prosopographical research of legislators, May 2018. submitted
15. Nelson, R.K., Winling, L., Marciano, R., Nathan Connolly, E.A.: American panorama. In: Nelson, R.K., Ayers, E.L. (eds.) (2015). https://dsl.richmond.edu/panorama/
16. Pollitt, A.S.: The key role of classification and indexing in view-based searching. Technical report, University of Huddersfield, UK (1998). http://www.ifla.org/IV/ifla63/63polst.pdf
17. Roberts, B.: Biographical Research. Understanding social research, Open University Press (2002). https://books.google.fi/books?id=04ScQgAACAAJ
18. Ruecker, S., Radzikowska, M., Sinclair, S.: Visual interface design for digital cultural heritage: a guide to rich-prospect browsing. In: Visual Interface Design for Digital Cultural Heritage: A Guide to Rich-Prospect Browsing, pp. 1–197 (2011)
19. Sacco, G.M.: Dynamic taxonomies: guided interactive diagnostic assistance. In: Wickramasinghe, N. (ed.) Encyclopedia of Healthcare Information Systems. Idea Group (2005)
20. Tunkelang, D.: Faceted Search, Synthesis Lectures on Information Concepts, Retrieval, and Services, vol. 1. Morgan and Claypool, New York (2009)
21. Verboven, K., Carlier, M., Dumolyn, J.: A short manual to the art of prosopography. In: Prosopography Approaches and Applications. A Handbook, pp. 35–70. University of Ghent (2007). http://hdl.handle.net/1854/LU-376535
22. Whitelaw, M.: Generous interfaces for digital cultural collections. Dig. Hum. Q. **9**(1) (2015). http://www.digitalhumanities.org/dhq/vol/9/1/000205/000205.html

CHISTA: Cultural Heritage Information Storage and reTrieval Application

George E. Raptis[1]([✉]), Christina Katsini[1], and Theofilos Chrysikos[2]

[1] Human Opsis, Patras, Greece
{graptis,ckatsini}@humanopsis.com
[2] Wireless Communications Laboratory,
Telecommunications and Information Technology,
Department of Electrical and Computer Engineering,
University of Patras, Patras, Greece
txrysiko@ece.upatras.gr
http://www.humanopsis.com, http://www.wltl.ee.upatras.gr

Abstract. More and more people use software applications and the Internet in their daily routine. Cultural heritage has been a favored domain for using such interactive software systems. Heritage sites, cultural institutions, and travel agencies provide visitors with digital applications, such as information retrievers and guides, aiming to enhance their visit experience. However, such applications support mainly visits at indoor than outdoor environments, are site-dependent as the information is provided for limited and specific cultural heritage items, and they are not customizable to store new information. Our previous work [9] overcome such issues, and in this paper, we extend that work by leveraging the recent technological advances in the telecommunications and the computer science domains. In this paper, we present the design and the preliminary evaluation of CHISTA (In Iranian and Persian mythology, Chista was the goddess of knowledge who led the mortals to the right way in life by providing them with meaningful information), which is an application for storing and retrieving information related to cultural heritage artifacts, sites, facts, etc. using computer vision techniques. We envision that CHISTA will be used by visitors and travelers to obtain cultural heritage information, which is provided by authorized third parties, using common technologies, such as their smartphones and the Internet.

Keywords: Cultural heritage · Computer vision · Mobile application
Tourism · Web-based interactive system

1 Introduction

People use smart mobile devices in their everyday lives for a number of reasons, such as communicating, getting entertained, and connecting with friends. Focusing on the cultural heritage domain, mobile devices have been widely used to enhance visitors' experience in heritage sites, based on either online or on-site

© Springer Nature Switzerland AG 2018
M. Ioannides et al. (Eds.): EuroMed 2018, LNCS 11197, pp. 163–170, 2018.
https://doi.org/10.1007/978-3-030-01765-1_19

interactions. Due to the multidiverse nature of the cultural heritage domain, mobile devices have been used across varying case studies, such as outdoor site exploration throughout different periods of time, based on augmented reality [5], monuments interactive walk-throughs using virtual reality environments [17], interactive storytelling across time and space [7], and 3D visualizations in immersive environments [11].

A common use of mobile devices in the cultural heritage domain is the implementation of guides which provide the visitors with information about a heritage artifact using varying technologies such as location-aware services [1], QR codes scanning, [14], NFC tags matching [3], visual recognition [13], and visual markers [2]. These mobile applications support various functionalities and purposes along with information retrieval, such as educational tasks, gamified context, bookmarking, navigation, visit planning and tracking [6]. However, such mobile applications, which are based on retrieving information from points of cultural interest, support mainly visits at indoor (e.g., museum, art gallery) than outdoor environments (e.g., archaeological sites). This results from the limitations that the outdoor settings introduce, such as the precision of the geo-location of the heritage point of interest, the cost of the Internet connection (especially when traveling aboard), the sensitivity and the non-adaptivity of the mobile apparatus in the changeable outdoor settings (e.g., weather), etc. Various techniques and mechanisms have been used to overcome such issues, such as pattern and object recognition techniques to identify a heritage artifact [10] and techniques to connect indoor and outdoor experiences [12]; however, they were still under evaluation and do not leverage on the recent advances in the computer science and engineering domains (e.g., deep learning, computer vision, and 5G capabilities).

In our previous work [9], we presented a mobile application that overcomes such issues as it retrieves static information using visual markers (e.g., scanning of QR codes). However, it introduces limitations which are as a result of the availability to the end-users (e.g., visitors of an archaeological site, tourists exploring an urban area), the ease of providing new content, the dependence on local authorities and structures of the supported points of interest. Three years later, the use of mobile devices and applications has been exponentially increased and the cost of connecting to the Internet is relatively low even when traveling abroad, since many municipalities and local communities offer free WiFi access or the cost of roaming has been decreased (e.g., according to European Union's "roam like at home" program, travelers do not pay any additional roaming charges when traveling within European Union[1]). Therefore, in this paper, we take advantage of the upward trend of mobility and the recent technological advances in the telecommunications (e.g., 5G networks) and the computer science (e.g., computer vision) domains, and we re-design our mobile application, which will be used by travelers and visitors to retrieve information about a cultural point of interest (e.g., painting, sculpture, building) either in indoor or outdoor settings, aiming to enhance visitors' experience.

---

[1] https://europa.eu/youreurope/citizens/consumers/internet-telecoms/mobile-roaming-costs.

2   CHISTA Mobile Application

2.1   Design

Several factors characterize a mobile device such as the operating system, its functionalities, the screen size, etc. The design of our mobile application should consider such factors; hence, we adopted a hybrid design approach, as it combines the best features of the native and pure web worlds, it is not costly, it is quick, it can be deployed for the most of the operating systems, and it is a widely used approach [8]. The architecture of the mobile application is depicted in Fig. 1.

A typical scenario that is supported by CHISTA is: the end-user (e.g., visitor) uses CHISTA mobile application to take a picture/video of a heritage object; the captured media along with position information are sent to the Computer Vision module (CV-m), which attempts to identify the captured object; once it is identified, the end-user receives the information about the captured object; the information is provided by authorized third parties and stakeholders (e.g., local authorities, museums) that uses CHISTA authoring tool to import the information into the system remote databases.

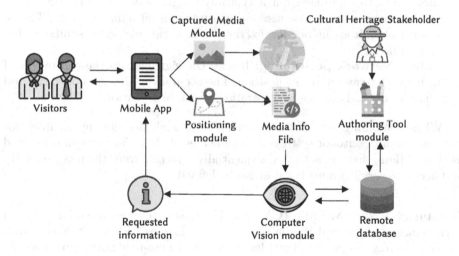

Fig. 1. High level architecture of CHISTA

Authoring Tool Module (AT-m): The authoring tool is a web service which is offered to authorized stakeholders who want to import new information (e.g., import a new heritage object) or edit stored information (e.g., change information about a heritage object). For each object that is imported in the system databases, a series of photos along with its geo-location must be provided.

Captured Media Module (CM-m): To capture the media (i.e., take a photo or record a video of a cultural heritage object), the built-in camera of the mobile device is used.

Positioning Module (P-m): The Positioning module (P-m) identifies the location of the end-user, exploiting the functionalities of the mobile device and the network input parameters. In particular, it is based on:

- **Global Positioning System (GPS) receiver:** GPS-enabled devices are typically accurate to within a 4.9 m radius under open sky [4]. However, the accuracy worsens near buildings, bridges, and trees. Focusing on Europe, European Union turned on *Galileo*[2], which is expected to include 24 live satellites by 2020 (now it includes 18) achieving accuracy within 1 m.
- **Wi-Fi positioning system:** It uses SSID and MAC address of access points, and by measuring the intensity of the received signal and by "fingerprinting" it detects the location of the mobile device. Wi-Fi location databases (e.g., Combain Positioning Service, Mozilla Location Service) are used to determine the position. The accuracy depends on the number of positions that have been entered into the database, but it typically ranges between 0.6 to 4 m. In the near future, it can also be used for an indoor positioning system (IPS) to perform ubiquitous indoor localization on a worldwide scale, similar to the GPS outdoors [16].
- **Mobile Network positioning:** It uses the signals from the cell towers of the network to ascertain the position. The accuracy of this method varies and it heavily depends on the concentration of cell base stations.

When combining any of these techniques a high positioning accuracy for both indoor and outdoor settings can be achieved [15]. They can also be used as three pillars, that are activated sequentially (starting from the more sensitive and accurate service) until the position is defined.

Computer Vision Module (CV-m). The Computer Vision module (CV-m) derives insights from multimedia material (e.g., images, videos). It detects various objects (e.g., popular natural landmarks and man-made structures) within images and through a modeling and classification approach, it identifies the object. The classification is based on a threshold score of the prediction algorithm (e.g., 0.50 out of 1.00). Various APIs can be integrated into the CV-m, such as Cloud Vision API[3] and Microsoft Azure[4]. New sets of labeled images can be inserted in the CV-m and, after a number of training sessions, they can be used to detect an object via multimedia classification.

---

[2] http://ec.europa.eu/growth/sectors/space/galileo_en.
[3] https://cloud.google.com/vision.
[4] https://azure.microsoft.com/en-us/services/cognitive-services/computer-vision.

2.2 Evaluation

The evaluation of our prototype was based on the following scenario: a visitor of an archaeological site sees a building and wants to know about it. She/he takes her/his smart-phone; launches CHISTA mobile application; takes a photo; sends the photo to CHISTA server; the computer vision module identifies (or not) the captured object after using machine learning/classification services and matches it with a database instance; the server sends the requested information to the CHISTA mobile application. The preliminary results about the response time and the accuracy of the computer vision module follow.

Response Time. To take a photo, our participants needed about 2 s per photo. The total time depends on the number of the taken photographs, the quality of the photographs, whether the user needs to traverse some distance to cover different angles, etc. For the scope of our evaluation study, we stick to the simplest scenario (i.e., one photo). The photo is uploaded to the CHISTA server. The upload time depends on the Internet connection and the filesize. We used a typical smartphone to capture a 1920×1080 photo of about 3.5 MB. The upload time is expected less than 7 s with a typical line or 3G/4G connection. 5G speeds will shorten the time to less than 1.5 s. The computer vision module runs in remote powerful web-servers and completes its prediction processes in less than 5 s, considering that the approximate location of the capture object is provided. The download of the matched information depends on the network connection, but it typically needs less than 1 s. Hence, the user receives information about a heritage object in less than 12 s. The time is acceptable, but further work is needed to optimize the processes of the computer vision module and to compress more efficiently the captured media.

Prediction Accuracy. For the computer vision module, we trained and evaluated the prediction mechanism following Microsoft Azure Vision services. The more popular a cultural heritage object (e.g., monument) is, the more accurate the prediction is (i.e., more than .950). In case of less popular cultural heritage objects, more labeled images are required, in varying environmental conditions, to train more efficiently the prediction mechanism and achieve results with high accuracy. It is worth mentioning that when the position, within a tolerance range, of the cultural heritage object was considered for the prediction process, we achieved accuracy higher than .950.

3 Discussion, Lessons Learned and Impact

We used advanced but common technologies to design a robust software system that can be used (a) by authorized cultural heritage stakeholders to store information and (b) by visitors/travelers to obtain information about a cultural heritage object. The preliminary results of the small-scale evaluation study indicate that CHISTA delivers the information in a short time with high accuracy.

Conventional technologies can adequately deliver such results. Everyday smart devices can be used to capture an image/video of a heritage object, and, through web services, remote and powerful computer vision modules can identify the captured object and send textual/graphical information about it. However, further work is needed to optimize the process (both in terms of classification accuracy and delivery time) to provide better cultural experiences to the end-users (e.g., visitors, travelers). Moreover, an important parameter of the CHISTA approach is its social impact. We summarize it into the following pillars:

- **Promotion of cultural heritage.** The heart of our application is each item or experience that has a heritage story to tell; it can be either a historic relic, an art exhibit, or an archaeological site. The ultimate goal is to transfer the historical knowledge through the provided technological platform.
- **Growth of the touristic flow.** The efficient and effective promotion of the application is expected to contribute to the growth of the touristic flow, which in turn will benefit economically and commercially rural areas with rich cultural heritage. In addition, the possibility of providing gamified experiences through our application (e.g., hidden treasure game), could contribute to the increase of the touristic flow in wider areas, stimulate the local economies and increase the public revenue for local and regional authorities.
- **Inclusion to the information society.** The use of our application contributes to the inclusion to the information society of the historical relics, art exhibits, archaeological sites etc. and of the local communities where they are located. The digitization of cultural heritage entails not only the creation of a rich database for the art exhibits, the historical relics etc., but also of a dynamic constantly growing and evolving information society of the cultural wealth of a country.
- **Knowledge acquisition and sharing.** Through the gamification elements and the configurable content of the platform, knowledge acquisition is achieved at a preferable pace and way for the user. Each one is a member of a worldwide cultural community with multiple benefits both for the user and the community, including the communication with other users and the sharing of the acquired knowledge, the socialization and the virtual empathy.

4   Conclusion and Future Work

In this paper we presented our preliminary work on designing and evaluating CHISTA software system, that we envision that will be used (a) by visitors and travelers to retrieve information about cultural heritage objects and (b) by content providers (e.g., museums, heritage institutions, local authorities) to store information about cultural heritage objects. We anticipate that CHISTA will trigger (a) the active participation of the users and arousal of the public for exploring, evaluating and formulating cultural information and (b) the movement towards the adoption of a worldwide framework for interconnecting cultural heritage stakeholders (e.g., visitors, curators, institutions). As an impact of the aforementioned anticipated results, we expect CHISTA to contribute to (a) the promotion of the cultural heritage of diverse areas, (b) the growth of the touristic flow, (c) the inclusion to the information society, and d) the knowledge acquisition and sharing. Our immediate future steps consist of (a) expanding our dataset, (b) testing and evaluating various classifiers and deep learning algorithms to improve the precision and the accuracy of the prediction procedure, (c) testing the effectiveness and efficiency of our system in remote areas (e.g. rural areas) and when having increased traffic load.

References

1. van Aart, C., Wielinga, B., van Hage, W.R.: Mobile cultural heritage guide: location-aware semantic search. In: Cimiano, P., Pinto, H.S. (eds.) EKAW 2010. LNCS, vol. 6317, pp. 257–271. Springer, Heidelberg (2010). https://doi.org/10.1007/978-3-642-16438-5_18
2. Ali, S., Koleva, B., Bedwell, B., Benford, S.: Deepening visitor engagement with museum exhibits through hand-crafted visual markers. In: Proceedings of the 2018 Designing Interactive Systems Conference, DIS 2018, pp. 523–534. ACM, New York (2018). https://doi.org/10.1145/3196709.3196786
3. Blöckner, M., Danti, S., Forrai, J., Broll, G., De Luca, A.: Please touch the exhibits!: using NFC-based interaction for exploring a museum. In: Proceedings of the 11th International Conference on Human-Computer Interaction with Mobile Devices and Services, MobileHCI 2009, pp. 71:1–71:2. ACM, New York (2009). https://doi.org/10.1145/1613858.1613943
4. van Diggelen, F., Enge, P.: The worlds first GPS MOOC and worldwide laboratory using smartphones. In: Proceedings of the 28th International Technical Meeting of The Satellite Division of the Institute of Navigation, ION GNSS+ 2015, pp. 361–369 (2015)
5. Duguleana, M., Brodi, R., Girbacia, F., Postelnicu, C., Machidon, O., Carrozzino, M.: Time-travelling with mobile augmented reality: a case study on the Piazza dei Miracoli. In: Ioannides, M., et al. (eds.) EuroMed 2016. LNCS, vol. 10058, pp. 902–912. Springer, Cham (2016). https://doi.org/10.1007/978-3-319-48496-9_73
6. Emmanouilidis, C., Koutsiamanis, R.A., Tasidou, A.: Mobile guides: taxonomy of architectures, context awareness, technologies and applications. J. Netw. Comput. Appl. **36**(1), 103–125 (2013). https://doi.org/10.1016/j.jnca.2012.04.007
7. Liestøl, G.: Along the Appian Way. Storytelling and memory across time and space in mobile augmented reality. In: Ioannides, M., Magnenat-Thalmann, N., Fink, E., Žarnić, R., Yen, A.Y., Quak, E. (eds.) EuroMed 2014. LNCS, vol. 8740, pp. 248–257. Springer, Cham (2014). https://doi.org/10.1007/978-3-319-13695-0_24
8. Malavolta, I., Ruberto, S., Soru, T., Terragni, V.: Hybrid mobile apps in the Google play store: an exploratory investigation. In: Proceedings of the Second ACM International Conference on Mobile Software Engineering and Systems, MOBILESoft 2015, pp. 56–59. IEEE Press, Piscataway (2015). http://dl.acm.org/citation.cfm?id=2825041.2825051
9. Raptis, G., Katsini, C., Chrysikos, T.: Design of a mobile computing system to obtain information from cultural heritage sites. In: Proceedings of the Pan-Hellenic Conference on Digital Cultural Heritage, Volos, Greece, pp. 371–378 (2015)

10. Ruf, B., Kokiopoulou, E., Detyniecki, M.: Mobile museum guide based on fast SIFT recognition. In: Detyniecki, M., Leiner, U., Nürnberger, A. (eds.) AMR 2008. LNCS, vol. 5811, pp. 170–183. Springer, Heidelberg (2010). https://doi.org/10.1007/978-3-642-14758-6_14

11. Verykokou, S., Ioannidis, C., Kontogianni, G.: 3D visualization via augmented reality: the case of the middle Stoa in the ancient Agora of Athens. In: Ioannides, M., Magnenat-Thalmann, N., Fink, E., Žarnić, R., Yen, A.-Y., Quak, E. (eds.) EuroMed 2014. LNCS, vol. 8740, pp. 279–289. Springer, Cham (2014). https://doi.org/10.1007/978-3-319-13695-0_27

12. Wecker, A.J., Kuflik, T., Stock, O.: AMuse: connecting indoor and outdoor cultural heritage experiences. In: Proceedings of the 22nd International Conference on Intelligent User Interfaces Companion, IUI 2017 Companion, pp. 153–156. ACM, New York (2017). https://doi.org/10.1145/3030024.3040980

13. Wein, L.: Visual recognition in museum guide apps: do visitors want it? In: Proceedings of the SIGCHI Conference on Human Factors in Computing Systems, CHI 2014, pp. 635–638. ACM, New York (2014). https://doi.org/10.1145/2556288.2557270

14. Wolff, A., Mulholland, P., Maguire, M., O'Donovan, D.: Mobile technology to support coherent story telling across freely explored outdoor artworks. In: Proceedings of the 11th Conference on Advances in Computer Entertainment Technology, ACE 2014, pp. 3:1–3:8. ACM, New York (2014). https://doi.org/10.1145/2663806.2663829

15. Yokoi, T., Oikawa, K.: Utilization of weak received signal strength for accurate indoor position estimation. In: 2018 IEEE/ION Position, Location and Navigation Symposium, PLANS, pp. 228–233. IEEE (2018)

16. Youssef, M.: Towards truly ubiquitous indoor localization on a worldwide scale. In: Proceedings of the 23rd SIGSPATIAL International Conference on Advances in Geographic Information Systems, SIGSPATIAL 2015, pp. 12:1–12:4. ACM, New York (2015). https://doi.org/10.1145/2820783.2820883

17. Zikas, P., Bachlitzanakis, V., Papaefthymiou, M., Papagiannakis, G.: A mobile, AR inside-out positional tracking algorithm, (MARIOPOT), suitable for modern, affordable cardboard-style VR HMDs. In: Ioannides, M., et al. (eds.) EuroMed 2016. LNCS, vol. 10058, pp. 257–268. Springer, Cham (2016). https://doi.org/10.1007/978-3-319-48496-9_21

Digital Applications for Materials
Preservation in Cultural Heritage

Ancient Sandbox Technique: An Experimental Study Using Piezoelectric Sensors

Trishala Daka[iD], Lokesh Udatha[iD],
Venkata Dilip Kumar Pasupuleti[✉][iD], Prafulla Kalapatapu[iD],
and Bharghava Rajaram[iD]

Mahindra École Centrale, Hyderabad, India
dakamalakondareddy@gmail.com,
lokesh9.udatha@gmail.com, {venkata.pasupuleti,
prafulla.kalapatapu, bharghava.rajaram}@mechyd.ac.in

Abstract. Ancient Indian temples are accredited for their immaculate style of construction. These temples are resistant to most natural calamities due to their geometry, material and construction technique. Of these, the foundation is considered to be the major contributing factor for their structural stability. Research on ancient foundation techniques can bring about a huge impact on today's foundation technologies. This paper presents a study on the *Sandbox Technique* for foundations, which was used around the 11th century, by the Kakatiya Dynasty in Telangana (South India). The sandbox technique was used to build the foundation for two major temples in Telangana viz. Ramappa temple and 1000 pillar temple. As part of our study, we carried out experiments on sand (dry and wet) and wet Red soil materials by building a model which mimics the Sandbox technique. In this context, piezoelectric knock sensors are used to capture the vibrations. We determined the dampening of vibrations for sand (dry & wet) and wet Red soil for various types of loads. Our analysis of the results obtained shows that sand with water absorbs more vibrations as compared to dry sand and wet Red soil.

Keywords: Indian temples · Sandbox technique · Earthquake resistant
Piezoelectric knock sensor

1 Introduction

Ancient and historical structures have always impressed the current generations. Especially, a few of these structures are not only visually attractive, but are extremely stable owing to the kind of architecture and materials used in building them. These structures stand as a testament to time and the frequency occurrence of natural calamities like earthquakes, floods, etc. While most of these structures are observed to have a certain order or pattern with spiritual and/or cosmological meaning, only in the recent decades have scientists and engineers started to give scientific/logical reasons behind the architecture, materials and a structures weathering over the ages.

In India, especially, most of these historical structures are temples. Even though their geometry is not similar, their purpose is assumed to be the same. An Indian temple

© Springer Nature Switzerland AG 2018
M. Ioannides et al. (Eds.): EuroMed 2018, LNCS 11197, pp. 173–184, 2018.
https://doi.org/10.1007/978-3-030-01765-1_20

is an architectural entity imbued with certain concepts about Gods and human beings developed somewhere around 4500 years ago during the initial stages of Indus civilization [1]. Although constructions in several parts of India make use of material local to them to construct stable structures (like bamboos), their lifespan is limited to at most 40 years. Ancient temples, however, are constructed from stone so that they can retain their stability for several centuries, even millennia [2]. Temple architecture is observed to follow a set of guidelines or rules known to be from "*Vaastu shastra*" [3]. A temple is typically constructed on a square or rectangular plot as they provide good structural grid and aesthetic appeal. Vaastu emphasis on symmetrical structures in both plan and elevation.

Most of the studies carried out so far concentrate more on super structures like architecture, material, arrangement, order, pattern, science behind the distribution of spaces, reasons behind the scripts, evolvement of construction techniques, role of five elements of nature, comparison of human body and temple architecture and shapes inspired from nature. But there has been noticeably less study on the foundations of historical structures, especially Indian temples, since most of these temples are still living and it is very difficult to access or get permission to excavate to understand the nature of foundations. Foundations are very vital for the stability of these structures. This study focuses on one special technique known as the *"Sandbox technique"* which was used to construct foundations of two temples in south India and is said to be resistant towards earthquakes.

2   Background

Restoration of historical structures has become a priority in recent days owing to the increased degradation of these structures due to exposure to man-made and natural calamities. Foundation restoration is particularly a difficult task. Two famous historical monuments which had a problem in their foundations and restored later are the Tower of Pisa and the Cathedral of Mexico City [4]. Most of the ancient structures were built on shallow foundations consisting of stone or brick and different types of mortar. Generally, these foundations are made by dropping rubble or debris into excavation, equal to or slightly wider than the underground structure, and pour poor mortar onto it. Foundation size usually depended more on the available space than on active loading and bearing capacity. The review of historical building foundations done by Przewłóck et al. [5], deal with Romanesque foundations, Gothic foundations, Renaissance, Baroque era, Neoclassical period foundations. Methodologies changed according to the age of structures built. While providing description of historical cities situated in the bank of rivers, along the rivers where high groundwater levels are available, the authors do not provide any information on the sandbox technique. During that period the existing techniques have not allowed for deeper excavations below ground water level for laying foundations leading to non-removal of soft or organic soils underlying foundations with sands or gravels, which is very similar to "Sandbox" technique. Even in the early days, the foundations constructed on soft soils are in the form of several beds of large stones or bricks resting on wooden piles or rafts. So there is no literature actually available on "Sandbox" technique and reasons supporting it to be earthquake resistance. Gokhale [7] has discussed on architectural heritage and seismic design with reference to Indian temple architecture, but as described earlier even this paper restricts itself to the super structure architecture in both plan and space. The ancient literature of Brahma Samhita, which is said to consist of 107 chapters on science and technology, describes earthquakes and various aspects with reference to earthquake resistance of the Indian temples [6]. Indian temples, which are standing with an unsurpassed allure and glory against the forces of nature, are the living shreds of evidence of structural efficiency and technological mastery of craftsmen in those days [7]. These temples are resistant to earthquakes, floods, heavy winds and also man-made disastrous with minimal damage. One of the major reasons for structural stability is its foundation, geometry and arrangement of construction material. Foundations, especially, provide the necessary reinforcement against natural calamities. As there has been no significant work or literature on the Sandbox technique, a small experimental study is carried out to understand it's characteristics.

3 Ancient Indian Temples Built Using Sandbox Technique

There are many ancient historical structures in India that withstood natural disasters. For our study, we considered two major temples viz. the Ramappa temple and the Thousand Pillar temple, both constructed by the Kakatiya dynasty at Warangal, Telangana, India. These are said to be constructed using Sandbox technology.

3.1 Ramappa Temple

Ramappa temple is an architectural marvel and described as "The brightest star in the galaxy of medieval temples in the Deccan". This temple is located in a valley, and is constructed with light bricks which can float on water. The structural base stood on a 6 ft tall, star-shaped platform [8]. The Ramappa temple is an excellent example of their art, music and dance which can be seen in the intricate sculptures embellishing walls, pillars and ceiling of the marvelous edifice. The main structure is built with reddish sandstone, but the columns outside the temple have large brackets of black basalt. These are carved as mythical animals, female dancers, musicians; which depicts "the Kakatiyas art, for their delicate carving, sensuous postures and elongated bodies and heads" [9]. We visited both the sites to investigate three major parameters: dimensions, various materials used and damage portions. Few pictures taken by us at Ramappa temple are shown in the Fig. 1.

3.2 Thousand Pillar Temple

Another one of the Kakatiyas' constructions that remained undisturbed was Thousand Pillar Temple as shown in Fig. 2 situated in Warangal, Telangana, India and its foundation Technique is referred as Sandbox technique, constructed by King Rudra Deva in 1163 A.D. It has its own unique style of construction and took 72 years to complete the construction; there were 1000 pillars although no pillar obstructs to see the God.

Fig. 1. (a) Ramappa temple (b) Main Sanctum (c) Removed elements (d) Base distortion due to earthquake

Fig. 2. (a) Thousand pillar temple (b) Rearrangement and reconstruction of damaged temple (c) Close view of pillars construction

3.3   Sandbox Technique

For Sandbox foundation, a minimum 3 m depth is dug with infill mixture of sand, granite, jaggery, and Terminalia Chebula. This sandbox acts like a cushion so the structure built on this sand foundation will survive an earthquake as most of the vibrations of the earthquake lose their strength by the time they are transferred through the sandbox to reach the actual foundation. As there are no written evidences of this technique and no prototype models are available, there can be two approaches to prove the phenomenon one being site investigation and other experimental testing. As the former one would be very difficult as it is sub structure and foundation of ancient structure. So an experimental study has been carried out, and is presented in the following sections.

4   Experiment

4.1   Experimental Setup

In order to evaluate the sandbox technique, we constructed the apparatus as shown in Fig. 3. The upper plank emulates the bed rock on which the foundation and super-structure are placed. Vibrations of the super structure and the bedrock are measured simultaneously in order to determine whether the foundation inhibits propagation of any external vibrations.

Fig. 3. Complete experimental setup a. Prototype of structure, b. Piezo sensor, c. Micro controller, d. base-1, e. Spring as specifications shown in Table 1, f. base-2, g. M8 Bolt

The mechanical suspension system is built with two plywood's kept apart by four fixed springs. The plywood at the top is entitled as base-1 and plywood at the bottom is entitled as base-2 and specifications of these are shown in the Table 1. Piezoelectric knock sensors are used to capture the vibrations and an Arduino Uno R3 is used for data acquisition. In our setup, two sensors are used, one to encapsulate vibration on the bedrock and the other for the structure. A box (10 cm × 10 cm × 6 cm) made up of 1 mm thick iron sheet, filled with different types of soils is glued to base-1 and a plastic rectangular cuboid (2.5 cm × 0.5 cm × 11 cm) is assumed as the structure is placed at the center of the box that is filled. One sensor is placed at the top of this structure and another sensor is placed on small box (4 cm × 4 cm × 4 cm) made up of 1 mm thick iron sheet is glued to base-1. Arduino is connected to pc and data is collected using MATLAB.

Table 1. Specifications of springs

Specification	Value
Spring constant	2.154 N/mm
True maximum load	75.580 N
Diameter of spring	1.40 mm
Inner diameter of spring	9.00 mm
Free length of the spring	116 mm
Number of active coils	15

4.2 Soil Samples Considered

Rajagopal et al. [10] describes various soil types found in and around the Warangal region. Two samples available nearer the site are considered for these studies which are shown in the Fig. 4. Properties of soil are given in Table 2. Major reason for considering red soil is to compare its behavior with sand during earthquakes or during the floods if they have been used for foundation. But this study concentrates more on the behavior of sand with and without moisture. Water content considered for this study for the sand is 10% of its volume, whereas for red soil, the soil is tested in its natural state.

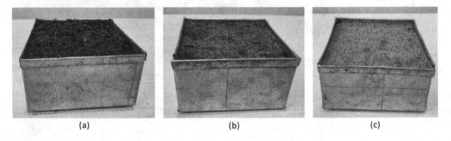

(a)   (b)   (c)

Fig. 4. Soil samples considered for this study a. Red soil with moisture, b. Sand with water, c. Sand without water

Table 2. Properties of sand and red soil

Properties	Sand	Red soil
Density (kg/m3)	1682	2650
Fineness modulus	2.75	3.1
Specific gravity	2.656	2.64

4.3 Load Conditions

For this study, three load conditions have been considered; impact force, initial displacement and forced vibration. Although the main motive of the experiment is to understand the behavior of the sandbox under seismic loading (vibrations), impact force was also considered as one of the load conditions since there were blasting done nearer to the temple using gelatin sticks for water tunneling. Impact force is given to the system as shown in Fig. 5. As it can be seen from the zoomed image of Fig. 5, there is an indication of initial and impact distance. The bob which is attached to the axle blade is given an impact distance which would hit exactly at the center of the base plate-1 causing the impact force. The distance for initial condition is 6 cm and bob is displaced by another 6 cm to generate inertial force. So the total distance for impact force considered is 12 cm and for second load condition to generate free vibration an initial displacement of 1.5 cm us given to base plate-1. Cyclic displacements are given to base plate-1 to have a feel of forced vibrations.

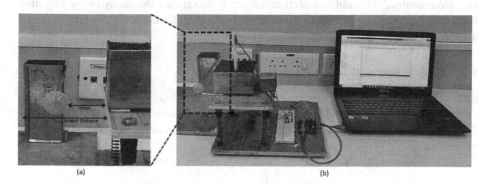

Fig. 5. Experimental setup showing load application for impact load

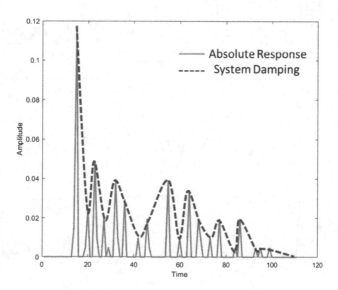

Fig. 6. Damping response of the system

5 Observations and Interpretation

The first task we performed was to validate the experimental setup itself and calibrate the Piezo sensors used with respect to the absolute displacement. For validation of the system, frequency analysis is carried out to calculate the natural frequency of the system. We checked if this natural frequency of vibration is the same throughout the system. We observed that both the bedrock and the superstructure vibrated at the same frequency. This natural frequency only changes when modifications are made to the superstructure. After all the validations have been carried out, results were computed to understand the damping present in the system. Figure 6 shows the plot of the free vibration obtained with red soil with moisture; it also shows the decay in the vibration from which the damping of the system can be computed. Below are the results obtained for three different cases considered for this study.

5.1 Case-1: Red Soil with Moisture

Red soil with natural moisture is considered for this study. Figure 7 shows three different graphs for three different load conditions. For impact force and free vibration the peaks are observed to be at the same location, which indicate the natural frequency of the system.

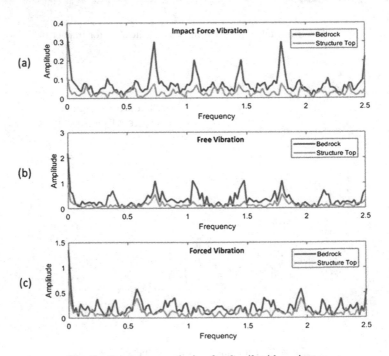

Fig. 7. Frequency analysis of red soil with moisture

From Fig. 7(a) and (b), it can be interpreted that there is a drastic reduction in the amplitude of the vibration. That is the main principle of the sandbox technique, by the time earthquake wave reaches the structural base, it loses its energy. Plot in Fig. 7(c) represents a forced vibration and peaks cannot be observed properly. The frequency of the system is 0.55 Hz.

5.2   Case-2: Sand with Water

See Fig. 8.

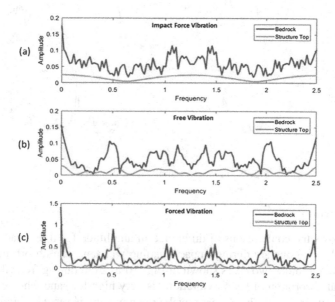

Fig. 8. Frequency analysis of sand with water

5.3   Case-3: Sand Without Water

Figure 8 shows the frequency response of the sand with water and its frequency is much lesser when compared to red soil with moisture. The frequency of the system is observed to be 0.22 Hz which is 40% of the red soil with moisture discussed in case-1. Another important observation is be the amplitude difference which is very large between the bedrock and structure top; henceforth, sand with water can absorb the necessary seismic waves more compared to red soil. Also the amplitude of the structural top is almost constant for impact and free vibrations.

Similarly Fig. 9 shows the frequency response of sand without water. Surprisingly the frequency of the system is observed to be 0.11 Hz, actually much less than both the cases above. Energy dissipation is also found to be similar to wet sand, but it is not much of constant. Forced vibration frequency analysis is almost similar in both the cases except the amplitude difference which is larger in the wet sand.

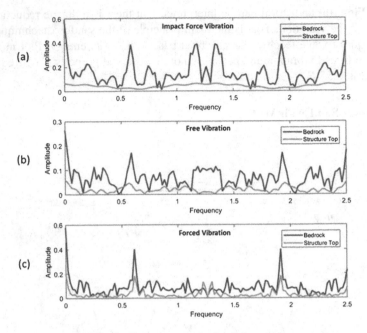

Fig. 9. Frequency analysis of dry sand

5.4 Comparison

Figure 10 shows the comparisons of difference in amplitude for three load conditions. Few major observations are during impact loading wet sand can absorb more energy when compared to other two cases shown in Fig. 10(a). And during free vibration, it is very clear that absorption of lateral vibrations is very high for sand when compared to red soil as shown in Fig. 10(b). As earthquake phenomenon is forced vibration, Fig. 10 (c) is a comparison of forced vibrations and analysis made that sand with and without water can absorb lateral vibrations.

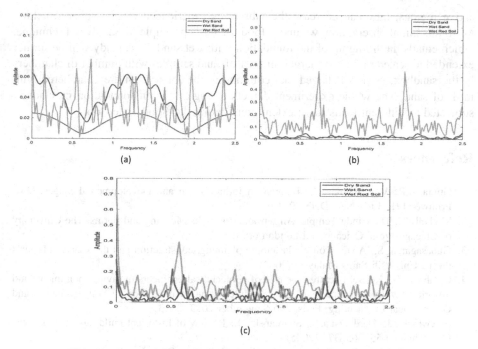

Fig. 10. Comparison plots between different soils for different loads.

Table 3 shows the percentage reduction in amplitude for the three cases discussed in above sections along with three different load conditions. Results indicate the absolute difference between the bed rock and structure at top. Thus, structural top vibrations are very less for the sand with water when compared to other two cases.

Table 3. Percentage of reduction in amplitude for different soils and different loads

S. no	Type of force	Reduction in amplitude (%)		
		Red soil with moisture	Sand with water	Dry sand
1	Impact force	51.4	70.8	59.6
2	Free vibration	32	61.9	45.6
3	Forced vibration	27	79.1	57.49

6 Conclusion

The Sandbox foundation technique has not been well explored in literature, although they are supposed to be resistant to earthquakes. In this context, this paper presented a preliminary study to understand the sandbox technique; through the experiment on three soil materials and a prototype model built to mimic a sandbox. Our study concludes that if sand with, and without water, is used for the foundations in seismically active regions, they can decrease the vibrations experienced by the super structure. From this initial observation, we understood the basic principle of Sandbox Technique, which entails the filling up of the foundation with wet sand. This study will be further extended to scaled models for larger number of sand samples with number of chambers in the sandbox, as it is believed that columns in the foundation are chambered with infill of sand. The whole experiment depicts a single column foundation in sandbox subjected to different loads to an extent considering the flood water too.

References

1. Gupta, S.P., Vijayakumar, S.: Temples in India: Origin and Developmental Stages. D.K. Printwood (P) Ltd., New Delhi (2010)
2. Michell, G.: The Hindu Temple: An Introduction to Its Meaning and Forms. The University of Chicago Press, Chicago and London (1988)
3. Gunasagaran, S.: A study on hindu temple planning, construction and the vaastu. Master's thesis. Universiti Sains Malaysia (2002)
4. Calabresi, G.: Kerisel Lecture - the role of geotechnical engineers in saving monuments and historic sites. In: Proceedings of the 18th International Conference on Soil Mechanics and Geotechnical Engineering, Paris, 2–6 September 2013 (2013)
5. Przewłócki, J., Dardzińska, I., Świniański, J.: Review of historical buildings' foundations. Geotechnique 55, 363–372 (2005)
6. Acharya, P.K.: An Encyclopedia of Hindu Architecture. QUp, London (1946)
7. Gokhale, V.A.: Architectural heritage and seismic design with reference to indian temple architecture. In: Proceedings of 13th World Conference on Earthquake Engineering, Vancouver, B.C., Canada, 1–6 August 2004 (2004)
8. Telangana Tourism Home page. http://www.telanganatourism.gov.in.html
9. Wikipedia. https://en.wikipedia.org/wiki/Ramappa_Temple#cite_note-4
10. Rajagopal, V., Prabhu Prasadini, P., Pazanivelan, S., Balakrishnan, N.: Characterization and classification of soils in Warangal district of Central Telangana zone. Madras Agric. J. 100 (4–6), 432–437 (2013)

Application of Non-destructive Techniques (Raman Spectroscopy and XRF) into an Icon by Michael Damaskinos

Nikolaos Gkoultas[1], Theodore Ganetsos[1(✉)], Maria Peraki[2],
Dimitrios Tseles[1], and Nikolaos Laskaris[1]

[1] Department of Industrial Design and Production Engineering,
School of Engineering, University of West Attica, Athens, Greece
ganetsos@puas.gr
[2] School of Mining and Metallurgical Engineering,
National Technical University of Athens, Athens, Greece

Abstract. The tremendous growth of technology, aims to serve human and scientific methods, which serve the analysis of the study of our cultural heritage. Initially, most techniques developed, applied to different fields of the cultural heritage, however along the way it was observed that they serve in the analysis of works of art. Such techniques are Raman spectroscopy (Raman spectroscopy) and X-ray Florescence (XRF). In this thesis, we present the study of these techniques on a portable icon of Michael Damaskinos of the Cretan School of the 16th century. Specifically, a study will be conducted on the chemical composition and pigment detection of qualitative and quantitative data in a portable picture of Michael Damaskinos of the Cretan School of the 16th century. The object of this study, is associated with P.G.C. (Post Graduate Course) as it includes innovative applications of automation technologies. The study will cover the gap in the literature of icons and inferences will be made on the use of Raman Spectroscopy and XRF.

Keywords: Spectroscopy · Raman · XRF · Michael Damaskinos

1 Introduction

The town of Galaxidi which is located in the southeastern part of the Prefecture of fokida West of Krisaios Bay is a coastal town that is built on the site of the ancient city of Oianthia or Chalaion. It has approximately 4,000 years of history with a very important role in the struggle of 1821. The town of Galaxidi is 215 km from Athens. It is one of the oldest maritime States both as far as building ships is concerned and for its maritime commercial fleet.

1.1 Sights of the Town of Galaxidi

The Church of Agios Nikolaos, Agia Paraskevi of Galaxidi. The monastery of the Transfiguration of Christ and the Church of St. John the Baptist, which dates back to 1833 is a small one-aisled church without a dome. Inside the church you find the icon

© Springer Nature Switzerland AG 2018
M. Ioannides et al. (Eds.): EuroMed 2018, LNCS 11197, pp. 185–195, 2018.
https://doi.org/10.1007/978-3-030-01765-1_21

of Agia Anna painted by Michael Damaskinos in the 16th century. The icon depicts the Holy Virgin, Anna, Christ, St. Nicholas and St. Anthony. The icon dimensions are 102×73 cm. The icon depicts Saint Anne on the throne, holding in her arms the Virgin Mary, who is holding the little Christ and these three forms are located on an axis. Left and right, the Saints Nicholas and Anthony respectively (see Fig. 1).

Fig. 1. Icon of Agia Anna painted by Michael Damaskinos

1.2   Byzantine Art

The term Byzantine art was originally coined to name the artistic production of the Byzantine Empire from the 4th century until 1453 with the fall of Constantinople. Furthermore, the term of Byzantine art applies to art that faithfully followed the same principles outside the spatiotemporal boundaries of Byzantium. The Empire's capital Constantinople was the most important centre of Byzantine art. The Byzantine art spread rapidly throughout much of the Mediterranean world from Eastern Europe to Russia and Armenia.

When Christianity prevailed and the Christian imperial power was established in the Byzantine Empire, Byzantine art was the principal medium for the visualization of the transcendental world and a means to spread the messages of the new religion and the new socio-political ideology. The creation of works of Byzantine art was to cover a wide range of practical needs (worshiping, teaching, sociopolitical and private). The aim of the artist was the artistic integrity and it was not an easy task to generate these austere forms that prevail in Byzantine art. To serve the aesthetic pleasure but at the same time to serve as a medium for the utilitarian function they performed. In this sense, the Byzantine art is "militant".

The periods of Byzantine Orthodox hagiography are as follows

- Earliest Christian period (30 BC–AD 325)
- Early Christian period (4th–7th century AD)
- Iconoclasm (726–842 AD)
- Macedonian dynasty (867–1057 AD)
- Comnenan dynasty (1057–1185 AD)
- Paleologou run 14th century
    - Macedonian school
    - Cretan school
- 16th–17th century. Acme of portable icons. There's a hcyday of portable icons with main representatives: Michael Damaskinos, Lampardo, Victor, Poulakis, Mosko, Jane, etc.
- 18th–19th century folk art (see Fig. 2).

Fig. 2. Madonna Della misericordia

1.3   Late Byzantine Period

After the occupation of Constantinople from the Franks and up to its fall, is the time frame where the boundaries for the late Byzantine art lie. Byzantium, during this period does not exist anymore as a powerful political and cultural centre of the post-Byzantine era. The illustrations of the late Byzantine period base their principle on elements of the post-Byzantine era, and are gradually enriched with themes of childhood and the passions of Christ or the life of the Virgin Mary. As it is very common to use expressions of the old testament they are considered to be foretelling the New Testament.

The painting of this period, displayed naturalistic elements most vividly, while quite a few artists gradually seek a more subjective depiction of the traditional subjects they develop, with the result of highlighting the expressions of persons or the movement of the figures depicted. During the late Byzantine period, the art of the portable icon reaches its greatest heyday, with lots of pictures surviving until today (see Fig. 2).

1.4   Michael Damaskinos

Michael Damaskinos was a painter of Cretan origin who lived in the second half of the 16th century. Born between 1530–1535 in Heraklion, Crete which at the time was occupied by Venetians and was known as Candia, he is one of the most important figures of post-Byzantine painting of the Cretan school. He was taught the art of icon painting in the school of the Holy Catherine Sinaitwn in Heraklion. Then at the age of 32, he worked and studied for a long time in Venice. In Venice he came into contact with all modern styles of art. In his works the influence of Western painting and Renaissance art is evident though he chose to rely more on the characteristics and peculiarity of the Greek technique (maniera greca) and to a lesser extent on Latin technique (maniera latina) Michael Damaskinos had multiple influences from various Italian painters of the Renaissance such as Raffaello, Leonardo da Vinchi and he was influenced especially by "the last supper", which also inspired the depiction of space with the use of geometric perspective in relevant work of his.

2   Spectroscopy

The number of techniques by which the interactions of electromagnetic radiation in connection with the matter, such as atoms, ions and molecules are analyzed, are called spectroscopic methods. With each interaction transition of energy levels in them can be triggered or even a redefinition of their direction. More specifically it appears:

- Scattering: the interaction of radiation causes redirecting of matter and there may also be transfer of energy sometimes.
- Transmission: It is displayed when there is a transition from a high level to a lower one and throughout the process a transfer of energy is displayed in the radiation field.
- Absorption: when the radiation occurs when a molecule or atom moves from a low energy level to a higher one and within the process a transfer of energy to it occurs.

The results arising from the interactions between matter and radiation can be used for the analysis of the structure of molecules and atoms [1]. In addition, there can be a qualitative and quantitative determination of inorganic and organic compounds with the help of fasmatometers which record the intensity of radiation emitted by an object and then it can be compared to the volume of the reference beam [2].

2.1   Electromagnetic Spectrum

The term Electromagnetic spectrum applies to the area's range of frequencies occupied by electromagnetic waves. The wavelength of the electromagnetic spectrum is 10^{-9} nm, with a limit on the radio waves with a wavelength exceeding 1000 km. The electromagnetic spectrum depending on the characteristic properties of electromagnetic waves, is split into the following categories.

- X-rays
- gamma rays
- ultraviolet radiation
- visible radiation
- infrared radiation
- radio waves
- microwaves.

In all regions of the electromagnetic spectrum, molecular, electronic and nuclear changes are observed and are responsible for energy transfer (quantum) of the condition of the chemical molecules. In the region range of x-rays and γ-rays observed ionizations and cuts of molecules are observed. In the ultraviolet and visible region, energy fluctuations that correspond to vibrations of the atoms and molecules are stimulated, while in the infrared region there is a stimulation of energy levels. In the area of radio waves swirling particles movements, the spin of the electron and nuclear spin appear (NMR) [3].

2.2   Advantages of Spectroscopic Techniques

The spectroscopic techniques are applied in many fields nowadays such as the medical, pharmaceutical, in geology, biology, in agriculture even in culture. They are mainly used for solving problems that are related to the structure of the identification and quantitative analysis of some compounds and they have some important advantages:

1. Measurements aren't time-consuming
2. In many occasions we need no sample for examination
3. Great sensitivity and accuracy of measuring
4. Usability in using the method
5. Early results with the help of computer
6. Quick identification in accordance with the databases that exist [4].

2.3   Materials Examined by the Spectroscopic Techniques

There is a wide range of materials that are analysed with the use of spectroscopic techniques. In everything that has to do with the cultural heritage and civilization in general, we can get information about the materials. More specifically with raw materials and their manufacturing technology and particularly what the materials are:

Pigments, varnishes, paints and coatings
Paper, wood, papyrus, leather

Glass and enamels
Metal and alloys found in coins, jewelry and tools
Ceramics and terracotta objects
Bones, hairs remains of animal and vegetable tissues
Mortar, plaster, cement and bricks
Stone artifacts, minerals, precious and semi-precious stones, and volcanic rocks [2].

2.4   Selection Criteria for Spectroscopic Method

The selection criteria for the best suited spectroscopic method depend on the sample and what exactly we want to study. The criteria taken into account are the following

- Initial reflections and questions that are to be answered.
- The archaeological value, uniqueness or multiplicity of the sample.
- The original form and shape of the object, which should normally remain unchanged.
- The type of sample material.
- The maximum quantity that can be taken for analysis.
- The minimum amount of sample that can be analyzed with the selected method.
- The need for a full or only superficial analysis and ability for on-the-spot analysis.
- The physical condition of the object and the possible alterations.
- The ingredients or properties that must be specified [2].

2.5   Spectroscopic Methods

The spectroscopic methods used for the analysis of objects of archaeological interest are based on the measurement of radiation from a specific region of the electromagnetic spectrum. These areas are given approximately as the electromagnetic spectrum is continuous and there is overlap of their areas within their limits [2]. The methods used are, XRF, XRD, FTIR, UV-VIS, LIBS and Raman.

2.6   X-Ray Fluorescence Spectroscopy

XRF Spectroscopy has as a basic principle of operation the x-ray fluorescence spectroscopy. as the sample to be analyzed emits x-rays and that is achieved as we cause the sample to emit x-rays with the help of x-ray bulbs [2]. The XRF spectroscopy gives us information on the quantitative and qualitative analysis, biological, environmental, geological and other specimens. It is a non-destructive method with fast results, multielemental and can be applied to a wide range of concentrations. As it is a handy technique it does not require any special preparation of the sample before the study and it is easy to analyse the spectra [5].

The wavelengths or energy emitted by x-ray in the sample provide information for the analysis of its chemical elements and by the intensity of the x-rays we understand the concentrations of components. The depth of the sample to analyze, ranges from 1 mm to 1 cm and it depends on its composition and the energy of the emitted x-rays [6].

The XRF Spectroscopy can be used to make analysis of gas, solid and liquid samples. It can analyze chemical elements with a higher atomic number than that of aluminum (Z = 13). Within a short period of time it can detect and identify several elements simultaneously, and, to give reliable measurement results, the sample can be irradiated more than once.

Drawbacks presented in XRF Spectroscopy is that it is not sufficient for analyzing organic materials, as light elements such as hydrogen, oxygen, carbon and nitrogen cannot be analysed. Another disadvantage is that the samples to be studied should have flat surfaces, as irregular shapes are unlikely to give an accurate output [2].

2.7 The Raman Effect

The phenomenon of light scattering named Raman had previously been mentioned by A.G. Smekal (1923) and Kramers and Heisenberg (1925) respectively. It was finally named after Indian physicist Sir C.V. Raman (1888–1970), who proved it experimentally after systematic studies on the molecular scattering of light. In 1928 Sir C.V. Raman studied the phenomenon of scattering light and found that when a single cold light beam radiates on a substance, then the ray leaving vertically from the original direction is not monochromic but contains other radiations of different frequencies, which are characteristic of the nature of any material [7].

Raman Spectroscopy examines the phenomenon of change of frequency, when the light is scattered by molecules. How great the change will be, is reported as Raman frequency and the total of frequencies scattered from each kind is Raman spectrum [8].

When a pure substance in the region of the visible spectrum is eradiated, then a small part of it, of about 0.001% will be scattered by the sample in different directions than the incident radiation [9].

2.8 Advantages of Raman Spectroscopy

The advantages of Raman spectroscopy are

- That it is used for identification in inorganic and organic materials.
- Is a non-destructive method as it does not cause wear on the subject under observation and more importantly one doesn't have to take a sample from it.
- The object to be examined needs no processing before the examination.
- Raman spectroscopy is a mobile device and has the ability to examine each object in the place that it is found without having to transfer it to a specialized laboratory.
- The examination of the sample is not time-consuming [2].

2.9 Pigments

The study and identification of pigments is a research field of many scientists because it is very important to study and understand the materials and techniques used by the artists painting in different periods and regions. Through identification and analysis of pigments we are given information about the composition of pigments and the artist's color palette.

The picture of Michael Damaskinos according to historical information dating back to the 16th century. It is the first time studies are made on the identification of colours in the icon and specifically with Raman Spectroscopy and x-ray fluorescence spectroscopy (XRF) to examine and to make known what the hagiographer's used pigments are.

2.10   Color Layer

By the term color layer we mean a colored material that is applied in a thin layer over the sublayer. The thickness of the layer ranges from 1 mm up to 200 μm and depends on the technique of painting and the aesthetic result that the artist wants to give.

The color layer applied during the preparation contains one or more pigments, which are in the form of granules, scattered in organic medium where they solidify over time. The key components of the color layer is: dyes or paints, glue and solvent [10].

2.11   Pigment Materials

The materials used for colouring depending on the nature and use of them, are divided into colors or pigments and dyes. The dyes are mostly organic compounds and used to dye fabrics. Colours (pigments) are fine colored materials, forming mists with the organic medium in which they are dispersed. They do not show chemical affinity with the other components of the color layer and therefore it is necessary to use glue. The colours originate from a wide range of organic and inorganic substances, natural or artificial. Among the inorganic pigments oxides and sulphur, carbonates, sulfates, chromates and silicates of certain metals are included [10]. The most important property of a pigment is the color, which first of all determines the usefulness of it. The term colour is used to denote the chromatic sense of sight, when this reacts to external irritations or from subjective experience [11]. The cause of color existence is the property of matter to interact with electromagnetic radiation, which falls onto the surface.

The speck of paint in a pigment plays the most important role. Because its size and shape determine the uniform and easy colour layer coating, as well as the creation of a smooth surface.

The fine pigments show best results in painting as well as having good revealing ability. Another property that characterizes an ideal pigment, is the chemical stability in terms of temperature, humidity, radiation and oxygen in the atmosphere in order to avoid discoloration. A very important role is played by the specific gravity of a pigment as it should be taken into consideration when creating color layers. There have been cases where the use of mixtures of heavy and light colours, causes separation of ingredients when the colour layer is applied to a horizontal surface [10].

2.12   Pigments Used Between the 15th and 17th Century

The main colors used in the 17th century are: Red: tyrian purple derived from shells and used mainly for textile dye, cinnabar, the minium and rouge anglais. Blue pigments: azurite, Egyptian blue, indigo, verditer, cobalt blue, ultramarin and Rho blue of Prussia. Green coloring: malachite, green earth, verdigris and various plant greens.

Yellow pigments are ochre, citron, and orpiment. Brown pigments used were the ompra (baked and brute), siena (baked and brute). Whites: chalk and plaster. In a study conducted on the icons of Angel Hand of the 15th century it has been found that for white they used white lead, for black carbon black, for Red cinnabar, red lacquer and hematite, for blue azurite and lazurite, and for green, green earth and malachite was used [12].

2.13   Instrumentation

For the study of the colours of the icon, a portable Raman spectrometer of DeltaNu was used, more specifically the Rockhound 785. The measurements were made on the spot in the church where the icon is found without the need to sample and transfer it into a laboratory. There was no need for any special process or extra equipment for the installation and acquisition of spectra. The spectrometer is integrated with a color camera, which, in collaboration with the digital microscope Nu Spec, defined the focal length from which the receiving of the spectrum would take place. The maximum magnification of the objective lens of the microscope reached 100x. The wavelength of the laser was in 785 nm and that was chosen because the fluorescence phenomenon is minimized. Diode laser was used with a focus size of 35 μm and with a resolution of 5 cm^{-1}. The data obtained from measurements was processed through software program, where NuSpec is embedded inside the gauge. The range of Spectra ranging from 200 to 2000 cm^{-1}. Then, after taking the spectra that appear in the computer too, processing and studying takes place. The database used for their identification was Clark's list.

2.14   Raman Measurements

16 measurements were taken from different parts of Michael Damaskino's picture and the taking of measurements was spot on with the portable Raman spectrometer of Delta Nu. In the same places there was a second taking with x-ray fluorescence XRF Spectroscopy (Fig. 3).

Fig. 3. Portable Raman spectrometer of Delta Nu

3   Conclusion

In this work thesis we studied the colours of an icon of Michael Damaskinos found in the area of Galaxidi, prefecture of Fokida. The measurements for the study of colours made in situ on the picture with a portable Raman spectrometer and with a portable x-ray fluorescence spectrometer (XRF) (Fig. 4).

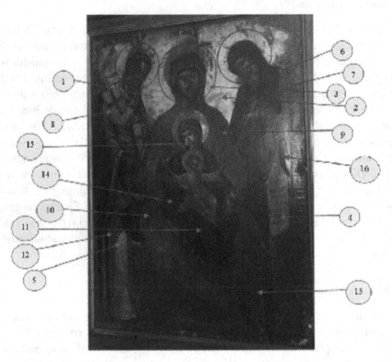

Fig. 4. Measurements were taken from different parts of Michael Damaskino's (Color figure online)

The results of the measurements showed that the pigments used for the creation of colors are: white lead, plaster, titanium oxide, zinc white, red vermillion, red ochre, red minium, carbon black, Indian yellow, citrine ocher, azurite, lazurite and blue cerulean.

The areas with white color where a combination of white lead, white plaster, zinc white, vermillion red, black coal citrine ochre and Indian yellow. The areas with Green was a combination of black carbon's yellow ochre, azurite, lazurite blue cerulean, zinc white and plaster white. The areas in red were a combination of vermillion red, Indian yellow, lead white, black carbon, zinc white and red ochre. In measure 14 in the himation of Virgin Mary, the red pigment contains lazurite and red minium. And areas with ochre was the combination of zinc white, red vermillion, the yellow ochre and red ochre. According to the results of the measurements it was observed that in measuring 7 and 11 where a green area was examined, a blue dye appeared as the basis. This is due to oxidized varnish of the icon that has a tendency to yellowing when oxidized, resulting in the blue pigment combined with a yellow film to give the impression that it is a green pigment. Also observed in virtually all measurements was the plaster white which is probably owing to its being a component of icon preparation.

References

1. Upatras Eclass. http://eclass.upatras.gr/modules/document/file.php/CMNG2173/Section1-introductiontoSpectroscopy.Pdf. Accessed 14 Aug 2018
2. Ganetsos, T.: Lecture Notes: Archaiometria I-Resolutions, Chronologiseis, Prospecting, Portable Instrumentation. University of the Aegean (2018)
3. Xeilakoy, H.: The application of spectroscopic and non-destructive methods to characterize, in control of wear and preservation-restoration of historical works. Doctoral thesis. NTUA, 6-86, Athens (2011)
4. UOA e-class. https://eclass.uoa.gr/modules/document/file.php/PHARM173/EASTER/ch7EISAGWGISTISFASMATOSKOPIKESTECHNICAL.Pdf. Accessed 14 Aug 2018
5. Zacharias, N.: Notes for the course: methods of spectroscopy, scanning electron microscopy: applications through the study of vitreous, metallic and composite materials. University of the Aegean (2016)
6. TEIAth eclass. http://physics.teiath.gr/activities/XRF_LAB/ylika/SAET_XRF_ppt.pdf. Accessed 14 Aug 2018
7. Merkopanas website. merkopanas.blogspot.gr/search?q=raman. Accessed 14 Aug 2018
8. Karoyntzos, C.: Raman spectroscopy as a tool for qualitative Study of Tungsten compounds in Molten Alkali Chlorides and Quantitative Phase Transformation analysis of Polycrystalline Zirconia, pp. 3–5. Ph.D. thesis. University of Patras (2003)
9. Tarantilis, P.: http://docplayer.gr/37817832-Fasmatoskopia-raman-raman-spectroscopy-petros-a-tarantilis.html. Accessed 14 Aug 2018
10. Alexopoulou-Agoranoy, A., Hrisoulakis, G.: Science and Art Projects, Ghonis SLE, 21-38, Athens (1993)
11. Kontaxakis, G.: Color Theory and Practice I, p. 20. Synepipedwn Color Association, Athens (1999)
12. Nun, D., Minopoyloy, E., Andrikopoulos, K., Karapanagiotis, J.: Analysis of organic and inorganic pigments and their application techniques in painter's pictures, pictures with the signature "Angel's Hand". Benaki Museum (2008)

Pigments Identification in Oil Paintings of 18th–19th Century from the Museum of Post-Byzantine Art of Zakynthos Using Raman Spectroscopy and XRF

Katerina Koutliani[1,3], Theodore Ganetsos[2](✉), Christina Merkouri[3], Maria Perraki[4], and Nikolaos Laskaris[2]

[1] Department of Mediterranean Studies, University of the Aegean, Rhodes, Greece
[2] Department of Industrial Design and Production Engineering, School of Engineering, University of West Attica, Athens, Greece
ganetsos@puas.gr
[3] Ephorate of Antiquities of Zakynthos, Ministry of Culture and Sports, Athens, Greece
[4] School of Mining and Metallurgical Engineering, National Technical University of Athens, Athens, Greece

Abstract. The aim was to use non – destructive spectroscopic techniques in selected paintings of the Ionian School of the Museum of Zakynthos, under the supervision of the Ephorate of Antiquities of Zakynthos. We used Raman and XRF spectroscopy in order to identify the pigments of the paintings. n our investigation, the use of these techniques for the first time at the Museum of Post-Byzantine Art of Zakynthos is more than essential due to the historical particularities of the Island. A massive earthquake, followed by a wildfire within the city bounds devastated the Island of Zakynthos in August, 1953 and its archival wealth was almost altogether ruined. These resulted in bibliography gaps and lack of archival material. The scarce scientific information for the understanding of the materials used by the post-Byzantine artists during the 18th–19th century, with the only exception being the artists' manuals and the absence of identified paintings led to the use of analytical techniques in order to answer questions that the History of Art could not answer. The study was focused on four paintings of the temple of Saint George of Petroutsos in Zakynthos, which has been moved after the destruction of the church due to the earthquake of 1953 to the Church of Ascension in the centre of Zakynthos. As well, the paintings that were examined were separated from the temple and today are exhibited in the Museum of Zakynthos.

Keywords: Pigments · Raman · XRF

© Springer Nature Switzerland AG 2018
M. Ioannides et al. (Eds.): EuroMed 2018, LNCS 11197, pp. 196–203, 2018.
https://doi.org/10.1007/978-3-030-01765-1_22

1 Introduction

1.1 Historical Frame

In the 15th century the Ottomans conquered the greatest part of Greece, as shown in the parts highlighted in yellow, but they didn't succeed in conquering the Ionian Islands. After the fall of the Byzantine Empire in 1453, the Ionian Islands came under the Venetian rule.

In 1453 the Byzantine period comes to its end and begins the post-Byzantine era, which lasted circa until the middle of the 19th century.

During the post-Byzantine era, two important schools of painting the Cretan School and the Heptanesian School were developed.

The fact that Crete was under Venetian Rule leads to the blooming of the Cretan School. Initially, the Cretan artists were following the strict rules of the Byzantine art of iconography, but because of the cultural influences that they received by Venice, they gradually adopted western characteristics in their art.

The end of the Venetian Rule in Crete in 1669 by the Ottoman invasion meant the end of the Cretan School. After that, begun a migration of the Cretan artists to several areas of Greece, and mainly to the islands of Ionion (Corfu, Cephalonia, Zakynthos) and to Venice. As a result, the cultural centre has been transferred from Crete to the islands of Ionion which remained under the Venetian Rule for four centuries until 1797. Under these circumstances the Heptanesian School (Seven Islands - Ionian Islands School) flourished.

The Heptanesian School of painting appeared in the middle of the17th century and flourished only in the Ionian Islands until the middle of the 19th century. The Ionian Islands School abandoned the Byzantine tradition and adopted the Western European painting standards, mostly that of Venetian mannerism of the 16th century and the Italian baroque and rococo.

Pioneer of this change is the painter Panayiotis Doxaras (born in Mani in 1662 - and died in Corfu in 1729) who with his treatise "Περί Ζωγραφίας" (about painting), written circa 1726 invited his contemporary artists to depart from the Byzantine tradition, which was the dominant painting trend in the largest part of the Helladic area, towards the Western European art. In this document, he described methods and materials of this era, along with personal ideas with especial reference to the oil painting. Having as a guide the works of Paolo Veronese he would paint the roof of the Church of Saint Spyridon in Corfu in 1727.

The most important changes that Heptanesian School introduces are the three dimensional perspective, the use of oil painting on canvas instead of the byzantine egg tempera technique on wood panel, the naturalistic depiction of the human form, the introduction of the secular subject, the use of chiaroscuro technique (which is the light and shade technique) and the focus on the emotional expression leading to the secularization of art and the change to the iconography plan of the churches.

Born in 1741 in Zakynthos, Nikolaos Koutouzis is considered the most important and talented painter of the Heptanesian School and the most prominent portrait painter of his generation. During the years 1760–1764 and probably later on, he travelled to Venice twice or more to study painting. He is referred to as an eccentric, versatile and prolific personality. Among other things he was a satirical poet that criticized his period's ethics, while in 1777 he was ordained a priest. His eccentric ways and caustic poems resulted in condemnation by the clergymen and his dismissal from office. His work includes secular and religious paintings. The most notable of the religious art-works are the assortments in the churches of Saint Spyridon of Flambouriaris, Saint Anthony of Andritsis and Saint George of Petroutsos in Zakynthos.

Here we can see some of his paintings that are exhibited in the Museum of Post-Byzantine art of Zakynthos.

Our paper is focused on the paintings of Saint George of petroutsos church (see Fig. 1). We meet a change to the iconography plan of the temples, as a consequence of the adoption of the western influences, on the temple of Saint George of Petroutsos in Zakynthos. After the earthquake in 1953, only the temple of the church was rescued and the assortment of its paintings was split apart. All icons are painted with oil on wood panel and are characterized by the effort of rendering the human dimensions of the depicted figures, contributing in this way to the secularization of the ecclesiastical art of Zakynthos.

The two Angels with the symbols of the Passion which adorned the sidelong sanctuary doors of the temple of Saint George of Petroutsos church and today are displayed in the Museum of Zakynthos are attributed to the same artist or to his student.

These sanctuary doors framed the painting Ecce Homo, attributed also to the circle of Koutouzis, which was the central sanctuary door of the temple, seen today in the church of Ascension in the centre of Zakynthos.

The icon of Lament, Nicodemus and Joseph remained in their original position on the temple. The remaining four icons of Mary Magdalene Mary of Clopas, John the Evangelist and Apostle Peter were detached from the temple, later transferred to the Museum of Zakynthos and since then have been part of the permanent exhibition [1].

2   Instrumentation

The site of the analyses was the Museum of Post-Byzantine Art of Zakynthos. The analytical techniques used were Raman and XRF spectrometry in order to identify the pigments used. Analyses were performed using two portable non-destructive instruments [2, 3].

A portable Raman and a portable XRF analyzer have been used. Namely, we used the DeltaNu RockHound handleld Raman Spectrometer for the determination of the chemical compounds. It has a near infrared 785 nm diode laser in order to minimize fluorescence of the organic medium. The resolution is 8 cm^{-1} (minus one). The spectra were acquired in the wavenumber range of 200– up to 2000 cm^{-1} (minus one).In addition, for the qualitative and quantitative determination of chemical element has been used the handheld XRF analyzer Skyray EDX pocket III, which provides rapid and simultaneous analysis of elements in the range from Sulfur, (S) (16) to Uranium (U) (92) [4].

Fig. 1. Paintings of N. Koutouzis from the Saint George of petroutsos church

3 Measurements

Here we can see the preselected points of the paintings on which the Raman technique was employed. More specifically, it has been a selection of the Light red, Dark red, Blue, Green and Yellow. At the same time, we measured using XRF at exact the same points of the paintings on which we also employed Raman, aiming at confirming the pigment based on the presence or the lack of elements.

For this presentation we selected to present the best quality spectra of two paintings, namely the painting of Mary of Clopas and the Angel with the symbols of the Passion. (nails, hammer, pliers, crown).

For the Angel with the symbols of the Passion, the measurement was made on the nose of the Angel aiming to identify the red pigment. The Raman peaks are very closely related to the red lead as compared to the Pigment's Checker database (see Fig. 2).

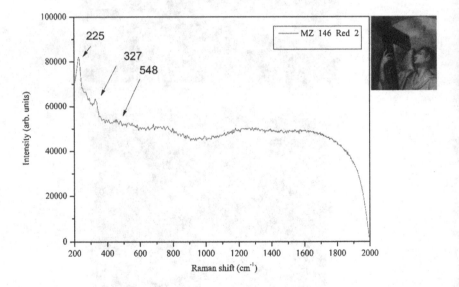

Fig. 2. Angel with the symbols of the Passion pigment identified as red lead (Color figure online)

On the painting of Mary of Clopas the Raman measurement was made on the himation for the identification of the red colour. The Raman peaks for the red ochre are very closely related to the database of Pigment's Checker with a variation of 10 cm^{-1} (minus one) (see Fig. 3).

On the XRF measurement at the same point of the painting confirmed the presence of iron oxide, identifying the presence of red ochre on the artwork. On the same painting the sample of blue colour was selected from the depicted sky. The use of Raman technique revealed the presence of Prussian blue as is indicated by the alignment of the experimental data with the bibliographical data.

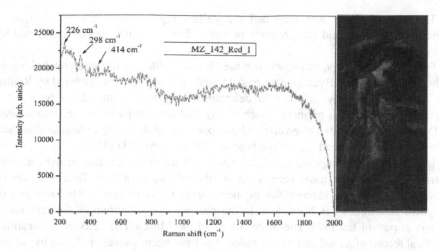

Fig. 3. Mary of Clopas, pigment identified as Red Ochre (Color figure online)

Moving on to the next point of measurement the green color was selected from the vestment of the woman's figure. The Raman peaks of our spectrum proved the presence of Terre verte colour as indicated by the corresponding peaks of the database of UCL.

As regards the yellow colour the selected point was on her shawl. The Raman peaks showed the presence of Lead tin yellow type II, as suggested by the peaks presented in the Database for this specific colour, which presence is unusual.

This pigment is confirmed by the presence of Lead (PB) and Tin (SN) as we can see from the XRF Spectrum shown here, in comparison with XRF database.

4   Final Results - Conclusions

A synopsis of the results is shown on this Table. From left to right we can see the data for each painting which are the sample colour of the painting, the identified pigment, the sample pigment, its chemical composition, the Raman shifts respect to the UCL database and the elements identified by the XRF.

On the painting of Angel with the symbols of the Passion, Red lead was identified by Raman for the Dark red colour, confirmed by the presence of Lead. Calcium is also present.

On the painting of Mary of Clopas, on the Light red sample, Red ochre was identified and XRF showed presence of Iron (Fe). Also showed the presence of Calcium.

As regards the Prussian blue, the Raman results confirmed the pigment for the blue colour and XRF showed the presence of Copper and Iron.

On the green sample, Raman identify the presence of Terre verte and XRF showed Copper, Calcium, Iron and Magnesium.

The yellow colour was identified the yellow pigment lead tin yellow type II according to Raman and the presence of Lead, Tin and Calcium was confirmed by XRF.

Four greek paintings, made between the 18th and 19th century and now belonging to the Museum of Post Byzantine art of Zakynthos collection, were analysed by Raman and XRF Spectroscopy in order to determine the pigments that have been used. Together with common pigments, such as (a) Red lead, (b) Red ochre (iron oxide). (c) Prussian blue and (d) Terre verte and a copper-containing green. Unusual materials were identified, like Lead tin yellow type II (PbSn(1-x)SixO3) [5].

In regards of the importance of this study it's the first time that analytical, non-destructive techniques have been used in the Museum of Post-Byzantine art of Zakynthos in order to identify the pigments used in its artworks. The only use of analytical techniques has been done in the past by Eleni Kouloumpi for restoration reasons as part of her PhD. The pieces of art of the Museum of Zakynthos constitute historical record of a land and a civilization that have been severely inflicted by natural disasters. In particular, the works under study constitute a part of the main body of the religious works that are preserved from the 1953 major earthquake and according to the bibliography are attributed to N. Koutouzis by reason of the primary role the artist has served within the domain of the Ionian Art.

As a consequence, common pigments have been identified like: Red lead, one of the earliest pigments artificially prepared. It was in common use during the Byzantine period and also commonly used in European manuscripts and paintings. Red ochre (iron oxide), used from prehistoric era, continuously in use by painters throughout the Middle Ages and the Renaissance. Prussian blue, is the first modern, artificially manufactured colour, available to artists by 1724 and extremely popular throughout the

Table 1. Identified pigments in the paintings of N. Koutouzis of Saint George of petroutsos church

Painting	Sample Color	Pigment	Sample pigment	Chemical composition	Raman bands(cm⁻¹)	XRF-elements
Angel with the symbols of the Passion MZ_146_Red_2	Dark Red	Red lead		dilead(II) lead(IV) oxide Pb₃O₄	122vs, 149m, 223w, 313w, 340vw, 390w, 480vw, 548vs	Pb, Ca
Mary of Clopas_ MZ_142_Red_1	Light red	Red ochre		iron(III) oxide chromophore (Fe₂O₃+ clay + silica)	220vs, 286vs, 402m, 491w, 601w	Fe, Ca
Mary of Clopas_ MZ_142_Blue_1	Blue	Prussian blue		iron(III) hexa-cyanoferrate(II) Fe₄[Fe(CN)6]3 14-16H₂O	282vw, 538vw, 2102m, 2154vs	Cu, Fe
Mary of Clopas_ MZ142_Green_2	Green	Terre verte		Variations on K[(AlIII,FeIII)(FeII,MgII)],(AlSi₃,Si₄)O₁₀(OH)₂	145vs, 399w, 510w, 636m, 685m, 820vw, 1007m, 1084m	Cu, Ca, Fe, Mg
Mary of Clopas_ MZ142_Yellow_1	Yellow	Lead tin yellow type II		silicon substituted lead(II) stannate, PbSn1-xSixO₃	138vs, 324m (br)	Pb, Sn, Ca

three centuries since its discovery, Terre verte, used since antiquity. Medieval Italian painters used green earth for underpainting middle and shadow flesh tones. In addition, an unusual material for this period (18th–19th century) in Greece was identified, like the Lead tin Yellow type II. We believe that the Lead tin yellow type II is the actual pigment because two different techniques from a different point of view give the same result. Raman spectrum with the chemical bonding and XRF spectrum with the presence of important elements according to identify pigment. It has been found principally in Florentine, Venetian, and Bohemian paintings. It was used on works by Giotto, the workshop of di Cione, Veronese, and Tintoretto (see Table 1).

References

1. Mylona, Z.: Archaeological Receipts Fund, Athens, pp. 352–357, 360–371, 386–387 (1998)
2. Vandenabeele, P.: J. Raman Spectrosc. **35**, 607–609 (2004)
3. Bersani, D., Madiaraga, J.M.: J. Raman Spectrosc. **43**, 1523 (2012)
4. Ganetsos, Th., Katsaros, Th., Greiff, S., Hartmann S.: Int. J. Mater. Chem. **3**, 5–9 (2013)
5. Burgio, L., Clark, R.J.H., Theodoraki, K.: Spectrochimica Acta Part A **59** (2003)

A Status Quaestionis and Future Solutions for Using Multi-light Reflectance Imaging Approaches for Preserving Cultural Heritage Artifacts

Vincent Vanweddingen[1,2]([✉]), Chris Vastenhoud[1], Marc Proesmans[2],
Hendrik Hameeuw[3,4], Bruno Vandermeulen[4], Athena Van der Perre[3],
Frederic Lemmers[6], Lieve Watteeuw[5], and Luc Van Gool[2]

[1] eCollections, Royal Museums of Art and History (RMAH), Brussels, Belgium
vincent.vanweddingen@esat.kuleuven.be
[2] ESAT/PSI, KU Leuven, Leuven, Belgium
[3] Faculty of Arts, KU Leuven, Leuven, Belgium
[4] ULS Digitisation and Document Delivery, KU Leuven, Leuven, Belgium
[5] Book Heritage Lab, Illuminare, Faculty of Theology and Religious Studies,
KU Leuven, Leuven, Belgium
[6] Digitization Department, Royal Library of Belgium, Brussels, Belgium

Abstract. Single-Camera Multi-Light scanning methods like Reflectance Transformation Imaging (RTI) and Portable Light Dome (PLD) are being widely used in the cultural heritage sector. Both technologies followed a long development track in collaboration with cultural heritage partners, resulting in matured technologies. In this short paper, we highlight recent progress with this technique (capturing and modeling reflectance, multi-spectral pipelines, material classification) and present ongoing work of how both technologies can be brought closer together. Finally, we address RTI's and PLD's challenges and possible solutions in terms of long term preservation and valorization by the scientific community.

Keywords: RTI · PLD · 3D imaging · Relightable images
Photometric stereo

1 Introduction

Researchers or museum curators who want to study, document or disseminate cultural artifacts have a vast toolbox of HD imaging methods and 3D scanners at hand. A careful choice must be made, depending on the shape, size, location and materiality of the artifact and which characteristic is of interest. In the PIXEL+ project, of which we are providing preliminary ideas and work-in-progress results, we are focusing on single-camera multi-light imaging methods.

© Springer Nature Switzerland AG 2018
M. Ioannides et al. (Eds.): EuroMed 2018, LNCS 11197, pp. 204–211, 2018.
https://doi.org/10.1007/978-3-030-01765-1_23

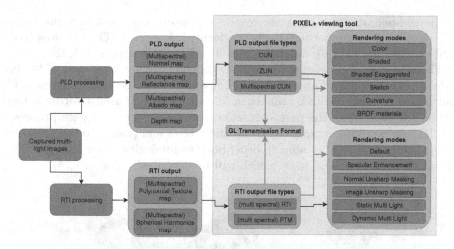

Fig. 1. Overview of RTI's and PLD's processing and shading blocks and what the PIXEL+ viewing tool intends to incorporate. Note that PLD's MS pipeline is all-in-one and fully automated, whereas RTI requires consecutive recordings.

Reflectance Transformation Imaging/Polynomial Texture Mapping [11] and the Portable Light Dome [20,22,23] are multi-light methods that require a stationary camera and a point light source at several known positions. Each time the object is lit from another angle, a photo is taken. Both methods rely on this altering information to learn more about the surface of an object and create so called interactive 2.5 dimensional (2.5D or 2D+) images that can be virtually re-lit. Various shaders can be selected to accentuate a specific property of the surface, varying from the shape (e.g. of cuneiform script [23]) to the reflective properties (e.g. to investigate pigments [18,22]). For dissemination purposes the photo-realistic shader is typically used, which displays interactive models [12] (Fig. 1).

RTI and PLD have followed their own specific development trajectories. RTI has a strong focus on low-cost solutions and ease of use. Any single light source, a camera and a reflective sphere suffice to capture multifuctional RTI data. The hand-held setup is adaptable to a large array of object sizes, making it a widely used tool in the cultural heritage domain. RTI typically focusses on virtually relighting objects, but can recover surface characteristics as well. The methodology assumes the camera to be orthographic, and the light sources to be at infinity, therefore there is less attention to the accuracy of the measurements.

The PLD-dome was originally designed to support the digitization of collections with numerous similar objects. Since [23], in collaboration with the cultural heritage sector, it has evolved into several industrial prototypes, catering specific needs [22]. Figure 2 shows a collection of prototypes with different sizes and illumination. Each device is tailored to a specific object size. Because of its rigid structure, it has the benefit that environmental effects can be alleviated and optical effects like quadratic light falloff, vignetting and non uniform light emission can be compensated for. As such, results are more consistent and qualitative analysis of surface properties can be performed. Likewise, RTI has adopted a number of similar capture methodologies in the form of domes [1,4,21].

The approach and benefits of the PLD pipeline are not restricted to the use of the PLD-domes only. Lab-tests at KU Leuven with datasets derived from RTI-domes have successfully been brought in line with the rendering algorithms used in the PLD viewers. In the past, datasets created with the PLD were processed with RTI software [14] as well. Based on these tests and thanks to the similarity of both methods, PIXEL+ aims to bring both technologies closer together. This can be achieved in several ways, which will be described below (Fig. 4).

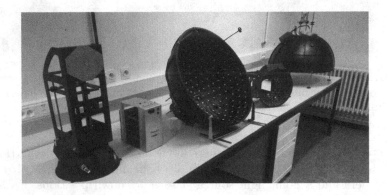

Fig. 2. Selection of different dome prototypes with varying sizes and illumination

Fig. 3. A PLD file of cuneiform tablet NP47 (KU Leuven Archaeological Collection), opened in PLD viewer

Fig. 4. A PTM file of a small stone Ancient Egyptian stele (RMAH E.02431) opened in RTIViewer 1.1.0

2   PIXEL+ Viewer

Displaying both PLD and RTI files with their respective shaders is the core of the PIXEL+ viewer. To achieve this, an OS viewer (Windows 10, Mac OS X and Fedora) as well as a web viewer are being developed. The OS viewer will take full usage of the hardware capabilities allowing more demanding algorithms like depth profiles to be calculated and shown. The web viewer has the same viewing functionality, but is targeted more as a dissemination utility, allowing collection holders to display 2.5D files of their artifacts. It can also be linked to an online database to directly open and view the 2.5D files.

2.1 Combining PLD and RTI Shaders

Traditionally, photometric stereo (PS) [24], the principle behind the PLD, is used with Lambertian surfaces (e.g. Fig. 3). The intensity of reflected light of these materials is directly proportional to the cosine of the angle between the orientation of the surface and the direction of the incident light. The recovered surface orientation (e.g. relief) is typically very detailed. The PS algorithm has been extended to non-Lambertian materials [17]. With standard Lambertian shading however, renderings of non-Lambertian materials won't look photo-realistic. To incorporate specularity, the PLD system has included Phong shading (Figs. 5 and 6).

Fig. 5. Screenshots with 'color' and 'shaded' shaders of KU Leuven Libraries, Special Collections: BRES-Ms. 1333; A and B details with measure tool activated, rendering PLDviewer 7.0.05., HQ: DOI: 10.5281/zenodo.1256576

Fig. 6. Screenshots with 'color' and 'sketch1' shader of Archives Old University Leuven: 22 (KU Leuven University Archives), front of pendant seal Emperor Charles V, rendering PLDviewer 7.0.05., HQ: DOI: 10.5281/zenodo.1256588

RTI can be seen as an interpolation technique between the input images under different light. Polynomial Texture Mapping [11], Hemispherical Harmonics [5] are typically used to fit the reflectance. As such, effects like specularity and self shadowing will be captured, resulting in photo-realistic renderings. To allow a more careful study of the surface, PTMviewer [2] has included several (non photo-realistic) shaders like Specular Enhancement and Unsharp Masking as well to display gradients or exaggerate surface curvature. Recently [16] proposed a strategy to represent RTI datasets in a compact and web-friendly manner.

The future PIXEL+ tool will allow PLD files to be shown with RTI shading and vice versa, providing the end users with more flexibility in displaying 2.5D files and thus alleviating some of the disadvantages of both methods.

2.2   Photometric Stereo: From Lambertian Shading to General BRDF Models

Another way of tackling PLD's rendering quality of non-Lambertian materials is by leveraging more extensive shading information. A Bidirectional Reflectance Distribution Function (BRDF) [13] is a mathematical function which describes how light is reflected at an opaque surface. By capturing and modeling the BRDF, very photo-realistic renderings can be made. In the current PLD viewer software a subset of the BRDF can already be captured [22] in the form of so called reflection maps, which display the reflectance of the local surface structure for each LED, positioned in the same way as the LEDs are placed on the dome (Fig. 7).

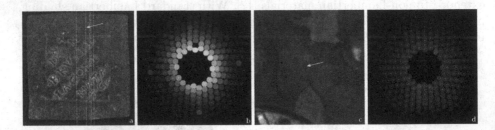

Fig. 7. Reflection maps using white light PLD; Golden medallion CBIB W827 (a) and detail frontispiece Anjou Bible (c); (b) and (d): reflection maps corresponding to one pixel, see green arrows (©RICH & ESAT-VISICS, KU Leuven) (Color figure online)

These reflectance maps can serve as an input to model lower dimensional analytic or tabular BRDFs which will allow more realistic shading of (non-)Lambertian surfaces for any multi-light imaging dataset [17].

3   Multi-spectral Multi-light Imaging

3.1   Broader, More Detailed View of the Spectrum

Traditionally cameras mimic how we see the world. Like our eyes, RGB cameras can be seen as tristimulus integrators of the visible spectrum - the entire spectral information at a specific pixel is summarized in 3 numbers. From a scientific point of view, one ideally would like to image a larger part of the spectrum and bin it into more and finer grained intervals, as a lot of information can be found outside the visible part of the spectrum as well as in the power spectral density of reflected light. Recently, multi-spectral imaging was introduced to multi-light single-camera scanning [7,8,10]. Likewise, the MS-version of the PLD provided new abilities, this dome consists of 5 narrow bands (NIR (850 nm), R (623 nm), G (523 nm), B (460 nm), UV (365 nm)) allowing users an all-in integrated wider look into the electromagnetic spectrum [22].

3.2   Luminescence Imaging

Multi-light reflectance imaging, especially with the stable pre-assembled acquisition domes (mostly long exposure times are needed), provide as well new research possibilities towards MS imaging techniques which make use of the luminescence/fluorescence phenomenon. Recently, lab-experiments conducted by the KU Leuven/RMAH teams on coins, stone seals and Ancient Egyptian coffins have revealed promising new insights in the effect of luminescence on the estimation of normals and for the identification of pigments in combination with an understanding of the relief (Visible-induced Luminescence). Equally [9] has proven firmly the potential of this approach. Depending on the intended luminescence phenomenon, both acquisition methods/devices applying only white lights emitters as well as setups with separate narrow band emitters in the UV and/or VIS can be used [19].

3.3   Material Analysis

The reflectance maps as captured and computed by the PLD not only provide information to aid in photo-realistic rendering, they can also serve as cues to classify materials. [6] has shown that reflectance cues can be used to visually recognize materials. Material classification algorithms based on reflectance can easily pick up wrong cues (e.g. shape or texture) to infer the material type. Reflectance maps are calculated per pixel and are shape invariant, so that classification results will not depend on the object's shape or texture, but only on the reflective behavior of the material.

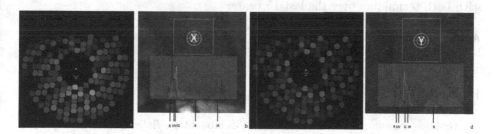

Fig. 8. In the RGB images (b) and (d) both azurite (b) and ultramarine (d) appear as blue, but have distinctive MS reflection maps (a) and (c) corresponding to marked pixels and histograms (b) and (d) corresponding to areas marked by a yellow rectangle (©ESAT-PSI, KU Leuven) See also [19] (Color figure online)

In Fig. 8, the MS reflectance maps are used to distinguish between two different blue pigments, azurite and ultramarine respectively.

In the context of RTI, experiments have been carried out to use the interpolation coefficients to classify materials. Results are shown in [15,21].

4 Archiving Challenges

Both RTI and PLD are matured technologies in terms of the recording strategies and processing principles. Because of the special type of their output data, some hurdles still need to be overcome. RTI and PLD store their results in highly specific file formats. The issue is that these files will perhaps one day not be able to be opened any more. While this is true for any file type, 2.5D (or even general 3D) file types are extra vulnerable because they are not so widespread as say JPG or TIFF for storing image data. While the ability to parse the current 2.5D formats needs to be kept, PIXEL+ will also introduce a conversion/exporter tool to GL Transmission Format (glTF) [3] and reflect on which meta-data, i.e. EXIF, acquisition procedure related meta-data, data ownership needs to be saved. Although this still cannot guaranty future accessibility, the authors nevertheless believe that storing 2.5D files in a by the Khronos Group specified open file format as well as documenting thoroughly how to display them, is a first to follow strategy towards a sustainable file format.

5 Conclusion

In this short paper, we introduced preliminary work on how RTI and PLD, both interesting 2.5D/3D scanning methods for the cultural heritage sector, can be combined. These methodologies will be brought closer together in a single software environment, allowing visualization modes of one method to be applied to the other. It will open the potential to share and combine the strongholds of both approaches and revive many of the ten thousands of datasets acquired with both techniques over the last 15 years.

Acknowledgments. This work is part of the PIXEL+ project, funded by Belspo's BRAIN-be (Pioneer) Program.

References

1. Building an automated RTI dome - LATIS labs. http://labs.dash.umn.edu/aisos/building-an-automated-rti-dome/. Accessed 30 May 2018
2. Cultural heritage imaging — reflectance transformation imaging (RTI). http://culturalheritageimaging.org/Technologies/RTI/. Accessed 30 May 2018
3. glTF Overview - The Khronos Group Inc. https://www.khronos.org/gltf/. Accessed 30 May 2018
4. Earl, G., Martinez, K., Pagi, H.: Reflectance transformation imaging (RTI) system for ancient documentary artefacts (2010)
5. Gautron, P., Krivanek, J., Pattanaik, S.N., Bouatouch, K.: A novel hemispherical basis for accurate and efficient rendering (2004)
6. Georgoulis, S., Vanweddingen, V., Proesmans, M., Van Gool, L.: Material classification under natural illumination using reflectance maps. In: IEEE Winter Conference on Applications of Computer Vision (WACV), pp. 244–253. IEEE (2017)

7. Giachetti, A., Ciortan, I., Daffara, C., Pintus, R., Gobbetti, E., et al.: Multispectral RTI analysis of heterogeneous artworks (2017)
8. Hanneken, T.R.: New technology for imaging unreadable manuscripts and other artifacts: Integrated spectral reflectance transformation imaging (spectral RTI). Ancient Worlds in Digital Culture, p. 180 (2016)
9. Kotoula, E.: Reflectance transformation imaging beyond the visible: ultraviolet reflected and ultraviolet induced visible fluorescence. In: CAA 2015, p. 909 (2015)
10. Kotoula, E., Earl, G.: Integrated RTI approaches for the study of painted surfaces. In: Computer Applications and Quantitative methods in Archaeology, pp. 22–25 (2014)
11. Malzbender, T., Gelb, D., Wolters, H.: Polynomial texture maps. In: Proceedings of the 28th Annual Conference on Computer Graphics and Interactive Techniques, pp. 519–528. ACM (2001)
12. Mudg, M., et al.: Principles and practices of robust, photography-based digital imaging techniques for museums (2010)
13. Nicodemus, F.E.: Directional reflectance and emissivity of an opaque surface. Appl. Opt. 4(7), 767–775 (1965)
14. Palma, G., et al.: Telling the story of ancient coins by means of interactive RTI images visualization. In: Archaeology in the Digital Era, p. 177 (2014)
15. Pintus, R., Ciortan, I., Giachetti, A., Gobbetti, E., et al.: Practical free-form RTI acquisition with local spot lights (2016)
16. Ponchio, F., Corsini, M., Scopigno, R.: A compact representation of relightable images for the web. In: Proceedings of the 23rd International ACM Conference on 3D Web Technology, p. 1. ACM (2018)
17. Shi, B., et al.: A benchmark dataset and evaluation for non-lambertian and uncalibrated photometric stereo. In: IEEE Conference on CVPR, pp. 3707–3716 (2016)
18. Van der Stighelen, K.: Young anthony van dyck revisited: a multidisciplinary approach to a portrait once attributed to peter paul rubens. Art Matters: Int. J. Tech. Art Hist. 6, 21–35 (2014)
19. Vandermeulen, B., Hameeuw, H., Watteeuw, L., Van Gool, L., Proesmans, M.: Bridging multi-light & multi-spectral images to study, preserve and disseminate archival documents. In: Archiving Conference, vol. 2018, pp. 64–69. Society for Imaging Science and Technology (2018)
20. Verbiest, F., Van Gool, L.: Photometric stereo with coherent outlier handling and confidence estimation. In: IEEE Conference on CVPR, pp. 1–8. IEEE (2008)
21. Wang, O., Gunawardane, P., Scher, S., Davis, J.: Material classification using BRDF slices. In: IEEE Conference on CVPR, pp. 2805–2811. IEEE (2009)
22. Watteeuw, L., et al.: Light, shadows and surface characteristics: the multispectral portable light dome. Appl. Phys. A 122(11), 976 (2016)
23. Willems, G., Verbiest, F., Moreau, W., Hameeuw, H., Van Lerberghe, K., Van Gool, L.: Easy and cost-effective cuneiform digitizing. In: The 6th International Symposium on Virtual Reality, Archaeology and Cultural Heritage (VAST 2005), pp. 73–80. Eurographics Assoc. (2005)
24. Woodham, R.J.: Photometric method for determining surface orientation from multiple images. Opt. Eng. 19(1), 191139 (1980)

Digital Cultural Heritage Learning and Experiences

eHERITAGE Project – Building a Cultural Heritage Excellence Center in the Eastern Europe

Mihai Duguleană[✉]

Transylvania University of Brasov, Brasov, Romania
mihai.duguleana@unitbv.ro

Abstract. eHERITAGE ('Expanding the Research and Innovation Capacity in Cultural Heritage Virtual Reality Applications') is a twinning project which was accepted for financing by the European Commission under the topic H2020-TWINN-2015. The coordinating organization of the eHERITAGE project is University Transilvania of Brasov (UTBv). This institution aims to significantly improve its expertise in the field of virtual heritage by collaborating with 2 other organizations, experts in this area: Jožef Stefan Institute from Ljubljana, Slovenia, and Scuola Superiore Sant'Anna from Pisa, Italy.

UTBv is based in Transylvania, a geographical area full of historical landmarks and with a well-defined regional strategy for marketing and promoting cultural tourism. eHERITAGE tries to mold on this strategy and to uplift some of the activities foreseen in it. Our staff interacted on several occasions with local authorities for exploiting and disseminating history through virtual applications. The measures foreseen in eHERITAGE have already influenced the social, economic and cultural environment from Romania in an exponential way, making room for partnerships with other research institutes or with companies which want to use our expertise in order to gain more market traction.

The main objective of this initiative is to provide the means for the research staff of UTBv to obtain excellence in "virtual heritage". The aim of this paper is to present the activities and the results of our consortium and to present our expertise to stakeholders, in the hope of establishing new sustainable research cooperation schemes.

We strongly believe that cultural heritage can be enriched with the help of new technologies, and we hope that our activities have already contributed to proving this.

Keywords: eHeritage · Project · Twinning

1 Introduction

1.1 What Is a "Twinning" Support Action?

The last few years, I have been asked on multiple occasions about the project that I coordinate. People usually want to know what it does and what its purpose is. They tend to question the idea of twinning. I usually start the explanation by a comparison with the concept of "twinned" cities.

© Springer Nature Switzerland AG 2018
M. Ioannides et al. (Eds.): EuroMed 2018, LNCS 11197, pp. 215–223, 2018.
https://doi.org/10.1007/978-3-030-01765-1_24

The key idea behind this type of projects is the following: Western European research centers have a great scientific and technological advance. For this reason, Eastern European research institutions and centers cannot compete with them on various grants and research projects opened by the European Commission (EC) under their frameworks. "Twinning" is a support action that aims to diminish these disparities. Speaking of disparities, this problem is unfortunately more severe than officials thought in the beginning. In Fig. 1, we have illustrated the main financial movements in different clusters of countries.

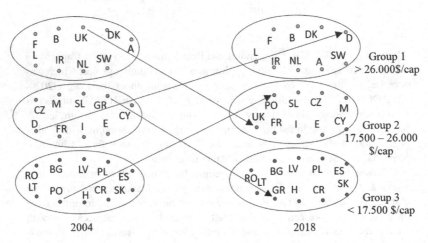

Fig. 1. Movements among EU countries in the last 14 years, considering the average GDP/cap

As one can see, the disparities aren't really diminishing, at least not at the financial level. Trying to fix problems at a more detailed level is one way to solve this situation. Thus resulted the "twinning" support actions proposed by the CE under the H2020 umbrella.

1.2   eHeritage Consortium

The coordinator of the eHERITAGE is *University of Transilvania of Brasov* (UTBv), a public higher education institution from Romania which also has a great interest in research. This organization participated in a wide variety of national/international research projects. The Virtual Reality and Robotics Department (VRRD – merged into Department of Automotive and Transportation) is the key drive of this project. Our department has undergone scientific studies in multiple areas such as robotics, human computer interaction, interfaces, autonomous and intelligent systems, mechatronics and more recently, automotive and driver assistance systems.

Jožef Stefan Institute (JSI) is one of the 2 partners of this project. JSI is also the biggest research organization in Slovenia. JSI ranks in the top of the research centers regarding European involvement. This institute is comprised of 28 departments and sustains hundreds of researchers and PhD students. JSI is a well-known institute at the international level, thanks to its continuous involvement in research initiatives.

The main department which is involved in eHERITAGE is the Department of Intelligent Systems (DIS). DIS experts work with in human-computer interaction paradigms, mixing various artificial learning techniques. Their staff has built various multi-agent systems with direct application in cultural heritage. Moreover, they have a good expertise in speech and language recognition and synthesis, assets which can be easily inserted in virtual heritage applications.

Another partner of the eHERITAGE consortium is *Scuola Superiore Sant'Anna* (SSSA). This is an Italian public university that has a unique interest in heritage. SSSA researchers have various publications, patents and spin-off companies that show the ability of the SSSA to foster and uplift intellectual property. The SSSA experts which joined eHERITAGE are part of the PERCRO (Perceptual Robotics) laboratory. PER-CRO is invested in doing both research and education on virtual environments, augmented reality and cultural heritage.

1.3   eHeritage Project Objectives

eHERITAGE project started on the 1st of November, 2015 and ends on the 30th of October, 2018. The main project objective is to increase the know-how and the visibility of the research staff of VRRD on a specific theme - virtual heritage, or better said, building an excellence center which will be able to successfully integrate virtual reality technologies in preservation and elevation of cultural heritage.

What does "being an expert" in virtual heritage mean? Experts are the ones who have a wide range of patents and publications in top indexed journals, have international openings in the sense of organizing conferences, engaging in society, appearing on television, etc. Specialists are usually easily recognized by reviewers because they know them, read articles written by them, have accepted the projects they have proposed to implement. Becoming an expert in any research field is sometimes hard to qualify, so here is the project in numbers [1].

2   eHERITAGE Project – Context and Numbers

eHERITAGE had 9 consortium meetings, out of which 3 also hosted exploration visits, workshops, awareness days of similar types of events. More than 200 days were spent by UTBv members at the premises of our partners, in external internships and other forms of meetings which enabled the transfer of knowledge.

The members of our consortium have participated in other events such as summer schools, workshops of other projects or exhibitions (e.g. TEDx Constanta 2017, Researchers Night 2017, EU Open Day 2018, History Museum of Brasov First World War expo 2017, ICIF 2018 from Shenzen, China, AFCO 2018 and so on). Tens of thousands of people had the chance to interact with our technologies and to find out more about our project.

Other interesting activities were related to the organization of major events such as the 1st International Conference on VR Technologies in Cultural Heritage (VRTCH'18) conference, the Advanced Study Institute – an event which includes a series of 6 workshops in the area of cultural heritage or the Brokerage event – an expo within the Internet Festival 2017 from Pisa, Italy.

The interaction with the CE presumes the completion of more than 30 deliverable, as well as reaching KPIs such as 10 conference articles, 10 indexed journal articles, 3 media appearances (newspapers, magazines, TV) and others.

The consortium has submitted several other H2020 project proposals, and is interested to submit many more in the near future.

The staff of eHERITAGE is maintaining the eHeritage.org portal (in bilingual format, with the Repository section which offers 3D models for free).

eHERITAGE undergoes activities which are integrated into international, national and local development strategies. For example, 2018 is the year of the European Cultural Heritage. This resulted in a suite of activities undertaken by the consortium, including the organization of an international conference, a press conference with the local media, meetings with curators, museum directors and art gallery owners.

Other examples are the proposal of several cultural projects for the local city hall, participating in workshops with cultural heritage experts such as the one hosted by VIMM, in which we tried to establish a European research guide in this thematic area, participating at the 14th Shenzhen International Cultural Industry Fair (ICIF 2018) in China or at the EU Open Day from Brussels, Belgium (see Fig. 2).

Fig. 2. eHERITAGE stand at the EU open DAY 2018

3   eHERITAGE Project – Technologies and Competences

Throughout the project, our team gained competences in several research fields, including Augmented Reality, Haptics, Mixed Reality, Holography, Human-Computer Interaction, 3D Reconstruction and Photogrammetry.

3.1   Augmented Reality

During the project, we have built a series of AR scenarios, among which we can list the various aspects from the life of Ovid roman poet, the reconstruction of the Cecina Etruscan Tomb, or a gallery with famous Romanian paintings. The AR applications are supported by AR Core and the obsolete Google Tango technologies [2] (Fig. 3).

Fig. 3. Ovid poet, virtual avatar and house reconstruction at Creative Summer School 2017

3.2   Haptics

Haptics is any form of interaction involving touch. The term derives from the ancient Greek word "haptikós" which means "able to come in contact with". Haptic equipment provides the tools for kinesthetic communication. This means that haptic devices are able to artificially deliver the sensation of touch by the use of small inertial of vibrating forces. Haptic stimulation is used to give to virtual objects from a computer simulation their physical dimension.

Our team has a wide experience with haptic systems [3]. We can develop innovative systems which combine multi-sensory input, allowing users to experience a high-quality kinaesthetic haptic feedback. We can also integrate several concepts and technologies, including artificial intelligence, sensors, haptics and mechatronics. We present in Fig. 4 the case of a haptic bow, one of our recently developed haptic devices which is used in an interactive VR scenario.

Fig. 4. The haptic bow tested at ICIF 2018 from Shenzen, China

3.3 Digitization

The UTBv and SSSA teams collaborated to capitalize a vestige in the warehouse of the History Museum in Brasov. This is the Constitutio Criminalis Theresiana (also known as Nemesis Theresiana or only Theresiana), a criminal code drafted in Austria during the reign of Maria Theresa, Archduke of Austria, Queen of Bohemia, Queen of Hungary [4]. The book ensures the uniform application of Criminal Law in Austria and Bohemia.

A copy of this book was in the store of the History Museum in Brasov [5], not accessible to the general public. Members of eHERITAGE thought of making a change in this regard. We have built a stand (see Fig. 5) which hosts a digital book which

Fig. 5. The 3D book presented at Researchers Night 2017

featured dynamic 3D elements, ready to be accommodated within the cultural institution mentioned above [6].

3.4 Photogrammetry and Holography

In order to output information about the fortified churches from "Țara Bârsei" (a small region from Transylvania, Romania) to visitors of a museum, gallery or any other kind of cultural heritage related exhibition, we have built a system which incorporates several technologies. Making use of the holographic effect obtained from the reflection of the image outputted by flat monitor into a glass pyramid, the holographic stand can display various 3D models, animations and other types of visual effects. Thus, it is perfect to showcase the small yet very detailed 3D models of the fortified churches from our region. In order to make the system more interactive, the physical device was coupled with a smartphone application which allows users to select their desired monument from a stylized historic map of the area. The application contains information on the most important fortified churches, which are both interesting touristic sites as well low marketed destinations.

The holographic stand (see Fig. 6) uses the classic principle of holography: the image emitted from a highly luminous 4 K TV screen is reflected by a single-side reflexive glass mounted at an angle of 45 degrees. Inside the glass construction, a white base lighten by a weak light source breaks the reflection sensation and creates the

Fig. 6. The holographic stand at EU Open Day 2018, showcasing Prejmer fortified church

feeling of having the image reflected being inside the pyramid, instead of being on the surface of the glass. Thanks to the 3 reflections offered by the 3 sides of the pyramid, users can experience a greater sense of immersion.

The 3D models were constructed based on photogrammetry. Tens of thousands of pictures were used to build the 3D models of several fortified churches from "Țara Bârsei", including Prejmer, Harman, Vulcan, Sanpetru, Maierus and Feldioara.

The system (in various versions) was presented at various events such the VRTCH'18 from Brasov, Romania, the EU Open Day 2018 from Brussels, Belgium, AFCO 2018 from Brasov, Romania, Researchers Night from Brasov, Romania, Internet Festival 2017 from Pisa, Italy and the Lubec 2017 from Lucca, Italy. The system was very well received by all the participants of this study. Many praised the idea and the content, and even promised they will visit some of the fortified churches presented in the holographic stand, in the near future.

4 Conclusions

eHERITAGE has successfully attained all its objectives. The members of the UTBv team interacted with experts and researchers from several EU countries. We had the opportunity to collaborate with librarians, curators, museum directors and all the other related stakeholders. We have learnt how to work under common methodologies and how to use best practices. We have organized a conference during which we've come together with other people which share our interests, and exchanged ideas, experiences and know-how. We hope we will continue to organize future editions of this conference.

Based on the increased profile of our department, we are now ready to participate to future research initiatives having as central point the use of virtual reality technologies for the preservation, exploitation and the marketing of European cultural heritage.

Acknowledgement. This paper is supported by European Union's Horizon 2020 research and innovation programme under grant agreement No 692103, project eHERITAGE (Expanding the Research and Innovation Capacity in Cultural Heritage Virtual Reality Applications).

References

1. eHERITAGE Project. http://www.eheritag.org
2. Girbacia, F., Duguleana, M., Postelnicu, C., Girbacia, T., Voinea, D.: A mobile application for discovering brasov monuments using augmented reality. In: Proceedings of the 2016 International Conference on Augmented Reality for Technical Entrepreneurs (2016)
3. Antonya, C., et al.: Haptic interface design for experiencing ancient works. In: Proceedings of the 19th International Multi-conference Information Society (2016)
4. Feješ, I.: Constitutio criminalis theresiana. Zbornik radova Pravnog fakulteta, Novi Sad **43**(2), 261–288 (2009)
5. History Museum in Brasov. http://www.brasovistorie.ro/
6. Lorenzini, C., et al.: An interactive digital storytelling approach to explore books in virtual environments. Informatica **40**(3), 317–322 (2016)

Migration Experiences: Acknowledging the Past, and Sustaining the Present and Future

Paul Longley Arthur[1]([⊠]) [iD], Marijke van Faassen[2], Rik Hoekstra[2],
Nadezhda Povroznik[3], Lydia Hearn[1], and Nonja Peters[4]

[1] Edith Cowan University, 2 Bradford St, Mt Lawley, Perth 6050, Australia
paul.arthur@ecu.edu.au
[2] Huygens ING, Oudezijds Achterburgwal 185, 1012 DK Amsterdam,
Netherlands
[3] Perm State University, Ulitsa Bukireva 15, 614990 Perm, Russia
[4] Curtin University, Kent Street, Perth 6102, Australia

Abstract. Australia is recognised as one of the world's most culturally and ethnically diverse nations. Immigration has historically played an important role in the nation's economic, social and cultural development. There is a pressing need to find innovative technological and archival approaches to deal with the challenge to digitally preserve Australia's migrant heritage, especially given the ageing of the European communities that were the first to come under the postwar mass migration scheme. This paper reports on plans for a national collaborative project to develop the foundational infrastructure for a dynamic, interoperable, migrant data resource for research and education. The Migration Experiences platform will connect and consolidate heterogeneous collections and resources and will provide an international exemplar underscoring the importance of digital preservation of cultural heritage and highlighting the opportunities new technologies can offer. The platform will widen the scope and range of the interpretative opportunities for researchers, and foster international academic relationships and networks involving partner organisations (universities, libraries, museums, archives and genealogical institutions). In doing so, it will contribute to better recognition and deeper understanding of the continuing role played by immigrants in Australia's national story.

Keywords: Migration heritage · Intangible heritage · Transnational history Digital humanities · Research infrastructure · Australia · Netherlands Russia

1 Introduction

1.1 Background: Worldwide Migration

In recent years international mobility has become a major issue in political, social, economic, security and human rights terms. Border crossing is increasing exponentially, and we are experiencing the largest displacement of individuals since World War II [1]. According to an estimate by the UN Population Division in 2017, the

© Springer Nature Switzerland AG 2018
M. Ioannides et al. (Eds.): EuroMed 2018, LNCS 11197, pp. 224–234, 2018.
https://doi.org/10.1007/978-3-030-01765-1_25

number of international migrants worldwide was approximately 258 million (3.4% of global population) [2]. The enormous increase in people movement around the world in recent times, whether in forced or chosen circumstances, has destabilised national boundaries and disrupted traditional concepts of home, identity, citizenship, community and nation. In this era of shifting and porous borders, Benedict Anderson's phrase 'imagined communities', coined in the 1980s, is highly relevant [3]. Individuals and communities that are no longer anchored in physically bordered spaces need to create communities, real or virtual, with which they can identify and where they can engage, be supported and seek a sense of belonging and security [4]. There are many reasons for migration, ranging from voluntary migration to asylum-seeking due to political conflict, resettlement following natural disaster, labour migration and migration undertaken for educational or economic or family reasons. However, in most cases the reasons commonly involve the undertaking of a journey (by choice or pressure of circumstances) to leave one's home environment to travel to a place that is foreign in terms of language and culture [5; 6]. Whatever the reasons for undertaking them, the journeys represent transitions, disruptions and upheavals in people's lives, and for each individual migrant the years and generations that follow are indelibly marked by that crossing and, in many cases, shaped by it. Under the global statistics lie smaller-scale groupings of specific communities with growing collective histories and individual stories of migration that are part of collective history and identity but exist mostly in fragmented, dispersed and often ephemeral forms in government records and reports, in a handful of dedicated museums and in the memories and memorabilia of immigrants and their families.

1.2   Project Overview

Australia is recognised as one of the world's most culturally and ethnically diverse nations, and over recent decades there has been increasing community interest and extensive scholarly research on immigration to Australia from the time of settlement in 1788, especially post-WWII immigration. With the establishment of government-supported migration museums followed by 'a veritable explosion of exhibitions about immigration' from the late 1980s until the late 1990s [7], data – in the form of information, artefacts and stories relating to migrant heritage – has been accumulating in these and other repositories.

Immigration has historically played an important role in the economic, social and cultural development of Australia. In addition to supporting the Australian government's ongoing cultural commitment to developing as a diverse and culturally inclusive society [8], immigration continues to be of vital importance for practical reasons, such as the maintenance of a stable level of population and, in the context of an ageing society, the future maintenance of services. The 2016 census results, published by the Australian Bureau of Statistics, show that 'Nearly half (49%) of all Australians were either born overseas (first generation) or have at least one parent born overseas (second generation)' [9]. Most importantly, Australians, including many Aboriginal and Torres Strait Islander people, therefore have links to one or more of the 200 immigrant source countries around the world.

In Australia large-scale digitisation of cultural heritage resources has been led by national collecting institutions. While much has been achieved in this arena, digital preservation of migrant cultural heritage remains a major challenge that now needs urgent attention. The massive population shifts since WWII, characteristic of the postwar period, have stretched most museums' financial capacity to house collections that reflect Australia's ethnic diversity. As was typical of postcolonial countries, by the 1990s Australian museums were housing mainly scientific specimens relating to Australia's flora and fauna and artefacts that reflected the experience of its dominant Anglo-Celtic culture. The word 'museum' was still generally 'reserved for collections in natural history, science and technology, anthropology and ethnology', and according to the writers of the 1975 Committee of Inquiry on Museums and National Collections, the word itself had 'a musty effect' [10]. The study of Aboriginal history only truly came into being in the early 1990s. Australia's two immigration museums, Adelaide (established in 1988) and Melbourne (1997), have been limited by the dictates of traditional museum practices even as their remit has expanded in the digital era. There is a pressing need to find innovative new technological and archival approaches to deal with the challenge of digitally preserving Australia's migrant heritage, especially given the ageing of the European communities that were the first to come under the postwar mass migration scheme.

This paper reports on plans for an international collaborative project to create and develop the foundational infrastructure for a dynamic, interoperable, migrant data resource for research and education. The development of this resource will not only benefit the communities themselves in terms of citizenship, it will also facilitate cross-cultural understanding by providing access beyond the individual communities. It will create a reliable, expandable source of information and data to inform policy and to support the diverse and extensive array of migration scholarship being pursued nationally. This project was initiated by Nonja Peters, who over a period of decades has made a major international contribution to mutual heritage understanding, in particular in relation to Dutch-Australian history. Although there have been prior efforts to establish such a platform through the Australian Research Council's Linkage Infrastructure, Equipment and Facilities (LIEF) projects scheme involving members of the project team, to date these have not been successful and so there remains no integrated platform or data resource in Australia for the preservation of immigrants' cultural heritage. The broader ambition is to expand and build on the authors' established bilateral Netherlands-Australia research program in migration and mutual heritage studies to include further international partners. In doing so this paper responds directly to the Euromed Conference's call to 'Refine, amend and publish main ideas and visions of any technological platforms opened to the entire field of CH in the context of preparation of the EU Horizon 2020 Framework Programme (2014–2020)'. Migration is a global phenomenon; by approaching it in a global and collaborative way, it is possible to better understand European migration in a world context.

Innovation in the humanities and creative arts is increasingly dependent on enabling infrastructure to support research excellence. The Migration Experiences platform will connect and consolidate heterogeneous collections and resources for the field of migration studies and will provide an international exemplar underscoring the importance of digital preservation of cultural heritage and highlighting the opportunities new technologies can offer [11]. The platform will widen the scope and range of the interpretative opportunities for researchers, and foster international academic relationships and networks involving partner organisations (universities, libraries, museums, archives and genealogical institutions). In doing so, it will contribute to better recognition and deeper understanding of the continuing role that immigrants play in Australia's national story.

2 Designing a Digital Platform for Preserving and Accessing Migrant Cultural Heritage

The Migration Experiences platform is in the early phases of development, focusing on consultation and scoping that will guide the formulation of a prototype schema funded through the 'Digital Preservation and Documentation of Australia's Migrant Cultural Heritage' grant awarded by the Australian National Commission for UNESCO (2018–19). The platform is intended to enable:

- Research and analysis of the migration experience – from selection through to resettlement, including the array of human emotions without which the immigration story would be incomplete, which consists not only of loss, grief, despair and homesickness, strangeness, anxiety and relief but also the joy of reunion and the satisfaction of 'making it' in a new land; and
- Digital preservation of Australia's immigrants' cultural heritage – which is, at the same time, also a part of the heritage of the migrants' former homelands.

Heritage can be defined as 'that which comes or belongs to one by reason of birth; an inherited lot or portion; or something reserved for one' [12]. However, while we most often refer to material possessions in discussions about our cultural heritage (historic buildings, archaeological sites and artefacts held in museums, archives and libraries), Vasiliki Nihas, speaking as chair of the Cultural Council of the Australian Capital Territory, has maintained that the inheritance we most often receive and leave behind is 'our experience and our expression of culture, individually and collectively. Because . . . it represents a metaphor for the human condition of growth and discovery, [and because] the stories it evokes are powerful and can create connections across cultural [and national] boundaries' [13]. While this is challenging in all cases, it is even more so if the inheritance is international and the heritage objects that cast light on different aspects of culture are dispersed over different countries and many repositories, as is inevitably the case for migrant heritage.

As set out in the UNESCO Charter on the Preservation of the Digital Heritage (2003), 'The purpose of preserving the digital heritage is to ensure that it remains accessible to the public' [14]. The Migration Experiences platform will be built on the principles of a collaborative international research framework and the open sharing of datasets.

The project will be developed in two main stages. The first phase will involve the scoping and design of core features, plus a preliminary data schema focused on interoperability and open data standards, tested using available digitised materials. Later iterations will enhance the data repository schema, introduce further interoperability protocols and explore links with other national and international repositories, refining the design as needed and developing domain-specific research tools. Pilot studies will then set out to capture, share and preserve text-based migrant stories and multimedia records/data of individual migration experiences in order to test the approach and for feature refinement. These studies will be informed by the prior experience of developing the Dutch Australians at a Glance (DAAAG) archive and repository. A diverse range of resources available digitally will be identified and linked in order to test the data model. Resources will include published research findings relevant to migration experience; migrant group histories; digitised diaries, letters, oral histories, voice recordings, films, documentaries, virtual exhibitions, photographic indexes, research bibliographies and artefact databases; migrant biographies held by ethnic communities, migrant families and individuals; and links to shipping lists, immigration records, registration migration cards of 'aliens' [15], citizenship requests held by Australian and overseas collecting institutions and genealogical records.

The second phase of the project will focus on identifying relevant records, located in Australian and international collecting institutions, which are currently unavailable or minimally available in digital form and seek to digitise a selection of these, initially to test data matching and linkage methods, but also to expand the platform's content. There is enormous practical and economic benefit in connecting the data from such research institutions. This phase of the project will build upon the successful cooperation already established amongst a diverse range of researchers working in key Australian and overseas universities and collecting institutions.

While the focus of the Migration Experiences project is currently on Australian migration data, the infrastructural framework is intended, as noted, to be a scalable model and template that can ultimately be reapplied in other national contexts. The vision is for this platform to become a key resource for researchers to utilise for accurate, up-to-date and scholarly research findings, as well as oral history and bibliographic, genealogical and archival material available via databases in Australia and around the world on immigration experiences that relate to Australia. In designing this infrastructure, the project will follow a 'bazaar' model (concept developed at an NIAS-Lorentz workshop organised by members of the project team in Leiden in 2016), in which every heritage custodian, individual or institutional, has the opportunity to contribute and connect their materials to the larger heritage ensemble without over-reliance on a central organisational steering mechanism that would be difficult to devise or operate in such a diverse and international setting. To achieve this, the project will need to address legal and cultural barriers to data sharing: specifically, copyright and data reuse issues around digital collections, and tools to expedite the execution of data/image sharing agreements between partner organisations. The platform is envisaged to ultimately allow individual researchers and institutional collections to link, share and critically evaluate information pertaining to many facets of the migration experience. The intention is for the site to also be relevant on a personal, family and community level – for research and education now and into the future – to the nearly 200 ethnic groups that constitute Australian society.

3 Data Sharing, Integration and Interoperability

3.1 Data Models

The Migration Experiences platform will be specifically informed by and will incorporate features of the following leading international migration, digital history and digital infrastructural projects – which the authors of this paper have led or with which they are actively involved.

The Migrant: Mobilities and Connection project developed by Hugyens ING, Netherlands, offers a best-practice example of **data sharing and analysis** [16]. The project focuses on immigrants who moved to Australia from the postwar Netherlands and their life histories, including longitudinal perspectives (origins, religion or health), and it investigates how these can be reconstructed on the basis of the registration systems used at the time. Underlying the project is the Timbuctoo/Anansi open-source repository system developed by Huygens ING in the context of CLARIAH (Common Lab Research Infrastructure for the Arts and Humanities), to support academic research in the arts and humanities, which 'often yields complex and heterogeneous data' [17]. The project database enables **data comparison and linkage** of emigrant registration cards from the National Archives of the Netherlands with Australian migrant dossiers from the National Archives Australia. This is intended to facilitate research that bridges the gap between migrant agency and policy by reconstructing life-courses of migrants, and mapping and analysing the networks surrounding them, to make visible their influence on individual lives.

The online resource Digitalhistory.ru, a major digital history project developed by the Perm Center for Digital Humanities, Russia, has recently extended its metadata fields to include migration data, and it provides an example of data aggregation, developed in the Russian context but incorporating data and projects from many parts of the world [18]. Aggregated data can help to show otherwise hidden linkages and patterns of connection between entities, as well as resolving ambiguities or contradictions in data held across diverse online or digitised resources. Digitalhistory.ru is a recent example of best practice in **information retrieval and documentation** for digital cultural heritage resources. It provides a catalogue of history-oriented information systems and demonstrates their application in the humanities for research and for education. It includes fields for the standardised description of organisations, authors, countries and links to web resources, as well as an extensive list of thematic descriptions of content (for example, geography, time, types of primary sources and fields related to the description of migration history and cultural heritage). The project takes a multiresource approach to linking data from virtual museums as well as other information focused on the representation of historical sources and cultural heritage, including electronic archives and libraries, and online collections [19].

In Australia, the Humanities Networked Infrastructure (HuNI) provides an existing model for **data aggregation and integration**, incorporating rich biographical data to enable new understandings of social trends and phenomena in the study of Australian people, history and culture, including aspects relevant to migration studies [20]. HuNI brings together data from 30 of Australia's most significant humanities and creative arts datasets and makes them available for use by researchers across the arts and humanities and more widely by the general public. The project's objectives are to make Australia's wealth of cultural resources more accessible and connected; to break down barriers between humanities disciplines and support collaboration and data sharing between researchers, nationally and internationally; to create efficient workflows for researchers working with cultural data centred around enhanced discovery, analysis and sharing; and for the HuNI data aggregate service to lay the foundation for collaborative cross-disciplinary online research capability into the future.

HuNI was funded by the NeCTAR (National eResearch Collaboration Tools and Resources) project, which is part of Australia's strategic investment of over $2.8 billion, made between 2005 and 2016 via the National Collaborative Research Infrastructure Strategy (NCRIS), to provide accessible, nationally networked research infrastructure. Yet the humanities have not historically benefitted from major investments in digital research platforms in Australia. The initial investments from 2005 to 2011 were guided by the 2006 National Research Infrastructure Roadmap, which had a science and technology emphasis, although humanities and social sciences were introduced into the 2008 edition [21]. Much energy in the education sector later went into developing a 2011 roadmap, and while it included a humanities-focused capability area, the roadmap was not finally implemented. Adjacent and intersecting programs, such as the Australian Government's SuperScience Initiative and its Education Investment Fund, separately contributed over $2.3 billion from 2009 to 2015 for the construction and development of teaching and research infrastructure, mainly in the university sector. This included national projects and programs that remain current, such as ANDS (the Australian National Data Service), RDS (Research Data Services, and before this RDSI, or Research Data Storage Infrastructure), and NeCTAR (National eResearch Collaboration Tools and Resources).

The Migration Experiences platform will contribute to national and international digital humanities and creative arts infrastructure by collaborating with other providers that are working toward the efficient discovery and sharing of data. To ensure long-term interoperability it will adhere to interoperability protocols developed for NCRIS projects such as HuNI. This approach will also maximise searchability of data, ensuring that researchers can find pertinent search results quickly and efficiently.

3.2   Migration Museums as Models

The project is also informed by the example of the digital strategies of migration museums. The Statue of Liberty-Ellis Island Foundation, which funds the Ellis Island Immigration Museum via corporations, foundations and private contributions, launched the "Family History Centre" in 2001. Its database contained the given name and surname, ethnicity, last town and country of residence, date of arrival, age, gender, marital status, ship of travel, port of departure and the line number on the manifest of 22 million immigrants, passengers and crew members who passed through the Port of New York between 1892 and 1924, the peak years of Ellis Island's processing [22]. This data, which was taken directly from microfilms of the ship's manifests provided by the National Archives and Records Administration, had never before been available electronically. This searchable collection has now been extended to contain over 51 million passenger records [23].

In Europe, emigration to the 'promised land' is on par with war and memoriali-sation as a focus for museums. For example, in 2007 Germany opened the Auswan-derers Haus German Emigration Center Theme Museum, in Bremerhaven. At a cost of 21 million euros, this 'stellar center' is dedicated to the seven million emigrants who gathered in Bremerhaven between 1830 and 1974 to board a ship headed for the 'new world'. A few months later, the engaging Ballinstadt Emigration Museum was opened in Hamburg. It records the story of the five million emigrants (Germans, Central and Eastern Europeans) who left their homelands – due to dire poverty, hunger and hopelessness, or political and religious persecution – via the port of Hamburg in search of a better life across the Atlantic. In Italy an emigration museum opened in Rome in 2009, and there are many other such examples over the past decade of museums recording the exodus of citizens [24].

The displays in these two German emigration museums are impressive in that they provide easy access to both the big picture and the detailed human stories that underlie it. At the Auswanderers Haus there are spectacular digital initiatives that have been created using linked data resources. In the Gallery of the Seven Million, basic docu-ments and shipping list information are recorded for the overwhelming majority of the emigrants. However, in some cases, visitors can also listen to the stories of individuals and identify their artefacts throughout the museum displays. As a representative sample, these exhibits are relevant for all the emigrants who left Germany to settle in a host country, and to the wider population that seeks to better understand the history of emigration to America.

These are only a handful of examples of the many migration museums that have developed digital resources for public engagement and access that the Migration Experiences project will draw upon and learn from in order to ensure successful implementation.

4 Conclusion

One of the greatest challenges facing society today is the need to rethink the con-struction and transmission of historical knowledge in an increasingly globalised world of fluid national identities, mass migration and an Internet accessible to a vast general public. Cultural historian Maria Grever noted a decade ago that 'digital interactivity is set to revolutionise the preservation and study of all forms of history, . . . every day the Internet attracts thousands of visitors, representing various publics' [25]. The Migration Experiences platform will acknowledge immigrants' contribution to Australian society, including the diversity and wealth of their original cultures. At a broad level it will also provide a positive sense of dual belonging for immigrants and their descendants by raising public awareness of the many facets of migration experience and thus building cross-cultural understandings and empathy. It will support inclusiveness by educating the public to question and challenge cultural stereotypes. The central aim of the project is to create a structure that, through its use of existing successful models, and its linkages with other national and international data infrastructure, can develop a resource that will be economical, scalable, lasting and sustainable for future generations to build upon and use.

The United Nations Educational Scientific Cultural Organisation (UNESCO) and the International Council on Monuments and Sites (ICOMOS) have both acknowledged the urgent need to preserve intangible and tangible heritage resources in the face of the accelerated pace of cultural and economic globalisation. As the UNESCO Medium-Term Strategy (MTS) for 2014–2021 points out, 'The world is growing closer together' [26]. This is occurring not only in physical terms through exponential growth in air travel, global trade and international tourism but also as a result of the communications revolution, especially the rapid uptake of digital media in people's daily lives around the world. The technological advances of information and communications also offer an opportunity to link and connect the dispersed records of migration to create new infrastructures for migration research. The Migration Experiences project responds directly to UNESCO's call for 'new intersectoral approaches and partnerships' [27]. This research is underpinned by the key principles and priorities of UNESCO's 2018–2021 Draft Programme, specifically 'inclusivity . ..; the fight against poverty and the reduction of inequalities; the overarching goal of peace, peaceful societies, intercultural understanding and global citizenship; the fight against gender inequality; . . . supporting populations in crisis, conflict and disaster situations'. UNESCO's 2018–2021 agenda gives 'unprecedented recognition of cultural heritage and cultural diversity' [27].

From an Australian perspective, by integrating and preserving immigrants' cultural heritage for posterity, and viewing it, following Nihas, as an 'active long-term and ongoing contribution to the evolving narrative of Australian identity, Australian nationhood and the Australian politic', the Migration Experiences project aims to strengthen immigrants' sense of belonging and identity as citizens while enabling a deeper understanding of the many strands and influences that make up a nation's history in a globalised world.

Acknowledgement. This research is supported by the research grant 'Digital Preservation and Documentation of Australia's Migrant Cultural Heritage', Australian Department of Foreign Affairs and Trade, United Nations Educational Scientific and Cultural Organisation (UNESCO), 2018–2019.

References

1. Amit, K., Bar-Lev, S.: Immigrants' sense of belonging to the host country: the role of life satisfaction, language proficiency, and religious motives. Soc. Indic. Res. **124**(3), 947–961 (2015)
2. United Nations: Department of Economic and Social Affairs, Population Division. International Migration report 2017 (ST/ESA/SER.A/403) (2017)
3. Anderson, B.: Imagined Communities. Rev. ed. Verso, London (1991)
4. Arthur, P.L.: Things fall apart: identity in the digital world. Life Writ. **14**(4), 541–550 (2017). Cardell, K., Douglas, K. (eds.) Locating Lives
5. Papastergiadis, N.: The Turbulence of Migration: Globalization, Deterritorialization and Hybridity. Wiley, Hoboken (2018)
6. Arthur, P.L.: Transcultural studies in Australian identity. In: Arthur, P.L. (ed.) Migrant Nation: Australian Culture, Society and Identity. Anthem, London (2018)

7. Szekeres, V.: Museums and multiculturalism: too vague to understand, too important to ignore. In: Griffin, D., Paroissien, L. (eds.) Understanding Museums: Australian Museums and Museology. National Museum Australia, p. 8 (2011). http://nma.gov.au/research/understanding-museums/index.html

8. Tudge, A.T.: Celebrating Australian multiculturalism on harmony day, 21 March 2018, Press release. http://minister.homeaffairs.gov.au/alantudge/Pages/celebrating-australian-multiculturalism-on-harmony-day.aspx

9. See Australian Bureau of Statistics data. http://www.abs.gov.au/ausstats/abs@.nsf/lookup/Media%20Release3. See also Nihas, V.: Migration heritage: Beyond the memory box. MHC Forum (1999). http://www.migrationheritage.nsw.gov.au/mhc-reports/forum99/nihas.html

10. Museums in Australia: 1975 Report of the Committee of Inquiry on Museums and National Collections including the Report of the Planning Committee on the Gallery of Aboriginal Australia, p. 5 (1975). http://www.nma.gov.au/__data/assets/pdf_file/0018/1269/Museums_in_Australia_1975_Pigott_Report.pdf

11. Peters, N., Marinova, D., van Faassen, M., Stasiuk, G.: Digital preservation of cultural heritage. In: Zacher, L.W. (ed.) Technology, Society and Sustainability, pp. 107–114. Springer, Cham (2017). https://doi.org/10.1007/978-3-319-47164-8_7. See also Arthur, P.L., Ensor, J., van Faassen, M., Hoekstra, R., Peters, N.: Migrating people, migrating data: digital approaches to migrant heritage. J. Jpn. Assoc. Digit. Hum. (accepted, forthcoming in 2018/19)

12. Macquarie Dictionary, p. 831. https://www.macquariedictionary.com.au

13. Hunt, E.: Barely half of population born in Australia to Australian-born parents. The Guardian (Australia edition), 27 June 2017. https://www.theguardian.com/australia-news/2017/jun/27/australia-reaches-tipping-point-with-quarter-of-population-born-overseas

14. UNESCO: Charter on the Preservation of the Digital Heritage, UNESCO Organisation des Nations Unies pour l'éducation, la science et la culture (2003). https://www.unesco.nl/sites/default/files/dossier/charter_digitaal_erfgoed.pdf?download=1

15. See Australian Government Aliens Act 1947. https://www.legislation.gov.au/Details/C2004C01845

16. Migrant: Mobilities and connection project. Huygens ING, The Netherlands. https://www.huygens.knaw.nl/migrant-mobilities-and-connection/?lang=en

17. Timbuctoo (open source repository system). Huygens ING, The Netherlands. https://www.huygens.knaw.nl/timbuctoo/, https://www.clariah.nl/

18. Centre for Digital Humanities, Perm State University, Russia. Digitalhistory.ru

19. Povroznik, N.: Virtual museums and cultural heritage: challenges and solutions. In: Mäkelä, E., Tolonen, M., Tuominen, J. (eds.) Proceedings of the Digital Humanities in the Nordic Countries 3rd Conference, Helsinki, Finland, 7–9 March (2018). http://ceur-ws.org/Vol-2084/short14.pdf

20. Humanities Networked Infrastructure (HuNI). https://huni.net.au

21. The 2008 Roadmap included recognition of the Humanities area: 'Six capability areas have emerged as a result that essentially incorporate the former priority capabilities . . . together with a new capability recognising the important and pervasive influences of the Humanities, Arts and Social Sciences' (p. viii), and 'A new capability in the Humanities, Arts and Social Sciences (HASS) has been identified in recognition of the wide-ranging contributions these disciplines make to the national interest. Investment in this area would relate to a HASS eResearch infrastructure including data creation and digitisation of research materials' (p. 17)

22. Statue of Liberty-Ellis Island Foundation. https://www.libertyellisfoundation.org/AFIHC-celebrates-grand-opening

23. Statue of Liberty-Ellis Island Foundation. https://www.libertyellisfoundation.org

24. Other examples of emigration museums include the new Irish Emigration Museum in Dublin, Ireland; the House of Emigrants in Vaxjo, Sweden; and the Red Star Line Museum in Antwerp, Belgium

25. Grever, M.: Fear of plurality: historical culture and historiographical canonization in Western Europe. In: Epple, A., Schaser, A. (eds.) Gendering Historiography: Beyond National Canons, pp 45–64. Verlag, Frankfurt (2009)

26. UNESCO: 37 C/4 Medium-Term Strategy 2014–2021. UNESCO, Paris (2014)

27. UNESCO: 39 C/5 Volume 1 Draft Resolutions First Biennium 2018–2019. UNESCO, Paris (2017)

A Progressive Web Application on Ancient Roman Empire Coins and Relevant Historical Figures with Graph Database

Kun Hu(✉) and Jianfeng Zhu(✉)

Kent State University, Kent, OH 44240, USA
{khul, jzhul0}@kent.edu

Abstract. In the past years, information and computer technologies have radically changed cultural heritage sceneries. Cultural heritage institutions have
faced challenges: extracting from heterogeneous data sources, requiring techniques for system improvements and designing better functions and interfaces to
promote user experiences. To enhance user experience, many organizations and
researchers engage in merging advanced technologies to cultural heritage digitization to leverage knowledge both with their organization and external users.
In this report, we describe a process beginning from refining datasets of Roman
coins and historical figures to a final progressive web application. We present
the main technologies that support the digital cultural heritage system to presents
a collection of interesting information to users.

Keywords: User experience · Progressive web app · Cultural heritage
Cultural heritage digitization · Linked data

1 Introduction

Cultural heritages and histories are treasures awaiting more advanced approaches to
reveal more secrets among them. Museums, galleries, libraries and archives already
have their rich collections and datasets developed for many years which have been
organized by domain experts. These datasets are valuable resources to integrate into
databases and even some information systems, which can be accessed online by all
users. Along with developments of recent techniques and tools, it is essential for
modern applications to digitize and manage information of diverse cultural contexts in
a more systematic and friendly way.

In this paper, a modern prototype information system on ancient Roman Empire
coins and related historical figures on their sides are proposed to achieve better user
experiences, richer modern application features and more intuitive data managements
for cultural information applications. Additionally, a complete process of the prototype
system construction is presented, including fetching data of Roman Empire numismatic
information as well as some Wiki data of historical figures, constructing a graph
database of linked data with necessary data elements, and building up a feasible progressive web app system. The system focuses on the information of each coin and
relevant historical figures on coin sides.

© Springer Nature Switzerland AG 2018
M. Ioannides et al. (Eds.): EuroMed 2018, LNCS 11197, pp. 235–241, 2018.
https://doi.org/10.1007/978-3-030-01765-1_26

2 Status

Digitizing cultural heritages seems promising, but some problems still exist. Most of cultural heritages are easy to search online, but standard and systematic information or datasets are hard to collect. Despite some highly structured datasets can be found, not all of them are free, open or sharable to all users. A lack of technical skills especially in small museums and developing countries make essential data hard to exploit because of bad data organizations, poor user interface (UI) design, complex operations, low performance and old system architectures. Besides, there are very few complete and standard strategies or approaches for data management in fields of culture and humanity, which causes the fact that people need to deal a lot with datasets in complex but diverse metadata or even a pile of unstructured datasets. Moreover, most of cultural information systems rely on some past techniques, especially some quite old ones. There is no doubt that they are working, but they don't work well because some techniques are unfriendly, hard to use, in poor performance, out of date or even deprecated. Due to all concerns, cultural heritage data collection, cultural heritage knowledge transformation and standardization, information retrieval technologies, and data visualization are critical tasks in the future.

3 Technology Trend

3.1 Progressive Web App (PWA)

PWAs [3, 7, 8] are a category of web applications with specific features from fusions of recent techniques, friendly designs, better performances, and modern application requirements with specific functions. This category of apps is safe, responsive, installable, discoverable, linkable, re-engageable, always up-to-date, connectivity-independent, interactive with a feel like a native app for better user experience from multiple different aspects.

Not all web apps are PWAs so there is a baseline for the judgment [9]. A PWA should be responsive on multiple devices with different viewports, and of course work cross-browser. The app should be served over HTTPS (Hyper Text Transfer Protocol Secure), and each page can be linkable with a valid URL (Uniform Resource Locator). Smooth page transitions and fast first load on even 3G network are required. Accessing URLs offline on certain contents and adding to home screen make the app "native". For a large, complex and complete PWA, more features need considerations, such as History API (Application Programming Interface), canonical URLs, metadata for searching and sharing, caching strategies, app notifications, friendly UI design, Credential Management API for login, Payment Request API and so on.

3.2 Graph Database

Graph database literally is a database using graph structures. Fast growth on graph databases recently indicates good characteristics of graphs to depict relations and benefits of organizing datasets into graph structures for diverse application requirements. Graph database, compared with traditional databases, has a better performance on queries and analytics thanks to the inherent indexed data structure in the graph model which never works on irrelevant data. Besides, graph database is more intuitive and natural on data modeling because without strict rules in relational databases or complex data organization strategies in some NoSQL databases, vertices for objects and edges for relations lead to a friendly and semantic mode for datasets. Additionally, flexibility of data structure trans-formation makes the database adapt to dynamic use cases on changes of schemas, attri-butes and relations for elastic expanding or shrinking on the data model. For real-time data stream, graph databases can even support simultaneous updates and queries.

Graph databases are in five categories [10]: operational graph databases for a broad range of transactions and operational analytics, like JanusGraph, OrientDB and Neo4j; databases of knowledge graph/RDF which are suitable for operational contexts but have inferencing capabilities and index requirements, such as AllegroGraph, Virtuoso, Blazegraph, Stardog and GraphDB; multi-modal graphs to support different model types for compound requirements, including Microsoft Azure Cosmos DB, ArrangoDB and Sqrrl; analytic graphs focusing on 'known knowns' problems or 'known unknowns' and even 'unknown unknowns', for example, Apache Giraph; real-time big graphs to deal with massive data volumes and high data creation rates and to provide real-time analytics, and an instance is TigerGraph.

3.3 Linked Data and JSON-LD

According to standards of World Wide Web Consortium (W3C), linked data [1, 2] is one concept under Semantic Web. Linked data is the collection of reachable and interrelated data on the web. It empowers people that publish and use information on the web. It provides a way to create a network of standards-based, machine-readable data across web. JSON-LD [4–6] is a lightweight JSON-based Serialization for Linked Data of W3C. It is easy for humans to read and write. It is based on the JSON format and provides a way to help JSON data interoperate at web-scale. JSON-LD is an ideal data format for programming environments, REST (REpresentational State Transfer) web services, and document-based NoSQL databases. Compared to other formats or standards for linked data, JSON-LD is easier to transfer, transform, interoperate and store.

4 Implementation

4.1 Data Sources and Tools

The data used in this project is from three data sources: MANTIS (A Numismatic Technologies Integration Service) for coin entities, OCRE (Online Coins of the Roman Empire) for coin series and DBpedia for historical figures information from Wikipedia. There are over 44000 coins entities, more than 11000 types of coin series and beyond 150 historic figures.

The whole system is built up with Node.js, the JavaScript runtime. ArangoDB is the database to store datasets of coins, historical figures and their relations into a graph.

Koa is for the prototype server. Vue.js is for web components used on the page. Element-UI is for the web UI widgets and design. Fetch API polyfill is for sending requests to the server. Webpack is the module bundler for packaging code files of Vue and Element-UI. Lighthouse is the tool to check the quality of web pages for PWAs. Let's Encrypt is the certificate authority for configurations of HTTPS.

4.2 System Architecture

As a prototype system, there are three main parts: front end pages, back end server and the database. Apart from these, there is a mini program for data integration, and this part is currently standalone because datasets are not real-time. Front end pages are the client part which interacts with users with brief UI design and responsive layout. Back end server is small and simple to deal with incoming requests, send responses back and conduct some operations on the database. The database, operated by logical codes in the server, stores the graph of coins, historical figures and relations among them. Mini program will store elements of the graph (Fig. 1).

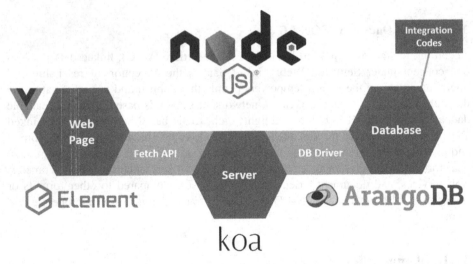

Fig. 1. System architecture

4.3 Data Integration

As the complexity on data integration is not so high, the strategy is simply the batch processing not real-time. The goal of data integration is to get all necessary datasets, synthesize data fields from both coin entity type and coin series type into a more general and refined coin type, simplify data fields of historical figure datasets from DBpedia, and rebuild relations between the refined coin type and the simplified historical figure type. There are three steps to acquire the needed dataset: fetching, preprocessing and aggregating. Data fetching is downloading data files since MANTIS, OCRE and DBpedia all provide APIs of structured datasets. All downloaded files are in JSON or JSON-LD formats because MANTIS and OCRE both have JSON-LD APIs, and DBpedia has JSON API. Data preprocessing is to select required fields in each JSON structure, which is the core part in integration. Data aggregating is to combine data fields from both coin entity type and coin series type into the coin type based on relations in the JSON-LD files from MANTIS and OCRE and recreate relations between coin type and historical figure type according to data files from OCRE and DBpedia. The last step of aggregation is to add schemas to the context and standardize all key terms into IRIs based on the JSON-LD standard. The JSON-LD standard used is the version 1.0, and schemas are from multiple sources: Schema.org for some general annotations, Nomisma.org for some professional numismatic descriptions and some W3C schemas for complements as needed. Due to relationships among coins, coin series and historical figures from fetched data files, coin datasets should be downloaded firstly, then coin series datasets can be downloaded secondly after getting related coin series IDs from coin data, and finally historical figure datasets are downloaded when acquiring related historical figure IDs from coin series data (Fig. 2).

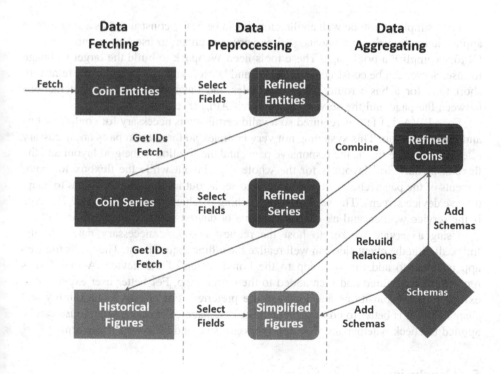

Fig. 2. Data integration flow

4.4 PWA Construction

The general workflow to build up a PWA is to build up a responsive web application first, then add necessary and some optional features of a PWA based on application requirements, and finally use Lighthouse to check how well the application works for later plans on existing problems or optimizations (Fig. 3).

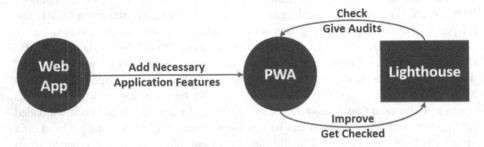

Fig. 3. PWA conversion chart

For a simple prototype web application, it can be easily constructed as a single page application with web components, so it is very convenient to use Vue.js and Element-UI to accomplish a brief page. These tools need Webpack to build the target webpage for use. Server can be constructed with Koa and latest JavaScript features in a relatively short time for a basic router, response codes and database operations. Interactions between the page and the server are via Fetch API for requests.

For a PWA, HTTPS is required so a valid certificate is necessary for configurations and the application. This system is not very complex so three main parts are necessary after HTTPS. The first is the responsive page, and the solution is the grid layout and the flexbox layout. Grid layout is for the whole page layout while the flexbox for components of the page. The most important is to set layout in different viewports to adapt diverse device screens. The second is the caching mechanism for offline use. The core is the service worker, and all cached contents or datasets rely on IndexedDB API.

Using a service worker to host the request and save necessary data into the IndexedDB at the client side can well realize the offline requirement. The last is the web app manifest to add the web app to the home screen of the device. A manifest is required to configured and then added to the current app. For better user experiences, extra efforts on transitions and loadings are preferred. For effective indexability and shareability, it is better to edit the meta tags of the page. Above all, Lighthouse can be applied to check whether the web app is progressive and how well it performs.

5 Conclusion

With the workflow of this PWA, a prototype of modern cultural information system is done, and the app has good features of PWAs indeed, which is one way to solve problems of web applications on multiple platforms. Web components increase the reusability and reduce duplicate developments. Module bundler can partition large modules to smaller ones and emphasize the hierarchy of the system. Fetch API awaits its maturity in the future to totally replace the existing AJAX so the polyfill library is applied. Graph database still needs more concerns and applications during the transition from NoSQL to NewSQL. For this system, a lot of new techniques, skills and tools requires acquisitions and proficiency, which can be current humanity realms. For larger cultural information systems, the architecture can be more complex. For huge relation graphs and real-time uses, TigerGraph can be a good choice. Diverse datasets can be transformed into linked data with some advanced methods from data mining or artificial intelligence and standards for Semantic Web from W3C and further presented as Knowledge Graphs. Server cache can be useful for some data reuses. Large distributed servers can be used for some enterprise-level applications. Excessively many functions can be spread into individual modules of a large microservice application. There can be exceptionally considerable strategies and approaches for information systems of humanity.

References

1. Bizer, C., Heath, T., Berners-Lee, T.: Linked data-the story so far. Int. J. Semant. Web Inf. Syst. 5(3), 1–22 (2009)
2. Bizer, C., Heath, T., Idehen, K., Berners-Lee, T.: Linked data on the web (LDOW2008). In: Proceedings of the 17th International Conference on World Wide Web, pp. 1265–1266. ACM (2008)
3. Hume, D.A.: Progressive web apps. Manning Publications Co. (2017)
4. JSON-LD homepage. https://json-ld.org/
5. JSON-LD 1.0. https://www.w3.org/TR/json-ld/
6. JSON-LD 1.1. https://www.w3.org/2018/jsonld-cg-reports/json-ld/
7. PWA from Google developers. https://developers.google.com/web/progressive-web-apps/
8. PWA from MDN. https://developer.mozilla.org/en-US/docs/Web/Apps/Progressive
9. PWA checklist from Google developers. https://developers.google.com/web/progressive-web-apps/checklist
10. Xu, Y.: A look at the graph database landscape (2017). https://www.datanami.com/2017/11/30/look-graph-database-landscape/

Multidisciplinary Experiences of Virtual Heritage for the Documentation of Architecture and Archaeology Within the *DigitCH Group* - Digital Cultural Heritage Group

Paola Puma(✉)

University of Florence, 50121 Florence, Italy
paola.puma@unifi.it

Abstract. Here we address the roadmap of the Digital Cultural Heritage research group DigitCH group, which was set up in 2013 at the Department of Architecture, University of Florence. The aim of DigitCH group was to realize the link between scientifically validated methodologies and contents, innovative storytelling, and technological instrumentation. The spread of electronic devices has enabled rapid and easy technological fallout of research in the field of the acquisition-representation of the survey data expanding audiences and accelerating even an innovative approach to the whole knowledge of CH.

Among the objectives that the DigitCH group seeks to achieve is the strengthening of the concrete experience of visitors through the use of technological potential; this allows the promotion of CH in all categories of citizens and the renewal of approaches and languages through more active and interactive educational activities. Moreover, DigitCH aims to increase knowledge of CH gained through experience within bespoke digital environments. A selection of case histories from DigitCH shows how we have designed solutions that promote interactions within a broad context, aiming to establish a communication strategy that "opens the educational box" to the territory (to get in touch with the identity of the visited places), new languages (to foster the links between different kinds of cultural heritage: architecture, archeology, artistic heritage), and to a new public (to create a shared cultural habitat among different institutions).

Keywords: Virtual heritage · Architectural survey · Digital representation

1 Scientific Background

The New European Agenda for Culture [1] has recently entered its final phase of drafting and changes the vision for those involved in CH, including those engaged in the acquisition, dissemination, and valorization. The New European Agenda for Culture also changes the public debate; in particular, this vision does not consider CH as only a way to preserve the memory of the past but rather as part of an ecosystem. Within this new ecosystem, cultural policies must be connected to European research policies and digital innovation policies.

© Springer Nature Switzerland AG 2018
M. Ioannides et al. (Eds.): EuroMed 2018, LNCS 11197, pp. 242–252, 2018.
https://doi.org/10.1007/978-3-030-01765-1_27

Briefly, the temporary framework that is emerging suggests that the new direction on which the European cultural policy will be set will be strongly connected with the other already active policies (health, environment, job, competitiveness and social cohesion) so that all work in synergy.

In this framework, it is evident how the field of Digital Cultural Heritage (DCH) can play a key role enhancing its characteristic of being from its origin at the intersection of Digital, Culture, Research. The current culture is formed with a continuous evolution that makes the formulation of strategies for the activation of knowledge very complex, especially if we refer to a "significant" knowledge (we borrow the concept of "meaningful learning" of Ausubel and Novak): the knowledge produced through networks of relationships between people and contents that, using different languages and even distant from each other, makes it possible to re-contextualize the meaning of each experience in a novel way. In this sense, we can build a bridge between contents from humanistic knowledge and high-tech fruition if we work by choosing as a working method the contamination between fields of similar knowledge and a multidisciplinary approach: a bridge that benefits from tangible and intangible CH in a mature and evolved way [2].

2 Strategy, Goals and Program of DigitCH Group

This premise represents the strategic thread of the Digital Cultural Heritage-DigitCH group, which has operated from within the Department of Architecture of the University of Florence since 2013, engaging the research group coordinated by the author in the dissemination of architectural and archaeological cultural heritage by strong synergy between knowledge of the investigated assets and sustainable use of technology for their fruition.

Our guidelines aim to encourage innovative information models and are aimed at achieving objectives based on four axes:

- Experiencing the slow beauty of cultural heritage: when we talk about tourist fruition of CH, DigitCH works to prevent the "tourist selfies" and tourist consumerism; this means inducing more mature ways of visiting and means to promote tangible CH not so much for its abstract beauty but for the slowness and depth resulting from its birth and evolution over time; this produces encouragement for every visitor to approach culture in a direct and emotionally involving way;
- Activate the museum as a factory of knowledge: when we talk about museums we use museographic language to introduce further levels of knowledge on the conception-gestation of the artefact (art as techne) and induce engagement of new public, promoting an "information architecture" that favors the transformation of the museum from a depository to a place to explore one's own creativity;
- Reinforcing the link between the artifact and its context: to promote a truly meaningful cultural experience it is necessary to foster a deeper knowledge of the provenience of the artifacts, of the authors and of the communities of origin: this is one of the main prerequisites for a really wide knowledge of the contents and with a positive impact on the communities involved.

- Maximize the accessibility: the overall information architecture of the DigitCH work program has been principally expressed through the representation of the investigated artifacts so that they are more physically accessible, accessible in contents, and accessible in the space-time line; the general aim of the DigitCH Program, created to facilitate the "smart" fruition of architectural and archaeological heritage (whether museumized or not) through computer-based information architectures, focuses on updating the traditional methods of public dissemination by adding to the original contexts some "information devices" represented by multiple material and immaterial conformations with variable accessibility to the objects themselves.

Already in 2008, the *Icomos Charter for the Interpretation and Presentation of Cultural Heritage Sites* [3], and then in 2009, the *London Charter for Computer-based Visualization of Cultural Heritage* [4], gave the scientific community the problem of rigorous definition of contents, methodologies, and results for the correct proposal of cultural products aimed at public dissemination.

The subsequent application about the archaeological heritage [5] - represented by areas, remains and finds- is also based on the seven principles established in 2011 by the *International Principles of Virtual Archeology* [6], aimed at defining guidelines and best practices in this specific field.

Based on these principles, in 2010, DigitCH began experimenting with the use of low-cost techniques of 3D survey and representation for the documentation and dissemination of the cultural heritage.

The research activity's program has focused on four main lines:

(1) keeping on the critical balance aspects of the scientific context: to realize cultural contexts that can be used collectively and not limited to technical virtuosities individual, DigitCH operates aiming at the use of Surveying and Representation as tools and not as a scope of the process;
(2) to work according to rigorous scientific standards in the measurement and representations for visual reconstructions and contents based on the detailed collection and systematic analysis of historical and environmental data; it means to disseminate contents strictly validated in historical terms and far from easy "special effects";
(3) experimenting with the theoretical and applicative model on different scales, including urban context to architecture, to archaeological areas, to mobile finds;
(4) to achieve greater diffusion and impact of the work by using only entry-level technologies, low-cost or open access hardware and software, and rapid procedures.

In all three cases - in the documentation of the urban landscape, in architecture and in archeology - the group has therefore worked to increase public understanding by avoiding imaginative reconstructions and working to obtain results deriving from a process of logical interpretation based on multidisciplinary work and collaboration between architects, archaeologists, art historians and ICT experts.

In the last 10 years, a new approach to CH communication has emerged based on the use of scientifically reliable metadata [7, 8]. Today, such metadata can be easily activated using an operating chain Survey-Representation-Visualization - Communities of the data that digitalization has strongly integrated and speeded.

Using high-definition 3D models of archaeological finds, for example, presents the undoubted added value of a series of advantages linked to the possibility of visual and perceptive contact (or in some cases, even of the interaction) with an object unavailable in time or in place or not accessible for conservation reasons; this allows, for example, to present the find at a much larger scale, thereby revealing details otherwise not visible to the naked eye [9].

This methodological and instrumental approach [10] enabled DigitCH to create systems of "interactive heritage" in an increasingly flexible manner, where the LS has been progressively joined by the SFM: in particular, the availability of photo modelling has allowed multidimensional data to be used for innovative cultural communication strategies - and according to multidimensional outputs in advanced results, which today has a very wide range of devices and languages, from 3D reconstructions and animations to Augmented Reality, to Virtual Reality and immersive, to virtual scenes.

3 Nine Cases Study by DigitCH Group

3.1 Architecture

Title: Ponte Vecchio in 3D: The architectural survey for the visualization the of post-war reconstruction of the Florentine historic center

Where and when: Florence historic center, 2008–2011;

Description: In 1944, the Nazis retreating from Florence mined and they blew-up the bridges over the Arno and a substantial part of the area of the historic center surrounding the Ponte Vecchio. The research is aimed at producing visual documentation for the knowledge and disclosure of this very special urban piece between the Piazza della Signoria and the Ponte Vecchio.

Outcome: The production of this 3D model represents a tool for the reconstruction of the relationship between project and building, as well as a communication tool to allow tourists to better understand the place; consisting of an easy-to-consult 3D model. Data were collected from the integrated survey and traditional graphic elaborations, as well as the 3D models of the area.

Financing: the research has been funded by University of Florence in Research programs 2009, 2010.

Official acknowledgments: University of Florence - Dept. of Architecture: Paola Puma, Municipality of Florence.

Title: Project Augmented Reality Tbilisi-ARTbilisi

Where and when: Tbilisi, Georgia, 2013;

Description: The project represented the first application of Augmented Reality for documentation and spreading of assets selected from Georgian architectural and archaeological heritage [11]. In 2013 no tools were available for tourists and professionals to investigate the city, except for a few traditional guides, without the sufficient information such an important architectural and archaeological heritage merits.

Due this needing, the Italian-Georgian research group developed ARTbilisi - a multidisciplinary project involving archaeology, informatic engineering, and media arts

- designed by the Italian-Georgian research group to make it possible to visit the Old Tbilisi and the National Archaeological Museum of Georgia in a more in-depth and innovative way. ARTbilisi provides a demo of educational apparatus to show how AR can be used to know info and the educational contents.

Financing: University of Florence, Tbilisi State Academy of Art, Ministry of Culture and protection of monuments of Georgia.

Official acknowledgments: University of Florence - Dept. of Architecture: Paola Puma, Tbilisi State Academy of Arts- Dept. Media Arts: Nana Iashvili, Ministry of Culture and protection of monuments of Georgia, National Agency for CH preservation of Georgia, Italian Embassy in Georgia, Georgian Embassy in Italy, Tbilisis Hamkary, Architectural League of Tbilisi.

Title: FIrenze Mura-FIMU Project

Where and when: Florence historic center, 2016;

Description: The ancient city walls of Florence represents the theme of the Project FiMU [12], with a focus on the survey and digital representations. The short segment of walls we can visit today is the result of the overlapping of traces and circuits that have been, the leading sign of the urban form, up to the caesura of the XIX century, when the entire segment on the north side of the river has been demolished and replaced by boulevards, interspersed with squares designed around the ancient doors.

Outcome: DigitCH has carried out architectural LS surveys, producing 2D drawings and 3D models as tools for visiting the wall circuit and its valorization.

Financing: the project has been funded by University of Florence in Research programs 2014, 2015.

Official acknowledgments: University of Florence - Dept. of Architecture: Paola Puma.

Title: FlorenceImagingMap

Where and when: Florence historic center, 2016;

Description: This research intends to map the material and immaterial characteristics that are profoundly changing the place investigated; through architectural surveys and digital representations (LS survey, 2D and 3D models intended for interactive use), we studied the transformations that an important part of the center of Florence - very representative of its genius loci- faces for some years, due the pressure of tourism mass, the risk of trivialization of places and their image consumption.

Outcome: FlorenceImagingMap, which is still in progress, has given output in the homonymous platform in progressive Web App format: to operate from the website makes it easy to work while the interface from mobile app facilitates intuitive use and promotes the collaborative construction of the repository.

Financing: the research has been funded by University of Florence in Research programs 2015.

Official acknowledgments: University of Florence - Dept. of Architecture: Paola Puma, Giuseppe Nicastro, Dept. of Educational Sciences: Stefano Oliviero.

Title: Yerevan Virtual Heritage Project

Where and when: Yerevan, Armenia, 2017;

Yerevan Virtual Heritage is a didactic research project realized in cooperation between DigitCH and National University of Architecture and Construction of Armenia, Department of Theory of Architecture.

Today the church of Katoghike Tsiranavor Church of Avan has no roofing and is one of the oldest examples of a tetraconca church with cylindrical niches on the diagonals in Armenia: the workshop entitled "The enhancement of the Armenian architectural historical heritage: surveys and representations of the Avan church in Yerevan" has been held meaning the architectural survey as a tool for the reconstruction of its original shape.

Outcome: The project is ongoing. Architectural surveys have been done by SFM and drone, and digital 2D drawings and 3D models have been produced.

Financing: University of Florence, National University of Architecture and Construction of Armenia.

Official acknowledgments: University of Florence - Dept. of Architecture: Paola Puma, National University of Architecture and Construction of Armenia- Dept. of Theory of Architecture: Emma Harutyunyan.

3.2   Archaeology

Title: Project Baratti in 3D

Where and when: Archaeological Park of Baratti and Populonia; Archaeological Museum of Populonia, Piombino, Tuscany, 2007–2013 and 2015, respectively;

Description: Fufluna was the only Etruscan city born on the sea, in front of the Tuscan Archipelago, and was an important and rich city because of its iron production and position adjacent to important trade routes in the Mediterranean Sea.

From the VII century B.C., the most powerful families of Populonia build the Monumental Necropolis, a complex of tombs so rich in luxurious grave goods that were called "the tombs of the princes".

Outcome: The Monumental Necropolis consists of a large number of tombs that were surveyed and represented in 2D drawings and 3D models between 2007 and 2013; then, to virtually "relocate" the finds from the necropolis – exhibited in the Archaeological Museum of Populonia and in the National Archaeological Museum of Florence – in 2015, we undertook the first campaign for the documentation of two burial sets, to realize reconstructions by metrically reliable 3D models [13].

Financing: the project has been funded by UE POR 2007 and University of Florence in Research programs 2014.

Official acknowledgments: University of Florence - Dept. of Architecture: Paola Puma, Archaeological Museum of Populonia: Silvia Guideri, Soprintendenza per i beni archeologici della Toscana: Andrea Camilli.

Title: Project A museum in every sense

Where and when: Archaeological Museum of Populonia, Tuscany, 2014–2016;

Description: This project favored an innovative approach to museum communication, thinking of it as a place of true social inclusion: the storytelling system was born to reverse the traditional approach of many Italian museums – "forbidden to touch" – perpetuating an old concept in which more emphasis is placed on the sacralization of the finds than on the promotion of what they can teach.

Outcome: The project uses the techniques of virtual heritage, applying low-cost techniques to ensure greater involvement of the public through the construction of installations consisting of interactive reproductions of the three emblematic finds of the museum of Populonia (see also the Baratti in 3D Project): the precious Anfora di Baratti, the Tomb of the Chariots, and the mosaic on the marine scene. Working in cooperation with archaeologists, museum curators, and electronic engineers, DigitCH has realized an informative architecture [14–16] where the visitor "queries" to the object that answers: each of the three replicas, made in 3D models by rapid prototyping, has six touch-sensitive points that activate visual and vocal devices that provide information about the three artifacts.

Financing: the project has been funded by UE POR 2013- Regione Toscana.

Official acknowledgments: University of Florence - Dept. of Architecture: Paola Puma, Archaeological Museum of Populonia: Silvia Guideri, Soprintendenza per i beni archeologici della Toscana: Andrea Camilli, Municipality of Piombino.

Title: The Castellum aquarium of Poggio Murella in 3D

Where and when: Manciano, Tuscany, 2016;

Description: This virtual heritage project is aimed at documenting an important artifact currently in a state of neglect, with the goal of triggering subsequent enhancement initiatives. The cistern looks like an imposing stone and brick construction, surveyed by DigitCH for the first time in all its characteristics, whose size and position indicates the possible presence of a typical III century B.C. villa, of which today the Castellum remains the only permanence. The preserve has a volume of approximately $11 \times 35 \times 5$ ml and is made of many kinds of opus. Today, the state of disrepair makes it impossible to walk on the original level and to appreciate the vaults.

Outcome: After the acquisition of morphometric data (carried out through SFM with topographical survey), we produced 2D drawings and 3D texturized models for the Virtual Tour, thereby making the artifact understandable through texts and visual contents. The virtual tour was created as a responsive, multi-channel fruition system (accessible from desktops, laptops, totems, tablets, and smartphones).

Financing: the project has been funded by the Municipality of Manciano and University of Florence.

Official acknowledgments: University of Florence - Dept. of Architecture: Paola Puma, Municipality of Manciano: Giulio Detti.

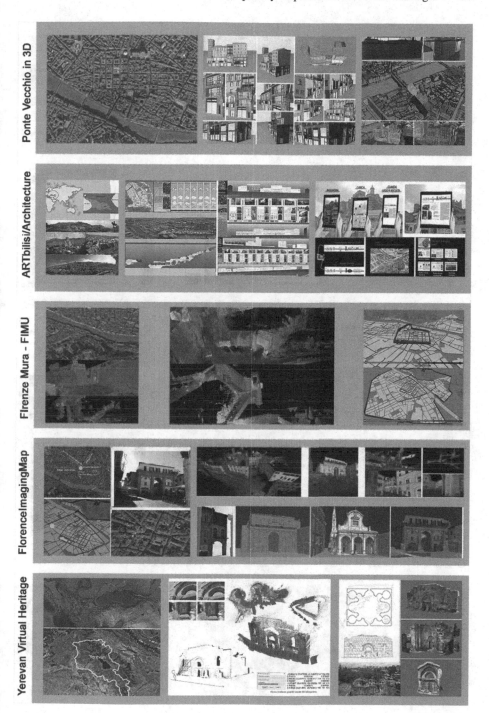

Fig. 1. Synopsis of the study cases of the DigitCH group related to architecture.

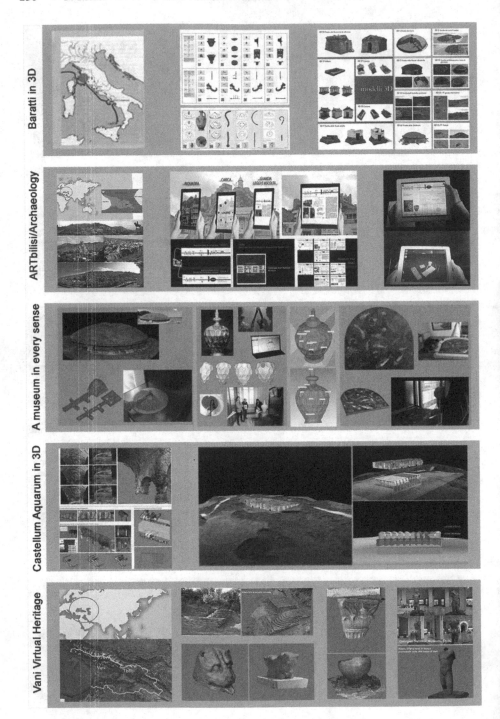

Fig. 2. Synopsis of the study cases of the DigitCH group related to archaeology.

Title: Vani Virtual Heritage

Where and when: Vani, Tbilisi, Georgia, 2017;

Description: Vani Virtual Heritage is a didactic and research project undertaken jointly by Italian and Georgian groups in 2017, in cooperation with Tbilisi State Academy of Arts, Media Arts Department; the workshop "The enhancement of the Georgian archaeological heritage: surveys and representation of remains and finds from Vani" has been conceived to prepare the first modern documentation of the important archaeological heritage of Vani, the ancient capital of Colchis;

Outcome: This project realized surveys of the remains and finds in the Vani Archaeological Museum and the National Archaeological Museum of Georgia in Tbilisi and is in the progress of producing 2D and 3D representations.

Financing: University of Florence, Tbilisi State Academy of Art, National Archaeological Museum of Georgia.

Official acknowledgments: University of Florence - Dept. of Architecture: Paola Puma, Tbilisi State Academy of Arts- Dept. Media Arts: Nana Iashvili, National Archaeological Museum of Georgia: Darejan Kacharava, Sulkhan Kharabadze.

References

1. A New European Agenda for Culture. https://eur-lex.europa.eu/legal-content/IT/TXT/?uri= COM:2018:267:FIN. Accessed 08 July 2018
2. Puma, P.: Local cultures, global heritage: surveying, collecting, communicating - new information models for knowledge and dissemination of cultural heritage. In: Niglio, O. (ed.) Paisaje Cultural Uurbano E Identitad Territorial, pp. 600–608. Aracne, Roma (2012)
3. The charter for the interpretation and presentation of cultural heritage sites. Ratified by the 16th General assembly of Icomos. Quebec, CA. http://www.icomos.org/charters/ interpretation_e.pdf. Accessed 08 July 2018
4. London Charter for computer-based visualization of cultural heritage. http://www. londoncharter.org/fileadmin/templates/main/docs/london_charter_2_1_en.pdf. Accessed 08 July 2018
5. Bertocci, S., Arrighetti, A.: Scires-it 5(2). http://caspur-ciberpublishing.it/index.php/scires-it/ issue/view/756. Accessed 19 Sept 2018
6. Principles of Seville, International Principle of Virtual Archaeology. http://sevilleprinciples. com/. Accessed 08 July 2018
7. Ippoliti, E., Meschini, A.: Tecnologie per la comunicazione culturale. Disegnarecon. https:// disegnarecon.unibo.it/issue/view/276/showToc. Accessed 08 July 2018
8. Pescarin, S.: Scires-it 6(1). http://caspur-ciberpublishing.it/index.php/scires-it/issue/view/ 772. Accessed 08 July 2018
9. Remondino, F., Campana, S.: 3D Recording and Modeling in Archaeology and Cultural Heritage. Theory and Best Practices. BAR International Series 2598. Archaeopress, Oxford (2014)
10. Brusaporci, S.: Handbook of Research on Emerging Digital Tools for Architectural Surveying, Modeling, and Representation. IGI Global, Hershey (2015)

11. Puma, P.: The Tbilisi project: architecture's survey and advanced models for the Atlas and the AR visit of Old Tbilisi. In: Vernizzi, C. (ed.) 36° convegno internazionale dei Docenti della Rappresentazione, Italian survey and International experience, pp. 695–704, Gangemi, Rome (2014)
12. Puma, P.: Tourism and heritage: integrated models of surveys for the multiscale knowledge and dissemination of the historical towns, the architecture, the archaeology. In: Pinto, L. (ed.) The Book of Heritage vs Tourism, an International Point of View, pp. 120–132. Universidade Lusiana, Lisbona (2017)
13. Puma, P.: The Digital Cultural Heritage - DigitCH programme: experiences of documentation and survey for the smart fruition of archaeological heritage. Scires 6/2, pp. 151–164 (2016). http://caspur-ciberpublishing.it/index.php/scires-it/issue/view/779. Accessed 08 July 2018
14. Gershenfeld, N.: When Things Start to Think. Henry Holt, New York (1999)
15. Puma, P.: From survey to 3D: the representation of the archaeological heritage in the project "A museum in every sense". In: Aa, V.V. (eds.) 39° convegno internazionale dei Docenti della Rappresentazione, "Territories and frontiers of the representation", pp. 1113–1120. Gangemi, Rome (2017)
16. Resmini, A., Rosati, L.: Pervasive Information Architecture. Elsevier-Morgan Kaufmann, Amsterdam (2011)

Is E-learning Really Flexible? Ideas for Building Effective Interactive Learning Environments for Cultural Heritage

Afroditi Kamara[1]([✉]), Despoina Lampada[2], Yorgos Tzedopoulos[3], and Kleopatra Ferla[1]

[1] Time Heritage, Papagou, Athens, Greece
{aphrodite, cleopatra}@timeheritage.gr
[2] NTUA and Time Heritage, Athens, Greece
thespoina@yahoo.gr
[3] Academy of Athens and Time Heritage, Aghia Paraskevi, Athens, Greece
tzedoy@gmail.com

Abstract. The paper deals with the use of e-learning platforms in courses concerning digital cultural heritage. The authors draw from their experience in the use of e-learning modules in the context of Erasmus+ projects focusing on adult/VET education on cultural heritage, and suggest an e-learning approach that focuses on personification, modularity and interactivity. As the authors argue, the above three concepts are particularly important for aiding an adult audience understand and implement basic notions of cultural heritage management and enhancement as well as for introducing them in the world of digital cultural heritage. The paper examines possibilities of employing methodologies which will induce personified and interactive knowledge for the creation of e-learning platforms for digital cultural heritage adapted to the needs of diversified target groups. Such e-learning platforms become more and more a necessary counterpart to several digitization projects, as many agents responsible for cultural heritage management and enhancement do not necessarily possess all the skills needed for accomplishing such projects. Therefore, they should be diversified, adaptable to different realities and include various levels as well as stages of self-assessment of users' needs and self-evaluation of users' accomplishment.

Keywords: E-learning · Distance learning · Digital cultural heritage
Digitization · Adult education · Heritage management

1 Introduction

The use of technological innovation in education is not a new phenomenon. Radio waves and television had been recruited for educational purposes in the United States already in the first half of the 20th century. The first computer-supported courses were created in the 1980s and 1990s, until the development of the World Wide Web helped establish electronic learning, a term that today includes all forms that employ

© Springer Nature Switzerland AG 2018
M. Ioannides et al. (Eds.): EuroMed 2018, LNCS 11197, pp. 253–261, 2018.
https://doi.org/10.1007/978-3-030-01765-1_28

"electronic or digital media for the presentation and distribution of learning material and/or the support of human communication" [1].

As the 2000 Lisbon Strategy proclaims, lifelong learning and digital literacy through the use of the Internet and multimedia resources provide a background of a "knowledge society" within a globalized economy and communication [2]. But is this enough?

According to Ally [3] e-learning "involves more than just the presentation and delivery of the materials using the Web". It focuses on a triple interaction (with the content, the instructor and the other learners), which employs the potential of digital communication and multimedia versatility.

Thus, e-learning responds to the educational needs the digital world has created, enabling distant learners "to obtain support during the learning process, in order to acquire knowledge, to construct personal meaning, and to grow from the learning experience" [3]. Taking a deeper plunge into cognitive psychology, e-learning has to abide to the basic precepts of Universal Design of Learning, namely to answer to the "What?", "How?" and "Why?" of learning as stressed by Meyer, Rose and Gordon [4].

2 Scope and Basic Precepts

In this paper we are going to discuss some ideas and concerns on the use of e-learning platforms specializing in digital cultural heritage; we will focus on the need to maximize personification, modularity and interactivity. This discussion draws from our involvement in creating content and educational material for e-learning courses on cultural heritage management and new technologies in the context of two Erasmus + projects, namely Cultour+ [5] and DEN-CuPID [6], at which Time Heritage participated as partner. Both programmes introduced the parameter of technological means for enhancing skills, background knowledge and qualifications on Cultural Heritage, Cultural Tourism and Cultural Routes in people professionally linked to those fields but without having necessarily solid academic background in those fields. In the former case [5], the trainees were young entrepreneurs and professionals interested in cultural tourism, particularly that related to Religious Pilgrimage Routes and to Thermal Tourism; in the latter [6], they were professionals in institutions responsible for (but not exclusively dedicated to) drafting cultural policies (cultural organizations, municipalities) and/or managing cultural heritage (the above plus museums, galleries etc.), as well as aspiring entrepreneurs in this field. In both cases, the trainees stemmed from the local communities and their projects were centred on local development and local perspectives. Beside the actual internships and transnational training activities supported by the Ersmus + framework, both projects involved e-learning as Intellectual Outputs, in order to facilitate dissemination and involvement of larger audiences professionally interested in the above mentioned fields.

In both projects, the partnerships involved at least one academic partner, who was responsible for the development of the e-learning courses. This resulted in a rather academic-oriented approach and structure. However, the actual needs of our trainees, with their various educational and professional backgrounds, seemed not always compatible with this approach; also, the use of moodle platforms, which had been customized according to the needs of quite different courses and learners, presented us with many limitations as to the media and formats which we could use. Therefore, we often found ourselves unable to integrate in our e-learning courses the hands-on methodologies of non-formal learning which we had employed at the physical workshops implemented in the context of these same projects; paradoxically enough, this caused the web-based part of our training courses to be less innovative in its approach. We have explored partly the reasons why this happened and, as associates of a company which aims at further focusing on developing digital content and investing on educational innovation for digital environments, we present them here more in a desire to induce discussion and brain-storming rather than as final results of a research.

3 Defining the Target Group(s)

The need for training and education on all levels for professionals involved with aspects of Cultural Heritage management is a recurring discussion, accentuated by the multifaceted questions pertaining to the digitization of culture and cultural heritage. At a recent Consensus-building workshop in the context of Horizon 2020 Vi-MM project, held in Berlin in April 2018, there was increased awareness of the need for training of heritage professionals and for ensuring "continuous training through DUI (Doing, Using and Interacting) and DWO (Doing With Others) methodologies". This will enhance "awareness of and openness to digital initiatives, as well as promote innovation in Education" [7].

This suggestion does not refer primarily to e-learning, but does include it. It is important that in its formulation various target groups are being taken into consideration. The administrative staff of Local Governments, for instance, may involve individuals with different backgrounds, but with a common scope (or even duty), namely to incorporate innovative technologies into the management of local cultural heritage. The diversity within the learners' group(s) should be taken into account when assessing the needs and possibly trigger versatility in the design of the e-learning course and activities. On the other hand, the structure and scope of an e-learning course for Digital Cultural Heritage (DCH) addressed to historians, archaeologists etc. may be more strictly defined from the start, given that there is ample academic material to rely on and that the target group is highly competent in absorbing structured, formal knowledge.

Aside from the need for trainers and designers of e-learning courses to consider target groups which might better be conceived as "communities of practice" rather than learners with a specific academic profile, we must also address the question of how individual learners are assisted in identifying and choosing the courses most suitable for their needs.

This was a serious issue in both e-learning courses we implemented for the aforementioned Erasmus+ projects. In Cultour+ we had to have in mind a blended audience, consisting of university students[1] from different countries, as well as of

---

[1] Our student audience consisted particularly of students enrolled in the curricula of the three leading universities, namely University of Extremadura in Spain, University of Tras os Montes y Alto Douro in Portugal and Varna Free University in Bulgaria.

professionals and entrepreneurs. A major problem was the language barrier as the e-learning was in English, although we soon realized that not all participants had the same level of English knowledge and that for some of them language barriers were a real obstacle for taking the course. On the other hand, our attempt to create a homo-geneous, palatable-to-all course ended up in units that seemed tedious to part of the audience, not offering enough challenge to make them want to go through with it. However, the modular design saved the day, as participants could chose some of the modules to match their own interests. In DEN CuPID, our target groups did not include students but rather people interested in different aspects of cultural and cultural heritage management and with different levels of background knowledge as well as different roles in the management procedure. Municipal employees, for example, had to focus on resolving administrative issues whereas people involved in voluntary cultural activities through clubs, associations etc. were more interested in innovative funding methods and creating Public-private synergies. Our aim was thus to try and create units as autonomous as possible, so that participants could chose the ones most suitable for their own needs. Language barriers are still an issue, but less so. What seemed to be a challenging and stimulating factor in the physical training courses was the blending of trainees in working groups which could thus share experiences and look at projects from different angles: in the e-learning this is more difficult, however the platform does have a collaborative space for sharing ideas although the courses themselves are designed in a linear, structured way not necessarily inducing use of the collaborative space.

4   Personification and Modularity

Horizon 2020 has funded several projects for cultural heritage digital enhancement, run by higher degree and research institutions all over Europe. "Cross-Cult" [8], "Pluggy" [9], "EMOTIVE" [10] are some of them, sharing, as common denominator, the ambition to "personalize", to some extent, the information offered or shared by administrators and users alike. This tendency to avoid generic, stereotyped information is evident in many fields of digital communication. We believe that it emanates from the feeling that "information" is not enough anymore. With so much of it available on the web, users often feel tired or at a loss. It has been therefore a desideratum of research to find ways to address users not as a mass, not even as "target groups" but, rather, as individuals. The element of free choice, the desire to form one's own nar-rative and to develop one's own interpretation (to some extent) of cultural heritage and culture in general have been proven crucial for appreciating, understanding and further transmitting heritage-related knowledge.

Personification, as understood and put forward through the abovementioned pro-jects and many more, involves the design of specific platforms through which e-learning courses are offered. Normally, in most platforms, we have a short presentation of each course, describing its scope, units, anticipated results, and maybe the target group that the instructor has in mind. In the light of the cognitive theory briefly discussed above we are now at a stage where we need to think of further providing the learner with criteria and informed suggestions about possible courses to choose, by employing personalization processes used in various content-sharing platforms. Such processes might be enriched by enabling learners to tag courses, as part of their feedback, and by designing statistics & analytics grids which can provide correlation between learners' profiles and level of satisfaction for specific courses and/or specific units, so that target groups and profiles associated with these courses & units can be accordingly revised and updated by teachers and content managers. In order to achieve that, design of e-learning platforms and courses should be executed in the future in a modular way, in order to facilitate users to choose the modules they need and are able to assimilate.

Let us elaborate on our initial example: an e-learning course on cultural heritage management for non-specialists (e.g. local agents, municipal employees etc.), such as the one we implemented for DEN CuPID, may address people with completely different educational background. On a local level it may address also entrepreneurs, organizers of events, tourism professionals etc. This course should therefore be designed in a way that each participant could choose the modules that he/she could follow and that could be of greater interest. A self-assessment in the beginning of the course via a mock exercise could help prospect users identify their needs, position themselves within the course and decide which modules would be most useful for them based on their background. For example, if the course is taken by an engineer working in the technical services of the municipality, it would be good to choose modules related to the ethics of conservation of historic buildings, preservation of historic landscapes, creation of a SWOT analysis for restoration projects, drafting a feasibility study etc. Modules on the educational values of cultural heritage are probably less useful for him/her. This, however, means that each module has to be designed in an autonomous way, yet pointing out to other, relevant entities.

5 Interactivity and Enrichment

A way to render an e-learning course more interactive would be to introduce a teacher's "persona". The human voice or even the human face helps users loosen up and feel more secure than when they have to face an impersonal page with instructions. It would be, therefore, advisable, to adopt one of the following strategies. Depending on our audience, our resources and the general "style" of our e-learning course, we could: (a) use an introductory video in which an expert explains the methodology of the platform and the way to use the modules; (b) use videos as the core of our presentation, accompanied by short texts to summarize what the "teacher" says; (c) use an animated figure as guide of the users through the platform; in this case the figure can interact with a basic lesson structure in power-point or text and help make the course more lively or draw attention of the user to the most interesting/important parts or, finally, "pop up" in order to ask the user to do something and thus become part of the knowledge conveyed [11].

The element of video is an excellent tool for learning, which makes a course much more appealing and easy to follow. Apart from digital video presentations of the exact material of the course, which is an expensive procedure, embedded videos or links to videos already extant on the web (provided license can be obtained) can be used for enhancing the main course or for offering additional information. For example when we address the issue of heritage preservation one can embed videos from UNESCO's world heritage series or from other international organizations working on rehabilitation projects. The incorporation of "home-made" videos from physical learning events, such as workshops, is an option commonly adopted but not always technically adequate. Through our experience from DEN CuPID we learned that such videos have usually poor sound, which makes them difficult to follow for long.

Even more important than videos, however, are the embedded toolkits that can be used for offering the user the necessary methods, lists, charts, tables and other tools that might help him/her to understand, design and implement a project. For example, when the issue of a course is project management, one could have an interactive SWOT analysis form embedded in the e-learning course, for users to fill in. The difference between a simple printable toolkit and this one is that the user stays within the learning environment and can use each separate "tool" in conjunction with others or even share his/her "tools" with other users, i.e. his colleagues in a project and thus get feedback or accomplish part of a project's implementation while learning.

Access to further reading and related materials is an important addition to an e-learning course, but constantly updating the relevant repositories in an e-learning platform may not always be possible. In order to address this need, it might be advisable to employ a focused crawler (data mining bot) for mining bibliography and references beyond the pre-selected ones. In order to avoid useless entries, and to reduce searching time, a basis of 4–5 keywords might be set for each search.

Another point that is closely connected to both interactivity and enrichment is the formation of a community among trainees. According to the triple interaction schema we mentioned above, one side of the triangle concerns "interaction with other learners". This is a step towards the formation of a peer community for the facilitation of the learning process on the basis of digital sociability. The communication between the learners and the exchange of opinions and experiences, as mentoned above on the basis of or DEN CuPID experience, may help them identify their needs, put to test and solidify their knowledge through discussion and mutual support, and end up with the creation of an engaged community.

6 Assessment and Self-evaluation

An issue that has to be taken into account when aiming at creating more personalized e-learning courses, is the assessment type. Nowadays, for reasons which have to do with the sustainability of the e-learning module even after the completion of the project for the purpose of which the course has been created, the most usual way to assess the user's knowledge is the quiz with multiple choice selections. Multiple choice offers a standard assessment, with automatically generated results, which do not need an expert at the other end for assessing the answers. However, this by default does not help the users deepen their educational experience nor to develop skills, which is often the required goal of any educational activity, particularly in adult and non-formal education [12].

E-learning courses are addressed largely to adults who either want to acquire new knowledge or to blend the "bits" of knowledge they have acquired "on the field" into an integrative whole. The fact that the learners do not have always to start from scratch, as well as their expectations about being able to put in action the acquired knowledge in a constructive and effective way point to the incorporation of specific evaluation features.

A fruitful way would be, instead of insisting on multiple-choice queries and quizzes, to employ a more playful, sequential and creative evaluation structure, which could involve the learners' psychological and emotional powers towards self-realization. We suggest an evaluation process that follows a modular structure in a game-type series of exercises with correct responses to the challenges leading to further challenges until the completion of a specific action. Drawing from our experience with the specific target groups we mentioned above, such "evaluation games" could include scenarios concerning a conservation initiative, an educational activity, a dissemination strategy for a cultural event, a scenario for cultural digital storytelling etc. This type of gamification brings the evaluation process near to real-life implementation and compels users/trainees to think in real-life terms for completing the exercises.

To give a more concrete example: upon evaluating the participants' understanding of creating a funding scheme for their cultural heritage management project, a drill could be to build a hierarchical ladder with all possible funding sources (public funds, private donors, crowdsourcing, ticketing etc.); wrong answers would be dismissed by the system (like what happens with on-line jigsaw puzzles). Or, similarly, to decide upon the steps to take for effectively using social media for enhancing their project (from starting the account to establishing an audience and checking the insights or Google analytics to control the effectiveness of their use of each specific medium). However, if the resources allow it, a complete on-line game could be organized which could be played by each user individually or even by different users with role-assumption. Given on our experience from Cultour+ this could include for example the virtual travellers' needs along a pilgrimage route and how these are met by local businessmen; based on our DEN-CuPID experience, on the other hand, the gamification aspect could include the gamification of a project such as the restoration of an old factory to house a museum: each participant could assume a role and decide upon one's steps to be taken towards the accomplishment of this goal.

Although gamification may refer at first instance to practices suitable for children and adolescents, the truth is that it is appealing also to adults and helps embed not only knowledge and information but also create the sense of procedure and set milestones along it, so that the experiential aspect of learning is triggered.

7   Conclusion

E-learning theory has already covered a lot of ground since the emergence of the concept and practice of distance learning via digital channels [13, 14]. With the spread of e-learning courses on the web, the necessity for designing effective courses is so evident, that one can now find both University modules - see for example King's College, London [15] - and online courses - as the ones offered by the e-learning provider Alison [16] - aiming at enabling educators to make the most out of e-learning as a teaching tool.

In designing and planning an e-learning application it is always advisable that the people taking part in it, rather than differentiating between the distinct roles of "content creator", "designer" and "programmer", blend their contributions into a common, inclusive methodology. In this process, all elements of the e-learning structure are constantly interacting with each other in the creation of a particular module. Design affects the presentation and integration of the content; programming affects the degree of interactivity; content is constantly re-formulated in order to respond to requirements of authenticity and agency. This requires, however, very good collaboration among members of the team and a sense of collective work which does not always come easy for the respective parties, particularly in what concerns cultural heritage and humanities. An initial remedy to this is to help creators of e-learning modules to think both as creators and addressees, as teachers and students at the same time. However, a lot of research and experimentation has to be carried out in order to create templates and functions which would facilitate upload of content on a more interactive substratum and thus facilitate e-learning in the fields of Digital Humanities and Digital Cultural Heritage.

The collaborative environments created under major EU-programme platforms such as Horizon 2020 or Erasmus+ are ideal for promoting such research, as they observe the function of e-learning also in multi-lingual and multi-cultural environments. However, as e-learning platforms are usually proposed as deliverables, there seems to be a repetition in the methodology followed in these platforms. Following our experience we think that EACEA and perhaps other European agencies should invest more on research regarding effectiveness, originality and functionality of e-learning based on the precepts proposed above and perhaps provide some basic templates or guidelines through its portal. Furthermore, it has to be understood that funding should be more generous in Erasmus+ for implementation of e-learning and educational tools in general, in order for partnerships to be able to make use of more and up-to-date resources.

References

1. Kerres, M.: Mediendidaktik: Konzeption und Entwicklung mediengestützter Lernangebote, 4th edn. Oldenbourg Verlag, Munich (2013)
2. Lisbon European Council 23 and 24 March 2000: Presidency Conclusions. http://www.europarl.europa.eu/summits/lis1_en.htm. Accessed 27 July 2018
3. Ally, M.: Foundations of educational theory for online learning. In: Anderson, T., Elloumi, F. (eds.) Theory and Practice of Online Learning, pp. 3–31. Athabasca University, Athabasca (2004). https://auspace.athabascau.ca/bitstream/handle/2149/411/?sequence=1. Accessed 22 June 2018
4. Meyer, A., Rose, D.H., Gordon, D. (eds.): Universal Design for Learning: Theory and Practice. CAST, Wakefield (2014)
5. Cultour Plus: Innovation and Capacity Building in Cultural Tourism, Entrepreneurship for European Cultural Routes. http://www.cultourplus.info/en/. Accessed 30 June 2018

6. DEN-CuPID: Digital Educational Network for Cultural Projects Implementation and Direction. http://den-cupid.eu/en/den-cupid-welcome/. Accessed 5 July 2018

7. Virtual Multimodal Museum: Propositions and polling from the joint consensus-building workshop of all thematic areas, Berlin, 12–13 April 2018. https://www.vi-mm.eu/wp-content/uploads/2018/04/ViMM-Propositions-following-Berlin-for-platform-inc-poll-results.pdf. Accessed 5 July 2018

8. Cross-Cult: Empowering reuse of digital cultural heritage in context-aware crosscuts of European history. https://www.crosscult.eu/. Accessed 8 July 2018

9. PLUGGY: Pluggable Social Platform for Heritage Awareness and Participation. https://www.pluggy-project.eu/. Accessed 13 June 2018

10. EMOTIVE: Storytelling for Cultural Heritage. https://emotiveproject.eu/. Accessed 30 May 2018

11. Sofos, A., Kosta, A., Paraschou, V.: Online remote education: from theory to practice. In: Greek: Online εξ αποστάσεως εκπαίδευση: Από τη θεωρία στην πράξη. HEALLINK, Athens (2015)

12. Yasunaga, M.: Non formal education as a means to meet learning needs of out-of-school children and adolescents. Background paper, UNESCO Institute of Statistics and the United Nations Children's Fund, Global Initiative of Out-of-School Children (2014). http://allinschool.org/wp-content/uploads/2015/01/OOSC-2014-Non-formal-education-for-OOSC-final.pdf. Accessed 5 July 2018

13. Haythornthwaite, C., Andrews, R.: E-learning Theory and Practice. SAGE, London (2011)

14. Haythornthwaite, C., Andrews, R., Fransman, J., Meyers, E.M.: The SAGE Handbook of E-learning Research. SAGE, London (2016)

15. King's College, London: E-learning theory and practice (module). https://www.kcl.ac.uk/study/courses-data/modules/7/E-learning-Theory-And-Practice-7ssem021.aspx. Accessed 25 July 2018

16. Alison: Introduction to E-Learning Theory and Practice. (Free On-line course). https://alison.com/course/introduction-to-e-learning-theory-and-practice. Accessed 5 July 2018

Eco Sustainable Graphic Heritage Drawing for a Contemporary Territories Learning and the Creating Smart Cities

Alessandro De Masi[✉]

School of Design, Milan Polytechnic, Via Durando 38 A, Milan, Italy
alessandro.demasi@polimi.it,
alessandro.demasi@unina.it

Abstract. The research Eco Sustainable Graphic Heritage Drawing (ESGHD) is intended as development of representation models for architecture and urban landscape both in the measurement phase and simulcast description of information. With this premise the research will enable to pursue the knowledge and communication of the processes of modification for Cultural Landscape with the construction of a "visual model", which can be implemented, for "typologies of representation" and the creation of Smart City.

Keywords: Operative reading · Semiotic interpretation · Visual frameworks
Sensitivity levels · Modeling in HBIM · WEB GIS

1   Introduction

The study proposes a methodological advance on the dimensions identities of research in representation in the mapping of the cultural and natural features of Historic Urban Landscapes (HUL), Green Contemporary Territories and Smart City (SC); it will be directed to recover the loss of human contact with landscape components for to verify a comparison with natural historical culture and the places of history for support the contemporary territories and SC. As regards the impacts in creating SC Eco Sustainable Graphic Heritage Drawing (ESGHD) will produce the developing process of open innovation in the urban environment through sensitive analysis of new urban uses, territories stakes, prototypes, green technologies and operating process of users' collaboration. ESGHD is intended as development of representation models for architecture and urban landscape both in the measurement phase and simulcast description of information. This through a vision related to the new "Informational Dimension of Survey" based on the relationship between continuous models and photorealistic 3D models (photomodeling), Heritage (H) - Building Information Modeling (BIM) and geo-databases. It will go in the direction of constituting: (1) Levels of "documentation – monument" [20] on the status of architectural goods with disciplinary advances on 3D modeling methods. The methods of analysis and classification will highlight the architectural structure of algorithms and objects with categories and parametric data. Cataloging the goods will be understood as a sequence of images, according to Gestalt, associated with the emotional and perceptual dimension of the observer. (2) A "continuous representation model" for metadata to geographic and geographical entity,

© Springer Nature Switzerland AG 2018
M. Ioannides et al. (Eds.): EuroMed 2018, LNCS 11197, pp. 262–270, 2018.
https://doi.org/10.1007/978-3-030-01765-1_29

monitoring of the state of preservation of goods. In this case, the "3D relational geo-database" will aim to archive geographic entities and catalog attributes, geo-referenced multiscalar architectural/typological elements. (3) A "thematic representation of monumental and urban systems" to allow the geometric description of primitive graphs with functional relationships. (4) Knowledge and communication of the processes of modification of both the CH and the *genius loci*, according to Norberg-Schulz named "spirit of the place", of the landscape with the construction of a "visual model", which can be implemented, for "typologies of representation" and different categories related to "temporal and not temporal dimensional apparatus". This will allow, through the grid of knowledge and nodes, to represent, in scalar reading the "sensitivity levels" both on a landscape scale (cultural - archaeological, urban, productive) and architectural systems through historical signs and modifications [11]. (5) An "operative reading" to identify criteria and address lines in environmental insertion techniques. This will highlight the material culture of the place and the *genius loci*. In addition to connect the constructive cultural traditions. (6) The UNESCO Recommendations (2011) on the HUL with the European Union's territorial policy processes.

2 Research Methodology

The methodology, oriented both to the knowledge and communication of the modifications of landscape and constructed reality, can be based on a "operative reading" through methodologies and techniques for architectural, urban and environmental drawing. The "informational dimensions of the survey" together the material-constructive, spatial and formal characters highlight the processes of laceration in the urban fabric that influences the perceptive quality. The ESGHD can allow communication of critical complexity by comparing multiple compartments and their representation methods. This with particular regard to the following Classes (C) and Subclasses (SC):

L1 - Grid of Landscape Knowledge: C1 - "Physical, Identity and knowledge Landscape Elements" for understanding the aspects of aerophotogrammetric documentation of landscapes (Entirety, Criticality, Vulnerability) and landscape units in relation to landscape plans. SC1.1 "Study of Environment and Landscape Units" (between these Anthropological Semiology Charter and Absolute Visualisation Charter). SC1.2 "Methods of Survey and Visual Evaluation of the Morphological Characters of the Landscape" with the study of visual frameworks [21] - (Fig. 1). SC1.3 "Evaluation of Complexity through Indicators at Different Dimension Space-Time". Between these integrity and fragility of open and closed urban spaces, permeability and porosity of anthropic environment, integrity and connection of spaces to green [13]. C2 - "Scalar Reading of Sensitivity Levels" for read the modifications and evaluations of data within the area interest landscapes. It allows the development of a "visual model" that returns a reading of CH by the "sensitivity levels" of historical signs and knots. It identifies "patterns related to typologies of representation" for a "temporal and not temporal dimensional" images of Cultural Landscapes (Fig. 2).

L2_Grid of knowledge at Architectural Unit level: C1 - "General Elements of the Architectural Unit" for a comparative reading of localisation, geographic-

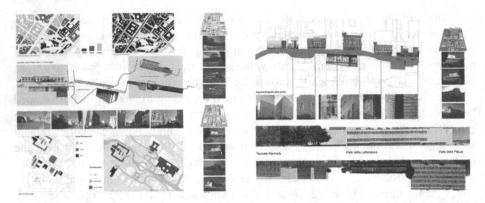

Fig. 1. From the left, study of visual frameworks for recognisability and identity of places (Sede della Gioventù italiana del Littorio and Palazzo dei Ricevimenti e dei Congressi, Rome) - Course of Techniques of Representation, University of Rome III (A. De Masi)

Fig. 2. From Left, Sensitivity Levels of historical signs and knots (Residential building "Casa Rustici" and Palazzo per Uffici De Angeli Frua, Milan), Virtual model that identifies the wood model and the geometric structure according to the Morphosis architects (Sede della Gioventù italiana del Littorio, Rome). Courses of Architecture Representation, Milan Polytechnic and University of Roma III (A. De Masi)

administrative data with the cartographic documentation. C2 - "Elements of Recognition and Evaluation of the Identity Character of CH" for read the typological/structural data related to the elements of particular interest. SC2.1 "Integrated Digital Survey: Acquisition and Data Recording". SC2.2 "Digital Restitution and Modeling" with the reading of the formal, functional and dimensional aspects through the representation methods; Creation of an integrated 3D system of dimensional and formal data manipulable for the purpose of preservation and checks geometry, topology and photometry data (Fig. 3). SC 2.3 "Reading of Identity

Characters, Pre-existence and Utilizations" for supports of CH through both the restitution made by orthogonal representation methods and the management of 3D urban models. SC2.3.1 –"Reading Methods of Three-Dimensional Representation" that allow to emerge the different modifications and evaluations of data on CH. SC 2.3.3 - "Hypermedia Systems" to facilitate both computer dialogue between different 3D modeling methods and communication of modification processes. This through "temporal and not temporal dimensional apparatus" for the purpose of sharing of aspects related to the relationship between perception and representation, knowledge and understanding of current Urban Landscape (UL). C3 - "Sensitivity levels in Scale Reading" through the representation of historical signs, permanence, modifications, and subsequent comparing of data of different functional, historical, geometric, typological and structural categories with topological, photometric and geometric characteristics [11]. C4- "Elements of Provision for the Restoration of CH".

Fig. 3. From left, Temporal and not Temporal Dimensional Model's Interpretation by 3D system (Residential and office building, Milan). Course of Architecture Representation, Milan Polytechnic (A. De Masi)

2.1   The Grid of Landscape Knowledge: Semiotic Interpretation of HUL and Aesthetic/Perceptive Theory

In the ESGHD visual perception and aesthetic theory are structural part of the complex system of recognition and translation. In particular: (1) Landscape is image of reality with the recognition of characters and signs as a "document" of relationship between nature and culture. Further meanings lie in the distinction between objective and subjective meanings. For a semantic value of vision, the landscape is as visual perception reveals it and from the circumstance in which such context is perceived as reported by Italo Calvino (1923–1985) in "Esercizi di Descrizione". (2) The process of identification is possible through an isomorphism relationship between the relevant part of the stimulate information and a mnesic visual information pattern: a sort of gestaltic schema [2]. (3) Each object has its own expressive connotation that immediately affects our vision [3]. (4) For an analytical and objective method, assuming a sort of a priori knowledge of things that have a typical or categorical character to be privileged with respect to the subjectivity according to Norberg-Schulz (1926–2000). (5) Each model is based on a plastic and iconic reading according to Algirdas Julien Greimas (1917–1992). (6) The relationship between perception and cultural context determines the awareness of landscape values in the light of Kevin Andrew Lynch's visual framework (1918–1984).

2.2 Grid of Knowledge at Architectural Unit Level: Utility and Beauty in Schinkel's Architectural, Pictorial and Scenic Representations and Design of American Architects Between Illusion and Advertising

The grid of knowledge at Architectural Unit includes, beyond the restitution and modeling of architecture, the representation of context and landscape (Fig. 4a). The idea of landscape as representation belongs at the concept of pictorial representation that is at the representation. The villas of Andrea Palladio (1508–1580) are an example of "visual" integration with landscapes. The perspective representation is intended as scenography for a reading of the sequence of scenes and discontinuity of the spaces. Furthermore, it is in line with the nature of the interpretation of paintings of the 500 Venetian and the representation of literary myths. Also the pictorial and scenographic representation of Karl Friedrich Schinkel (1781–1841) show particular attention to the representation of the landscape with a surprising graphic restitution for the different pictorial and scenographic expressive modes. Moreover, denotes a focus on Roman pictorial decoration and the representations of the nineteenth century "Pensionnaires". An example is shown in the drawings of the French School that reconstructed Pompeii's building structure with accurate reproductions both the frescoed walls and the architectural structure all harmoniously incorporated into the landscape. Between 1805 and 1816 the Schinkel's pictorial representation will be understood among other things as: (1) Physicality's study of architecture and its context for critical reading. (2) Representation element of the cultural landscape without the mere representation of nature. Between 1819 and 1840 the elaborates denote the rigorous application of oblique projections according to the eighteenth-century Venetian vedute aimed at highlighting the technique of representation and the representation of natural elements with chiaroscuro effects to underline the interior of representation (Fig. 4b). From 1834 to 1841, in the Royal Palace on the Acropolis (1834), Schinkel integrates, surprisingly, architecture and context, both inside and outside, for the imperial residence in Orianda (1838) of the tsarina Alexandra. The representation of the environments of the Crimean Museum and the temple-belvedere is entrusted to the central perspective views

(a)   **(b)**   **(c)**

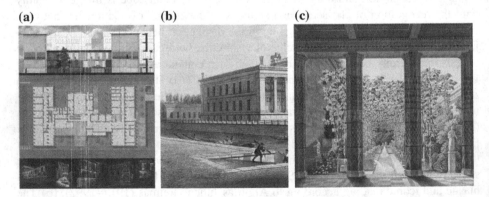

Fig. 4. From Left, Sede dell'Unione Fascista dei Lavoratori dell'Industria, Como. Course of Architecture Representation, Milan Polytechnic (A. De Masi), K. F. Schinkel, Atles Museum, 1830 and Crimea Museum, Orianda. Section Prospective

elaborated according to the model of the Pompeian School with the observer that inspects from a window (Fig. 4c).

Also American architects, in the last century, have been innovative in the representation/communication of architecture and landscape. In particular the perspective, after 1820, will be indispensable to relate the volume to nature and the site as in the case of Richard Upjohn (1802–1878). Map and prospect drawings, according to the influence of Beaux-Arts, will feature planimetric composition representations, while the landscape will go to the background (Fig. 5a). Frank Lloyd Wright's drawings (1867–1959) will be an exception in which plan drawing predominates in design with attention to landscape and nature. The drawings, since 1970, will highlight an executive component for the request of environmental impact. Also, the design of Morphosis architects are characterized by: (1) A capacity to illustrate the richness of the composition of the landscape, the cultural and social dynamics of the contemporaneity. (2) Complicated sculptural forms for the diverse organizational systems present and intrinsic of emotionalism, of sensationalism that escape from geometric control (Fig. 5b).

(a)   (b)

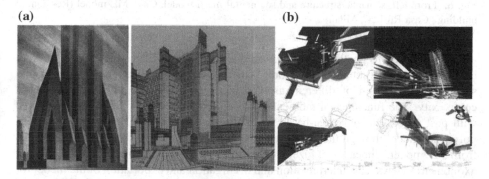

Fig. 5. From Left, H. Ferriss, Study for Maximum Mass allowed by 1916 New York, 1922, A. Sant'Elia, Drawings for a Futurist City, 1911, Morphosis, projects 1993–97. Virtual model, that identified the wood model, and geometric strcture

2.2.1 Modeling in HBIM Environment, Integration into WEB GIS and Hypermedia Systems to Facilitate Both Dialogue Between Different 3D Modeling Methods and Communication of Modification Processes

Parametric modeling allows a model to be modeled using real-world prefabrication methods by integrating a segmented and semantic BIM modeling. This to return: (1) The values of the landscape components. (2) An innovative approach to hypertextuality and interactivity also on GIS platform for conservation. The integration of the 3D model from HBIM into a 3D GIS is possible with CityGML (Open Geospatial Consortium) for detailed semantic framework of CH modelling, the geometry of a heritage site and visualising and analysing geographic data (Fig. 6). (3) Procedures for CH models with 3D information and 3D data obtained by 3D architectural libraries for main architectural elements. The data coming from different sensors will be segmented and represented with different levels of accuracy and detail. This is to describe geometric shapes with libraries created by Generative Modeling Language (GML) systems in union with 3D survey technique. (4) Consultation and historicization of interventions's scheets (Fig. 7). The process begins with survey data (photogrammetry) and then proceeds with integration from a library of parametric objects of modeling technique using a Geometric Descriptive Language (GDL) to repeat objects (windows and portal) of modelling for the construction of the walls of the buildings. The 3D model is converted into CityGML with geometrical and semantic information using an application for Google SketchUp for to insert additional information.

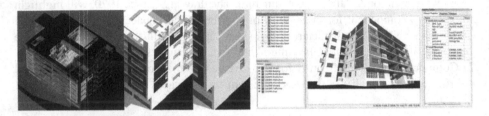

Fig. 6. From left, semantic structure and segmental mesh model, CityGML model (Residential building "Casa Rustici", Milan)

The applications photogrammetry made for two CH of Milan were carried out both by the method of restitution of the outer surface and the application of textures, and survey for the return of different aspects in order to acquire levels of geometric complexity. The fundamental moment has been extracting and filtering data captured with post processing of image-based modeling data for the transition to the textured polygonal model through the use of images. Next return of two-dimensional drawings from 3D model, dimensional size measurement and extrapolation of perspective or axonometric views, data interpretation and divulgation and exportation of the model for controlled mosaic creation. The post-processing phase was subdivided into the generation of the photorealistic mesh model and digitisation. Accurate application was carried out with multi-store photo datasets for the acquisition of geometric and metric data using image-based photogrammetric systems. This is to allow, with Autodesk 123D Catch and ReCap Photo, a dependable 3D polygonal photographic model both metric and visually. The comparison in Meshlab allows metric data to be retrieved from the mesh model and transmitted to a mathematical model for cleaning, filtering and editing phases (Fig. 8a). With ReCap Photo, you can take advantage both important point beatens (selecting a point in the image and coordinating input x, y, z), and using the reference lengths (measured with direct relief through two points taken as reference) (Fig. 8b). With the "spherical panorama" hybrid application is possible to retrieve metric inputs with other rilief methods (topographic, laser scanners) booth for to combine different photographs to eliminate the distortions of the lens and to take large spaces (Fig. 8c).

Fig. 7. Photomontages of UL complexity assessment (Residential building "Casa Rustici", Milan. Course of Architecture Representation, Milan Polytechnic (A. De Masi)

(a)   (b)   (c)

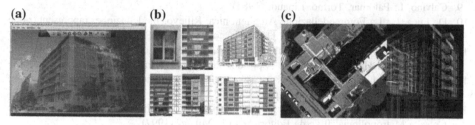

Fig. 8. From left, ReCap Photo reconstruction mesh in wireframe and automatic extraction of profiles with Rhinoceros, and 123D Catch, External acquisition, mesh reconstruction in texture and wireframe view, Orthographic view from a point clouds and with application of spherical panorama (Residential building "Casa Rustici", Milan)

3 Result and Conclusion

The research collects the results obtained as a senior expert of the MiBACT and proposes a methodological advancement on the changing identities of research in representation. This in the mapping framework of cultural and natural characteristics of the UHL. The ESGHD is identified with the development of representation models both in the "measurement" phase and simultaneous description of information for architecture and UL. The results achieved are: (1) Knowledge and communication of the processes of modification of both the CH and the *genius loci*. (2) An "operative reading" to identify reading criteria and addressing lines in the environmental insertion techniques. (3) To the quality of knowledge communication and social infrastructure with the development of a language that highlights the relationship between semantic and parametric dimension of architecture in the BIM and GIS. (4) The informational dimensions of the survey through a "operative reading". Advanced technique can to support applications to improve urban life and urban informatics.

References

1. Amistadi, L.: Paesaggio come Rappresentazione. Clean, Napoli (2008)
2. Arnheim, R.: Visual Thinking. University of California Press, Los Angeles (2004)

3. Arnheim, R.: Art and Visual Perception: A Psycology of the Creative Eye. Regents of the University of California, Berkeley (1954)
4. Atkinson, K.B.: Close Range Photogrammetry and Machin Vision, Whittles Publishing (2001)
5. Beraldin, J.A.: Acquisizione 3D e modellazione poligonale. McGraw-Hill, Milano (2010)
6. Rodriguez Navarro, P.: Automated Digital Photogrammetry versus the systems based on active 3D sensors. In: EGA, no. 20 (2012)
7. Brusaporci, S.: Handbook of Research on Emerging Digital Tools for Architectural Surveying, Modeling, and Representation. IGI Global, Hershey (2015)
8. Cabezos-Bernal, P., Cisneros-Vivó, J.: La restituzione fotogrammetrica 2D/3D di elementi architettonici e l'integrazione dei modelli virtuali sulle fotografie dell'intorno reale, mediante programmi CAD, software liberi e fotocamere convenzionali. In: Disegnarecon, vol. 6, no. 12 (2013)
9. Calvino, I.: Palomar, Torino, Einaudi (1983)
10. De Luca, L.: La Fotomodellazione Architettonica. Rilievo, modellazione, rappresentazione degli edifici a partire da fotografie. Dario Flaccovio Editore, Palermo (2011)
11. De Masi, A.: Campania (Italy), cultural landscape and rural environment governance. In: Proceedings of Heritage 2008, vol. 2, pp. 607–617. Green Lines Istituto, Barcelos (2008)
12. Fangi, G.: Further developments of the spherical photogrammetry for cultural heritage. In: 22nd CIPA Symposium, Kyoto, Japan (2009)
13. Ferrara, G., Campioni, G.: Tutela della Naturalità Diffusa, Pianificazione degli Spazi Aperti e Crescita Metropolitana, Il verde Editoriale s.r.l., Milano (1997)
14. Gaiani, M.: La rappresentazione riconfigurata. Un viaggio lungo il processo di produzione del progetto, POLI.Design, Milano (2006)
15. Gaiani, M.: I portici di Bologna. Architettura, modelli 3D e ricerche tecnologiche, Bononia University Press, Bologna (2015)
16. Gartner, H.: Schinkel Studien, Seemann, Leipzig (1984)
17. Greimas, A.J.: De l'Imperfection, Paris, Falanc, P. (ed.) (1987)
18. Kolbe, T., Gröger, G., Plümer, L.: CityGML – interoperable access to 3D city models. In: International Symposium on Geo-information for Disaster Management, Delft (2005)
19. Le Goff, J.: L'immaginario urbano nell'Italia medievale (secoli V-XV). In: Storia d'Italia. Annali 5. Il paesaggio, Enaudi (1982)
20. Le Goff, J.: Documento/Monumento, Enciclopedia Einaudi, Torino, vol. V, pp. 38–43 (1978)
21. Lynch, K.: The Image of City. The Technology Press & Harvard University, Cambridge (1960)
22. Mueller, P., Zeng, G., Wonka, P., Van Gool, L.: Image-based procedural modeling of facades. In: ACM Trans. Graph. 26(3), Article ID 85 (2007)
23. Norberg-Schulz, C.: Architettura: presenza, linguaggio e luogo, Skira ed. Milano (1996)
24. Pevsner, N.: Schinkel. J. R. Inst. Br. Archit. (59) (1952)
25. Pogacnik, M.: Karl Fiedrich Shinkel Architettura e paesaggio, Motta editore, Milano (1993)
26. Remondino, F.: Rilievo e Modellazione 3D di siti e architetture complesse. In: Disegnarecon, vol. 4, no. 8 (2011)
27. Rizzo, E.: La modellazione 3d applicata ai beni culturali: la Pieve di San Giovanni Battista a Caviglia, in Archeomatica no. 3 (2013)
28. Semino, G.P.: Schinkel. Serie di architettura, Zanichelli, Bologna (1993)
29. Schikel, K.F.: Raccolta di disegni di architettura, F. Motta, Milano (1991)
30. Socco, C.: Semiotica e Progetto del paesaggio, Torino (1996)
31. UNESCO: Recommendation on the Historic Urban Landscape (2011)

Automatic Verification Framework of 3D Scan Data for Museum Collections

Jeong-eun Oh[✉] and Jeongmin Yu

Department of Cultural Heritage Industry, Graduate School of Convergence
Cultural Heritage, Korea National University of Cultural Heritage,
Buyeo-gun, Chungcheongnam-do, Korea
{ohelly878, jmyu}@nuch.ac.kr

Abstract. 3D digital archiving of cultural heritage has been conducting actively all over the world. Although the applications using the obtained digital 3D scan data are widely developed, their data management and quality verification does not conducted properly. To overcome this problem, we propose a novel verification framework based on the comparisons of shape and color information between an original image and an image from 3D scan data (i.e., mesh data with color mapping). Firstly, to verify that they are the identical object, we use the shape contexts information based on a machine learning technique. Secondly, we compare the color information between them for verifying its quality of color mapping. Utilizing the proposed framework, we expect that non-experts can verify the quality of 3D scan data automatically, thus, museum itself will be able to manage the 3D scan data systematically and reliably.

Keywords: 3D scan · Shape alignment · Correlation-based methods
Color comparison · Verification framework

1 Introduction

Recently, acquiring shape information of cultural heritage is regarded as an evitable process for conservation and analysis, and its big data has been accumulated through 3D digital archiving of cultural heritage over the years. The Cultural Heritage Administration of South Korea is conducting the prototype archiving of nationally designated cultural properties, and each local government and museum have its own 3D digital archiving of cultural heritage. Although the researches and applications utilizing the obtained digital 3D scan data are widely proceeding, its management and verification does not performed well.

For museums, they have a large number of collections, which requires systematic data management. However, since most of 3D scan archived data are provided by different service providers (they also used a different software), it is hard to verify the quality of data. Furthermore, it is difficult to accurate visual verification between color of 2D image and true color, due to illumination problem. And, it is hard to conduct accurate visual verification since the curator is not a 3D scanning expert, and there is a problem where verification takes a long time due to the large number of collections.

M. Ioannides et al. (Eds.): EuroMed 2018, LNCS 11197, pp. 271–278, 2018.
https://doi.org/10.1007/978-3-030-01765-1_30

Recently, verification of 3D scan data has been performed by detecting characteristic features using 3D measurement data and an input image data [9]. Similar to photogrammetry, this method allows an image data to be compared to 3D data by organizing interfaces or edges in a straight line in three dimensions. In [12], 3D curves are automatically extracted through 2D images and the extracted 3D curves are similar to the actual values. However, if the initial position of the image and 3D data are inadequate, the optimization result may be incorrect.

In this paper, we propose an automatic quality verification framework based on the following two steps: (i) confirmation the identical object by comparing original images and image from 3D scan data (i.e., mesh data with color mapping) using a machine learning technique, (ii) color information comparison between original images and image from 3D scan data. Unlike other existing manual verification, the proposed framework performs data verification automatically, and enables non-experts to verify the target data. From the proposed verification framework, we expect that a museum itself can systematically verify the 3D scan data, thus it is possible to manage the reliable 3D cultural database.

This paper is organized as follows: In Sect. 2, we briefly introduce the related works for shape alignment and color comparison. In Sect. 3, we explain the proposed method, and Sect. 4 is presented the initial experimental steps. Lastly, in Sect. 5, conclusions and future studies are discussed.

2   Related Works

In this section, we will explain how to optimize objects for 2D and 3D shape alignment and how to compare color information. This makes it possible to compare the similarity of the data.

2.1   Shape Alignment

This paper uses shape alignment to compare an original image and an image from 3D scan data prove the identical object. In this way, a method of optimizing objects by comparing distances and similarities is available.

The creation probabilistic network (GSN) method presented in [10] uses kernel density estimates to calculate weighted features. The comparison point density and distance characteristics are analyzed by a small number of data, resulting in faster calculation and reduced classification errors for higher-dimensional object recognition problems. Therefore, this paper design to using a shape context that connects multiple connection distances between shape studied recently.

2.2   Color Comparison

Higher accuracy is needed to reproduce primary colors in 3D scanning data. However, it is difficult to verify accurate comparison since only image that are not real are limited to reflections that occur during filming. This is because the effects of light reflecting, scattering, and absorbing the surface vary [13]. Therefore, it is necessary to compare

RGB values obtained from equipment to CIEXYZ, which is a measured data, since they are not in primary color. A method of obtaining and the validating bidirectional reflectance distribution function (BRDF) data can be used to generate HDR images with multiple image [11].

BRDF is a radioactive function that checks the accuracy of a realistic rendering system, which can typically identify which direction the incident energy is progressing on the surface [13]. Based on these data, it is possible to compare each BRDF's distance function [14]. However, no reference model has yet been prepared to standardize material representation.

3 Methodology

3.1 Prerequisite

The digital cultural heritage archiving takes place in both 2D images and 3D scanning, and 2D images data is set to true value to validate the 3D scan data. 2D images and 3D scan data obtained are then taken using special imaging equipment, rotating 360 degrees. It is also assumed that 2D images takes place under the same conditions to obtain accurate color values and reduce errors in actual colors (Fig. 1).

3.2 Shape Alignment

Step 1. Prototype Configuration. As the first step, we will extract the silhouette of 2D images through computer vision. [1] use this to set up a prototype that can be compared to 3D scan data. Because we need to be aware of unstructured objects, the prototypes create the number of deployed 2D images, not the number of each large and upper bound.

Step 2. Random Image Extraction of 3D Data. This step extracts the image from the 3D data using an image segmentation algorithm [7]. This is a step of extracting images to be compared with the prototype obtained by 360-degree shooting, and randomly extracts images for each object. At this time, the rotation axis and the rotation angle are randomly selected every time.

Step 3. Comparison Through Shape Alignment. The step of extracting the correspondence between the image extracted from the 3D scan data and the prototype calculates the average value and the standard deviation of the distance between the contour surfaces. Load prototypes and 3D extract images to identify and classify objects to see correspondence. In general, the values of curvature may not match exactly when comparing data. The goal is to find the best matching point and find shape context of both images. [8] Because there are multiple prototypes per object, it can be concluded that distinct data is not the identical data when it is discovered.

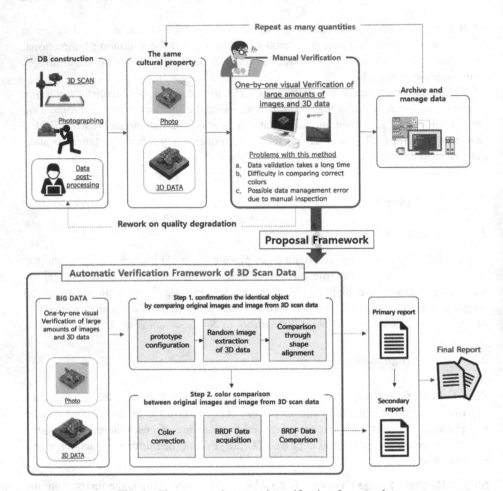

Fig. 1. The proposed automatic verification framework.

3.3   Color Comparison

Step 1. Color Correction. The images acquired by digital cameras are RGB (Red, Green, Blue), reflecting the effects of light. Therefore, in order to obtain true color information, first, the International Lighting Commission should convert the color matching function of the standard observer to the CIEXYZ value that can be expressed as the specified value. Second, in digital images, brighter places are expressed brighter, darker places are darker, and HDR is converted to HDRs close to what people see. The function that implements HDR is PQ (Perceptual Quantizer).

Step 2. BRDF Data Acquisition. HDR results may vary depending on the direction of rotation if you use an image shot 360 degrees rotated in a special way. This is used to obtain BRDF data by sampling only true color information. BRDF data obtained at this time can reduce true color errors caused by reflections.

Step 3. BRDF Data Comparison. It is a process of verifying whether the primary color is processed correctly by comparing the BRDF data converted from the image and the BRDF converted from the 3D scan data. The way to compare these two data is to use distance calculation differences, as in shape alignment, to compare the BRDF data obtained from the image to the true value. For the accuracy of the result value, all image patches of pixels are compared sequentially, and if the color is within the range set to be not exactly the identical color value, it is recognized as the identical color.

4 Initial Experiments

There are many similar types of artifacts or collections in the museum. Therefore, if we do not name the file correctly when managing digital 3D scan data, management may not be performed properly. In this section, we designed the proposed framework experiment to catch this error. The subjects of the experiment are two pieces of 'Korean official seals', which is a symbol of the authority of the royal family. In order to test cases that are properly managed based on 'Golden Royal Seal for the Bestowal of Honorific Title upon Queen Munjeong' and those that are managed with incorrect data, the report was compared with 'Jade Royal Seal for the Crown Prince Investiture of King Hyeonjong'.

4.1 Shape Alignment

Step 1. Prototype Configuration. The prototype was created by extracting the silhouette of the shape using the 2D image of the previously constructed 'Golden Royal Seal for the Bestowal of Honorific Title upon Queen Munjeong' (shown in Fig. 2).

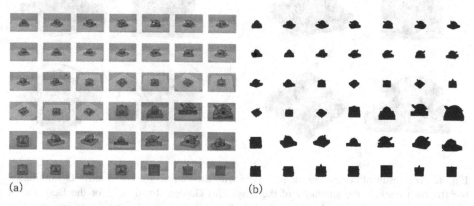

(a)   (b)

Fig. 2. Extract silhouettes to set 'Golden Royal Seal for the Bestowal of Honorific Title upon Queen Munjeong' 2D image as a prototype. (a) 2D image/(b) extract silhouettes

Step 2. Random Image Extraction of 3D Data. We extracted the outline of the image by randomly rotating the 3D scan data of 'Golden Royal Seal for the Bestowal of

Honorific Title upon Queen Munjeong' and 'Jade Royal Seal for the Crown Prince
Investiture of King Hyeonjong' (shown in Fig. 3).

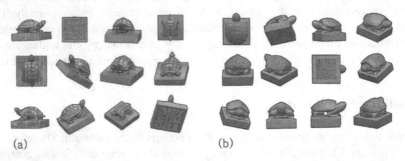

(a)   (b)

Fig. 3. Extracts images obtained by randomly rotating 3D scan data. (a) Golden Royal Seal for
the Bestowal of Honorific Title upon Queen Munjeong, (b) Jade Royal Seal for the Crown Prince
Investiture of King Hyeonjong

Step 3. Comparison Through Shape Alignment. When we compare the images
extracted from the prototype with the image from the second step, there is a similarity
of the silhouette because the data of 'Golden Royal Seal for the Bestowal of Honorific
Title upon Queen Munjeong' is the identical data, but there is no similarity of the
silhouette of 'Jade Royal Seal for the Crown Prince Investiture of King Hyeonjong'.
Therefore, it can be concluded that it is not the identical data (Fig. 4).

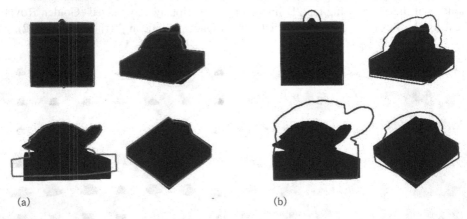

(a)   -   (b)

Fig. 4. As a result of comparing the prototype with the outline, (a) can confirm the similarity,
but (b) can't confirm the similarity of the shape. (a) Golden Royal Seal for the Bestowal of
Honorific Title upon Queen Munjeong, (b) Jade Royal Seal for the Crown Prince Investiture of
King Hyeonjong

4.2   Color Comparison

Step 1. Color Correction. 'Golden Royal Seal for the Bestowal of Honorific Title upon Queen Munjeong' is color calibrated. Using color charts, the RAW files were converted to RGB files as shown below, and then converted to CIEXYZ, which can be expressed as numerical values, and later to HDR (shown in Fig. 5).

RGB   CIEXYZ   HDR

Fig. 5. The color corrections give the true color information.

Step 2. BRDF Data Acquisition/Step 3. BRDF Data Comparison. We check whether the color information of test image is processed correctly by comparing the BRDF data obtained by sampling the true color. A patch of pixels can be verified by comparing it to a physical point in a digital image. In addition, if an error occurs because we can be digitized by color value, the image can be improved to the true color value for re-production. In order to verify this, we will compare colors with BRDF in future work.

5   Conclusions and Future Works

This paper proposes verification framework by comparing shape and color information between original image and 3D scan data image. Firstly, confirm to verify that they are the identical object, we use shape context based on machine learning techniques. Secondly, we compare the color information to check the quality of color mapping.

Utilizing the proposed framework, we expect non-experts to be able to automatically verify the quality of 3D scan data. thus, the museum itself manages the 3D scan data systematically and reliably.

Future works include the number of prototypes required for comparison through shape alignment and prototype setting automation that recognizes the characteristics of unstructured data by deep learning. Second, data accuracy verification by enabling edge extraction. Third, studies on criteria that can be recognized as the identical color for color comparison may be included.

Acknowledgment. This research is supported by 2018 Support Project for Academic Research on Traditional Culture in Korea National University of Cultural Heritage.

References

1. Tian, D., Gong, M., Su, L.: Generalized correlation for shape alignment. Inf. Sci. **363**, 40–51 (2016)
2. Sandhu, R., Dambreville, S., Tannenbaum, A.: Point set registration via particle filtering and stochastic dynamics. IEEE Trans. Pattern Anal. Mach. Intell. **32**(8), 1459–1473 (2010)
3. Li, H., Shen, T., Huang, X.: Approximately global optimization for robust alignment of generalized shapes. IEEE Trans. Pattern Anal. Mach. Intell. **33**(6), 1116–1131 (2011)
4. Dong, Z., Yang, B., Liu, Y., Liang, F., Li, B., Zang, Y.: A novel binary shape context for 3D local surface description. ISPRS J. Photogramm. Remote. Sens. **130**, 431–452 (2017)
5. Mehtre, B.M., Kankanhalli, M.S., Desai Narasimhalu, A., Chang Man, G.: Color matching for image retrieval. Pattern Recognit. Lett. **16**(3), 325–331 (1995)
6. Pang, G., Zhu, M., Zhou, P.: Color transfer and image enhancement by using sorting pixels comparison. Optik **126**(23), 3510–3515 (2015)
7. Zhang, S., Zhan, Y., Dewan, M., Huang, J., Metaxas, D.N., Zhou, X.S.: Towards robust and effective shape modeling: sparse shape composition. Med. Image Anal. **16**(1), 265–277 (2012)
8. Belongie, S., Malik, J., Puzichal, J.: Shape context: a new descriptor for shape matching and object recognition. Adv. Neural. Inf. Process. Syst. **2001**, 831–837 (2001)
9. Kim, H., Jung, K., Chang, M., Kim, J.: Feature detection using measured 3D data and image data. J. Korean Soc. Precis. Eng. **30**(6), 601–606 (2013). No. 267
10. Cárdenas-Peña, D., Collazos-Huertas, D., Álvarez-Meza, A., Castellanos-Dominguez, G.: Supervised kernel approach for automated learning using general stochastic networks. Eng. Appl. Artif. Intell. **68**, 10–17 (2018)
11. Yoo, H.J., Kim, K.Y., Kim, H.M., Seo, M.K., Ko, K.H., Lee, K.H.: Realistic representation based on measured BRDF data. In: HCI KOREA, pp. 1019–1024, 5 February 2007
12. Willcocks, C.G., Jackson, P.T.G., Nelson, C.J., Obara, B.: Extracting 3D parametric curves from 2D images of helical objects. IEEE Trans. Pattern Anal. Mach. Intell. **39**(9), 1757–1769 (2017)
13. Guarnera, D., Guarnera, G.C., Ghosh, A., Denk, C., Glencross, M.: BRDF representation and acquisition. Comput. Graph. Forum: J. Eur. Assoc. Comput. Graph. **35**(2), 625–650 (2016)
14. Havran, V., Filip, J., Myszkowski, K.: Perceptually motivated BRDF comparison using single image. Comput. Graph. Forum: J. Eur. Assoc. Comput. Graph. **35**(4), 1–12 (2016)

A Delivery Model for Cultural Heritage Services in Smart Cities Environments

Konstantina Siountri[1,2]([⊠]), Emmanouil Skondras[1],
and Dimitrios D. Vergados[1]

[1] Department of Informatics, University of Piraeus, Piraeus, Greece
{ksiountri,skondras,vergados}@unipi.gr
[2] Department of Cultural Technology and Communication,
University of the Aegean, Mytilene, Greece

Abstract. The cultural heritage of a city, both tangible and intangible, constitutes a resource of inestimable value that in the uprising digital era needs as well sustainable use and management. The transformation of heritage sites and cultural intangible fields into Smart Cultural Heritage environments implies to the development of Smart Cities. This paper introduces a new delivery model for providing cloud based cultural services to users, through advanced network infrastructures in Smart Cities environments. The proposed model is called Smart Cultural Heritage as a Service (SCHaaS) and aims to promote and preserve the cultural heritage through smart applications and participatory processes. This model also aims to be customized according the special cultural characteristics of a city and the needs of its citizens.

Keywords: Smart cities · Smart cultural heritage · Digital heritage
Digital culture · Fifth generation networks · Cloud computing
Mobile edge computing

1 Introduction

The cultural heritage of a city, both tangible and intangible, constitutes a resource of inestimable value, like water, energy etc., that in the uprising digital era needs as well sustainable use and management. The transformation of heritage sites and cultural intangible fields into Smart Cultural Heritage [1] environments implies to the development of Smart Cities. In this context, the digital city is considered as a complex system, which requires interdisciplinarity, in order its functionalities to be modeled.

So far, the design of a Smart City was structured on "Urban Factors" such us:

- The natural environment, the natural resources and the geological features.
- The city environment, including infrastructure such as roads, bridges, tunnels, buildings etc., and electrical and communication networks.
- The city services, including transportations or other commercial services.
- The social systems of the city, including citizens' interactions, laws, regulations and governance.

© Springer Nature Switzerland AG 2018
M. Ioannides et al. (Eds.): EuroMed 2018, LNCS 11197, pp. 279–288, 2018.
https://doi.org/10.1007/978-3-030-01765-1_31

There are over 120 city service indicators across 20 theme areas that include: education, energy, finance, recreation, fire emergency, response, governance, health, safety, solid waste, transportation, urban planning, waste water and water [2, 3]. But they do not include Smart Cultural Heritage Indicators and this has to change.

The cultural metrics of tangible and intangible heritage should be considered as key elements for the community infrastructure. Those elements shape the particular physiognomy of a city, not only in terms of its image but also its social composition through its customs and social morals. Smart cities must meet not only social, economic and environmental indicators, but also combine the current technological developments with the cultural wealth.

As far as it concerns the novel digital technologies, the means that enable the development of Smart Cities include:

- The use of sensors and digital systems for controlling and operating cultural heritage infrastructures.
- The evolution of the wireless communication networks beyond the fifth generation (5G), which allows the sensors to interact with each other, as well as with the respective Cloud infrastructures.
- The availability of computing systems with plenty of computational resources, which provide real time processing of the information gathered from the sensors.
- The evolution of Internet of Things (IoT) devices, which enable the remote control of cultural heritage infrastructures.

But a Smart Cultural Heritage city goal takes more than simply using ICT to link and manage infrastructure. Smart Cultural Heritage infrastructure metrics should be a measurement, quantification method and scale of the technical performance which:

- promote the diversity of cultural communities
- be applicable to the whole range of communities (e.g. geographical location, sizes, economic structures, levels of economic and cultural development, stages of infrastructure development).
- allow a holistic perspective of multiple infrastructures in cultural heritage fields
- have dynamic properties
- take into account the long-term aspects of culture

The **Smart Cultural Heritage** combines the (a) tangible and intangible heritage of the city, (b) all the "Urban Factors" and (c) novel digital technologies (Fig. 1).

Smart Cultural Heritage could be developed using Fifth Generation (5G) network technologies, including Cloud Computing (CC), Mobile Edge Computing (MEC) or Fog infrastructures, sensors and IoT devices and services within the cultural places. In this context, the "as a Service" model which indicates the ability to reuse the cloud resources on demand could be considered. The main approach of the "as a Service" model is called as Software-Platform-Infrastructure (SPI). SPI refers to the three main delivery models of cloud based services, as defined by NIST [4], namely the Software as a Service (SaaS), the Platform as a Service (PaaS) and the Infrastructure as a Service (IaaS). The entire cloud computing solutions are based on the SPI.

This paper introduces a new delivery model for providing cloud based cultural services to users through advanced network infrastructures in Smart Cities environments. The

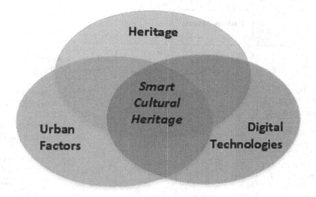

Fig. 1. The smart cultural heritage concept.

proposed model is called Smart Cultural Heritage as a Service (SCHaaS) and aims to promote and preserve the cultural heritage through smart applications and participatory processes. This model also aims to be customized according the special cultural characteristics of a city and the needs of its citizens.

The paper is organized as follows: Sect. 2 discusses the available delivery models for cloud services, Sect. 3 describes the proposed delivery model and, finally, Sect. 4 concludes our work.

2 Delivery Models for Cloud Services

The delivery models are referred to the way in which the service is delivered to the users. The main cloud computing delivery models are the Software as a Service (SaaS), the Platform as a Service (PaaS) and the Infrastructure as a Service (IaaS). As presented in Fig. 2, each one of the main delivery models contains a variety of delivery models described in the following subsections.

2.1 Software as a Service (SaaS)

Software as a Service (SaaS) provides cloud services to the end-users, while at the same time it prevents them from configuring the services' source code or controlling the underlying cloud infrastructure. The SaaS delivery model includes the following subcategories:

- User Communication as a Service (UCaaS): This delivery model [5] provides the necessary applications to the users, in order to be able to communicate with each other, by making voice or video calls, sending emails, using chat boxes etc.
- Data as a Service (DaaS): In a network architecture, data sourcing and data manipulation could be done from the cloud infrastructure using the appropriate applications. According to [6], DaaS allows users to retrieve data from the cloud, in order to avoid the permanent storage of big data sets to their devices.

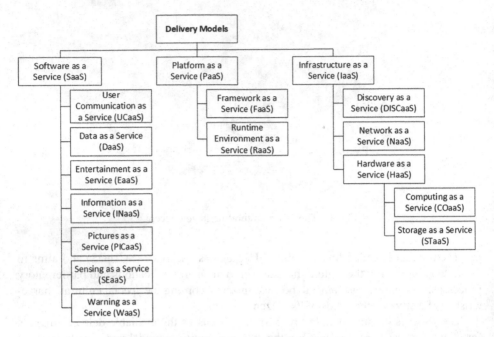

Fig. 2. The available delivery models for cloud services.

- Entertainment as a Service (EaaS): Modern network infrastructures offer media services such as video, music or advertisements to users [7]. EaaS defines that the provided media services are hosted to the cloud and broadcasted to users or offered to them on-demand.
- Information as a Service (INaaS): Users often need information related to events, points of interest (POIs) or emergency situations. The INaaS delivery model provides that information to the users. Indicatively, in [8] users share information about their location with other users as well as with a cloud infrastructure. Then, if a user needs information about a specific location, interacts with the cloud and subscribe to INaaS in order to receive it.
- Pictures as a Service (PICaaS): According to PICaaS operating principles described in [9], users are registered to a centralized cloud manager and periodically share their geographical coordinates. A customer user requests multimedia material about a specific geographic area. Thus, some users are selected according to their positions, to take photos or videos of the given area using their cameras. Finally, such multimedia material is sent to the consumer user.
- Sensing as a Service (SEaaS): Sensors are distributed to countryside to collect data about the respective environment. The data are collected to the cloud and, subsequently, they are broadcasted to the SEaaS users [10].
- Warning as a Service (WaaS): The cloud infrastructure collects information about emergency situations or disasters. Subsequently, warning messages are transmitted to users in respect of their locations [11].

2.2   Platform as a Service (PaaS)

In Platform as a Service (PaaS), the users are considered as application developers. Specifically, as mentioned in [12], PaaS provides computational and storage resources to users by hiding the underlying hardware infrastructure from them. Also, PaaS offers the necessary platform (e.g. the underlying Operation System - OS) to users in order their applications to be deployed. Users are able to remotely develop and deploy their applications, which should be compatible with the provided cloud platform. The following delivery models could be considered as PaaS subcategories [13]:

- Framework as a Service (FaaS): FaaS provides a framework for the implementation of user applications.
- Runtime Environment as a Service (RaaS): RaaS provides a deployment and execution environment for users' applications.

2.3   Infrastructure as a Service (IaaS)

Infrastructure as a Service (IaaS) refers to the provision of infrastructure from the cloud to the users in order to be able to set up a specific platform (e.g. an OS) to deploy their applications. The IaaS delivery model provides resources to users, including the following subcategories:

- Discovery as a Service (DISCaaS): This delivery model allows users to discover cloud recourses with specific characteristics [14].
- Network as a Service (NaaS): NaaS defines that the users with internet access can offer this facility to the users that have not [15].
- Hardware as a Service (HaaS): HaaS [16] defines that the user devices or the cloud with plenty computational resources can offer these to the users that need more resources. The HaaS model contains two subcategories, the Computing as a Service (COaaS) [12] and the Storage as a Service (STaaS) [17]. COaaS provides computational resources, such as Central Processing Unit (CPU) cores to users, in order to develop and run their applications. Accordingly, STaaS provides storage space to users to deploy their applications.

3   Smart Cultural Heritage as a Service (SCHaaS)

The Smart Cultural Heritage City Indicators should be standardized, consistent, and comparable over time and across cities, enhancing the ability of cities to observe trends and to facilitate comparisons with other cities, but in the same time to preserve or enhance their own special cultural characteristics.

Therefore, in this paper we will present how we use cloud services for communication, diffusion, monitoring and management of cultural heritage. As we focus on the services offered by a smart city we will call this delivery model Smart Cultural Heritage as a Service (SCHaaS).

The Smart Cultural Heritage as a Service (SCHaaS) model combines SaaS, PaaS and IaaS functionalities (Fig. 2), to provide a fully virtualized environment for services implementation, deployment, maintenance and usage. Specifically, IaaS provides the appropriate infrastructure for offering PaaS, since it lets the user to create a virtualized infrastructure consisted of several Virtual Machines (VMs) or platforms. Thus, VMs created using IaaS are provided as PaaS to software developers along with the specific usage rights. Consequently, PaaS provides the appropriate components for offering SaaS, since the applications created and deployed using PaaS, can be offered as SaaS to users.

Software as a Service (SaaS) model consists of a continuous turnover, where the provided Information (Data) is enriched through crowd sourcing, is evaluated and is given back to the community (Fig. 3).

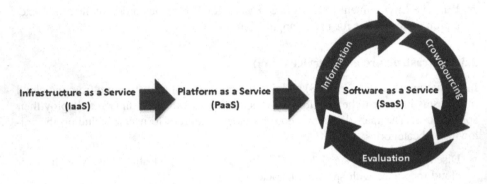

Fig. 3. The smart cultural heritage as a service (SCHaaS) design.

This process is necessary, as we have already mentioned that we want to build a sustainable model with holistic approach, which enables evolvement of the diverse communities and the local stakeholders (scientists, local market etc.).

The Smart Cultural Heritage as a Service (SCHaaS) should be designed to assist cities in monitoring their performance of city cultural services. For example a main aspect of creating smart service deals with the automation of infrastructure, that may improve the visitors' comfort to a smart museum [18], a smart monument, a smart archaeological site, Smart Libraries, etc. Also, a Smart City could apply innovative solutions such as smart road lighting, road traffic manipulation, navigation assistance and autonomous driving services to facilitate the access to the cultural wealth, enabling the creation of cultural routes [19]. Additionally, remote monitoring services could help the preservation and constant monitoring of cultural heritage or could enable alarm in cases of natural disasters. The above mentioned cases are only a small part of the services that Smart Cultural Heritage can offer. For that reason, a Software Defined Network (SDN) controller may provide centralized control of the entire system.

The fully virtualized architecture of SCHaaS, which includes a Cloud and a Fog infrastructure, is presented in Fig. 4. The Cloud includes a set of VMs which are created using IaaS. Each VM hosts cultural heritage services which are implemented and deployed using PaaS. Also, these services are offered to the users using SaaS applications. Accordingly, the Fog infrastructure incudes a heterogeneous network access environment consisting of LTE and WiMAX Macrocells and Femtocells, as well as of WiFi Access Points (APs). Also, sensors and Internet of Things (IoT) devices exist into the Fog infrastructure. The Fog is deployed to sites with cultural interest like museums, monuments, archaeological sites, libraries etc.

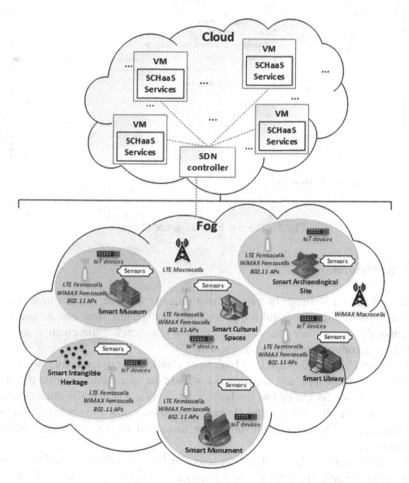

Fig. 4. The proposed architecture.

The sequence diagram of Fig. 5 presents the SCHaaS functionality. Specifically, the user interacts with the Fog infrastructure and requests a cultural heritage service. If the requested service already exists to the Fog, it is immediately provided to the user. On the contrary, the Fog interacts with the Cloud infrastructure through the SDN controller, retrieves the requested service and, finally, provides the service to the user. In this case, the Fog caches the cultural service in its resources, in order to immediate provide it to a future user.

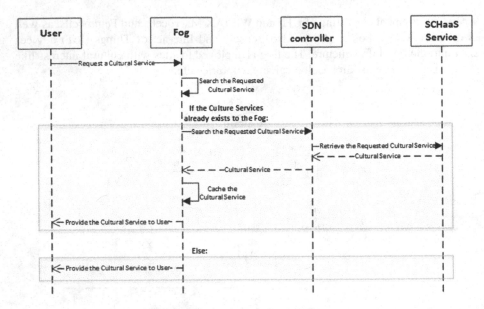

Fig. 5. The use case sequence diagram.

4 Conclusions

The Smart Cultural Heritage Index will help cities to become smarter in a sense that they can maximize their cultural footprint while at the same time can promote social and economic opportunities for their inhabitants (i.e. serving the creative industries) and thus to accommodate population growth.

The Smart Cultural Heritage City Indicators should enter dynamically to the core of the Smart Cities Design and the process should be standardized. But the desired standardization should not end to the horizontal overview of what is smart in cultural heritage. Even the slightest cultural element can be crucial for the preservation of the physiognomy of a place, like the image or the smell of the blossomed trees in a neighborhood.

The evolvement of the local society and the local stakeholders and the constant evaluation of the system are necessary, so as to assure the preservation of diversity and protection, monitoring and enhancement of the local cultural heritage. Finally, the network should all allow the management of infrastructure through a central controller system.

Acknowledgements. The publication of this paper has been partly supported by the University of Piraeus Research Center (UPRC).

References

1. Chianese, A., Piccialli, F., Jung, J.E.: The internet of cultural things: towards a smart cultural heritage. In: 2016 12th International Conference on Signal-Image Technology & Internet-Based Systems (SITIS), pp. 493–496. IEEE, November 2016
2. ITU-T Focus Group on Smart Sustainable Cities, Master plan for smart sustainable cities, ITU-T, FG-SSC, Telecommunication Standardization Sector of ITU (2015)
3. Smart community infrastructures-Review of existing activities relevant to metrics, Technical report, ISO/TR 37150 (2014)
4. Mell, P., Grance, T.: The NIST definition of cloud computing. Computer Security Division, Information Technology Laboratory, National Institute of Standards and Technology Gaithersburg (2011)
5. Priyank Sharma, D.V., Vaniya, S.: Communication as a service based cloud computing. In: IEEE International Conference on Emerging Technology Trends (ICETECT), Nagercoil, India, pp. 15–17 (2011)
6. Vu, Q.H., Pham, T.-V., Truong, H.-L., Dustdar, S., Asal, R.: DEMODS: a description model for data-as-a-service. In: 2012 IEEE 26th International Conference on Advanced Information Networking and Applications, pp. 605–612 IEEE (2012)
7. Lagraa, B.B.N., Lakas, A., Ghamri-Doudane, Y.: RCS-VC: renting out and consuming services in vehicular clouds based on LTE-A. In: Global Information Infrastructure and Networking Symposium (GIIS), pp. 1–6. IEEE (2015)
8. Hussain, R., Abbas, F., Son, J., Oh, H.: TiaaS: secure cloud-assisted traffic information dissemination in vehicular ad hoc networks. In: 2013 13th IEEE/ACM International Symposium on Cluster, Cloud and Grid Computing (CCGrid), pp. 178–179. IEEE (2013)
9. Gerla, M., Weng, J.-T., Pau, G.: Pics-on-wheels: photo surveillance in the vehicular cloud. In: 2013 International Conference on Computing, Networking and Communications (ICNC), pp. 1123–1127. IEEE (2013)
10. Ferretti, S., D'Angelo, G.: Smart shires: the revenge of country sides. In: 2016 IEEE Symposium on Computers and Communication (ISCC), pp. 756–759. IEEE (2016)
11. Hussain, R., Oh, H.: Cooperation-aware vanet clouds: Providing secure cloud services to vehicular ad hoc networks. JIPS 10(1), 103–118 (2014)
12. AbdelBaky, M., Parashar, M., Jordan, K., Kim, H., Jamjoom, H., Shae, Z.-Y., Pencheva, G., Sachdeva, V., Sexton, J., Wheeler, M., et al.: Enabling high-performance computing as a service. Computer 45(10), 72–80 (2012)
13. Kächele, S., Spann, C., Hauck, F.J., Domaschka, J.: Beyond IaaS and PaaS: an extended cloud taxonomy for computation, storage and networking. In: Proceedings of the 2013 IEEE/ACM 6th International Conference on Utility and Cloud Computing. IEEE Computer Society, pp. 75–82 (2013)
14. Mershad, K., Artail, H.: Finding a star in a vehicular cloud. IEEE Intell. Transp. Syst. Mag. 5(2), 55–68 (2013)
15. Hussain, R., Son, J., Eun, H., Kim, S., Oh, H.: Rethinking vehicular communications: merging VANET with cloud computing. In: 2012 IEEE 4th International Conference on Cloud Computing Technology and Science (CloudCom), pp. 606–609. IEEE (2012)
16. Stanik, A., Hovestadt, M., Kao, O.: Hardware as a service (HaaS): physical and virtual hardware on demand. In: 2012 IEEE 4th International Conference on Cloud Computing Technology and Science (CloudCom), pp. 149–154. IEEE, December 2012
17. Mandal, M., Landge, C., Gaikwad, P., Nagaraj, U., Abhale, A.: Implementing storage as a service in VANET using cloud environment. Int. J. Adv. Found. Res. Comput. (IJAFRC) 1, 70–76 (2014)

18. Chianese, A., Piccialli, F.: Designing a smart museum: when cultural heritage joins IoT. In: 2014 Eighth International Conference on Next Generation Mobile Apps, Services and Technologies (NGMAST), pp. 300–306. IEEE, September 2014
19. Skondras, E., Siountri, K., Michalas, A., Vergados, D.D.: A route selection scheme for supporting virtual tours in sites with cultural interest using drones. In: 2018 International Conference on Information, Intelligence, Systems, and Applications (IISA 2018) (2018)

Comparative Analysis of Inspection
and Diagnosis Tools for Ancient Buildings

Joana Gonçalves[1]([⊠]), Ricardo Mateus[1], and José Dinis Silvestre[2]

[1] CTAC, University of Minho, Guimarães, Portugal
arq.joanag@gmail.com
[2] CERIS, Instituto Superior Técnico, Universidade de Lisboa, Lisbon, Portugal

Abstract. The survey and inspection of the state of conservation of buildings is understood as an active process of selecting information to support decision making in the rehabilitation of the built heritage. The development of new technologies applied to the integrated management of the built heritage resulted in digital tools able to support the technicians in on-site procedures. The purpose of this study was to analyse existing methods for the survey and inspection of the state of conservation of ancient buildings. It uses a qualitative methodology, focused on bibliographical survey and comparative analysis. Only methods with identical characteristics were considered: evaluation based on visual inspection of buildings with heritage value. This research shows that structuring information in computer systems is a solution to overcome the main problems pointed out in previous studies related to survey and inspection: expensive, time-consuming, inconsequential procedures and dispersed information. However, this is only valid if computer-based methods are adapted to the different geographic and chronological contexts. Future research may contribute to the development of a method that brings together this added value with a simple but objective way to diagnose the condition of ancient buildings with heritage value.

Keywords: Built heritage · Inspection · Digital tools

1 Introduction

In the recent history of built heritage preservation, there is a constant concern to understand the building, through historical analysis and state of conservation assessment [1–6]. The evolution of this concept has essentially two vectors: the extension of the concept of heritage to groups of buildings and historic districts [7–9]; and the technological progress, which introduces new tools that empower management and design processes.

The "principles for the analysis, conservation and structural restoration of architectural heritage" [6] are aimed at ensuring "rational methods of analysis and repair methods appropriate to the cultural context" [6]. This document recommends diagnosis based on qualitative approaches, i.e. historical information, direct observation, but also quantitative, through trials and monitoring. However, the principles are not enough to support practitioner's decisions and imply the use of complementary resources.

© Springer Nature Switzerland AG 2018
M. Ioannides et al. (Eds.): EuroMed 2018, LNCS 11197, pp. 289–298, 2018.
https://doi.org/10.1007/978-3-030-01765-1_32

New technologies have followed the need to gather more information about the building, such as: the use of laser scanner and photogrammetry for detailed survey of historical buildings [10, 11], the non-destructive analysis of old structures through digital images and thermography [12], and the development of methodologies for the transposition of data collected to parameterized three-dimensional models [13]. All these studies confirm the survey as an active process, essential for supported decision-making. However, they are mostly oriented to interventions in monuments. Considering the need to "establish a cost-effective plan of activities proportional to the structure's complexity and which also takes into account the real benefit to be obtained from the knowledge gained" [6], such methods are usually not suitable for smaller buildings, such as historic dwellings of private owners.

A survey to practitioners in Portugal [14] concluded that, in the renovation of residential buildings, there is low budget and time available to resort to current detailed methods of inspection and diagnosis. This problem is aggravated by the scarcity of technical information and its dispersion. Only 74% of the respondents perform regular inspection of the state of conservation in this type of buildings. However the procedures used lack objectivity since they are based on photographic record and on previous experiences.

This research presents a comparative analysis of international methods to support inspection and diagnosis procedures in heritage buildings. The focus is to systematize their characteristics and identify the potential of their application in professional practice according to the needs expressed by practitioners in previous studies, e.g. [14, 15].

2   Methodology

This research uses a qualitative methodology, focused on bibliographical survey and comparative analysis of methods used in Portugal and internationally.

In the literature review, the tools were selected considering three criteria:

(a)   Tools most used in professional practice by technicians in Portugal [14];
(b)   Prominent tools in international scientific literature;
(c)   International tools aimed at practical conservation.

For each assessment criterion, two tools were considered. Only methods that have identical characteristics were considered: evaluation based on visual inspection and focus on buildings with heritage value. Thus, expert-systems not oriented towards heritage rehabilitation [16], or that have already been the subject of previous studies [17], were excluded.

The key variables considered in the comparative analysis were: support (type of storage by which information is communicated); format (structure for processing and displaying the data); type of buildings, end-user, and stage of the intervention; and outputs (type of results obtained).

3 Tools to Support Building Inspections and Diagnosis

3.1 Brief Description

This section presents the characterization of the analysed tools, as described in Table 1, contextualizing their scope and aim.

Table 1. Inspection and diagnosis support tools analysed.

Source	Tool	Country	Author	Year
Identified by Portuguese professionals	Reabilitação de Edifícios Antigos (REA)	Portugal	Appleton	2003–2011
	Método de Avaliação do Estado de Conservação de Imóveis (MAEC)	Portugal	LNEC	2007
Scientific literature	Monument Diagnosis and Conservation System (MDCS)	Netherland	Van Balen et al.	1995–Now
	Monument Damage Ontology (Mondis)	Czech Rep.	Caccioti et al.	2013–2015
International practice	Faith in Maintenance - Maintenance Co-operatives Project (FiM/MCP)	United Kingdom	SPAB	2007–2017
	Caring for your Home (CYH)	United Kingdom	IHBC	2016

Reabilitação de Edifícios Antigos. Rehabilitation of Ancient Buildings [18] is one of the publications most used by Heritage professionals in Portugal [14]. It was first published in 2003 and reissued in 2011, with the main goal of "contribute (…) to make a more efficient and widespread dissemination of information on architectural heritage" [18].

This technical publication gathers the main building defects, possible causes and intervention criteria. It is oriented to intervention in ancient buildings, defined as those "built before the advent of concrete (…) thus resorting to traditional materials and technologies" [18].

Método de Avaliação do Estado de Conservação (MAEC). Between 2003 and 2010, the National Laboratory of Civil Engineering (LNEC) developed different methods to evaluate the building' state of conservation, aiming to "support the implementation of public policies for the rehabilitation of building stock" [19]. The Method of Evaluation of the State of Conservation of Buildings (MAEC), although not specifically developed for use in buildings with a heritage value, is highlighted by Portuguese professionals in the rehabilitation sector [14].

It is a legal instrument that includes an inspection form and a supporting glossary. Its application is mandatory only under the Portuguese Urban Renting Regime [20], to determine the updating of the value of rental agreements.

Monument Diagnosis and Conservation System (MDCS). MDCS is an expert system oriented to Heritage professionals, "meant to furnish a support during inspection aiming at assessing the type and severity of the damage found" [21].

It is the latest version of a project started under an European program for R&D in 1993 [22]. Initially called Masonry Damage Diagnosis System (MDDS), it was aimed at "bridging the gap between scientific information and application of it in the field of architectural conservation" [23]. It brought together uniform terminology for the types of damages and theirs origins, and created the possibility of their identification through a computerized questionnaire of a diagnosis system, currently accessible through an online website [24].

Monument Damage Ontology (Mondis). Mondis is the result of a project funded by the Ministry of Culture of the Czech Republic, between 2012 and 2015, "aimed at enhancing data sharing and access, and integration of existing digital systems" [25] in the field of immovable cultural heritage.

Consists in a series of tools oriented to the introduction, edition and consultation of information by professionals. Its aim was to ensure "user accessibility, the reliability of contents and possibility of integrating other information systems already existent in the domain" [25]. However, after the end of the project the online platform is no longer available [26].

Faith in Maintenance – Maintenance Co-operatives Project (FiM/MCP). When William Morris 1877 exalted the need for a culture of preventive maintenance of monuments in 1877 [27], he launched the Society for Protection of Ancient Buildings (SPAB), in the United Kingdom. As one of the most important international associations in Build Heritage safeguard [28], SPAB promoted in 2007 the project Faith in Maintenance (FiM), aimed at safeguarding religious buildings, followed by the project Maintenance Co-operatives (MCP) [29].

To contribute to "more systematic informal inspections and routine maintenance of places of worship" [30], these projects developed an online toolkit with resources for the non-professional community such as baseline survey templates, instructions for assessment and a glossary of historic buildings terminology.

Caring for your Home. This is an online platform aimed at homeowners of traditional buildings, defined as "those built using local, indigenous building materials by craftsmen" [31]. Developed in 2016 by the Institute of Historic Building Conservation (IHBC), this tool is "intended to explain why maintenance is so worthwhile and help owners to look after their homes" [31].

It gathers information on the characteristics of traditional buildings, with instructions for periodic inspections, as well as recommendations for maintenance interventions.

3.2   Comparative Analysis

The tools described above were analysed comparatively, as presented in Table 2.

Table 2. Comparative analysis of key-parameters.

Tool	Support	Format	Type	End-user	Stage
REA	Book	N/A	Ancient buildings	Practitioners	Anamnesis
MAEC	Law-decree	Checklist	Rented properties	Practitioners	Value assessment
Mondis	Mobile app	Form	Monuments	Practitioners	Anamnesis
MDCS	Online platform	Questions	Monuments	Practitioners	Anamnesis
FiM/MCP	Online toolkit	Questions	Places of worship	Wardens and caretakers	Periodic maintenance
CYH	Online toolkit	Checklist	Traditional buildings	Building owners	Periodic maintenance

Support. In the last decade, it was possible to verify the use of digital technologies as a tool to help professional practice. There are different approaches and levels of digitalization: totally digital systems; systems based on the dissemination of information in digital media and non-computerized systems.

MDCS and Mondis are fully digital systems, based on the automation of information in databases. REA is the only fully non-computerized tool, among the analysed ones.

FiM and CYH make information available online, even though the procedure relies mainly on filling in paper forms (not automated). Also, the MAEC can be considered in this group, since although it is published in a law-decree, the support documents are available online and accessible in PDF format.

Format. Considering how the information is structured, it was possible to distinguish three approaches: checklists, forms and questionnaires. The REA does not provide any practical tool to support inspection, so this field was considered not applicable.

The checklists include predefined lists that guide the sequence of procedures to be adopted in situ. However, the ability to identify and describe anomalies dependent on the user's technical skills. In computerized forms, such as Mondis, this problem is minimized by limiting the user to the selection of standardized possibilities, depending on materials and building elements. It also has the advantage of providing specific information for each case, during the inspection.

The questionnaire format is the most effective to eliminates the inspector's subjectivity, as evidenced in the MDCS expert-system. It determines the anomaly through objective and closed-ended questions (Yes or No answers) that consider only the visible reality and not the user's technical knowledge in formulating hypotheses.

Type of Building. The majority of the analysed methods are oriented to the inspection and diagnosis of the state of conservation in buildings with heritage value. The main exception is the MAEC, "designed to be applied to buildings of any construction period" [19]. For the adaptation of the method to historical buildings, Pedro et al. [19]

suggest that inspection parameters should also consider "the heritage value of each functional element". However, the way of doing so is not clearly defined.

End-User. It was possible to distinguish two different approaches to the end-user: tools aimed at the technical community - expert systems - and tools directed to the non-technical community – toolkits.

The second group goal is to "enhance the skills expertise and personal development of volunteers" [30] in Heritage preservation.

In the tools of the first group, there is a concern to make inspection procedures accessible in everyday professional practice, as expressed by Van Balen [23]: "technicians, architects, engineers should be helped in executing correct analysis of the major part of (simpler) damage cases".

Stage of Intervention. The analysed tools can be used during the anamnesis and the periodic maintenance. Anamnesis designates the stage of investigation and diagnosis that must precede any intervention in Built Heritage. It consists in the collection of information "on the structure in its original and earlier states, on the techniques that were used in the construction, on the alterations and their effects, on the phenomena that have occurred, and, finally, on its present state" [6].

The tools developed to support periodic maintenance are aimed at "a set of simple but effective tasks" [32], that "carried out on a regular basis can safeguard the condition of a building" [31].

This classification does not, however, invalidate that the same tools can be used in different phases of rehabilitation processes, whenever they are needed to support decision-making.

Outputs. Each analysed method results in different types of information for the user: defect diagnosis, summary of condition, priorities' weighting and possible solutions, as shown in Table 3.

Table 3. Outputs of each tool.

Tools	REA	MAEC	Mondis	MDCS	FiM	CYH
Support defect diagnosis	X	X	X		X	X
Automated defect diagnosis				X		
Summary of the condition		X			X	
Priorities' weighting			X		X	X
Possible solutions	X		X			

The diagnosis of the identified damages can be supported by complementary literature, through glossaries, such as REA technical book or the MAEC support glossary. In the case of *Mondis* and *CYH*, the identification of defects is supported by predefined lists associated with the different building elements.

With a different approach, the MDCS expert-system automatically determines the defect identified - not depending on the technician's subjective judgment capacity.

The MAEC and FiM/MCP tools allow obtaining a summary of condition of each building element's state of conservation. Also using the weighting factors, the Mondis, FiM/MCP and Caring for your Home tools make it possible to prioritize conservation interventions.

Some diagnosis tools purpose possible interventions to solve the identified problems, through complementary literature (such as REA) or through computerized knowledge matrixes that relate causes and remedial actions (such as Mondis).

4   Discussion

The analysis recognizes some available tools to support the professionals in the inspection and diagnosis of the state of conservation of ancient buildings. It confirms that "while in building rehabilitation, each case is a unique case, the majority of occurrences of defects in non-structural elements can be solved in a systemic way" [17].

Unlike some of the Building Inspection Systems previously analysed by Ferraz et al. [17], the systems analysed in this research have in common the aim of developing practical tools capable of communicating scientific knowledge to daily practice. The methodologies developed by the English conservation associations (SPAB and IHBC) are the most illustrative: due to its simplified structure and accessible language they are "an effective support system in order to provide readily and freely accessible information across the range of media to assist volunteers" [30]. They evidence that it is possible to systematize tools that are sufficiently expeditious to perform inspection of the state of conservation to support decisions, even with few economic resources and little availability of time – the two main reasons pointed out by professionals in Portugal to not perform this procedure [14]. The conclusions of the Maintenance Co-operatives Project point to "an increased community awareness of the importance of maintaining historic places" [33], that may lead to "a shift toward maintenance type interventions on historic buildings instead of more 'heavy' restoration interventions" [23].

The tool MDCS was at the beginning of the project considered "very innovative", for being intended "to develop through scientific research a useful tool directed to possible end-users" [23]. This tool differs from other Building Inspection Systems analysed by Ferraz et al. [17], which, despite providing an online diagnosis, depend on the analysis of "experts in building pathology and rehabilitation" without "an actual visit from an engineer to the building" [17]. Although they support the pre-diagnosis of the building's condition, these tools are not real expert systems, understood as the transposition of "expertise into a computer system" [23].

Despite the growing interest in the computerization of systems, this is not yet a reality. Digitalization is often based on the provision of static online information or complementary tools, but not the entire method: "pathology catalogues are accessible through a website", and contribute to a greater dissemination of information, but are not enough "to provide users with an expedited solution to their needs" [17]. In other cases, despite the initial investment in the development of the systems, they still do not reach the professionals because of insufficient disclosure or lack of commercialization.

Most of the methods are based on the structuring of data in glossaries that support the filling of forms or checklists. The subjectivity of the decisions based on the individual knowledge of the technicians is one of the most evident concerns in the tools analysed. The questionnaire format contributes most to the objectivity of the results, but the forms with automated filling of standard fields have the advantage of making data more easily accessible in on-site operations, adapted to the circumstances and immediate needs of technicians.

The tools most used by Portuguese professionals - REA and MAEC - are still mostly non-computerized, explaining the difficult access to information and the poor efficiency identified in the research and learning process by the technicians [14]. Nevertheless, such tools [18, 34, 35] remain the only ones adapted to the reality of ancient buildings in Portugal, and that is why the professionals interviewed are positive about finding the information they seek in these databases [14]. Crossing the information in these databases with advanced models identified in the literature [24, 25], would make research and learning more effective and reduce the gap in technical knowledge [14]. It would be possible to improve the accuracy of inspections without significantly increasing the complexity of the procedures: maintaining the predominance of photo-assisted visual inspection, without intrusive techniques or costly equipment and procedures.

One of the most critical points for professionals is that inspection has no impact in the project results [14]. By including the possibility of weighing the priorities of intervention as well as information on the possible conservation actions to be taken for each damage, some of the tools analysed are useful to support decision-making, being adequate answers to the concerns expressed by the practitioners.

5 Conclusion

The purpose of this study was to make a comparative analysis of different methods of inspection and diagnosis for the Built Heritage. The literature review identified different approaches to the subject: databases, law-decrees, computerized expert-systems and toolkits for the non-technical community. In common, these tools rely on visual, expeditious and cost-effective inspections.

Databases and glossaries are not sufficient to support in situ procedures. Checklists, forms, and questionnaires can be used during the fieldwork to guide the technicians and reduce the subjectivity of the inspection.

To Implement the technical expertise in computerized systems favours the dissemination of information and its real time real time accessibility, and allows for more rigorous evaluations, less dependent on the user's individual experience. Linking these systems with information about intervention priorities and remedial solutions makes them decision support tools.

This paper demonstrated that the main problems pointed out by practitioners in previous studies (expensive, time-consuming, inconsequential procedures and dispersed information) can be solved by structuring information in computer systems. However, this is only valid if these systems are adapted to the different geographic contexts and construction periods.

Future research may contribute to the development of a methodology that brings together the added value identified in the different models, consolidating a tool that allows in a simple but objective way to diagnose the state of conservation of buildings with heritage value and to support the decision-making regarding the intervention.

Acknowledgements. The authors would like to acknowledge the support granted by the Portuguese Foundation for Science and Technology (FCT), in the scope of the Doctoral Program Eco-Construction and Rehabilitation (EcoCoRe), to the Ph.D. scholarship with the reference PD/BD/127853/2016 that was fundamental for the development of this study.

References

1. Viollet-le-Duc, E.: Histoire d'une Maison, 1978th edn. Berger-Levrault, Paris (1873)
2. Boito, C.: Questioni pratiche di belle arti, Milano (1893)
3. Giovannoni, G.: Questioni d'architettura, Roma (1924)
4. League of Nations: Charter for the restoration of historic monuments. In: First International Congress of Architects and Technicians of Historic Monuments, Athens (1931)
5. ICOMOS: International charter for the conservation and restoration of monuments and sites. In: 2nd International Congress of Architects and Technicians of Historic Monuments, Venice (1964)
6. ICOMOS: Principles for the analysis, conservation and structural restoration of architectural heritage. In: ICOMOS 14th General Assembly, Victoria Falls, Zimbabwe (2003)
7. Council of Europe: European charter of the architectural heritage. In: Congress on the European Architectural Heritage, Amsterdam (1975)
8. UNESCO: Recommendation concerning the safeguarding and contemporary role of his-toric areas. In: Records of the General Conference Nineteenth Session, Annex I, pp. 20–28. UNESCO, Nairobi (1976)
9. ICOMOS: Charter for The conservation of historic towns and urban areas. In: ICOMOS General Assembly, Washington, DC (1987)
10. Haddad, N.A.: From hand survey to 3D laser scanning: a discussion for non-technical users of heritage documentation. Conserv. Manag. Archaeol. Sites **15**(2), 213–226 (2013)
11. Balzani, M., Maietti, F.: Historic centres' surfaces. Integrated procedures for survey, diagnosis and conservation. In: Proceedings of 2nd International Conference on Preservation, Maintenance and Rehabilitation of Historical Buildings and Structures, Rehab 2015, vol. 2, pp. 705–714. Green Lines Institute, Porto (2015)
12. Moropoulou, A., Labropoulos, K.C., Delegou, E.T., Karoglou, M., Bakolas, A.: Non-destructive techniques as a tool for the protection of built cultural heritage. Construct. Build. Mater. **48**, 1222–1239 (2013)
13. Li, K., Li, S.J., Liu, Y., Wang, W., Wu, C.: Coordination between understanding historic buildings and BIM modelling: a 3D-output oriented and typological data capture method. In: International Archives of the Photogrammetry, Remote Sensing and Spatial Information Sciences, vol. 40, no. 5/W7, pp. 283–288 (2015)
14. Gonçalves, J., Mateus, R., Silvestre, J. D., Vasconcelos, G.: Survey to architects: challenges to inspection and diagnosis in historical residential buildings. In: 3rd International Conference on Preservation, Maintenance and Rehabilitation of Historic Buildings and Structures (REHAB 2017), pp. 3–10. Green Lines Institute, Barcelos (2017)

15. Gonçalves, J., Mateus, R. & Silvestre, J. D.: Experiências da prática profissional na reabilitação: análise de um grupo de foco. In: II Encontro Nacional Sobre Reabilitação Urbana e Construção Sustentável, pp. 147–156. iiSBE Portugal: Lisboa (2017)
16. Silvestre, J.D., Brito, J.: Inspection and repair of ceramic tiling within a building management system. J. Mater. Civil Eng. 22(1), 39–48 (2010)
17. Ferraz, G.T., Brito, J., Freitas, V.P., Silvestre, J.D.: State-of-the-art review of building inspection systems. J. Perform. Constructed Facil. 30(5), 04016018 (2016)
18. Appleton, J.: Reabilitação de Edifícios Antigos – Patologias e tecnologias de intervenção, 2nd edn. Edições Orion, Amadora, Amadora (2011)
19. Pedro, J.B., Vilhena, A., Paiva, J.V., Pinho, A.: Métodos De Avaliação Do Estado De Conservação Dos Edifícios: a Actividade Recente Do Lnec. In: Proceedings CLME'2011 - 6º Congresso Luso-Moçambicano de Engenharia e IIICEM - 3º Congresso de Engenharia de Moçambique, pp. 5–18. Edições INEGI, Porto (2012)
20. Ministério das Obras Públicas: Transportes e Comunicações & LNEC: Método de Avaliação do Estado de Conservação de Imóveis – Instruções de Aplicação. Ministério das Obras Públicas, Transportes e Comunicações, Lisboa (2007)
21. Naldini, S.: MDCS - A new system for the diagnosis of damage to monuments. In: Heritage and Architecture Publications 2015, pp. 39–40. TU/Delft (2015)
22. Van Balen, K., Mateus, J., Binda, L., Baronio, G.: Expert System for the Evaluation of the Deterioration of Ancient Brick Structures. European Comission, Luxembourg (1997)
23. Van Balen, K.: Learning from damage of masonry structures, expert systems can help! In: Lourenço, P.B., Roca, P. (eds.) Historical Constructions 2001 – Possibilities of Numerical an Experimental Techniques, Proceedings 3rd International Seminar, pp. 15–28. Multicomp, Guimarães (2001)
24. MDCS Homepage. http://mdcs.monumentenkennis.nl/. Accessed 28 June 2018
25. Cacciotti, R., Valach, J., Kuneš, P., Čeřňanský, M., Blaško, M., Křemen, P.: Monument damage information system (Mondis): an ontological approach to cultural heritage documentation. In: ISPRS Annals of the Photogrammetry, Remote Sensing and Spatial Information Sciences, vol. II-5/W1, pp. 55–60. Strasbourg (2013)
26. Mondis Homepage. http://www.mondis.cz/. Accessed 28 June 2018
27. Morris, W.: Anti-Scrape – The need for an association. In: Briggs, A. (ed.) William Morris Selected Writings and Designs. Penguin Books, Suffolk (1962)
28. Donovan, A.E.: William Morris and the Society for the Protection of Ancient Buildings. Routledge, Abingdon (2007)
29. SPAB Homepage. https://www.spab.org.uk/. Accessed 28 June 2018
30. Goddard, S.: Faith in Maintenance – Final Project Evaluation Report, March 2007 – January 2012. Oakmere Solutions (2012)
31. Caring for your Home Homepage. http://ihbconline.co.uk/caring/. Accessed 28 June 2018
32. SPAB.: Maintenance Co-operatives Project - Toolkit. SPAB, London (2014)
33. Oakmere Solutions.: Maintenance Co-operatives Project: Final Summative Evaluation. Oakmere Solutions (2016)
34. Freitas, V.: Manual de Apoio ao Projecto de Reabilitação de Edifícios Antigos. OERN, Porto (2012)
35. Teixeira, J.: Salvaguarda e valorização do edificado habitacional da cidade histórica. Metodologia de intervenção no sistema construtivo da Casa Burguesa do Porto (Doctoral dissertation). FAUP, Porto (2014)

Spaces and Cultural Assets of the Autonomous National University of Mexico

Catalina Naumis-Peña[1]([⊠]) [iD], Ariel A. Rodríguez-García[1] [iD],
Juan Ayala-Méndez[2] [iD], Natalia Velazco-Placencia[2] [iD],
and Ana E. Pérez-Martínez[3] [iD]

[1] Instituto de Investigaciones Bibliotecológicas y de la Información,
Universidad Nacional Autónoma de México, Ciudad de México, Mexico
{naumis,rgarciaa}@unam.mx
[2] Secretaría Técnica de Planeación y Programación, Coordinación de Difusión
Cultural, Universidad Nacional Autónoma de México, Ciudad de México,
Mexico
ayala.unam@gmail.com, natvelazcounam@gmail.com
[3] Secretaría Técnica de Vinculación, Coordinación de Difusión Cultural,
Universidad Nacional Autónoma de México, Ciudad de México, Mexico
anaelsaperez@gmail.com

Abstract. The UNAM's cultural spaces and assets have seen constant growth in order to better fulfil the University's commitment to artistic and cultural activities. A special collaboration was established between the cultural area and the librarianship in order to develop a project that would simultaneously facilitate the retrieval of information regarding cultural spaces and infrastructure, record the University's cultural heritage and carry out the scheduling of artistic and cultural activities. The Project was developed via the action research method: plan, act, observe/collect, reflect/review. These activities are carried out in cultural spaces expressly intended for this purpose, as well as in the different campuses and dependencies that make up this immense university. Due to the advances of the Project, a database has been created, gathering the necessary data to consult and recover the cultural resources the University possesses, enabling the University to program activities and make full use of the cultural infrastructure's capacity. Once the basic structure of the data to be organised had been established, the Object-Oriented Analysis and Design methodology was implemented in order to obtain a meta-structure of analysis relevant to the development of systems, with the Entities, Attributes and Relationships. International standards were adhered to throughout both the survey and certification of information.

Keywords: University cultural spaces · University cultural assets
Databases · Registration and retrieval of cultural information
Innovation of cultural heritage

Proyecto PAPIIT IT400318.

M. Ioannides et al. (Eds.): EuroMed 2018, LNCS 11197, pp. 299–310, 2018.
https://doi.org/10.1007/978-3-030-01765-1_33

1   Introduction

The Information System for the University Registration of Cultural Spaces and Assets (Sistema de Información para el Registro Universitario de Espacios y Activos Culturales, SI-RUEyAC) is being presented as a project with the purpose of highlighting the inter- and multidisciplinary research carried out to make the cultural heritage of the National Autonomous University of Mexico (Universidad Nacional Autónoma de México, UNAM) more visible by establishing a platform where this heritage is presented in its entirety. Not only will this facilitate the identification of that property, but also the programming of the institution's cultural activities.

The Project was developed via the use of the action research method: plan, act, observe/collect, reflect/review [1]. It consists of the construction of an online platform for the registration, cataloging, recovery and consultation of cultural infrastructure, artistic activities and cultural assets, that contribute to the integral development of university students through the dissemination of the artistic and/or cultural expressions of the UNAM.

The University City alone covers close to 7 km^2 (3.5 square miles), larger than some European cities and even some of smaller countries. Additionally, it has 18 foreign offices in Mexico and six extension schools in the USA, Canada, Spain and China. It also has several meteorological, seismological, ecological and oceanographic monitoring stations distributed throughout the country [2].

In 2007 its central campus was declared a World Heritage Site by UNESCO. In 2009 it was awarded the Prince of Asturias Award for Communication and Humanities.

The development of this information system combines the experience of those who carry out the University's arts outreach programs with the researchers in Library and Information Science to make a product that complies with the information standards for a better understanding of the data featured on the platform.

The main beneficiaries of the project are thought to be people involved in the cultural work of the UNAM's Department of Cultural Affairs, as well as its Subsystem and the coordinators of cultural activities in different headquarters, instances and places of higher education and higher media of the university (academic entities). This tool allows the university to become stronger in the field of arts outreach by registering and consulting its resources pertaining to the subject.

The theory of cultural capital developed by Pierre Bourdieu transcends as a backdrop in the perspective of university arts outreach as fundamental in the creation of conditions that broaden the horizons and perspectives of the community. "Cultural capital can exist under three forms: in the incorporated state, that is to say, in the form of durable organism arrangements; in the objectified state, in the form of cultural goods, pictures, books, dictionaries, instruments, machinery, which are the mark or the realisation of theories or criticisms of these theories, and of problems, etc., and finally in the institutionalised state, as a very particular form of objectification, because as it can be seen with the school title, it confers to the cultural capital - which must supposedly guarantee- to the totally original properties" [3].

"... three of Bourdieu's key arguments with which we engage: (a) the importance of cultural capital, (b) the homology between cultural fields, and (c) the role of culture in reproducing advantage." (Bennet 2009, 9).

In this sense, there are studies based on Bordieu's theory [4], with reference to young people (the main beneficiaries of the UNAM's cultural policy): "this is a period in which people make very important decisions, for which they may or may not feel responsible later, for which they may or may not be judged. And there is also no doubt that those decisions have been adopted under regimes of social reality that generate radically different conditions for some young people from the beginning" [5].

Youth, defined as the age between fifteen and twenty-nine years in the survey conducted by Gayo to support his hypothesis, contains a range of ages within which there is remarkable diversity. In this regard, the youngest among young people are the most participatory, which shows that the often-commented lengthening of youth does not hide the important changes that occur in periods of just a few years [6].

Effective programming and dissemination of the University's cultural activities requires knowledge of all its possibilities. There is a need, therefore, for systemised information on the available infrastructure, giving rise to the reinforcement of the growth of new forms of cultural outreach.

The integration of the spaces and cultural assets of the UNAM into an information system is useful because it systematises the functions, attributes, instruments and programs within the University's cultural infrastructure, and serves those responsible for staging cultural events, for which they either permanently or sporadically use or administer cultural infrastructure.

Objetives

- Promote institutional learning among the Department of Cultural Affairs, those responsible for cultural activities in the university's campuses and the subsystem's addresses, to detect needs and opportunities in the administration of cultural information.
- Carry out the registration of sites specialising in Arts Outreach, with the use of international standards for the survey and homologation of information.
- Provide the Coordination Subsystem directorates with a tool to consult cultural information that streamlines programming processes and supports planning criteria with quick and timely information.
- Contribute to a catalog of the cultural spaces and technical means of the UNAM education centres, to strategic line 10.13 of the Institutional Development Plan that reads: "Integrate weekly cultural activities in situ to schools and faculties, facilitate their understanding, cultivate their taste, enjoyment, allowing cultural inclinations to consolidate and become a recreational habit" [7].

At first glance, the fulfilment of these objectives might seem easily achievable. However, it is a big challenge for several reasons. The University has three objectives: teaching, research and arts outreach. All three are addressed separately from each other in each of the University's campuses. In addition, there is a central cultural infrastructure which serves not only the university, but also the population interested in the activities it promotes attending (2,246,148 people in 2017 [8]). The Department of

Cultural Affairs is responsible for this segment in addition to supporting the activities of the different university dependencies. The number of cultural spaces owned by the University are many, located in various parts of Mexico City, the states or even abroad. It is for this reason that the need arises to harmonise the knowledge of the spaces and assets that exist in each of them through a system with great functionality. Another aspect is the difficulty in determining which infrastructure should be reflected and represented by the database. Although it is evident through the defined objectives that the programming of cultural activities is the central aim, it is not always easy to separate what a coordination can offer as opposed to what the different branches of the University not belonging to that coordination consider to be of interest to them and to the communities they work for. This situation requires coordination to be able to respond to the varying needs of the University.

The expectation for the database is that it will provide a solution not only for the programming of activities, but also to interrelate the different university dependencies in their cultural activity in order to achieve better results and involve the student and teaching population.

The Project is scheduled to be completed within three years: the first one presents the design of the database, in the second the standardisation of the terminology and in the third the functionality tests. To this end, the work to be carried out was presented to the Support Program for Research Projects and Technological Innovation (Programa de Apoyo a Proyectos de Investigación e InnovaciónTecnológica, PAPIIT) [9], whose objective is to support and encourage the development of fundamental and applied research, technological innovation and the formation of research groups in and between academic entities, through research projects and technological innovation, whose design leads to the generation of knowledge published in the highest impact and quality media, as well as the production of patents and technology transfer. The program is part of the special supports offered by the University's General Directorate of Academic Personnel Affairs.

2 Methodology and Actions to Develop the Project

As mentioned at the beginning of this work, the methodology is action research most appropriate for projects related to cultural industries, the scope in which this project presented is circumscribed. Action research is designed to bridge the gap between research and practice. Action research is defined as:

"... a form of collective self-reflective inquiry undertaken by participants in social situations to improve the rationality and justice of their own social or educational practice... and the situations in which these practices are carried out... The approach is only action research when it is collaborative [and relies upon] the critically examined action of individual group members" [10].

In order to design the information system, it was necessary to define the formats that allow each type of space to be recovered, as well as the cultural assets that they comprise. The constitution of the system allows for the cataloging and indexing of resources in such a way that they are recoverable, both for cultural managers and for space managers (Fig. 1).

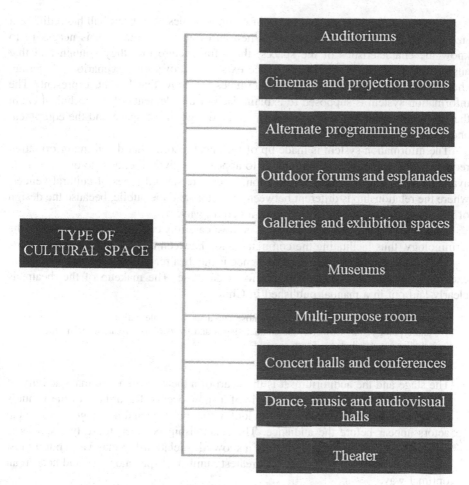

Fig. 1. Typology of cultural spaces. Due to the great complexity presented by the UNAM's various cultural spaces, it was concluded that most systems for classifying cultural spaces do not accurately reflect the spatial configuration of any of the University's cultural spaces. Under these constraints, the typology of cultural spaces was established based on a qualitative analysis of the various systems of classification in Latin America and the information gathered on technical visits, with the aim of guaranteeing a reliable result according to the multiple contexts in which the UNAM's many academic and cultural buildings were developed, channelling our efforts towards generating bespoke concepts and terminology that respond to university life.

There are different types and forms of cultural venues. A concert hall has a different size and shape different to a theatre. When an event is scheduled, it is necessary to know the characteristics of the spaces, the infrastructure that they contain and that answer the question: Where does a space exist that allows for a scenario with certain characteristics and infrastructure that facilitates the show that I want to present? The information system is supposed to explain each of the elements of the technical chain that are required for a given event, such as the design of the space and the equipment and amount of personnel available.

The information system is made up of technical records that detail the information required by an external company that is to appear at a given site: how to operate in the available space and plan that presentation. There are several types of cultural venues, where the relationship is different between the actors and the public, because the design of the space defines this relationship in a certain way.

Undoubtedly, one of the aspects that is most carefully curated in the database is the terminology, thus facilitating the communication between the system's different users.

One of the cultural venues par excellence is the theatre, which can easily be used to exemplify the access points necessary for a database. The makeup of the theatre is clearly laid out in a manual published in Chile:

"There are three main areas in a theatre, whose character and scale will vary according to the size and type of venue. However, the characteristics and the way they relate to each other are very similar across all cases. These are:

- The stage and the auditorium: it is the heart of a theatre where the main activity of presenting and experiencing the magic of a show occurs. Regardless of the venue's dimensions, the audience is seated to look upon the stage and the stage is where the actors appear before the audience. The relationship between these two spaces is crucial for the proper development of a show; this relationship may vary, but it must in any case be designed so that the greatest number of spectators see and hear in an optimal way.
- Reception or FOH (abbreviation in English of front of house, the front part of an enclosure): the area where the spectator waits to enter the auditorium. It also includes service areas such as toilets, cafeteria and ticket office
- Work areas of the theatre or Backstage: includes dressing rooms, workshops, warehouses, electrical or dimmers room, control room, etc. In summary, it corresponds to the work support zones on the stage." [11].

This example shows the terminological differences that exist between similar situations in different Spanish-speaking countries. In Mexico the word lobby in the theatre is taken to mean the same as the reception would in Chile, likewise is that which is referred to as the box office in Mexico also known as the box office in Chile [11]. In Mexico, the word cabin is more commonly used for that which is known as the control room in Chile. However, there are also differing terms used in Mexico for different theatres and their parts. In the oldest theatre in the city, built in the neoclassical style, the lobby is known as the foyer.

3   Observe/Collect

In the case presented, the system responds to the informational needs of the cultural spaces and assets available to the UNAM. Therefore, in order to represent them in the database, access points were defined with the purpose of structuring the system. To this end, the data was extracted on technical visits to the university campuses and through consultation with specialists. During this first stage of compilation of the database, the development team was under the stewardship of the Technical Secretariat of Planning and Programming of the UNAM's Department of Cultural Affairs, specifically the Coordination of Cultural Assets and Innovation, a group created specifically for the purpose of planning and developing the system, as well as the coordination of the interdisciplinary team consisting of architects, economists, specialist in the arts, librarianship and outside collaborators.

The gathering of information was carried out directly in the cultural spaces specifically dedicated to the arts as well as in the UNAM's establishments for secondary, higher and specialised education. In addition to that, specialists in the field of technical resources were consulted to ascertain the minimum characteristics necessary for the use of digital cinema platforms in order to be able to take them to educational venues. This allows the database to show the possibilities for the dissemination and programming of, in this case, the UNAM's General Direction on Cinematographic Activities. This same procedure was carried out to study the technical needs of some areas of the Subsystem of the Department of Cultural Affairs. It was tested on the comedy car, and with the Itinerant Festival in Contact with You, assigned to the Direction of Theatre and the Integral Training Coordination, respectively. Another aspect in which points of access had to be defined is in those cultural spaces existing within the confines of other cultural spaces, such as museums or educational facilities, that are managed in the category of administrative dependency to which said space corresponds.

In addition to systematising the data obtained for the development of the platform, the existing databases already dedicated to compiling information of the same type and with similar objectives to those represented in the RUEyACwere reviewed and analysed.

This project has been characterised by its collaborative nature, with institutions outside of the UNAM participating from the beginning, contributing to the construction of the platform. One of the main formats of analysation was used by the Ministry of Culture to request that states registration data concerning the categories that make up the MICultura project.

A pilot of the platform to be built was also carried out, with the support of the Cultural Information Centre of Hidalgo (CIC). This centre is focused on the conservation and dissemination of phonographic and bibliographic files, however, the overall work was fruitful to obtain the initial format for the collection of information.

Another source of data extraction was IBERMUSEOS, which aided in the standardisation of the museum data of the Ibero-American Network of Museums by providing data for the part of the database pertaining to museums belonging to the UNAM.

Over a period of two months, 42 formats were reviewed, from which a battery of 757 points of access was designed, distributed across 9 categories contemplating Infrastructure and Cultural Assets. The first record for data collection was created on Google Drive as a preliminary stage before the system was designed. The main takeaways for each cultural venue were:

- Cultural infrastructure
- General services
- Accessibility and security measures
- Location and contact information
- Technical resources
- Graphic material and photographic record.

The My Structured Query Language (MySQL), which allows the management of a few thousand records from small databases, to more complex structures with hundreds of thousands of records, was used as DataBase Management System (DBMS) for the definition, manipulation, validity and data relationship.

The processes for obtaining the data referring to the spaces and the infrastructure was systematised and defined from a battery of questions comprised of 1,064 items, for which the methodology of Object Oriented Analysis and Design (OOAD) was implemented, resulting in the mapping of all the 'abstract concepts' in terms of Entities, Attributes, Relationships and Roles which, as a whole, define the descriptive, structural and administrative metadata of the data set.

Once the basic structure of the data to be systematised was established, the aforementioned methodology of Object Oriented Analysis and Design was implemented in the second phase in order to obtain a meta-structure of analysis relevant to the development of systems using Entities, Attributes and Relationships.

In the case of the Roles, they are defined in the database through the profiles of the users and structured so that each one of them has sufficient access to the necessary information without compromising access to the entire database.

Some common diagramming techniques were used to illustrate certain aspects of the system. These diagrams are determined by the UNIFIED MODELLING LANGUAGE (UML). The UML is not a programming language, but a specific graphic notation for an object-oriented system. The UML describes over a dozen different diagrams. However, only the most common are used in this document (Fig. 2).

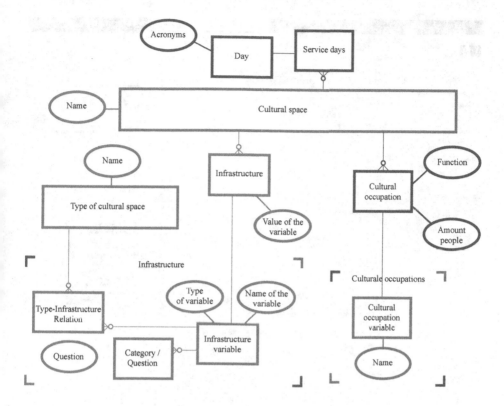

Fig. 2. Entity-Relation Diagram used to determine the logical data model that uses the system of information in regard to a cultural space. Cultural spaces depend on unity and a type of cultural space. Unity puts cultural spaces into groups and the type of cultural space determines its specific behaviour in accordance with its typology. The type of cultural space is a controlled catalogue.

A UML is a systematic way of describing and defining data or information related to a "business process". The process is modelled through components (ENTITIES) that are linked together by means of RELATIONS that express dependencies and requirements. For example: A building can be divided into zero or more departments, but a department can only be in a single building. ENTITIES can have many properties (ATTRIBUTES) that characterise them. The diagrams created to graphically represent such ENTITIES, ATTRIBUTES and RELATIONS are known as ENTITY - RELATIONSHIP DIAGRAMS (Fig. 3).

308   C. Naumis-Peña et al.

Fig. 3. Graphic user interface for the administration of variables in infrastructure. The type of reactive defines the behaviour it will display when capturing information on a cultural space (textual, numeric, boolean, etc.). The relation between a reactive and a cultural space makes it possible to generate a screen capture of personalised information that responds to the characteristics encountered on technical visits.

4   Reflect/Review

As recommended in the action research steps, a pilot study was carried out six months after the start of the development, prior to the study that would be carried out as part of the main project [1]. Once the design of the registry for filling out the cultural infrastructure had been defined, pilot tests were carried out with those in charge of arts outreach or figures close to this work profile in the university, with architectural students, theatre students, dance, music, university professors, professionals working in university culture and university authorities all interested in the subject.

This pilot test revealed the need to include photographs and diagrams of the various spaces, designed as a small drawing of the rooms or auditoriums. Based on the detection of this need, students of social service architecture who were interested in participating in the project were asked to complete this part of the registry.

This was very useful as a complement to the platform, because it offers a visual record of the spaces available for the development of cultural activities, which helps us get a general idea of them.

On the one hand, the information referring to the infrastructure of a cultural space: its dimensions, total area of the enclosure, height of the stage platform, capacity, physical components, connectivity (internet access and telephone lines), security (if the site has emergency exits, signage in the event of earthquakes or fires), human resources, location and contact data of the Coordinators of Cultural Activities in the University.

On the other, one can consult the technical resources in audio, lighting and video projection, and even musical instruments.

The total number of spaces and cultural assets has yet to be fully incorporated, but approximately 40% have been registered thus far.

In addition to cultural infrastructure, we are working towards the construction of the University's concept of cultural assets in order to perform the survey: Choirs, student musical groups, theatre companies, dance, classical music quartets, student radio stations, reading circles, etc.

The thesaurus that supports the terminology used in the project is being prepared to achieve an adequate communication between the different users of the platform. Lists of possible terms are being compiled for this purpose.

5 Conclusions

A project of this nature starts with very general objectives which require rectifications along the way from the very start of its development, as proven in the pilot test carried out in the sixth months it took to design the record sheet. For this reason, each stage of progress must include a pilot test before moving forward.

The Department of Cultural Affairs and those responsible for cultural activities across the University's campuses took interest in the Project and collaborated extensively in the registering of cultural spaces and assets.

Consultation bodies developing similar activities allowed us to better meet the standards required for the adoption of metadata on the platform.

The use of the data registered in the platform has lead to the recognition of the work undertaken, as well as comments made in this regard.

After a year of development, the RUEyAC offers the possibility for the capture, management and online consultation of a systematic inventory of real estate, services, social uses of spaces, activities and technical means of lighting, audio and video projection, through specialised forms for the collection of data on museums, esplanades and open-air forums, dance halls, music and audiovisual, cinemas, theatres and auditoriums, whose purpose it is to make, preserve, produce, program or disseminate cultural content in the UNAM.

References

1. Collins, H.: Creative Research: the Theory and Practice of Research for the Creative Industries. Bloomsbury Academic, London (2017)
2. Universia México: Universidad Nacional Autónoma de México UNAM (in spanish). http://www.universia.net.mx/. Accessed 01 June 2018
3. Bourdieu, P.: Los tres estados del capital cultural. Sociológica **2**, 12 (1987). (in Spanish)
4. Bourdieu, P.: Las reglas del arte, génesis y estructura del campo literario. Anagrama, España (1995). (in Spanish)
5. Gayo, M.: The theory of cultural capital and the cultural participation of young people, the Chilean case as an example. Ultimadécada **21**, 168–169 (2013). (in Spanish)
6. Gayo, M.: The theory of cultural capital and the cultural participation of young people, the Chilean case as an example. Ultimadécada **21**, 160 (2013). (in Spanish)
7. Graue, E.: Línea estratégica 10. Desarrollo Integral de los estudiantes. Plan de Desarrollo Institucional 2015–2019, UNAM, México (2017). (in Spanish)
8. Portal of University Statistics: Autonomous National University of Mexico. http://www.estadistica.unam.mx/numeralia/. Accessed 25 June 2018
9. Dirección General del Personal Académico: Programa de Apoyo a Proyectos de Investigación e Innovación Tecnológica (PAPIIT). http://dgapa.unam.mx/index.php/impulso-a-la-investigacion/papiit. Accessed 25 June 2018
10. Kemmis, S., McTaggart, R., Nixon, R.: The Action Research Planner: Doing Critical Participatory Action Research. Springer, Singapore (2014). https://doi.org/10.1007/978-981-4560-67-2
11. Campos-Berkhoff, D.: Manual de Escenotecnia, Consejo Nacional de la Cultura y las Artes, Chile (2014). (in Spanish)

Correction to: Reconstructing the Historic Landscape of Larochette, Luxembourg

Marleen de Kramer(iD), Sam Mersch(iD), and Christopher Morse(iD)

Correction to:
Chapter "Reconstructing the Historic Landscape
of Larochette, Luxembourg" in: M. Ioannides et al. (Eds.):
Digital Heritage, LNCS 11197,
https://doi.org/10.1007/978-3-030-01765-1_4

The original version of chapter 4 starting on p. 30 was revised. Inadvertently the funding institution was not mentioned in the original chapter. A footnote for the explanation was added on the first page of the chapter. The original chapter was corrected.

The updated version of this chapter can be found at
https://doi.org/10.1007/978-3-030-01765-1_4

© Springer Nature Switzerland AG 2019
M. Ioannides et al. (Eds.): EuroMed 2018, LNCS 11197, p. C1, 2019.
https://doi.org/10.1007/978-3-030-01765-1_34

Author Index